A PEDIATRIC APPROACH TO LEARNING DISORDERS

A PEDIATRIC APPROACH TO LEARNING DISORDERS

Melvin D. Levine, M.D., F.A.A.P.

Chief, Division of Ambulatory Pediatrics
The Children's Hospital Medical Center
Boston, Massachusetts
Department of Pediatrics
Harvard Medical School
Boston, Massachusetts

Robert Brooks, Ph.D.

Director, Outpatient Child Psychology
  and Psychoeducational Services
McLean Hospital, Hall-Mercer Children's Center
Belmont, Massachusetts
Department of Psychiatry
Harvard Medical School
Boston, Massachusetts

Jack P. Shonkoff, M.D., F.A.A.P.

Codirector, Child Development Service
University of Massachusetts Medical Center
Worcester, Massachusetts

A WILEY MEDICAL PUBLICATION
JOHN WILEY & SONS
New York • Chichester • Brisbane • Toronto

Library of Congress Cataloging in Publication Data:

Levine, Melvin D
    A pediatric approach to learning disorders.

    (A Wiley medical publication)
    Bibliography: p.
    Includes index.
    1. Learning disabilities.   2. Pediatrics.
I. Brooks, Robert, 1942- joint author.
II. Shonkoff, Jack P., joint author.   III. Title.

[DNLM: 1. Learning disorders. WS110 L665p]
RJ506.L4L48   618.9'28'588   79-21839
ISBN 0-471-04736-8

Printed in the United States of America

10 9 8 7 6 5 4 3 2 1

The authors wish to dedicate this book to children who have been labeled.

Foreword

Do pediatricians have a role in caring for children with learning disorders? Many, especially among other professions caring for children, would say No. It can be argued that the medicalization of more and more human problems is unwise and that other institutions, especially the school, are the more appropriate settings for dealing with such children. Indeed, I agree that the management of learning disorders must be carried out in large part in schools.

There are several reasons to support the argument that schools are an appropriate place for dealing with children with learning disorders. First, we must recognize that teachers are with a child for approximately 1,000 hours a year. On the other hand, the pediatrician, who can be characterized as a "hit-and-run" consultant, sees a child 10 to 20 hours a year, at most. In addition, we now have evidence, after a period of denigration, of the effectiveness of schools. Rutter has shown that certain kinds of schools are more effective in dealing with children with behavior and learning problems than others. But as this book makes clear, care of children (and their families) with the distressing problem of difficulty in learning is not the exclusive province of any one discipline.

Pediatricians do have an important role to play, especially since they are almost the only point of entry to services during the preschool period when the signs of some difficulties in learning are first perceived. In addition, the pediatrician has more continuity, often caring for a child from birth until adulthood, while any given teacher rarely cares for a child for more than a year (even though that one year might be quite intense). But to be better qualified to care for children with learning disorders, the pediatrician must be able to provide more than this initial entry service and general counseling. The pediatrician must have diagnostic skills equivalent to the medical skills of auscultation and therapeutic skills equivalent to the knowledge of medications.

This book is devoted to an explication of such skills. The first requirement is for the pediatrician to be the generalist within a group of specialists. The pediatrician is the *one* member of this team who can best balance biological and social factors without being a partisan for any one cause or any one therapy. It is clear that learning disorders are due to many causes. There are no simple answers. Pediatricians can serve children best by looking for the best approach for each child.

This book details the types of learning disorders and the diagnostic systems appropriate for their assessment. Pediatricians who have not had experience in this field might find it a bit awesome to be faced with such a large collection of new approaches and procedures. But they should not view the field of learning disorders as one which can be learned by reading this book alone. This beginning book outlines the skills and assessment procedures that can be used by pediatricians, but it is clear that practice (under supervision) and further reading will be necessary to make any pediatrician competent in this complex field. After all, merely reading Goodman and Gilman does not make one an accomplished therapist with drugs!

The interested pediatrician who reads this book may wonder, "But how do I put all of this material together when I see a child? It will take hours to apply all of these screening procedures, much less the definitive tests." Even with all the practical advice in the chapter on assessment, the pediatrician who wants to use this material must practice and learn to use the skills *efficiently*. He must also face the problem of economics. This is time-consuming work. Who is to pay for it? How much is it worth? Any pediatrician deciding to enter this field should think through these issues.

Finally the pediatrician will ask how much good these new skills will do for children with learning problems. As the authors point out, the book is in many ways premature. Studies have not yet been completed to show that the diagnostic approaches described here are predictive of which children are most in need of specific therapy or which therapy will be most effective for a given type of learning disorder. Further study is needed to determine the effectiveness of any one method of care for these children. In addition, the gap between disciplines will continue to remain large until there are some clear-cut demonstrations of how the pediatrician armed with this new skill and knowledge can best work with schools.

As the authors point out, children cannot wait. All professionals who deal with children are faced with the distressing problems of those who cannot learn. This book will help the pediatrician to learn skills appropriate for current screening and assessment techniques. New editions will be necessary in the future to bring this rapidly moving field up to date.

ROBERT J. HAGGERTY, M.D.
Clinical Professor of Pediatrics
Harvard Medical School

Acknowledgements

The authors wish to acknowledge the tolerance, consultation and active help of many professionals. We are grateful for the excellent special educational input from Dr. Jane Hyman, Dr. Terrell Clark, and Dr. Lynne Meltzer. We are grateful for the valuable secretarial help of Linda Evans, Katie Foley, Carol Green, Liz Serpa, and Rosemarie Greene.

We also acknowledge the excellent photographic contributions from the Needham, Massachusetts Public Schools Media Center and from the very talented Mr. Bradford Herzog.

A number of Fellows and staff in Ambulatory Pediatrics at the Children's Hospital Medical Center contributed advice and early support. They include Dr. Judith Palfrey, Dr. Frank Oberklaid, Dr. Ronald Barr, Dr. Craig Liden, and Dr. Paul Dworkin. In the speech and language and neuropsychology areas we have benefitted from the continuing counsel of Dr. Anthony Bashir and Dr. Irving Hurwitz.

Our ongoing research, training, and program development in this field has been fostered through the generous support of projects by The Robert Wood Johnson Foundation, The Carnegie Corporation, The Ford Foundation, and The Bureau of Education for the Handicapped (Office of Education).

Dr. Brooks would like to thank especially Dr. Sebastiano Santostefano for his ongoing support and creative contributions.

Dr. Levine would like to acknowledge the courage of Dr. Mary Ellen Avery in offering him unswerving encouragement, support, and career guidance for which he will always be grateful.

Most of all, we wish to acknowledge the unwavering support of our families, especially Marilyn Brooks, Bambi Levine, and Fredi Shonkoff. There are also ongoing inspiration from Richard and Douglas Brooks, Michael and Adam Shonkoff, and a certain gaggle of geese!

*A DISCLAIMER: OF GENDERS AND THE DISABILITIES
IMPOSED BY ENGLISH PRONOUNS*

In preparing this volume, the authors have bemoaned the unavailability
of a neuter gender pronoun. Early efforts were directed toward a
reconciliation between syntactical euphony and sexual neutrality (e.g.,
"He or she should not be placed on medication without the cooperation
of his or her parents, the knowledge of his or her teachers, and the true
consent of himself or herself"). Alas, the esthetics of prosody have
prevailed, necessitating the present invocation of a "neuter" "he" or
"him." This should not be taken to mean that the learning disorders of
females or the involvement of women physicians are neglected herein.
Readers are invited to decode such pronouns into either or both gender
associations.

Contents

A PEDIATRIC APPROACH TO LEARNING DISORDERS

1

Introduction: Where We Are Headed

The advantage of confining attention to a definite group of
abstractions, is that you confine your thoughts to clear-cut
definite thoughts, with clear-cut definite relations. . . . The
disadvantage of exclusive attention to a group of abstractions
. . . is that you have abstracted from the remainder of things;
accordingly it is of the utmost importance to be vigilant in
critically revising your *modes* of abstraction. A civilization
which cannot burst through its current abstractions is doomed
to sterility after a very limited period of progress.

Alfred North Whitehead, Science and the Modern World *(1925)*

This is a book about school-age children for whom school is a problem. It is a
book about clinical child development embedded in the discipline of pediatrics.
It is intended to provide a framework for constructive pediatric involvement in
the care of children with learning disorders. It is not intended to be a definitive
work on so-called learning disabilities, but rather a conceptual model of one
discipline's involvement. It is expected that this model will also have relevance
beyond pediatrics, extending into the fields of family medicine, nursing,
psychiatry, psychology, social work, and parenting.

It is intellectually hazardous and rather premature to produce a volume on
learning disorders at this moment in the history of ideas about children. This is a
subject area in which our knowledge and sensitivity are advancing rapidly. It
lacks clear definition; it has no widely accepted taxonomy or methodology; and it
includes few if any therapies that have been proven effective beyond reasonable
doubt. It is a field in which conceptual "hunches" rapidly solidify into pro-
fessionally accepted dogma—a field that must search for its basic science.
Despite the flux and uncertainty, an increased awareness of children's needs and
rights, growing harvests of data about the impact of chronic failure on adult
outcomes, and supportive legislative mandates have combined to make a
systematic approach to learning disorders essential now. The clinician or teacher
faced with the suffering of a failing child has not the luxury to await advances in
the state of the art. It is out of such necessity that this book is offered as a
systematic, but rather tentative, approach to a group of problems.

1

AN APPROACH

Diagnostic labels for children who are failing have never been in short supply. Figure 1 offers a historical perspective, providing a general overview of evolving terms for children who have difficulty learning. The roots of history have taken us through rigid moral, psychometric, psychiatric, and "organic" systems of categorization. During the last 20 years, with increasing recognition of physiologic (i.e., brain-based) sources of learning failure, there has been an extraordinary proliferation of "syndromes." A partial list of these can be found in Table 1. It has not been possible to attain consensus either between or within individual disciplines. The concept of learning disability has emerged to account for children who are struggling with some discrete area (or small number of areas) of endogenous information-processing weakness. One official definition of a learning disability conceptualizes this clinical entity largely as diagnosis by exclusion (see p. 38). Such a definition might be taken to imply a mutual exclusivity among sensory loss, experiential underexposure, emotional problems, global developmental deficits, and true learning disabilities. Alas, most clinicians recognize the absence of purity and the overwhelming preponderance of children whose learning disorders are manifestations of mixtures of predispositions.

Table 1. A Compendium of Syndromes and Labels for Dysfunction*

Association deficit pathology	Hyperactivity
Organic brain disease	Hyerkinesis
Organic brain damage	Hyperkinetic behavior disorder
Organic brain dysfunction	Hyperkinetic impulse disorder
Minor brain damage	Hypoactive—hyperactivity
Neurophrenia	Hyperkinetic syndrome
Organic drivenness	Hypokinetic syndrome
Cerebral dysfunction	Hyperexcitability syndrome
Organic behavior disorder	Character impulse disorder
Choreiform syndrome	Aggressive behavior disorder
Minimal brain damage (MBD)	Psychoneurologic learning disorder
Minimal cerebral injury	Psycholinguistic learning disorder
Minimal chronic brain syndromes	Psychogenic learning disorder
Minimal cerebral damage	Psychoneurotic learning disorder
Minimal cerebral palsy	Specific reading disability
	Dyslexia (dysograhia, dyscalculia, dysorthographia)
Cerebral dys-synchronization syndrome	Developmental dyslexia
Developmental Gerstmann syndrome	Primary reading retardation
Hemisyndromes	Perceptual deficit syndrome
Frontal lobe syndromes	Perceptual cripple
	Perceptually handicapped
Disconnection syndromes	Conceptually handicapped
Allergic brain damage	Language disabled
	Learning disability (LD)
	Strephosymbolia
	Attention disorder
	Interjacent child

*Adapted from Clements (1966).

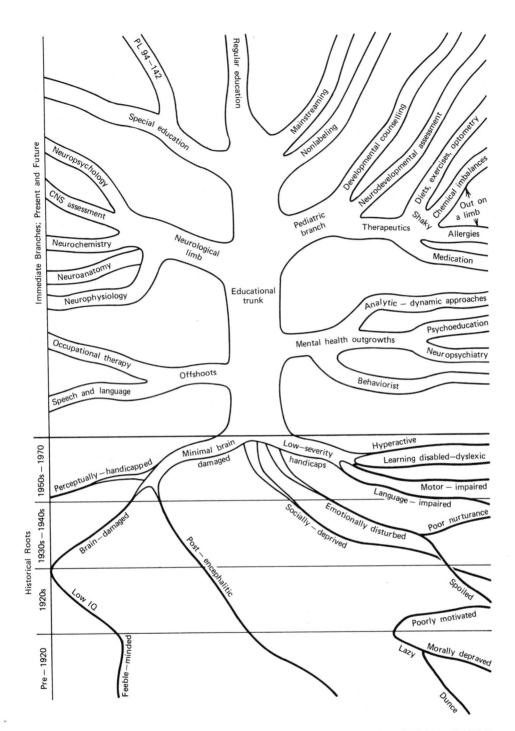

Figure 1. CHANGING CONCEPTS OF CHILDHOOD DYSFUNCTION: EARLY ROOTS AND CURRENT BRANCHES

3

In circles where public policy is formulated, the disorders of learning frequently are referred to as the *high-incidence–low-severity* handicaps of children. Such deficiencies are said to affect from 4 to 20% of school age children with a boy-girl ratio of between 6 and 8 to 1 (Minskoff 1973). The notion of *high-incidence–low-severity* handicaps can be useful in differentiating this population from those children who endure multiple or major handicapping conditions, including mental retardation, blindness, and severe hearing impairment. These latter are subsumed under the *high-severity–low-incidence* handicapping conditions.

When describing learning disorders, there are problems with the use of the word *disability*. For one thing, there is a gray area, an obscure borderland between subtle disabilities and cognitive styles. There are no perfect brains. Either by grand design or fortuitously, many human central nervous systems appear to be specialized. That is to say, they perform some jobs better than others. Certain brains seem particularly specialized for meeting the formal childhood academic expectations of our culture. Others may be well adapted to single aspects of education. Still others function superbly in a range of nonacademic areas while seeming to dissemble in formal learning situations. Further compounding the problem is the fact that certain so-called disabilities may in fact help potentiate mastery in other areas. Some individuals with significant impairments of receptive and spoken language, for example, may learn ultimately not to rely heavily upon verbal constructs for their thought processes. Such thinkers may become quite adept at sophisticated visual-spatial or symbolic processing, reaching illustrious levels of attainment in abstruse fields such as astrophysics and "higher" forms of mathematics.

Another issue inherent in discussions of disability and style is the observation that our definition of a disability can be very dependent upon the rigid standards adults create for children. Among the population of youngsters who have learning disorders, the clinician will encounter some who will make much better adults than children! In many respects it is easier to be a grown-up than a child. There are many more electives in adult life. The vast range of occupations and avocations for adults allows for endless accommodations to individual strengths and weaknesses. Such custom fitting of pursuits to strengths does not and probably will not exist within childhood educational institutions. A child who is highly distractible, one who is predisposed to "free flight of ideas," may present as an inattentive, disorganized, second-grade pupil. That very distractibility, that same "hyperkinetic mind," may blossom in a highly creative and imaginative adult (see Fig. 2). The very "handicap" of distractibility may be the source of great poetry or art. A child's free-ranging, ever-scanning, wide-angle focus that is maladaptive in a classroom may ultimately flow toward the discovery of new relationships, new inventions, and new metaphors blended from the disparate elements in the universe that a distractible mind could capture. Many children who have difficulty sustaining attention also have the characteristic of insatiability (see Chapter 3). This chronic difficulty in being satisfied, the steady hunger for stimulation and attention, the restless quest for gratification, may be condemned as a behavior problem in a young child yet in adult life may be favorably labeled "ambition." The doubled-edged nature of these so-called disabilities requires that adults working and living with such children maintain a broad and open-minded perspective with regard to their function, remaining vigilant not to extinguish future strengths. We must always ask what may be lost when we strive to change a child. Prognostic uncertainties, dilution effects, and possible determinants of outcome are illustrated in Figure 3.

The multifactorial complexity of children with learning disorders and the critical importance of recognizing their strengths argue strongly for a nondeficit-oriented approach. Moreover, the threat of self-fulfilling prophecy has been used as an argument against tattooing children with syndromes. Although frequently encountered clusters of symptoms may have value for future research, at present the clinical utility of specific syndromes is highly questionable. To pronounce that a youngster has "developmental Gerstman syndrome," for example, is unlikely to suggest specific services. Often syndromes or labels imply some consistency of etiology and/or treatment. Commonly applied tags for children with learning problems have no such attributes. For these reasons we are advocating (at least for the time being) a highly empirical approach to children with learning disorders, based on the assumption that the best services emerge from the best description of a child's strengths, weaknesses, coping strategies, styles, and patterns of behavior. The descriptors are valuable only insofar as they promote insight and generate services. The kinds of services that may be required to deal with or accommodate such characteristics are the subject of this book.

Several other assumptions underly this book. There is a recognition of the relative inseparability of behavior problems and the learning-developmental process for school-age children. In this age group a reciprocity between affect and learning is well established. Children with learning problems frequently have behavior difficulties that may arise from the same central nervous system substrate that is impairing learning. Alternatively, such problems may stem from personality changes secondary to chronic failure or may represent conscious or nearly conscious maneuvers designed for face saving. Conversely, children with significant emotional overload and psychosocial preoccupations may present to the clinician with apparent "learning problems." A complex interaction between the two (constitutional vulnerabilities and psychosocial stresses) necessitates clinical elaboration.

The clinician is often asked: "Is the problem organic or is it emotional? Do you think it is neurologic or psychiatric?" In school the child's assignment to a desk may hang in the balance between emotional disturbance (ED) or learning disability (LD). The sensitive clinician, after careful consideration of multiple failing children, can recognize the fallacious assumptions beneath these simplistic formulations. One can assume (in nearly all cases) that a failing child embodies the final common pathway of constitutional or endogenous (neurologic) predispositions, environmental and experiential factors, and the child's own repertoire of reactions and coping tactics. Rigid categorization, especially when it regards "emotional" versus "organic" disorder, is often inaccurate, almost always oversimplified, and frequently a moral injustice to the child. In many parts of the United States a diagnostic label is required in order to obtain community services. Regrettably, in such cases the clinician needs to accommodate to local constraints. It is hoped that such labels will be applied with some care and sensitivity and that they will not be excessively adherent.

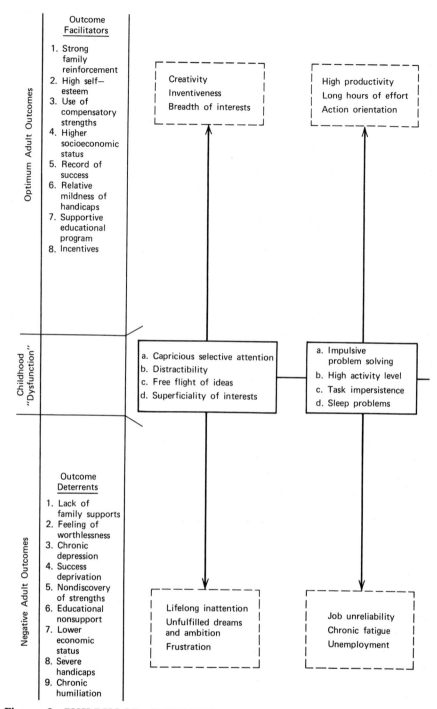

Figure 2. CHILDHOOD ATTENTION DEFICITS: THE ENIGMA OF PROGNOSIS

This diagram is intended to illustrate the variable prognoses for certain traits of inattention. The dashed rectangles at the top of the diagram represent positive adult outcomes, while those at the bottom illustrate some of the possible negative consequences of chronic inattention. The rectangles in the middle of the diagram describe some of the traits commonly seen in children with

6

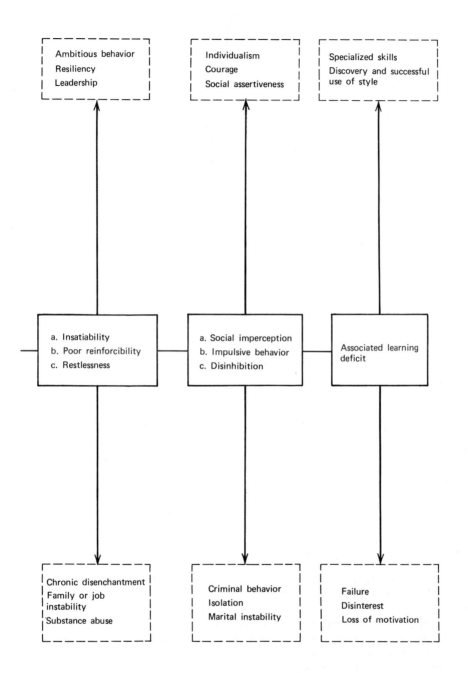

attention deficits. On the left-hand side is a list of some facilitators and
deterrents or factors likely to have an impact upon outcome. It should be
emphasized that mixed outcomes may occur in the same individual: Namely, a
particular inattentive child ultimately may develop both negative and positive
traits as an outgrowth of his dysfunctions. The figure depicts the complexity of
prognosis. For discussion of these traits accompanying attention deficits, see
Chapter 3.

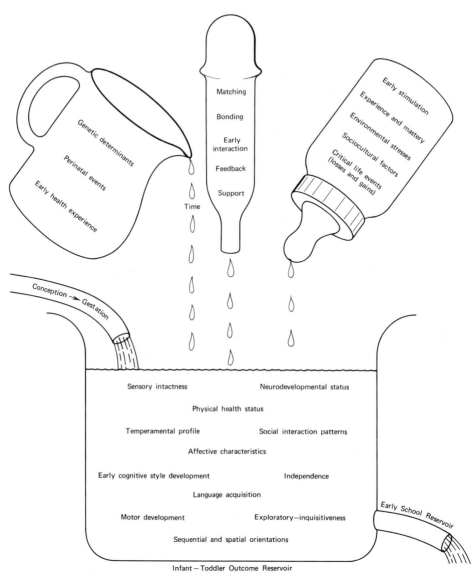

Figure 3. DEVELOPMENTAL DILUTION EFFECTS: PHASE I: EARLIEST INPUTS
AND INFANT-TODDLER OUTCOMES

One can conceptualize the processes of development as involving the constant admixture
of new with preexistent ingredients, each affecting outcome to a limited extent. There is a
constant accumulation and blending of factors that modify development. Simultaneously,
there is ongoing dilution, such that many of the earliest inputs are likely to become
increasingly less influential with age. In these diagrams three age groups are represented.
In the lower half of each figure is a reservoir in which the various influential ingredients
are intermixed in porportions that vary from individual to individual, resulting in unique
"solutions." Products from an earlier age contribute to the ingredients for a subsequent
developmental admixture (along with new inputs). Such a diagram suggests that any one
ingredient, be it biological, social, or educational, can be either neutralized or potentiated
by other inputs. A multifactorial conceptual model of development is thus illustrated and
suggested. This eclectic paradigm is implicit as one theoretical basis for this book.

8

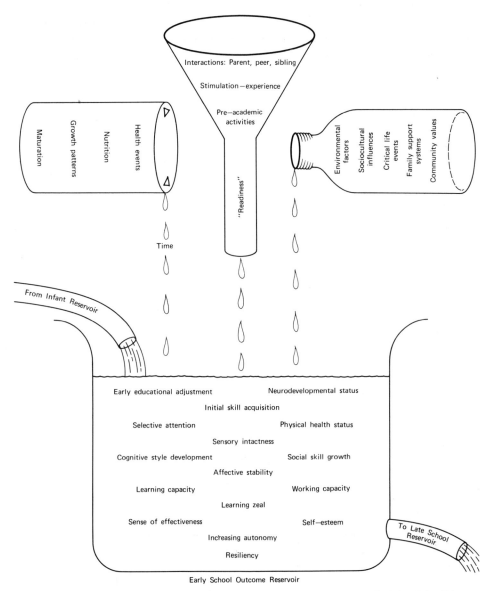

Figure 3. PHASE II: PRESCHOOL INPUTS AND EARLY SCHOOL OUTCOMES

Because this is *not* a book about the *syndromes* affecting learning in school-age children, it emerges as a volume dealing with developmental themes in this age group. The problems encountered in learning and behavior can be thought of as variations, deviations, or delays in the usual developmental processes. In the field of pediatrics the school-age child has been a victim of relative neglect, especially with respect to the study and clinical assessment of development. As a pediatric resident, one generally learns a series of developmental milestones (often committed to memory the night before a qualifying examination) whose checkpoints terminate abruptly just before entry into kindergarten (somewhere between copying a circle and a triangle). There is an implicit presumption in pediatric training that at the point of entry into public education development has closed down! Unwittingly, some child psychiatrists have supported this hypothesis by referring to the elementary-school years as *latency,* implying that little or nothing is happening! It may be that much of the turmoil over terminology in the field of learning disabilities has resulted from lack of clinical focus on the development of the school-age child. Thus, the careful study of

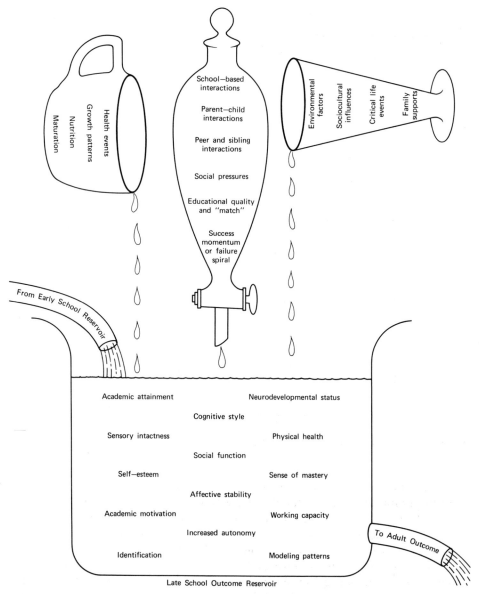

Figure 3. PHASE III: SCHOOL-AGE INPUTS AND LATE SCHOOL OUTCOMES

relatively subtle deviations may enable us to crystalize our understanding of the normal development of school-age chileren.

Honing our knowledge of specific and well-circumscribed developmental weaknesses in individual children may help us to understand better the more severely handicapped youngster. Mental retardation need not be looked upon as qualitatively different from a learning disorder. The severely and multiply handicapped child has the same kinds of disabilities encountered in a youngster with learning disorders, except that in the former such impairments are greater in number and in severity.

Another spin-off from the study of children with learning disorders regards its implications for younger children. The developmental themes woven into the lives of school-age children have their origins in the earliest days of life. With considerable current interest in newborn behavior and function and in early interactional dynamics, it is important that there be a continuing dialogue between the study of the school-age child and that of the infant.

A final aspect of the approach to learning disorders has to do with formulation. It was noted earlier that the suggested process be primarily empirical. The challenge for the physician and other team members is to develop an appropriate formulation of a child's problems, perhaps embodied in a narrative description. The emphasis must be placed on the ways in which observations can generate services. This subject is explored more fully in the section on systematic formulation (Chapter 5). There should not be an overreliance on psychometric test scores, nor an exclusive focus on psychodynamic issues. Instead there must be an effort to develop an eclecticism based on the collation of multiple contributing factors in order to describe and explain a child's current functional status. No exclusive fragment of evidence is ever accepted as anything but circumstantial, until it is corroborated by other reliable inputs.

DEVELOPMENTAL PEDIATRICS AND LEARNING DISORDERS

The discipline of developmental pediatrics is growing rapidly throughout this country. There is increasing concern with issues at the interface of behavior and learning. These areas are being considered to a greater extent in pediatric training programs. A recent report from the Task Force on Pediatric Education (1978) reemphasized the importance of training in this area. At present this is a discipline in flux. Curriculum content and pediatric role conceptualizations vary considerably from one training center to another. A number of basic principles appear to be emerging, however, that have relevance for a broad range of developmental disabilities and handicapping conditions. For the purposes of this book it might be helpful to summarize distinct features of the emerging discipline of developmental pediatrics:

A strong emphasis on a balanced perspective between nature and nurture. Pediatricians should retain their role as generalists. As such, they should maintain some "cleanliness" with regard to disciplinary biases. They should be spokespersons for balance between constitutional and environmental factors leading to dysfunction. As describers of children, pediatricians should be able to summarize neurodevelopmental observations and historical data and to describe a variety of constitutional or endogenous characteristics of a child. This information should be placed within an environmental-social matrix. The school-age child should be conceived of as a bundle of predispositions that have been acted upon in one way or another, sometimes fortuitously (see Fig. 3). This discipline should shy away from exclusive neurologic or psychodynamic determinism.

Departure from the traditional disease model. By dealing with strengths and styles, the pediatrician or health care professional deviates from a traditional disease orientation. For example, one might "diagnose" particularly superior motor skills in a child and suggest ways in which such an asset can be utilized. This requires a modification of the deficit-oriented medical model. As a physician, one is unaccustomed to palpating the abdomen and later declaring that: "This is the best belly I have felt in years!" Another shortcoming of the medical model is the realization that in many cases specific etiologic relationships are obscure. Moreover, their elucidation is not always a prerequisite for the formulation of a plan for intervention.

A nonaccusatory approach. In part because one cannot always determine causes with any degree of certainty, the field of developmental pediatrics is generally nonaccusatory. There is a deemphasis on blaming. The physician cannot always point a finger at any factor or group of factors as the definitive cause of a child's learning problems. One can believe that some things happen fortuitously. Thus, the medical role is largely supportive. The child becomes a hero for living under a maladaptive head; the parents receive respect for their efforts to help the child. All involved are viewed as "innocent victims." The emphasis is not on who caused the problem, but on what can be done to manage and minimize its effects.

A strong emphasis on advice giving. The pediatrician should become an increasingly rich source of developmental counselling. This is covered in detail in Chapter 9. A professional's growth in developmental pediatrics might be measured by the capacity to produce good and effective advice. Such advice should flow directly from systematic formulation processes as described in Chapter 5.

An emphasis on altering the environment. One of the major therapeutic strengths of developmental pediatrics is its potential impact upon environments for children. In many cases it is more helpful to alter conditions and expectations than to change the child. Modifications in educational programming, home structure, and recreational activities might be examples of such interventions. A developmental pediatrician can help to attain a constructive balance between modifying the workings of a child and altering the settings in which that child lives and learns.

The concept of dysfunction. One might identify dysfunction as a clinical phenomenon in which performance is impaired on the basis of characteristics that do not fit the traditional model of organic or emotional factors. The concept of a maladaptive style of learning fits this notion. It is neither a disease nor a psychiatric disorder. It represents, perhaps, unusual features in the "fine tuning" of the mind or body. These may be individual characteristics rather than pathologic findings. A child with encopresis might provide an example of dysfunction. Some of these children may really manifest a kind of dysfunction, rather than an organic or psychiatric disorder. Such a child may be active and playful to an extent where sitting on a toilet becomes a serious intrusion on recreation. He or she may inadvertently begin retaining feces, ultimately develop a megacolon, and lose bowel control. This problem does not really qualify as an organic disease, nor is it a sign of emotional disturbance. Rather, the "neutral territory" of dysfunction often best describes such a condition (see Chapter 9). The same model can be applied to many forms of learning disorders.

The process of demystification. Part of the counselling strategy in developmental pediatrics entails demystification by explaining the nature of symptoms to a parent, a child, or a teacher in terms that are understandable and that help all concerned to feel a sense of control (see Chapter 8). This necessitates the simplification of complicated terminology, professional jargon, and abstract-magical implications. The last of these is particularly important for counselling children. To tell a child that he is overactive because he does not know how to "control himself" tends to mystify rather than clarify. The child may have considerable difficulty seeing the relationship between his overactivity and an abstract concept like self-control. Besides, this formulation may be incorrect. On the other hand, reducing a child's behavior to more manageable terms can be redemptive and help to suggest specific therapies. For example, one might tell a child with auditory attentional problems that he has trouble "getting tuned in"—that his head is sometimes like a tuner on a radio that keeps drifting off the station. Further examples of such analogies are included in Chapter 9.

Interdisciplinary collaborations. The very nature of developmental pediatrics demands an interdisciplinary approach. Within the collaborative model there is often overlap between disciplines, and one should not construct rigid territorial boundaries. An educator can be an astute health case finder. A physician can make educationally relevant observations. A collaborative effort frequently involves a variety of specialists and therapists. Although developmental pediatrics frequently concerns itself with behavior problems, it should be perceived neither as quasi-psychiatric nor as competing with child psychiatry. In fact, the developmental pediatrician is likely to refer many youngsters to child psychiatrists, psychologists, social workers, and other mental health professionals (see Chapter 8).

JOB DESCRIPTIONS

It is hoped that this book will *not* become a definitive manual for pediatricians dealing with children who have learning disorders. Instead it should serve as a launching point for those who wish to be more responsive to the developmental needs of school-age children. Three levels of commitment might be anticipated:

The primary care physician with no special interest in the area. The pediatric generalist or family physician may have no special interest in developmental pediatrics but may incorporate the subject matter within his or her practice because of the prevalence of school problems among the physician's patients. In reading this book, such a clinician needs to become sensitized to the issues in order to enhance the quality of his advice-giving and referral patterns.

The primary care physician with a special interest in child development. It is not uncommon for primary care physicians to devote a portion of each week to a subspecialty. An increasing number of clinicians are acquiring this kind of focus with regard to developmental and behavioral issues. Such a physician might set aside one afternoon a week for extended developmental consultations. He or she might also spend time working (and teaching) in a learning or developmental clinic, acting as a consultant for a public school system, a special school or a variety of community service agencies. Such a physician may also participate in the training of interns, residents, and medical students.

The full-time consultant in developmental pediatrics. As medical centers become increasingly committed to the evaluation, management, and follow-up of learning problems, this aspect of developmental pediatrics is becoming part of a recognized academic subspecialty. In some centers this endeavor is contained within an ambulatory pediatrics program. In others a developmental pediatrician works within a self-contained unit for handicapped children. Such physicians may be involved in research, as well as in the design and implementation of training programs for future physicians and for personnel in other disciplines.

It is hoped that this book will be of interest to contemporary and future clinicians in all three of the above categories. Some may read these pages and feel that too much is being expected, that the approach being advocated is too time consuming, expensive, and logistically unrealistic. It is hoped, however, that readers will bite off and digest whatever portions of this content can be adapted readily to their professional environments, styles, and interests. This may range from simple appetite whetting or sensitization to a sizable commitment of space and time. The economic and political issues inherent in the life of a pediatrician in this field, although serious matters, will not be dealt with in this book.

Notwithstanding our recognition of a multiplicity of potential functions for pediatricians, it is helpful to list specific responsibilities that may constitute a basic pediatric role:

Facilitation of independent evaluations. As parents become increasingly wise consumers of educational and mental health services, there is increasing demand for evaluations that are independent of any political system and relatively free from disciplinary biases. In most cases evaluations within a school meet the needs of children with learning problems. In some instances, however, there may be the suspicion of inherent conflicts of interest. A school may be unlikely to suggest that a child has a language-processing problem, for example, if it has no speech and language therapist on the staff. Economic considerations, interstaff interactional problems, and assorted political issues may impinge upon the diagnostic process. For older children another potential conflict of interest exists: when evaluating such children, schools implicitly may feel they are evaluating themselves and the job they have done. This may lead to excessive defensiveness, to accusatory stances, and to undesirable adversary relationships between parents and school personnel or children and teachers.

The independent evaluation conducted outside a school can sometimes help in the mediation of actual or potential conflicts. Often the independent evaluation is sought by the school itself, especially when a child's problems are particularly puzzling, when health-related issues are suspected, or when an educational program has been utilized without measurable benefits. The pediatrician can either lead or participate in an independent evaluation process through a primary care office or within a medical center.

Early screening and detection. Because of his uniquely early access to children, the pediatrician may be the most important professional in the community with regard to the early detection of potential learning disorders. Routine screening of all youngsters (with particular emphasis on children considered to be at risk) can be incorporated into primary care services. The pediatric role in early screening has been described elsewhere (Dworkin and Levine 1979).

Continuity of care. The primary care physician is in a unique position to provide continuous longitudinal care for families. He is present in the newborn nursery after the birth of a child and ultimately available to perform a physical examination on the same child at entry into college. This enables the pediatrician to acquire a great deal of comprehensive knowledge about a child and his family while simultaneously establishing a trusting relationship. This can be particularly valuable in helping to formulate the problems of a youngster who isn't learning.

Providing a family perspective. The physician is privy to knowledge of other family members and the ways in which they interact with a child who is having difficulties. This kind of information can be helpful to a school and to other professionals working with a student with a learning problem.

Counseling and demystification. A potential pediatric role involves the opportunity to offer counseling as mentioned earlier in this chapter and elaborated upon in Chapters 8 and 9.

Community education. The physician can play a vital role in helping to elucidate constitutional, neurological, and health-related factors affecting all children with learning problems. Pediatric participation in inservice faculty programs can be helpful in sensitizing teachers to the problems of children with special needs. Lectures before parents' groups and community leaders can have a great impact. The primary care physician generally is viewed with respect by the community; his or her potential influence can be instrumental in obtaining services for all children.

Scientific consumer advocacy. Recently there has been an uncontrolled proliferation of pseudoscientific interventions for children with learning disorders. Such panaceas range from strict diets to elaborate exercise programs (see Chapter 7). Many therapeutic misadventures (some well-meaning, others fraudulent) are claiming increasing numbers of victims. It may be argued that in some ways they represent a defeat for pediatrics. It is essential that a pediatrician serve as a scientific advisor to families, helping them to discriminate between fact and anecdote, between well-established interventions and often expensive pseudoeducational placebos.

Medical and developmental consultation. The pediatrician has an implicit role as a resource regarding child development and related health issues. Such a professional is likely to be consulted by individuals from other disciplines as well as by parents. Familiarity with developmental issues is essential. Moreover, such a clinician needs assessment skills and the capacity to decode and integrate data generated by other disciplines.

Informed advocacy. In order to be an advocate for services for children, a physician needs to be knowledgeable about issues, diagnostic formulations, and available resources. In advocating for services, it is essential that the physician not be exploited unreasonably for his or her influence (see Chapter 8). For example, sometimes parents seek "a medical opinion" with the sole intent of obtaining a letter stating that the town should pay for a child to go to private school (for medical reasons). Such influence-gathering can represent a misuse of the pediatrician, while it sabotages special education within a community. In general the physician should concentrate on assessing the child and not on evaluating the school. It is helpful to avoid controversies about private versus public schools and, instead, describe the kinds of services a child needs, letting the community decide *where* these should be provided.

School health. Many school health programs across the country appear to be seeking redefinition. The pediatrician with a strong developmental orientation can serve as an on-site consultant for children with learning and behavior problems. Such consultations can be relevant and timely. Hopefully they will become an important aspect of the discipline of school health.

Follow-up and monitoring. In addition to his or her role on a diagnostic team, the physician can provide ongoing monitoring of the "titration" of services. Continuous availability can be particularly supportive to children and parents. Regardless of how or where a child is referred, it is essential that the physician remain involved in periodic review. Recommendations for specialized help should not be interpreted by the patient as terminations. If a referral does not succeed, a family should feel comfortable in returning to its physician for further consultation. A learning disorder needs to be managed like a chronic disease. Follow-up visits should be scheduled and therapeutic alterations recommended as needed.

Impact on public policy legislation. The pediatrician should remain informed and involved in the legislation at the local, state, and national levels. Groups such as the American Academy of Pediatrics will continue to be sensitive to public policy issues surrounding handicapped children. Developmental pediatric input into such legislation helps provide a well-balanced, responsible perspective.

THE DENOUEMENT

It is expected that the reader will be able to exploit this volume either as a reference source or as a cover-to-cover monograph. Chapter 2 reviews the history of learning disorders, highlighting the origins of specific concepts and the status of current controversies in the field. Chapter 3 describes some of the elements of development for the school-age child. In this chapter we adhere to an empirical approach, offering a description of clinical phenomenology or common manifestations of deficiencies involving each element. We then briefly consider historical clues, screening techniques, and standardized test instruments that might be used to elucidate a problem in a particular area of development.

Chapter 4 deals with school-related performance areas. It covers both normal function and deviation from what is expected. Some discussion of assessment techniques is provided. Chapter 5 explores the issue of assessment and systematic formulation. This awkward terminology has been used instead of *diagnosis,* which may suggest specific disease entities. The components of evaluation are summarized, and suggestions are made for medical participation.

The last four chapters deal with therapeutics. Sections are included on educational and medical interventions, and two chapters deal with alliance-building and developmental counseling.

There are several appendices. The first provides a survey of standardized examinations and a description of their content and use. The next is a glossary of common terms. Forms for the collection and reporting of clinical information are provided in the final section of this book.

This book presents one pediatric approach to learning disorders. It may also be a book about the rights of children.

2

Historical Overview: Where We Have Been

This passage quotes from a "certain Chinese Encyclopedia" in which it is written that "Animals are divided into: a. Belonging to the Emperor, b. embalmed, c. tame, d. sucking pigs, e. sirens, f. fabulous, g. stray dogs, h. included in the present classification, i. frenzied, j. innumerable, k. drawn with a very fine camel hair brush, l. etc., m. having just broken a pitcher, and n. that from a long way off look like flies." In the wonderment of this taxonomy the thing we apprehend in one great leap, the thing that by means of the fable is demonstrated as the exotic charm of another system of thought, is the limitation of our own, the stark and possibility of thinking *that*.

Michael Foucault, The Order of Things

Physicians have worked with public school systems for a long time. Their traditional responsibility has involved surveillance of children for "physical defects" and supervision of the school environment with respect to sanitation and the control of communicable disease. The role of the pediatrician in the assessment and management of the child with learning or behavioral problems, however, is a relatively recent phenomenon. It has evolved through a multitude of pathways which will be explored in this chapter (see Fig. 1, Chap. 1). Although the content of that role is not yet well defined, few contemporary critics have suggested that pediatric involvement in this area is unnecessary or inappropriate. Historical analysis of the subjects of learning disorders and special education will provide insight into the inevitability of medical-educational collaboration.

EARLY ROOTS

Until the late 1940s investigators in a number of disciplines were engaged in relatively independent and mutually isolated work that would later contribute to the development of the field of learning disorders in school-age children. The dramatic absence of significant cross-fertilization during this seminal period

18

underlines the striking diversity of these early sources and provides some insight into the reasons for the heated battle over definition that reached its peak in the 1960s.

The Genesis of Pediatrics

The subspecialty of pediatrics arose from within the medical profession at the end of the nineteenth century to deal with the challenges of infant nutrition. At a time when infant and early childhood mortality was unacceptably high, the physical health needs of older children were assigned a lower priority, and medical attention to the academic and behavioral performance of school-age children was understandably minimal. In fact, the preface to the first edition of *The Diseases of Infancy and Childhood* (Holt 1897) declared:

> The pathology and symptomatology of disease in children who have passed their seventh or eighth year really differ little from those of adolescents and young adults. It is in infancy and early childhood only that the peculiar conditions exist which separate pediatrics from general medicine and entitle it to be ranked as a special department.

The concerns of those in middle childhood, however, were not completely ignored, and, occasionally, voices were raised on behalf of their developmental needs as students. In 1900, in a book entitled *The Nervous System of the Child—Its Growth and Health in Education,* a British physician, Warner, wrote:

> In addressing this book to teachers I have endeavoured to indicate distinctly where help is required from medical science; as the opportunities for useful advice from the medical profession increase, it is necessary that there should be a common understanding as to the terms to be used in the descriptions of the conditions of childhood. For these purposes we must practice methods of observing children and making scientific inferences from what we see.

This pioneering book provided detailed descriptions of behaviors in school children that anticipated many of the later components of extended neurodevelopmental examinations, including tests for motor impersistence, choreiform twitches of outstretched fingers, and visual tracking. Other portions of the text advocated teaching theories that resemble the strategies articulated by some contemporary learning disabilities specialists:

> Training the general characters of brain action is a first step in mental hygiene towards developing the faculties in the child's brain which are to be acted on by your teaching: at the same time evolution of healthy action is encouraged and employed which renders the brain less liable to nerve storms in the form of emotion, nervousness, headaches, and other distressing conditions. There is a useless waste of brain power in the child when endeavors are made to correct and arrange thoughts that have only been partially formed in the brain; still, this seems often to be attempted too early by the employment of verbal instruction, and neglecting to train by impressions through the senses and by muscle sense.

Warner's, however, was truly a voice in the wilderness. Not until relatively recently did the concept of school health move beyond the traditional detection of sensory impairment or physical handicap and consider the careful observation of "healthy school children" with functional problems.

Aphasia as an Early Model

The earliest considerations of phenomena we now characterize as learning and reading disorders can be traced back through the extensive literature on *aphasia* in adults. The pioneer investigators were primarily neurologists, whose meticulous clinical examinations of adults who experienced sudden loss of speech often revealed concomitant loss of the ability to attach meaning to printed symbols. Early postmortem examinations of these patients revealed left-hemisphere lesions, which led to an anatomical classification of the various aphasias. According to Critchley (1970), Kussmaul, in 1877, was the first to describe the loss of reading ability, which he called *word blindness,* and ten years later Berlin (1887) suggested the term *dyslexia.* Although early studies were conducted solely on adults, children who failed to develop primary speech skills were generally perceived as having a lesion comparable to that found in adults with an acquired loss of previously normal language abilities.

The reports of a Scottish ophthalmologist on visual memory and word blindness in adults (Hinshelwood 1895, Hinshelwood 1896) prompted a British practitioner to describe a case of "congenital word blindness" in a 14-year-old boy with severe reading problems whose school master said he "would be the smartest lad in school if instruction were entirely oral" (Morgan 1896). In 1911, Town described congenital aphasia as a disorder in children that differed from the adult form in that it was not an inability to reproduce previously learned language, but rather a primary failure to "retain impressions." Despite these occasional pediatric reports, primary attention was directed toward the adult disorder, and the major thrust in the literature was toward identification and description of clinically observed phenomena, with less interest in remediation.

During the first quarter of the twentieth century, interest in the causes of primary reading difficulties grew. For some, the neuropathological lesions in adults with acquired alexia led to the hypothesis (never documented) that "congenital" reading disabilities resulted from structural defects in the angular gyri (Fisher 1910). For others, functional neuromaturational delays rather than anatomical abnormalities seemed to provide a more reasonable etiological model (Pipert 1924, cited in Critchley 1970). Out of this ongoing controversy, Samuel Orton expanded the neurological model and developed one of the first theoretical conceptualizations of reading disabilities in children. Based upon his work in the 1930s, Orton coined the term *strephosymbolia* ("twisted symbols") and postulated that mixed or incomplete cerebral dominance was the underlying reason for difficulties in learning to read. He based these views on his observations of frequent left-handedness or ambidexterity and the tendency toward reversals in writing and reading among the reading-disabled children he studied. Orton also believed that this abnormality of brain development was genetically determined, because of the increased incidence of the symptomatology he found within families (Orton 1928, Orton 1937). With his assistant, Ann Gillingham, he developed a variety of teaching strategies and remediation techniques that have endured longer than his theoretical premises (Gillingham and Stillman 1956).

Looking at the Eye

Although terms such as *word blindness* were commonly used to label learning problems associated with brain disorders without peripheral visual impairment, many investigators in the early part of the twentieth century explored the role of vision in the etiology of learning difficulties. In his classic monograph, Orton distinguished between reading and other visually dependent skills, and stressed that dyslexic children showed no significant evidence of visual deficits (Orton 1937). Whereas Farris (1934) demonstrated that problems in depth perception and ocular muscle balance in seventh-grade children were not associated with reading problems, and Fendrick (1935) found no relationship between ocular anomalies and the reading abilities of second- and third-grade children, Betts (1934) reported binocular coordination problems and considerable astigmatism in 90% of a reading-disabled population. Witty and Kopel (1936) repeated the latter study on a large school population and collected data which showed no significant difference in the incidence of visual defects among good or poor readers. They did demonstrate, however, that correction of marked visual problems in conjunction with remedial educational assistance resulted in im-proved reading skills. An extensive literature over the years has produced an accumulation of evidence to support the contention that peripheral visual problems play an insignificant role in the etiology of reading problems, but that eye problems can secondarily complicate a learning disorder and compromise the efficacy of educational intervention.

Early Concepts of Brain Damage

In 1902, the noted English pediatrician G. F. Still described a group of children with hyperactive behavior problems that were presumed to be a result of a variety of gross brain lesions and/or brain damage secondary to a documented cerebral insult. He distinguished these children from those with similar behavior not associated with demonstrable brain damage or central nervous system disease. The latter group had normal intelligence and was felt to have "defects in moral control." The "organic" problem was noted more often in boys than in girls. It was found frequently in children with unusual phenotypic features and was commonly first apparent in the preschool years. Often it had little relation-ship to the child-rearing environment, and it was generally described as resistant to punishment. Customary treatment at that time involved the use of medication and admission to a psychiatric ward (Still 1902).

The consequences of a major epidemic of Von Economo's encephalitis (encephalitis lethargica) in the United States and Europe in 1918 provided clinical evidence for an elaboration of Still's conceptualizations. Many adult survivors of the acute disease were found to have significant behavioral sequelae, including persistent hyperactivity, distractibility, irritability, affective changes, and antisocial tendencies without evidence of cognitive impairment. In 1921, a series of children was reported with apparently complete physical recovery from the disease. Psychological evaluation, however, showed dramatic behavioral changes including impulsivity, marked irritability, distractibility, and other deficits of attention. The authors believed that the substantial personality changes could be explained best on a purely physical basis. A treatment regimen of warm and wet packs, hydrotherapy, massage, and occupational therapy was prescribed (Leahy and Sands 1921).

The association of behavioral changes with a documented cerebral insult was further substantiated by Kurt Goldstein's studies of soldiers who survived head wounds during World War I. He referred to his patients as "traumatic dements" and documented significant psychological consequences of their cerebral injuries including perseverative behavior, perceptual difficulties involving figure-ground confusion, concrete behaviors, heightened responsiveness to a variety of stimuli, and catastrophic reactions characterized by marked emotional lability in conjunction with significant disorganization and disorientation (Goldstein 1936, Goldstein 1939). As a result of the studies of encephalitis and head trauma survivors, the linkage between hyperactive behavior and brain damage gained increasing acceptance. In fact, many clinicians began to hypothesize that when the behavioral disorder was observed in children without evidence for previous brain damage, one could presume that a cerebral insult had passed unnoticed and only became apparent with the demands of school (Ross and Ross 1976).

In 1937, Bradley published a study on the use of Benzedrine for the treatment of emotionally disturbed children in a residential center. He observed that those patients who received the stimulant medication exhibited increased interest in their school work, better work habits, and an improvement in their previously disruptive behavior. This first report in the medical literature on the beneficial effects of stimulant medication on the school performance of hyperkinetic children, however, had little initial impact. Many "hyperactive children" at that time, with or without organic brain damage, were expelled from schools, and physicians showed little inclination toward the use of such therapy on an ambulatory basis.

Although most early reports of behavioral disorders in association with brain damage dealt with well-documented neurological deficits, speculation also arose about the concept of clinically subtle, but behaviorally significant lesions. Arnold Gesell was one of the first to draw attention to the consequences of such "minimal" brain damage (Gesell and Amatruda 1941) when he wrote:

> The child with a selective injury is usually so obviously handicapped that sympathic understanding of his difficulties is a natural consequence. The child with only a minimal injury needs the very same recognition and understanding, and he too needs more than ordinary protection from stress and competition. . . . In all these cases, we are dealing with an extremely complicated interaction of developmental potentialities and dynamic forces. Even though the original motor injury was mild, the damages in the personality sphere may be considerable and more or less permanent. In the interpretation of the development of these infants, psychiatric concepts are often less helpful than an understanding of developmental neurology.

This concept of graded neurologic insult originating in early life was later expanded by Lilienfeld and Parkhurst (1951), who postulated a "continuum of reproductive wastage" extending from perinatal deaths to the consequences of subtle perinatal brain injuries such as learning disabilities and mild cerebral dysfunction. In 1961, Pasamanick and Knobloch suggested the alternative term "continuum of reproductive casualty" and included such entities as perceptual, learning, and behavioral difficulties. More recently, Sameroff and Chandler (1975) proposed the designation "continuum of caretaking casualty" to emphasize the potent impact of social and environmental factors on the ultimate developmental outcome of biologically vulnerable children (Rutter et al. 1970, Werner et al. 1971).

The Nurture Model

Although current research emphasizes the significance of constitutional disabilities, the primary role of emotional factors in the etiology of learning problems has traditionally been assigned considerable value by a number of clinicians and theoreticians. With the development of psychoanalytic techniques for children beginning in the 1920s, a recognition of the impact of early emotional conflicts led many investigators to emphasize the potent etiological effects on school dysfunction of intrafamilial emotional stresses. The behaviorists went even further by denying the existence of any inborn predispositions and characterizing the developing child as a completely passive victim (or beneficiary) of environmental influences. In a child-rearing book written for parents, John Broadus Watson (1928) wrote:

> Since the behaviorists find little that corresponds to instincts in children, since children are made not born, failure to bring up a happy child, a well-adjusted child—assuming bodily health—falls upon the parent's shoulders.

He went on to charge that:

> The vocation your child is to follow in later life is not determined from within, but from without by you, [the parents]—by the kind of life you have made him lead. . . . In a few cases where the child is physically defective, certain vocations become impossible, but these are so rarely met with that they need not influence our general conclusions.
>
> This doctrine is almost the opposite of what is taught in the schools at the present time. Professor John Dewey and many other educators have been insisting for the last twenty years upon a method of training which allows the child to develop from within. This is really a doctrine of mystery. . . .
>
> The behaviorists believe that there is nothing from within to develop. If you start with a healthy body, the right number of fingers and toes, eyes, and the few elementary movements that are present at birth, you do not need anything else in the way of raw material to make a man, be that man a genius, a cultured gentleman, a rowdy or a thug.

The combined influences of psychodynamic theory and behaviorism have had a potent effect on the way in which pediatricians have approached developmental issues in childhood. As late as 1954, the sixth edition of *Nelson's Textbook of Pediatrics* characterized the etiologies of reading problems as 75% personality imbalances, 10% poor teaching, and 2% to 3% neurogenic, with the remainder including miscellaneous combinations of factors. Although psychosocial and emotional issues were also raised in the early educational literature on learning disorders, they were never given as much etiologic emphasis as was found in the pediatric journals and textbooks.

Origins of Special Education—The Legacy of Mental Retardation

The concept of learning disorders in children with "normal" intelligence is a relatively young phenomenon in the field of special education, and its roots can be found deeply embedded in the history of mental retardation. Thus, when Binet and Simon set out in the early 1900s to develop an instrument that would help discriminate among the "mentally retarded," "poorly motivated," and "inadequately taught" children who shared the characteristics of poor school performance, the concept of "special learning disabilities" was never considered. Instead they classified all of the "abnormal" children into three groups:

> (1) the mentally defective; (2) the ill-balanced; (3) a mixed-type which includes those who are both mentally defective and ill-balanced. The simple defective do not present any well-defined anomaly or character, but they do not profit, or profit very little from the ordinary school teaching. The ill-balanced, who might also be called the 'undisciplined,' are abnormal chiefly in character. They are distinguished by their unruliness, their talkativeness, their lack of attention, and sometimes their wickedness. (Binet and Simon, 1914).

This simple dichotomy between "simple defective" and "Undisciplined" precluded any meaningful differentiation among the heterogeneous groups of children who failed to progress at an expected rate in school.

While attempting to classify the "defective child" for purposes of special class placement, E. R. Johnstone (1909) of the Vineland Training School in New Jersey observed that:

> The Medical college and the normal school make no effort to train their graduates to know them ["the defective children"], and yet, two or three out of every hundred patients and four to eight out of every hundred pupils should be recognized by the proper people [the doctor and the teacher] and steps should at once be taken to give them care, custody, treatment, and training.

Johnstone distinguished among:

> [the "idiot" who] is unable to do anything of value in the world . . . and in every way one from whom the average man or woman would shrink in disgust, [the "imbecile" who] may often be recognized by the physical signs . . . the uncoordinated gait, and the general air of stupidity or of excitability, [and the "feeble minded" who] may have a pretty face, a good form, and a pleasing way, [and whose "defective" nature] may only be apparent after careful study, but in most cases it will be seen that there is . . . squinting, twitching of mouth or blinking of eyes . . . incoordination of muscles, crankiness, obstinacy, indolence, inattention, or passion; imperfections of speech, sight or hearing; gross prevarication or exaggeration; pilfering and general lack of moral sense. . . . In some few cases none of these signs are sufficiently marked for anyone but the expert to detect them. The physician must look for adenoids, swollen tonsils, broken eardrums, tongue-tie, etc., for even slight imperfections often cause, for the immature brain, troubles out of all proportion to their apparent importance.

In a presentation to the National Education Association, Henry Goddard (1910) defined a "subnormal child [as] one who is unable to do school work at the usual rate, or any child who is behind his grade." He highlighted the confusion regarding terminology by classifying the "subnormal" population into two major groups.

> The temporarily subnormal . . . whose backwardness is due to sickness, physical impairment, or unfavorable environment, [and the permanently subnormal or "feeble-minded," which consisted of three subgroups—the "idiots" who] are totally

arrested before the age of three, [the "imbeciles" who] become permanently arrested between the ages of 3–7 [and the "morons" who] become arrested between the ages of 7–12.

Goddard described the educational presentation of these categories:

The idiots never get into the public schools. They are too low grade. The truant, incorrigible, and dullard may belong to any one of [the other] three grades. The truant is usually temporarily subnormal, sometimes a moron. The incorrigible and dullard are sometimes temporarily subnormal, but more often are morons, or imbeciles.

In his concern for the provision of "appropriate" schooling, Goddard clearly advocated a thorough diagnostic approach. He charged:

It would seem to be self-evident that the public schools should give special attention to every child that is a year or more behind grade. Generally a sufficient reason can be found for this backwardness. If it is defective sight or hearing, we send him to a specialist. If the reason lies in previous sickness or in the environment, the irregularity of attendance or change from one city system to another, the knowledge of the cause is sufficient explanation, and the child is not considered to need the special care. If no cause such as these can be discovered, then we must conclude that the child is either a moron or an imbecile.

The concept of educational differential diagnosis was publicly advocated in the early 1900s when the state of California enacted a remarkably progressive and prophetic Health and Development law, which included suggestions for the following:

1. The establishment . . . of annual physical examinations of school pupils and a follow-up service to secure the correction of defective development, thus maintaining continuous health and growth supervision of children and youth.
2. The adjustment of school activities to health and growth needs and development processes of pupils.
3. The special study of mental retardation and deviation of pupils in the schools.
4. [Provision for] a class of educators—experts in physiology, hygiene, and practical psychology—who can skillfully diagnose defective growth and development, and take more intelligent steps to grow children and youths.
5. [Facilitation of the] cooperation of this class of educators and all educators with skilled physicians (cited in The Training School, 1910).

Reaction to this legislation was not sufficiently supportive. An editorial in *The Training School* (1910) noted:

The law is permissive, not mandatory, but reads like a declaration of principles or a bill of rights, and is about as subversive in the field of education as the Communist Manifesto is in industry. Carried out to its full application, it would work a revolution in the public school system.

Unfortunately, a revolution in the American public school system did not take place, and pleas for considerable individuation of elementary education were rare and unheeded. Although special education techniques based upon the work of the early pioneers in the area of mental retardation were implemented, curriculum materials were uniform and applied to a variety of children with diverse educational handicaps. Their widespread dissemination was accompanied by little concurrent basic research. Moreover, despite a recognition of individual differences, a simple quantitative concept of "backwardness" was accepted in educational circles. Children were viewed as either normal or subnormal, competent or defective. It was not until Heinz Werner and Alfred Strauss began to talk about the importance of functional analysis of individual strengths and weaknesses rather than standardized test scores that the concept of retardation as a homogeneous condition was seriously challenged (Werner and Strauss 1939).

TRANSITION TO THE MODERN ERA (1940–1970)

A Critical Look at Mental Retardation

The emergence of an appreciation for the existence of specific learning handicaps came from the pioneering studies in the 1930s and 1940s of Alfred Strauss and Heinz Werner. In their work with brain-injured, mentally retarded children, they sought to investigate whether the psychological sequelae of brain damage that Goldstein had reported in adults could also be found in children. In order to test their hypotheses, Strauss and Werner popularized two categories of mental retardation—*endogenous,* which presumably was secondary to familial factors, and *exogenous,* which was felt to be secondary to a neurological deficit resulting from prenatal, perinatal, or postnatal brain insult. Through a series of elaborate psychological studies, they and their colleagues demonstrated that children with exogenous mental retardation, unlike the endogenous group, shared many of the psychological characteristics found in brain-injured adults, including perseverative behavior, conceptual disorders often associated with an inability to attend selectively to essential details, and a variety of perceptual disorders including auditory and visual-motor difficulties and problems with figure-ground distinctions. Deficits in fine and gross motor coordination were also noted. Behavioral differences included greater impulsivity, disinhibition, and socially unacceptable behavior in the exogenous group.

In *Psychopathology and Education of the Brain-Injured Child,* Strauss and Lehtinen (1947) emphasized the heterogeneity within the so-called exogenous group:

> The brain-injured group shows a great variety of brain defects. Some children are more disturbed in the perceptual field, others show no perceptual disturbance but a conceptual disorder, and still others may show only outstanding deviations in behavior.

In this classic monograph, the authors provided an overview of their group's work and suggested that the unique characteristics of the "exogenous children" required educational methods specifically directed toward their disabilities, and qualitatively different from teaching techniques that would be appropriate for the "endogenous child." They also cautioned that their findings concerned only mentally retarded children, but suggested that they might have implications for the education of other brain-injured children with or without intellectual deficits.

The specific educational recommendations formulated by Strauss and Lehtinen highlight the far-reaching influence of their work. Because of the "organic restlessness and distractibility" of the children, they suggested modification of the overstimulating classroom environment by removal to a small class setting (maximum number of 12), minimal visual stimuli on the walls, covered windows to reduce distractions from outside, and the use of cubicles or tables facing a wall. The academic and behavioral benefits of such classroom modifications were underlined by the authors:

> It is in such an especially adjusted environment that many children for the first time experience adequacy in meeting intellectual requirements. With decreased interference from the general organic disturbances comes an increased responsiveness to the learning situation. . . . The action of these processes is reciprocal: Control of behavior makes learning possible; knowledge gained makes possible more effective control of behavior.

Specific teaching materials, including perceptual motor training activities, were also recommended, but emphasis was placed on the need for a creative, individualized use of a variety of approaches by an insightful, flexible teacher (Strauss and Lehtinen 1947).

The work of Werner and Strauss can clearly be seen as the breakthrough that initiated the modern era in the field of learning disabilities. By underlining the critical importance of analyzing a child's strengths and weaknesses, they helped to destroy the myth of a homogeneous "mentally defective" population. In an area where theoreticians and educators had had virtually no meaningful dialogue, they combined a conceptualization of a neurologically determined handicap with a practical plan of classroom instruction. Their explanation for the "hyperactivity" and distractibility found in "exogenous children" provided a basis for understanding the problem of youngsters who were previously labeled as lazy, poorly motivated, evil, stupid, or emotionally disturbed. And finally, their emphasis on the importance of perceptual motor difficulties as a basis for learning disabilities had a major influence on the direction which this new field took.

Expanding the Spectrum of Brain Injury and Learning Disorders

The work of Werner and Strauss profoundly influenced an entire generation of investigators, who set out to explore its implications for a variety of educational handicaps. Under the direction of William Cruickshank and his colleagues, a number of important studies were undertaken in the early 1950s to explore the applicability of the Werner and Strauss findings for children with cerebral palsy and normal intelligence. This work provided substantial data demonstrating the increased prevalence of figure-ground discrimination problems, deficits in concept formation, visual motor difficulties, and problems in tactual-motor performance in this brain-injured population (Dolphin and Cruickshank 1951a, 1951b, 1951c, 1952). As a result of their studies, Cruickshank and Dolphin (1951) recommended major modifications of teaching programs for children with cerebral palsy, based upon the techniques proposed by Strauss and Lehtinen.

During the late 1950s, Cruickshank and his associates expanded their investigations to evaluate the usefulness of these same educational methods for the school management of children with normal intelligence, and the psychological characteristics of "exogenous" children studied by Werner and Strauss. Successful implementation of a demonstration project for these children with presumed "minimal brain injuries" provided compelling evidence in support of the growing belief that a cluster of behavioral and learning disorders were caused by brain damage and could be remediated through the implementation of specific educational techniques in a modified classroom environment (Cruickshank et al. 1961).

The Proliferation of Remediation

With the foundation laid by Werner and Strauss, and the demonstrated applicability of their concepts to physically able children with normal intelligence, a parade of educational theorists marched through the following decade advocating a variety of remediation techniques for children with learning disorders. A number of major figures adhered to the perceptual-motor model, whereas others adopted an increasingly popular linguistic approach. A monograph by Hallahan and Cruickshank (1973) provides an excellent review of the work of this era.

Among the proponents of the perceptual-motor approach was Newell Kephart, who worked with Strauss in his early years. For Kephart, perception and motor output could be best understood in terms of their relationship to each other. He placed a great deal of emphasis on the importance of the ability to distinguish between right and left on oneself as a prerequisite for differentiating between right and left in the outside world, which he viewed as essential for tasks such as shape and letter recognition. For children with perceptual motor problems, Kephart's book, *The Slow Learner in the Classroom* (1960), provided one of the most comprehensive discussions of the underlying theory and practical mechanics of remediation.

Gerald Getman, an optometrist, shared Kephart's emphasis on perceptual-motor abilities, with a particular focus on the assessment and remediation of visual-motor skills (Getman et al. 1964, Getman 1965). On the basis of his work with mentally retarded, brain-damaged, and perceptual-motor-disabled children, he provided much of the inspiration for the proliferation of eye-movement exercises and visual-perception motor-training programs that achieved a degree of popularity in the 1960s. Ray Barsch, who worked with both Getman and Kephart, developed the theory of "movigenics," which was based on the concept that learning depends upon the development of spatial movement patterns. In his program of remediation for learning problems, attention was focused on the development of muscular strength, dynamic balance, spatial awareness, body awareness, visual dynamics, auditory dynamics, kinesthesia, tactual dynamics, bilaterality, rhythm, flexibility, and motor planning (Barsch 1965, Barsch 1967).

Major emphasis on visual-perceptual skills formed the basis for an extensive program of diagnosis and remediation developed by Marianne Frostig in the 1960s. Her *Developmental Test of Visual Perception* provided a basis for evaluating abilities and designing a program of remediation for eye-motor coordination, visual figure-ground discrimination, form constancy, position in space, and spatial relations (Frostig et al. 1961, Frostig et al. 1964, Frostig and Horne 1964).

A. Jean Ayres developed a program of "sensory integration," whose objective was to facilitate the improved development of basic central nervous system functions such as perceptions and motor planning, with the assumption that the resultant increased abilities would be successfully applied toward academic tasks such as reading. Based upon an evaluation of such parameters as the status of primitive postural reflexes, equilibrium reactions, the level of excitability of the nervous system, and a wide variety of sensory perceptions (visual, auditory, vestibular, tactile, kinesthetic, etc.), a program was designed to enhance central nervous system integration through such activities as rubbing, swinging, spinning, hopping and climbing (Ayres 1965, 1972a, 1972b).

Although the language theorists in the area of learning disorders have only recently begun to achieve more prominence over the perceptual-motor advocates, a few notable adherents of the linguistic perspective established themselves as authorities in the 1950s and 1960s. Katrina deHirsch, a psychologist and speech pathologist who directed the pediatric language disorder clinic at Columbia Presbyterian Medical Center in New York, developed formulations of reading disabilities that drew upon perceptual-motor and psychopathological material, as well as a model of language pathology. In the early 1950s she described the receptive and expressive language disabilities of children with "dyslexia," including their difficulties with complex linguistic processing, word-finding, formulating of verbal output, and spatial and temporal concepts. Her studies of the prediction of reading failure in preschoolers were based upon a variety of perceptual-motor skills and body image, as well as a broad range of language measures (deHirsch 1952, deHirsch 1968, deHirsch et al. 1966).

Helmer Myklebust, another linguistically oriented figure in the field of learning disorders, began his work with hearing-impaired and aphasic persons, and, through his involvement in auditory disorders, he ultimately became interested in learning disabilities. Myklebust, who popularized the term *psychoneurological learning disability,* became interested in its etiological aspects and in the relationships between brain function and learning behavior (Myklebust 1968, Johnson and Myklebust 1967).

Clearly one of the most influential leaders in the field of learning disabilities has been Samuel Kirk, who spent the early stages of his career involved in the field of mental retardation. He is perhaps best known for his development in 1961 of the Illinois Test of Psycholinguistic Abilities (revised edition 1968) which is one of the most widely used instruments for the evaluation of learning handicaps (Kirk et al. 1968). Although the test was designed to assess psycholinguistic skills, it also contains some items that evaluate visual-motor function. The ITPA was designed to yield data that would have automatic applicability for planning teaching strategies, whose relevance would relate directly to the validity of the conceptual model on which it is based. Hallahan and Cruickshank (1973) noted: "In addition to the emphasis on language disabilities, it is this concern for the relationship between diagnosis and remediation which makes the work of Kirk and his colleagues so important to development of the field of learning disabilities."

Probably the most controversial treatment program for learning problems to arise in the 1960s was that developed by Glen Doman and Carl Delacato (Delacato 1959, Doman et al. 1960). From a theoretical point of view, the Doman-Delacato approach to reading problems was based upon the presumption of specific brain damage and the need for treatment procedures designed to promote improved neurological organization. This formulation was in marked contrast to other contemporary theories of remediation, which ignored the question of etiology and developed techniques based solely upon observed behavior. Components of the Doman-Delacato curriculum included a number of the more common perceptual-motor activities in conjunction with a variety of unconventional therapies such as passive manipulation of the child's limbs, and an attempt to improve unilaterality by forcing use of a dominant hand while inhibiting the use of the other. The pretension of a guaranteed, medically based cure for learning problems was viewed as seriously fraudulent by respectable medical authorities. The pseudoscientific approach of the Doman-Delacato group, its resistance to independent evaluation, and the extensive burden and potential guilt it imposed on the parents of handicapped children prompted strong critical statements from a number of professional organizations, including the American Academy of Pediatrics (1965) and the American Academy of Cerebral Palsy (1965). Although their high-pressure promotional methods continued, the proponents of the Doman-Delacato program were unable to produce any objective data to refute their critics and justify their treatment (Robbins and Glass 1969).

In summary, the decades following the seminal work of Werner and Strauss witnessed an enthusiastic expansion and implementation of their remediation techniques for children with learning disorders. Although most of the major figures during this period essentially followed the perceptual-motor standard, other perspectives, such as the language-disability model, gained some credibility. The proliferation of remediation programs, however, was not accompanied by a substantial amount of well-designed outcome evaluation studies. A review of the literature up to 1970 revealed a large and consistent increase in the number of articles dealing with brain-injured or learning-disabled children. A greater proportion of them, however, were characterized as theoretical in nature, rather than experimental or research-oriented (Hallahan and Cruickshank 1973). Thus, except for the censure received by the Doman-Delcato group as a response to its excessive promotional methods and undocumented claims for "miracle cures," most remediation programs continued with essentially no critical assessment of their efficacy. Moreover, as the identification of learning-disabled children became more widespread, parents' groups began to organize and demand increased implementation of "appropriate" special programs for their children in the public schools.

The Growth of Neuropsychology

While educationally oriented investigators searched for pedagogic breakthroughs, the traditional investigation of the neuroanatomical correlates of "aphasic" disorders was expanded by a new generation of neuropsychologists.

Based upon a reexamination of previously described syndromes, as well as a critical analysis of newly refined concepts, these researchers explored brain-behavior relationships for a wide range of clinical phenomena.

During the latter half of the 1950s, Arthur Benton reported a number of studies on the relationship between finger localization, right-left discrimination, hand preference, body schema, and finger praxis in normal, brain-injured, and mentally retarded children (Benton 1955, Benton 1959a, Benton 1959b). Although deficits in a number of these abilities previously had been demonstrated to be associated with left-hemisphere damage in adults, no consistent cerebral localization could be substantiated in children. Whereas concepts such as laterality had been considered important for the development of reading abilities by preceptual-motor theorists such as Kephart, Benton concluded from the available literature that right-left discrimination was *not* critical for reading. Although the significance of many of these specific developmental skills remained essentially equivocal, deficits in these areas were frequently observed in so-called learning-disabled children, and their relevance continued to be stressed by neurologically oriented investigators. In addition to his theoretical work, Benton developed a clinical instrument (Benton Visual Retention Test) designed to confirm a diagnosis of "brain injury" by evaluating the ability to reproduce geometric forms from memory (Benton 1963).

Much of the work in the field of neuropsychology has depended upon the availability of instruments to assess cerebral function. Ralph Reitan made major contributions to the development of a broad range of test batteries. Based upon modifications in the tests devised by Ward Halstead in the 1940s to study the psychological sequelae of brain injury in adults, Reitan developed a package for children that was eventually characterized as the Reitan-Indiana Neuropsychological Test Battery for Children. The areas of function assessed by this instrument include categorization abilities, tactual discrimination, rhythm analysis, auditory discrimination, conceptual and abstract thinking, and visual-motor skills. The availability of such batteries facilitated the completion of a broad range of studies on the psychological profile of "brain-injured" children and adults. Systematic attempts at lateralization of cerebral function demonstrated consistent association of gross verbal abilities with the left hemisphere and nonverbal abilities with the right in adults. For children, however, this simple differentiation was not consistently observed. Moreover, documentation of more specific localization in adults was generally equivocal.

Although much of the work in this field was conducted in the United States, important contributions were simultaneously made by a number of European investigators. MacDonald Critchley, a British neurologist who has written extensively about the sequelae of parietal lobe lesions in adults, produced a classic monograph on dyslexia (Critchley 1970). In the Soviet Union, A. R. Luria has written extensively about a wide variety of psychological tests used to evaluate a number of "higher cortical functions," and has contributed important work in the area of attention (Luria 1966).

The translation of neuropsychological data into educational planning has been problematic. Interestingly, as the work of the neuropsychologists became more sophisticated, the educational theorists and practitioners became less interested in matters relating to etiology and more oriented toward practical management and remediation issues. This conflict will be explored in more detail in the later discussion of the definition battles of the 1960s.

The Pediatrician's Response

At a time when the major theoretical figures in the field of learning disabilities were developing their models and beginning to have their impact on educational practices, pediatric participation in the overall evaluation and management of children with school dysfunction was quite limited. The concomitant availability of an increasing number of antibiotics and the development of new vaccines resulted in a major pediatric preoccupation with infectious disease in the two decades after Strauss and Werner opened the door to the modern era of learning disabilities. In this rapidly changing period in the history of pediatric practice, the prevention and treatment of acute disease received far greater emphasis than the long-term management concerns of chronic disability.

Children with persistent academic or behavioral difficulties in school were perceived by pediatricians in a variety of ways. In the fifth edition of Nelson's *Textbook of Pediatrics* (1950), in a chapter entitled "Neurotic Traits," Milton Senn and James Plant wrote about "nervousness" as "a symptom complex . . . applied to children who are abnormally and persistently restless, both physically and mentally, who fatigue easily and have a short span of attention, and who are over excitable or timid without apparent physical cause." In their discussion of the clinical manifestations of this emotional "symptom complex," the authors provided strikingly familiar descriptions of the characteristics currently applied to many children with primary attention problems and discrete areas of developmental dysfunction. These included observations on decreased inhibitory powers with exaggerated responses such as "flying off the handle," decreased tolerance for frustration, jerky muscular movements, sleeping difficulties, marked impulsivity, stammering, reading and writing problems, poor eating habits, fine-motor clumsiness, bowel problems, and general signs of "fatigue or of easily-produced fatigue of the nervous system." The management of the nervous child was believed to fall within the province of the family pediatrician, with the need for psychiatric assistance in the unusual case. The recommended components of an appropriate treatment program included "an abundance of mental and bodily rest," a well-balanced, nourishing diet, avoidance of scolding and ridicule, careful supervision, the provision of an appropriately designed school program, facilitation of association with other children, avoidance of parental catering to the child's whims, sedatives on rare occasions, and adherence to "the rule of not discussing the child's problems in his presence." "The nervous child," said the authors, "realizes that he or she cannot happily run his or her own life and welcomes the sturdy solidity of a routine that relieves him of this responsibility."

Over ten years before the term *minimal brain damage* was first introduced, "nervousness" was characterized by Senn and Plant as a much-abused term. They noted that:

Many parents speak of children as being nervous as an excuse for any sort of fault in upbringing; many physicians use the term to cover their ignorance of the underlying difficulty, and other physicians find its use a means of getting parents to ease the pressure being exerted on the child. The fact remains, however, that many children are brought to the physician because of nervousness, and even after the closest scrutiny some of them remain in this category. For this group of children some designation is necessary to catalog them and to define the procedures to be used in their treatment.

Little did Senn and Plant realize how enthusiastically that challenge to designate and categorize this symptom complex would be approached a decade later.

Reading disorders were also identified by pediatric textbooks as specific problems that were frequently brought to physicians and clinics for diagnostic purposes. In the fourth edition of Nelson's *Textbook of Pediatrics* (1945) they were classified as aphasic conditions. In the fifth edition (1950), after the publication of Strauss and Lehtinen's pioneering monograph (1947), reading disorders were presented as "disabilities (that) may have primary neurologic, ocular, endocrine, psychologic, and emotional origins." A broad-based, multidisciplinary evaluation process and a comprehensive management program addressing both academic and emotional needs was strongly advocated.

At a time when the neurological determinants of learning problems were receiving increasing attention, the psychodynamic approach to school failure remained strong in the pediatric literature. Laufer and Denhoff's (1957) description of a specific hyperkinetic behavior disorder presumably due to organic factors reflected an emergent concern with constitutional causes. Solnit and Stark (1959), on the other hand, acknowledged the role of "deviant visual-motor or auditory-motor coordination" in the evolution of learning problems, but stressed the major etiologic contribution of psychogenic and environmentally related factors. Perhaps the ultimate example of the psychodynamic perspective at that time can be found in the section on reading disorders by Ketchum in the sixth edition of Nelson's *Textbook of Pediatrics* (1954). Although the author characterized reading as "the most complex facet of the language function" which "calls upon the integrity and precise association of the major portions of the cerebral organization," he postulated that "adverse personality factors are becoming recognized as an important cause, not necessarily a secondary result, of learning disabilities." He then went on to say:

> For the preschool child, the average American home is a matriarchy. . . . The child's primary struggle for self-hood must, of necessity, be with the mother, owing to the father's daily absence. The child's initial school years are an extension of this situation; when these early relationships are reasonably healthy for the child, he usually does not present learning problems. When they are adverse, he lags in learning and generally his chief deficiency is in acquiring reading ability.

Children with reading difficulties were viewed as socially maladjusted, and this was presumed to be related to primary psychological problems rather than secondary to the burden of academic failure. In fact, the emotional basis for reading disability was so overwhelmingly accepted by some authorities that it was felt to account for such phenomena as letter or word reversals, omissions or substitutions of more familiar words in oral reading, and problems with reading comprehension in a child with well-developed decoding skills. Perceptual errors resulting in so-called mirror reading were said to be "of central origin" and their etiology "more likely to be psychogenic than neurogenic." When a child added words of his own to elaborate the context of an oral reading passage, it was presumed to be "symptomatic of psychologic maladjustment." If creative and flexible teaching could be provided, Ketchum declared that the general outcome for children with reading problems was good, with guarded prognoses reserved only for the relatively small numbers of children with "disorders resulting from organic factors" (Nelson 1954).

Generally speaking, during this period of increasing educational concern for the child with learning problems, those academicians responsible for the training of pediatricians did not consider such issues to be more than peripherally relevant to the practice of pediatrics. In fact, from 1940 through 1968 four successive editions of Holt's *Diseases of Infancy and Childhood,* even with its changes in principal editorship, reproduced its section on school difficulties without any revisions!

At the annual meeting of the American Academy of Pediatrics in October 1958, Leon Eisenberg spoke about the office evaluation of specific reading disabilities. He defined the pediatrician's responsibility as one of advocacy based upon a familiarity with community resources, and public involvement in the school system to assure the development of effective screening measures and appropriate intervention services (Eisenberg 1959). Although this model was generally adopted by practicing pediatricians, most pediatric training programs provided extremely limited and unsophisticated formal preparation for such a role.

With the publication of the seventh edition of Nelson's *Textbook of Pediatrics* (1959), a new section was added entitled "Behavior Problems Associated with Organic Brain Damage." This newly defined "diagnostic entity" was attributed to all children who demonstrated a variety of behavioral characteristics including distractibility, short attention span, perseveration, hyperactivity, impulsiveness, irritability, unpredictable variations in behavior, overreaction to stimuli, difficulty in abstract thinking, and figure-ground perceptual problems. The authors noted that this "syndrome" could occur in conjunction with motor and sensory deficits, seizures, and significant delays in the rate of mental development, or as the only manifestation of brain damage without associated disabilities. All degrees of severity were postulated and great variability in performance on psychological tests was noted. Although no definitive diagnostic studies were available, differentiation of this new entity from psychosis, mental retardation, and severe behavior problems secondary to psychodynamic factors was considered to be a pediatrician's clinical challenge. Special educational strategies, pediatric counseling, and occasional use of a variety of medications comprised the recommended treatment regimen. This overlap between educational and medical management of the school-age child with behavioral and academic difficulties became a major controversy in the turbulent decade that followed.

Expanded Visibility for a New Category of Children

The 1960s were a time of great political and social upheaval. In the United States, the images of "the New Frontier" and "the Great Society" created a climate of rising expectations and concern for "the disadvantaged" in conjunction with a persistent reassessment of many of the basic assumptions of the society itself. The traditional emphasis on formal education as the equalizer of opportunity contributed to an inevitable increase in interest in the problem of school failure. Socioeconomic factors and inadequate schooling were emphasized increasingly at a time when neurologically determined learning problems were receiving greater credibility than ever before. Divergent viewpoints and interdisciplinary isolation, however, had produced a tradition of fragmentation that precluded easy resolution of the controversies. During the decade of the 1960s, a new area of exceptionality achieved rapid recognition. Against a backdrop of a wide variety of inadequately evaluated intervention strategies and increasing parental pressure for appropriate services, a battle raged over definitions and management strategies for this new developmental classification.

The major battle line was drawn quite early between those investigators who concerned themselves with etiological questions and those who focused on behavioral characteristics and their remediation. The former group pursued the study of the neurological bases for dysfunction in learning and behavior, while the latter emphasized educationally relevant analyses with immediate pedagogic implications. For all, however, basic issues of terminology and taxonomy generated heated disagreements.

The classroom teacher at that time was generally isolated from the theoretical debates and their practical significance. Teacher training programs in the universities offered little if any preparation for the educational management of children with specific learning problems. Although there were college professors who knew about the special educational needs of mentally retarded children, they had little experience with the child with normal intelligence who failed to learn. To meet the demans of consumer groups, college programs were developed, but as Hallahan and Cruickshank (1973) noted, "It was the decade of the dilettante and the instant specialist in the university, as well as in the public school."

The Struggle for a Definition

A critically important theoretical formulation that arose in the 1960s was the shift from the model of "brain damage" to the concept of "dysfunction." In 1962 "minimal brain dysfunction" was first popularized in the American literature by Clements and Peters, while Bax and MacKeith were promoting the concept of "minimal cerebral dysfunction" in Britain. According to MacKeith, the Oxford International Study Group on Child Neurology decided that since the diagnosis was based on symptoms without documentation of actual damage, "the convenient but possibly illogical term of minimal brain dysfunction rather than the anatomical term of minimal brain damage" should be employed (Bax and MacKeith, 1963).

The article by Clements and Peters, on the other hand, was published in a major psychiatry journal, and its significance cannot be understated. The authors listed the symptoms frequently found in the "brain-damage behavior syndrome" and suggested that only a few may appear in a child with minimal brain dysfunction. These characteristics included specific learning deficits, perceptual-motor problems, general coordination difficulties, hyperkinesis, impulsivity, equivocal neurological signs, and either borderline or clearly abnormal electroencephalogram. Clements and Peters postulated that each child has his own unique cluster of symptoms, and the pattern of compensation varies with the child's intelligence and underlying temperament. The authors hoped that their message would persuade psychiatric facilities and guidance clinics to reexamine the predominant assumption that child-rearing patterns and interpersonal relationships are the primary causes of the described behavioral disorders. They suggested the need for a comprehensive diagnostic evaluation of such children, including a complete history and physical examination, neurological examination, a writing sample including a freehand drawing and a spelling test, and extensive psychological testing including the Wechsler Intelligence Scale for Children, the Bender-Gestalt Test, and a standard reading test such as the Gray Oral Reading. In their challenge to the psychodynamic heart of child psychiatry, Clements and Peters urged: "Granted the equal and often greater importance of experiential factors, we should not automatically fill the explanatory void with harsh fathers and overprotective mothers and give but cursory consideration to the organism which is reacting to such parents" (Clements and Peters, 1962).

Although many people regarded the contributions of investigators such as Clements and Peters to be important breakthroughs in the conceptualization of the "pathogenesis" of school dysfunction, others questioned its utility for educational therapeutics.

The existing confusion regarding the prevailing medical and educational terminology and the inadequacy of available teaching resources precipitated a succession of bold attempts to bring cohesion and clarity to this emerging field. In 1963 Samuel Kirk was invited to speak to a conference sponsored by a parents' group dealing with the needs of perceptually handicapped children. In his address he acknowledged the current semantic confusion and confronted the conflict between the etiological labels (brain injury, brain damaged, cerebral dysfunction, etc.) and the behavioral labels (hyperkinetic, learning disorder, perceptual disorder, etc.). He said (Kirk 1963):

> Research workers have attempted to correlate the biological malfunctions with behavior manifestations. . . . As I understand it, the task of the group meeting today, however, is not to conduct research on behavior and the brain, but to find effective methods of diagnosis, management, and training of the children. From this point of view, you will not be so concerned with the . . . category of concepts relating to etiology of brain injury or cerebral dysfunction, but with the behavior manifestations themselves and with the methods of management and training of the deviations in children.

After discussing the danger and relative uselessness of specific diagnostic labels, Kirk suggested the use of the term *learning disabilities* to describe a group of children who have disorders in development in language, speech, reading, and associated communication skills needed for social interaction. From this grouping he specifically excluded children with mental retardation and sensory handicaps, such as deafness and blindness. Kirk's presentation was so well received by the conference participants that they voted on the very next day to organize themselves as the Association for Children with Learning Disabilities (ACLD).

In 1965, Cruickshank organized a multidisciplinary seminar on "brain injured children" in which 27 of the foremost experts in the field of special education struggled with competing conceptualizations and problems of definition. As summarized by Hallahan and Cruickshank (1973), the debate between the medical-etiological and educational orientations was a major focus of controversy. James Gallagher rejected the term "brain injured" as being educationally useless and suggestive of a less hopeful prognosis. He proposed the alternative classification of "developmental imbalance," which he believed more accurately described the scatter of abilities characteristic of such children, and implied a "condition" more amenable to educational remediation. Elizabeth Friedus of Columbia University went even further and charged that the presence or absence of brain injury is irrelevant to a teacher. Sheldon Rappaport of the Pathway School in Norristown, Pennsylvania, on the other hand, argued that "brain injured" children should be made aware of their problem, and further charged that life-threatening neuropathology could be missed if etiological concerns were not addressed. William Gaddes, a neurophysiologically oriented researcher, criticized the absence of neurology in teacher education, and later he actually raised the question whether special classes should be designed differently for children with left- and those with right-hemisphere damage. Although issues of emphasis and definition were not resolved by this distinguished panel, the general flavor of the conference mirrored the clear trend in the literature of the early 1960s toward an increasing preference for educationally relevant behavioral terminology, and a decreasing concern among educators for etiology.

While the field of special education grappled with questions of management and remediation, the medical community similarly struggled with its own understanding of "dysfunctional children." Herbert Birch noted that "the fact of brain damage in children and the concept of 'the brain damaged child' are quite different matters." Because some children with documented brain damage do not exhibit the "characteristic" behavior pattern, and some children with "characteristic" behavior show no other verifiable evidence for damage to their brains, Birch proposed that the entity be considered a behavioral syndrome and not a neurological designation (Birch 1964).

In 1963 a series of task forces were set up jointly by the National Society for Crippled Children and Adults Inc.,the Easter Seal Research Foundation, and the National Institute of Neurological Diseases and Blindness of the U.S. Public Health Service to study the general subject of minimal brain dysfunction from the perspective of terminology, services, and research. In 1966 the report of the Task Force on Terminology and Identification was published. On the basis of a selected literature review, the members of the task force generated a list of 38 terms used to "describe or distinguish the conditions grouped as minimal brain dysfunction" (see Table 1). In an effort to incorporate a variety of emphases into a consensus working definition, the authors chose the term *minimal brain dysfunction syndrome* to refer to:

> Children of near average, average, or above average general intelligence with certain learning or behavioral disabilities ranging from mild to severe, which are associated with deviations of function of the central nervous system. These deviations may manifest themselves by various combinations of impairment in perception, conceptualization, language, memory, and control of attention, impulse, or motor function.

In their discussion of the diagnostic evaluation necessary to demonstrate the existence or absence of minimal brain dysfunction, the task force members emphasized the critical importance of both the medical and the behavioral-educational components (Clements 1966).

In 1968 the *First Annual Report of the National Advisory Committee on Handicapped Children* proposed the following definition (cited in Wiederholt 1974):

> Children with special learning disabilities exhibit a disorder in one or more of the basic psychological processes involved in understanding or using spoken or written language. These may be manifested in disorders of listening, thinking, talking, reading, writing, spelling, or arithmetic. They include conditions which have been referred to as perceptual handicaps, brain injury, minimal brain dysfunction, dyslexia, developmental aphasia, etc. They do not include learning problems which are due primarily to visual, hearing, or motor handicaps, to mental retardation, emotional disturbance, or to environmental disadvantage.

For each attempt toward synthesis and consolidation, however, there appeared another introduction of a new label and a somewhat modified perspective. On the basis of his early work in the areas of deafness and aphasia, Myklebust became interested in the critical importance of auditory disorders in the pathogenesis of learning disabilities, and he advocated the term "psychoneurological learning disability" to emphasize the brain-behavior interaction in learning problems (Myklebust 1968). In an important monograph in 1969, Chalfant and Scheffelin advanced the concept of "central processing dysfunctions," which attempted to solidify the marriage between the behavior-oriented and neurologically inclined. A number of theoreticians proposed a primary attentional model which provided an explanation for both academic and behavioral difficulties on the basis of maturational delays or deficits in the development of selective attention (Tarver and Hallahan 1974, Ross 1976, Dykman et al. 1971). Alternatively, Denhoff, Hainsworth, and Hainsworth (1971) developed an "information processing model" that provided a basis for the early detection of learning disabilities in the preschool years. As data began to emerge from their extensive longitudinal studies in New York in the early 1960s, Thomas, Chess, and Birch advanced the concept of congenital temperamental differences in children. This added yet another perspective to the armamentarium of the clinician seeking an understanding of behavioral issues in childhood.

For these investigators, psychological concepts such as attention span and distractibility were viewed as elements of an individual's emerging personality style, rather than signposts reflecting neurological deviance (Thomas et al. 1963, Thomas et al. 1968). Thus, the interaction between a child's temperamental characteristics and intra- or extrafamilial factors was felt to play a significant role in determining his or her function in school. When a child developed learning or behavior problems, it was considered that the cause might be a dissonance between school demands and the child's personality characteristics. Consequently, consideration of environmental expectations and temperamental matching (or mismatching) of child and adult were assigned greater legitimacy, as a variety of behavioral difficulties could be conceptualized and effectively managed through a "transactional analysis" (Thomas 1965).

With the introduction of fresh conceptualizations and new terms came the refinement of old definitions. Thus, in 1968, The Research Group on Developmental Dyslexia of the World Federation of Neurology (which included neurologists, psychiatrists, psychologists, and educators) updated their definitions of *dyslexia* ("a disorder in children who, despite conventional classroom experience, fail to obtain the language skills of reading, writing, and spelling commensurate with their intellectual abilities") as well as *specific developmental dyslexia,* which added the concepts of familial incidence, greater prevalence in males, characteristic reading and spelling errors, persistence into adulthood, and "fundamental cognitive disabilities which are frequently of constitutional origin" (cited in Critchley 1970). In the midst of the ongoing battle between those advocating a constitutional basis for "cerebral dysfunction" and those arguing for an environmental approach, Paul Wender, a psychiatrist, wrote a monograph on minimal brain dysfunction in children which sought to solidify the neurological approach by proposing a biochemical abnormality to explain the behavioral phenomena observed in children with learning disorders and hyperactivity (Wender 1971).

In the context of such vehement controversies, the pediatric literature of the 1960s reflected a predictably cautious, but earnest approach to the problem of etiology, diagnosis, and treatment of school dysfunction. Some published articles reviewed the causes of learning difficulties and stressed the need for pediatricians to sort through the variety of physical, emotional, and social etiological factors. (Glaser and Clemmens 1965, O'Sullivan and Pryles 1962). Synder and Mortimer (1969) characterized dyslexia as a major problem in pediatrics, and urged direct participation of the physician in comprehensive management. New chapters in the revisions of the standard pediatric textbooks reflected the rapidly changing terminologies by including such novel sections as "General Motor Restlessness" (Holt, McIntosh, and Barnet 1962), "Behavioral Patterns Associated with Minimal Cerebral Dysfunction" (Nelson 1964), "The Syndrome of Non-Motor Brain Damage" (Barnett 1968), "Cerebral Dysfunction (Brain Damage, Learning Disorders)" (Nelson 1969), and "Central Auditory Defects" (Nelson 1969). At a time when psychopharmacology was becoming a major factor in the practice of adult psychiatry, and a vigorous mass-media campaign by the pharmaceutical industry accompanied increasing public pressure for a "treatment" for children with behavioral disorders in school, the use of medication for dysfunctioning school children became widespread. Based upon limited empirical evidence, advocacy of drug treatment ranged from amphetamines for "hyperactivity" across a wide range of pharmacologic agents including major and minor tranquilizers, antihistamines, and anticonvulsants.

CURRENT STATE OF THE ART

While contemporary investigators and practitioners have continued to wage the traditional battles over etiologies and interventions, it is clear that a number of new perspectives and trends have emerged that seem to be representative of a developing consensus in the field of "school dysfunction." Whereas many of these new directions reflect a dramatic and refreshing shift in emphasis, it is likely that they too may ultimately be relegated to the status of "historically interesting" conceptualizations.

New Trends in Education

Despite the legacy of labeling school children according to their particular educational handicap, a major new orientation has evolved over the past few years. Instead of assigning specific diagnostic terms, such as perceptually handicapped or mildly retarded, increasing numbers of school systems have become part of what Janet Lerner calls "the non-categorical movement in education" (Lerner 1976). This new approach stresses the need for an individualized assessment of each child's unique combination of strengths and weaknesses, rather than an assignment to that diagnostic group whose essential characteristics he or she seems to match most clearly.

"Mainstreaming," the other major philosophical trend whose implementation has presented a revolutionary challenge to public education, provides a logical complement to the deemphasis on labeling. This principle embodies an advocacy of maximum integration of each child's educational experiences into a regular classroom setting. In practice, it may range from minimal remediation within a small group to the spending of a substantial portion of the school day in a highly individualized resource room. For multiply handicapped children who require intensive supervision that is not compatible with even minimal integration into a regular classroom, proponents of mainstreaming support the establishment of appropriate classes within the public school building itself. For those relatively few children for whom completely separate residential programming is clearly indicated, periodic reassessment regarding gradual reintegration into the public school setting is stressed.

The net result of the "nonlabeling" and "mainstreaming" philosophies has been an increasing appreciation for the variety of special educational needs that can coexist in a single public school. The problems created by this new approach, as well as the benefits, have been passionately debated. For some children, the net result has been the previously unavailable opportunity to attend their neighborhood school. For others, individualized modifications in curriculum have facilitated the achievement of success without sacrificing the continuation of nonacademic peer experiences.

In spite of pockets of opposition, it is clear that in the near future the mainstreaming trend will continue. Stimulated by the recent crusades for civil rights for all persons, as well as the more specific issues of the legal rights of children, legislative and judicial activity in the area of special education has rapidly expanded. An increasing log of parent-initiated litigation has confronted a number of public school systems with their legal responsibilities for the education of all their students. With the passage of Public Law 94-142, the federal government has provided the mandate for extending the right of a publicly funded, appropriately individualized educational program for *all* children.

The Neurologist's Response

While educational theorists and practitioners have grappled with a variety of teaching techniques for a multitude of learning and behavioral deviances, neurologists have sought ways to describe the unique characteristics of the central nervous systems of these same children. With the popularization of the expanded pediatric neurological examination over the past decade, a major diagnostic perspective was added to the evaluation of a child with school problems. Unfortunately, the early literature in this area did not demand a strict adherence to precise definition, and thus the confused concept of the "soft sign" came into general use without a clear understanding of what it represents. For some investigators, a soft sign referred to a subtle or equivocal manifestation of a classic neurological abnormality [what Martha Denckla (1978) calls a "pastel classic"]. Such examination findings were felt to reflect evidence of a mild but discrete brain deficit, which allowed the clinician to make a diagnosis of a localized lesion, albeit a "minimal" one. Because of their mild borderline nature, the identification of such soft signs was notable for a poor degree of interobserver reliability.

Unfortunately, the same terminology has been used in the literature for a qualitatively different class of positive neurological findings—namely, signs that are considered to be completely normal within a certain age group and deviant only beyond a specific chronological age. This class of soft signs has traditionally been associated with so-called neuromaturational delays or immaturity. Several papers, and Touwen and Prechtl's classic monograph (1970), attempted to provide standardized instructions for seeking and interpreting these developmentally relevant neurological signs. Although the degree of interobserver reliability for evaluating these examination items is better than that for the subtle classic abnormalities, cumulative normative data necessary for a valid interpretation are not completely available.

The significance of mild "abnormalities" or persistent immature responses is somewhat controversial. Those who assign the most value to the developmentally related findings perceive them to be what Denckla (1978) has called "next door neighbors to the substrate of constructs like attention, memory, and self-control for which we have inadequate examination correlates." Through guilt by association, many clinicians postulate that minimal deviation or immature responses on an extended neurological examination reflect minimal deviation or immature development of higher cortical processes necessary for successful learning. In an address before the American Academy of Pediatrics in 1972, Marcel Kinsbourne discussed this issue (Kinsbourne 1973):

> The part of the neurological examination which is relevant to reading is the physical examination of the association areas of the cerebral cortex. So you look back on the notes from medical school about the physical examination of the association areas. These are lacking. There is no such examination. When you do a physical examination, if you think you are examining a child for reading disability, you are mistaken. What you are doing is examining everything you know how to examine. You are in fact examining the rest of his nervous system—his spinal cord and brain stem—and your findings are relevant to those parts of the neuraxis. This does not make them totally irrelevant, because any agent that damages one part of the nervous system is quite likely also to damage another part of it. So, by a logic of guilt by association, if you find some hard and soft signs, that makes it somewhat more likely that the cognitive problem was also organically based. However, there are so many children without any physical abnormalities who have a reading disability that

is developmentally [organically] based, and so many children with nervous system damage all the way up to the cerebral cortex who do not have reading disability, that in the individual case you haven't gotten that much further.

A major recent theoretical analysis of learning disorders to evolve from the neurological model has been the concept of the *neuromaturational lag.* Kinsbourne adopted an extreme position when he remarked (Kinsbourne 1973):

> I have never seen a case of learning disability that was essentially any different from a younger child not yet ready to read. The kinds of difficulties that learning disabled children have are the kinds of difficulties in mastering the concepts that you would encounter if you were foolish enough to try to teach a three- or four-year-old child to read. . . . The possibility of further maturation always exists. The trick is not to change the maturation of the nervous system by some dramatic intervention—we have no way of doing that. It is rather to maintain the child in a climate in which he can benefit from further maturation, should it occur. This mainly means helping him to control his emotional reactions and get people off his back. This, I think, is the most valuable thing you can do.

The concept of neuromaturational lag as a unitary explanation for a learning disability is currently controversial among pediatric neurologists. For many, we seem to be entering a new phase characterized by development of a taxonomy of clinical syndromes defined by specific constellations of psychological, behavioral, and neurological findings (Mattis et al. 1975, Boder 1976, Denckla 1978b). As the table of proposed syndromes expands, the identifying combinations of attributes become more complex. For some, the number of discrete syndromes is as high as the number of theoretically possible combinations and permutations of developmental elements. Many argue that as each syndrome is divided into subclasses and variants, the concept of syndromology becomes less meaningful than simply describing the unique attributes of each child with school problems.

Contemporary Pediatric Roles

Pediatric roles in the assessment and management of school failure during the 1970s have been significantly influenced by rising consumer demands and the changing epidemiology of pediatric practice. Families, schools, and government agencies now seek medical assistance in evaluating a broad range of school-related academic and behavioral difficulties. Moreover, with the recent incorporation of adolescent health issues into the domain of contemporary pediatric training and practice, the natural history of school dysfunction and its relationship to later antisocial and delinquent behavior has received increasing attention.

While many pediatricians have welcomed this new area of responsibility with great enthusiasm, others have reacted with caution. As the time required to treat acute illness has diminished, and the need for frequent health maintenance visits has been questioned, many physicians have placed increasing emphasis on those aspects of the routine well-child examination concerned with anticipatory guidance and developmental assessment.

In 1973, the Council on Child Health of the American Academy of Pediatrics urged that multidisciplinary screening programs be established to facilitate early identification and follow-up of children considered at risk for learning problems. The literature of the 1970s has presented a variety of models for medical evaluation and subsequent management of a child who is failing in school. Suggestions have ranged from extensive pediatric neurodevelopmental assessment protocols, including laboratory studies and electroencephalogram, to assertions that reading problems are pedagogic concerns for which medical evaluations have minimal relevance (Kenny et al. 1972, Menkes 1976, Boder 1976).

In a study of 97 pediatric practices in New England in 1976, over 80% of the physicians endorsed the concept of preschool screening for potential learning disabilities in the primary care setting, and only 8% did not perceive school failure as an appropriate pediatric concern. The overwhelming majority of the primary care pediatricians interviewed defined their responsibilities in this area to involve some combination of direct school communication and individualized pediatric examination, with greater frequency of school contact and interdisciplinary team participation being found among younger physicians (Shonkoff et al, 1979).

The nature of the office examination and pediatric intervention for a school problem, however, remains poorly defined. This poor definition is somewhat related to the traditional pediatric relationship with psychiatry and neurology. As noted above, despite the growing literature linking "brain damage" with hyperactive behavior and psychological dysfunctions, the early pediatric approach to school failure was based upon a psychodynamic or behavioral model, which led to a search for emotional factors as contributory or primary causative agents. Beyond a faith and expectation that the school would provide appropriate instruction, the pediatrician offered family counseling for simple cases and referred more complex situations for psychiatric intervention. During the 1960s, the model of brain "dysfunction" gained increasing favor (and fervor). With the expanded emphasis on temperamental characteristics and their interaction with environmental contingencies, it has become increasingly appropriate to broaden the neurological model and talk about brain "variations" and learning or behavioral styles. Recent editions of pediatric textbooks have placed increasing emphasis on the issue of central nervous system organization, while continuing to stress the wide range of possible etiologies of school failure. Thus, although the role of neurological or constitutional factors is gaining substantial support, a transactional model that acknowledges the mutual contributions of constitutional and environmental factors is now most widely accepted.

Perhaps the most controversial aspect of the current pediatric role in the management of school problems lies in the realm of "hyperactivity." The literature in this area is extensive, yet inconclusive. Opinions range from a refusal of belief that the problem truly exists, to grim pronouncements of bleak prognoses (Kenny et al. 1971, Werry and Quay 1971, Ross and Ross 1976). Although many medical disorders have been reexamined and redefined as knowledge has increased over the past 100 years, no other symptom or syndrome has had its diagnosis and treatment so blatantly influenced by social and political forces. During the 1960s "hyperactivity" was generally accepted as a brain-damage syndrome for which stimulant medication was indicated and for which the prognosis for the adolescent years was considered good. After a decade of liberal use of medication for the treatment of the behavioral consequences of "minimal brain damage," questions were raised in the early 1970s about the use of drugs for social control, the general societal dependence on medication for solving problems, and the inadequate experimental evidence regarding the long-term effects of chronic medication in "healthy" children. Despite an abundance of research, methodological weaknesses have precluded the documentation of conclusive evidence supporting the relative efficacy of drug therapy as compared to a variety of other treatments for hyperactive behavior. As testimonials have been advertised in support of a number of alternative therapies, such as special diets and behavior modification techniques, the practicing pediatrician in the 1970s frequently has been asked to make recommendations based upon very few reliable data. This dilemma has been further complicated by the current recognition that so-called hyperactivity represents a spectrum of behaviors, rather than a diagnostic entity, with some clinicians suggesting that hyperactivity is often simply "that behavior which annoys the observer."

The general shift in emphasis away from acute medicine and toward the management of chronic physical disorders is another aspect of modern pediatrics that complements the increasing concern with developmental issues at all ages. Although they are relatively less prevalant than acute illnesses in the pediatric population, chronic diseases have become major health problems that present a whole new set of concerns for the practicing pediatrician (Pless and Pinkerton 1975). Medical and surgical breakthroughs have led to a dramatic decline in childhood mortality with a concomitant increase in children "living with a chronic disease." Unlike the child who recovers from an acute illness and returns to a "normal life," the child with a chronic medical problem must reconcile his biological handicap with the task of growing, developing, and learning. With the simple preservation of life now increasingly assumed, issues of quality have become more paramount. Thus, as the demand for comprehensive health care has escalated, attention to school function rather than merely school attendance has become a critical index of well-being. The traditional emphasis on acute hospital medicine in pediatric training programs has resulted in widespread concern among practicing pediatricians about deficiencies in their formal preparation. Repeated surveys have documented a clear desire for greater attention to chronic physical problems, such as allergy, and to chronic developmental issues, such as behavior problems and school failure (Becker 1978, Task Force on Pediatric Education 1978, Dworkin et al. 1979).

Where Do We Go From Here?

From its divergent roots in the fields of education, neurology, pediatrics, psychiatry, psychology, and psycholinguistics, the issue of learning problems in school-age children has clearly passed the point in histroy where any of these disciplines can continue productively in this area while remaining isolated from the others. This is not to say that adequate interdisciplinary communication has already been achieved. But it does highlight the essential, multidimensional nature of the problem.

For the pediatrician who wishes to become a developmental specialist with expertise in school problems, there is a critical need to collaborate with investigators who are seeking to understand the pathophysiology of inefficient learning and disordered behavior and with educational practitioners who will gauge the effectiveness of alternative teaching strategies. There is also a compelling need to develop evaluation techniques that can be used in pediatric settings to facilitate more meaningful and productive involvement in the total health care of children with school failure. All of these responsibilities must be integrated into the preparation of future generations of pediatricians for the demands of contemporary practice.

For the practicing pediatrician, the handwriting is on the wall: school-age children are a physically healthy group. Their performance in school has significant impact on self-esteem and their ultimate productivity and life quality. Function must therefore be a major health concern. The appropriate role for the primary care pediatrician in the care of a child with school failure is not yet engraved in stone. It is likely that much of what is proposed today will ultimately become a curious stage in the history of pediatrics. What will probably endure, however, is the pediatrician's role as an integrator of medical and developmental data, a demystifier of the "causes" of failure, and an advocate for the school-age child with special educational needs.

3

Some Elements of Development

I felt a cleavage in my mind
As if my brain had split;
I tried to match it, seam by seam,
But could not make them fit.

The thought behind I strove to join
Unto the thought before,
But sequence ravelled out of reach
Like balls upon a floor.

Emily Dickinson

As indicated in the Introduction, we assume that a description of the "elements" of development in the school-age child is likely to be more revealing than a laundry list of controversial syndromes. Future research indeed may lead to the establishment of dysfunction syndromes or the discovery of biochemical "lesions" (Shaywitz et al. 1978). Meanwhile, we hold that an infinite variety of profiles of strengths and weaknesses exist within a population of children.

This chapter describes clinical phenomenology likely to be encountered in children with specific functional deficiencies. An effort has been made to define each developmental element and to depict some common characteristics of children with clinical dysfunctions or variations. The elements were selected for their visibility, their association with learning failure, their fairly predictable dysfunctional manifestations, and their service implications. They do not represent *all* of the feasible dimensions of clinical assessment or of development.

When a youngster does not learn or acquire skills, the clinician may formulate a differential diagnosis based upon a careful and complete description of the child's developmental status in each of the elemental areas delineated in this chapter. The clinician may then seek convincing associations between specific developmental dysfunctions (or ineffective learning styles) and performance deficits in school. An evaluation should be considered incomplete if one or more elements of development have not been assessed adequately. •

46

The elements of development surveyed in this chapter are:

· Selective attention and activity
· Visual-spatial and Gestalt processing
· Temporal-sequential organization and segmental processing
· Receptive language function
· Expressive language function
· Memory
· Voluntary motor function
· Developmental facilitation
    Higher-order integration and conceptualization
    Cognitive strategy formation
    Working capacity
    Social cognition and adaptation

Introductory remarks concerning each element are followed by a description of the clinical phenomenology of dysfunction and a brief discussion of screening and assessment techniques. Later chapters deal with therapeutic approaches to dysfunction in each area.

SELECTIVE ATTENTION AND ACTIVITY

Most pediatricians are accustomed to dealing with issues of attention and activity under the clinical umbrella of "hyperactivity." Parents are likely to express concern about a child's activity level. Pediatricians often are consulted about a youngster who is ridden with impulses, who seldom finishes school assignments, and who is said to be distractible and fidgety. The process of discriminating between parents' or teachers' unrealistic expectations and truly problematic behavior is a common challenge for the pediatrician. Increasingly, investigators and clinicians are emphasizing one central aspect of this problem, namely selective attention (Ross 1976; Tarver and Hallahan 1974). An understanding of selective attention can help the clinician to manage a "hyperactive" child.

The progressive acquisition of selective attention is an important element in the development of the school-age child. Weak attention can create learning and/or behavior problems and, as we will attempt to show, learning problems in turn can weaken selective attention.

Attention is a perpetual, self-reinforcing selection process. At any given instant a display of internal and external stimuli compete for an individual's conscious focus. Such stimuli include immediate auditory or visual sensory data; information stored in long- or short-term memory; sensations originating in viscera, muscles, and joints; and fantasies, feelings, and associations (see Figs. 1 and 2). Through a process of selective attention, one (or a very few) of these incoming stimuli takes priority or achieves conscious saliency, while the others are relegated, at least tentatively, to the status of background or noise (beyond immediate conscious awareness).

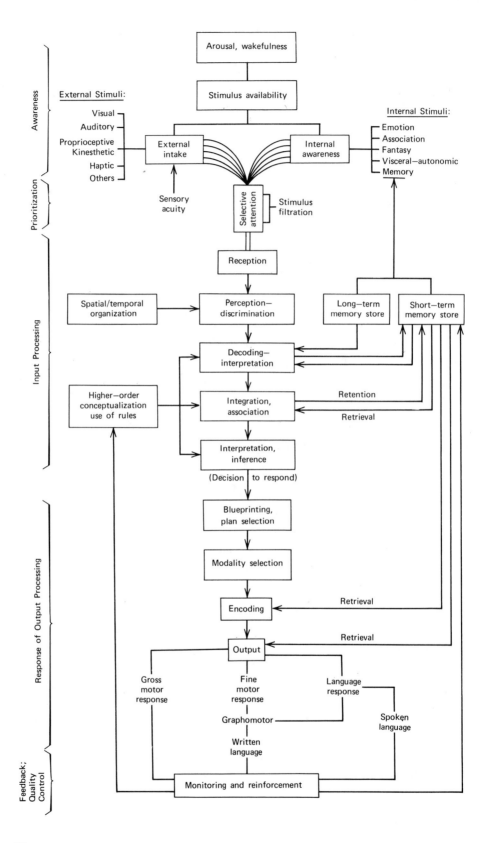

48

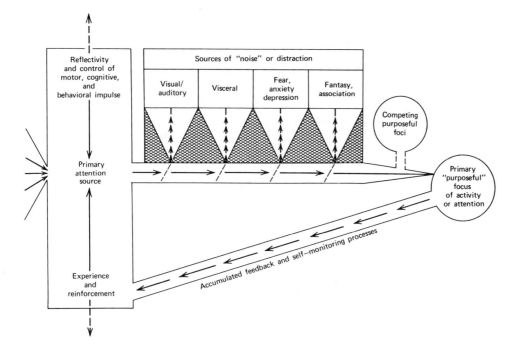

Figure 2. A CLINICAL MODEL OF ATTENTION AND ACTIVITY
This model illustrates the potential obstacles bypassed when a child focuses on purposeful stimuli. On the left side of the diagram is an abstract construct called the primary attention source. On the right side of the figure is a purposeful focus of attention or activity. Between the focus and the source are displayed a number of possible sources of distraction (sensory, visceral, emotional, and associative). Other competing purposeful foci also might deflect the "beam" of attention. The diagram illustrates that attention needs reinforcement; constant feedback and self-monitoring either make attention worthy of continuation or encourage tuning out. It is evident that the primary attention source can be either strengthened or weakened by experience and by the ability to mobilize reflective behavior. This kind of schematic diagram might be used to characterize an individual child's patterns of inattention—documenting, in particular, the form of distractibility, the extent of poor self-monitoring, and the role of emotional factors, impulsivity, and experience.

Figure 1. AN INFORMATION-PROCESSING MODEL
This model is not intended to represent the vast network of neuroconnections in the central nervous system. Rather it is a conceptual framework that can help to organize one's thoughts about the learning process in children. It can be seen that there are five basic levels of processing: awareness; prioritization; input processing; response of output processing; and feedback-quality control. Within this schema a variety of different types of sensory and internal stimuli are received, processed, integrated, stored, and used to program a response or communication.

In childhood, as in adult life, the process of selective attention allows one to focus on those stimuli that will be beneficial. When attention is optimal, one can concentrate for appropriate lengths of time on data that will lead to productivity, acquisition of knowledge, and enhancement of skills. When the machinery of attention is operating effectively, there is adequate immunity to distraction, together with an appropriately high level of reflection and persistence at tasks. Comprehension and problem-solving ability are optimized.

Participation in an activity can be similarly conceptualized. This, too, involves selectivity. From a wide range of possibilities at a given instant, a child chooses to engage in a particular activity. This may simply prolong what was pursued in a prior instant, or it may represent a change of agenda. Children who select activities purposefully are exploratory, efficient, and goal-directed much of the time; the level and quality of their movement adjusts to changing demands and environmental requirements.

Selective attention can be observed early in infancy. Numerous studies have documented the infant's growing awareness of distinctive detail in a mother's face, as well as an ability to ferret out discrepant or unusual stimuli (Fantz 1964). The tension between familiarity and discrepancy is part of a dynamic process of saliency determination which further affects the infant's choice of meaningful stimuli. In the toddler and preschool years, selective activity and attention become increasingly rational, efficient, and predictable. It is during such times, however, that a child may be perceived by adults as "hyperkinetic," inattentive, or erratic. A 30-month old toddler frantically pulling cans off the shelves in a supermarket may not be "hyperkinetic" but rather may be in pursuit of purposeful, exploratory objectives. The so-called "terrible twos" involves a series of intentional "expeditions" which, through trial and error, will enable toddlers to rehearse and enhance their processes of selection for both attention and activity. Parents may need a considerable degree of reassurance during this normal physiologic process.

By the time of entry into kindergarten a child should have developed an effective pattern of selective attention, a critical substrate for "educational readiness." The child should have begun to demonstrate purposeful attention with an increasing capacity to engage in reflective problem solving, to thwart impulses, to modulate activity, to persist at tasks, to adapt to the contraints of a chair, and to delay gratification.

Much of early academic success depends upon the capacity to select and sustain a focus. The acquisition of selective attention sufficient for learning is a triumphant developmental event between the ages of five and seven. As children proceed through elementary school, selectivity for both auditory and visual detail, along with sustained reflection, are requisites for knowledge and skill acquisition (Ross 1976). The retention of information rests heavily upon the intensity of initial focus. Those youngsters who are only superficially attentive are likely to retain less of what they have heard, seen, and experienced.

In late elementary and secondary school, the stress on attention is intensified to include demands for high volumes of written work and other forms of productivity. This will be discussed further in terms of working capacity. The child who cannot sustain attention or purposeful activity may have difficulty completing long assignments, finishing projects, and integrating information or data from multiple primary sources.

There is considerable confusion about the physiology of selective attention. Its precise neuroanatomical localization and its very primacy have been questioned. Is attention a neurophysiological process? Does it have its own network of neurons and a unique neurochemistry? Or, alternatively, is attention a clinical construct that helps us to explain normal and deviant phenomena? The considerable neurological and psychological literature on attention includes some useful reviews of the subject (Pick et al. 1975, Strother 1973, Hagan and Hale 1973, Donlas 1972). For purposes of clinical practice, selective attention and activity can serve as helpful abstractions and descriptors for the empirical characterization of certain failing school-age children.

Clinical Phenomenology

Attention deficits are often associated with academic, social, and behavioral failure in childhood. A series of examples taken from patient files offers some of the flavor of this phenomenon.

During an interview with a physician, a 14-year-old boy declared: "Doc, I'll tell you just what my head is like. It's like a television set. Only one thing: it's got no channel selector. You see, all the programs keep coming over my screen at the same time!"

A 9-year-old boy was sitting in the office of his pediatrician and listening intently as the physician described challenges and potential hazards of third grade. The physician, who had known of the child's chronic inattention for many years, was impressed by the sudden strength of the boy's focus. After three or four minutes of physician monologue, the boy interrupted. "You know, there's one thing I don't understand. I keep on hearing an air conditioner in this room, but I can't see it anyplace." So it was, while the physician thought that the child was focusing on his every word, the youngster was tuned in to the ventilatory sounds that he had selected as primary stimuli, relegating pediatric wisdom to the status of background noise!

In another instance, when a family moved to a new house, a young child who had a long history of attention problems and overactivity insisted that the wallpaper be removed from her new bedroom. She could not coexist with the stripes on the wall! She had difficulty filtering out this "visual noise" and became disorganized, inattentive, and preoccupied with this prominent covering, which her parents felt was not terribly "loud."

Many other examples could be cited. They would have in common the child's difficulty in focusing on the most purposeful stimuli, giving primary attention instead to stimuli usually considered extraneous or irrelevant.

There are widely conflicting estimates of the prevalence of attention deficits in children. It is well known that such symptoms affect more boys than girls, at a ratio of from six or eight to one (Ross and Ross 1976). In some cases the manifestations of attention weakness may be seen in early infancy with characteristic temperamental difficulties. In his description of children with minimal cerebral dysfunction, Paul Wender suggested that their common early temperamental attributes included irritability, unpredictability, and insatiability (Wender 1971). In other cases, children with attention deficits begin to manifest their problems in the toddler or preschool years. They may have difficulty "surviving" in a daycare center or other preschool setting. They may experience trouble with social interaction, skill acquisition and general behavioral organization. At home, they may be particularly recalcitrant. They may have chronic sleep problems, generally in the form of difficulty falling asleep at night. Some of these youngsters, as toddlers and preschoolers, are inordinately restless, whiny, and difficult to satisfy. They demand nearly constant attention, while refusing to share center stage with a sibling or with a parent's outside interests. Such a child can engender further conflict by alienating parents, peers, siblings, other relatives, and neighbors. In turn, aversive reactions (or overreactions) to the child can induce further isolation, anxiety, and behavioral deterioration.

In some cases, attention deficits are not evident until a child enters school, particularly when a youngster exhibits poor attention without overactivity. Normally active or, in fact, underactive inattentive children may be diagnosed later than those who display motoric "drivenness." Actually, such a "late-onset" attention deficit is likely to have been present throughout the earlier years. Often early demands for selective attention are not great, so that no problem is recognized. Only when such a child is confronted with developmentally appropriate complex tasks are attentional drift and poor selectivity observed. The added dimension of comparison with peers by nonfamily members is also significant. Recognition of poor attention depends to a large extent upon the standards and thresholds of the beholder. Individual parents and teachers may have widely varied levels of tolerance for weak attention, overactivity, impulsivity, and the like.

Table 1. Attention Deficits: A Summary of Common Concomitants

---

Propensity to tune in and out of selective focus capriciously. Poor vigilance to detail ranging inappropriately from perseveration to short span.

Distractibility. Difficulty prioritizing foreground-background phenomena; poor differentiation between noise or incidental data and central stimuli.

Impulsivity. Tendency to be poorly reflective, *not* to plan and monitor output, *not* to engage in forethought or deliberate problem solving, *not* to inhibit or "edit" inappropriate behavior.

Ineffective modulation of activity. Overactivity (in some cases), fidgetiness, purposeless motor output, inappropriate hypoactivity (in some cases).

Insatiability. Difficulty achieving a state of satisfaction or contentment; constant wanting; restlessness; whining (in young children); frequent irritability.

Poor reinforceability. Lack of adequate responsiveness to reward and/or punishment.

Easy fatigability. Difficulty remaining fully aroused and alert during day; frequent yawning; tendency to become excessively tired during cognitive activities.

Sleep problems. Especially difficulty falling asleep at night.

Task impersistence. Trouble finishing what is started. Diminished working capacity.

Developmental dysfunction. Neuromaturational delay or any conceivable combination of developmental dysfunctions. N.B.: Some children with attention deficits have *no* other developmental dysfunctions or information-processing weaknesses.

Incidental learning. A tendency to learn relatively trivial or less salient information as well as (or better than) more important or "central" data.

Free flight of ideas. The propensity to free-associate or daydream excessively.

Emotional lability. A tendency to change mood or affect unpredictably and often.

A variety of "symptoms" are encountered in association with attentional weakness; some have already been described. Such symptoms vary considerably, both in number and in level of penetration, from inattentive child to inattentive child. It is useful to understand how these behaviors are likely to affect interaction, personality development, and learning in the school-age child. The diagnostic evaluation of an inattentive child should include an adequate description of the specific clinical manifestations. Common observable signs and their clinical appearances are described briefly below (and summarized in Table 1).

Poor Selective Attention

The examples cited earlier typify the common kinds of difficulty with selective attention. A child may be overly sensitive to background noises and may attend better to incidental or irrelevant detail than to the central or most purposeful stimulus. There may be an eclipse of foreground/background distinction in virtually all modalities of input. A child who seems to be watching television attentively might, in fact, be concentrating on the knobs! A youngster might be better at overhearing than hearing. As one child commented, "Sometimes I can hear things three blocks away better than I can hear the teacher."

Experimental evidence indicates that many such children are as alert to incidental stimuli as they are to more central ones. Hagen and coworkers (1973)

Stimulus extinction is a minor neurological indicator that can be observed by the physician. A child sits with eyes closed. In succession each cheek and each hand is touched. Then one hand and one cheek are stimulated simultaneously. Very young children and those with neuromaturational delay are able to perceive only the proximal (rostral) touch during such simultaneous stimulation.

demonstrated that youngsters with attention deficits are nearly as adept at learning from a peripheral (incidental) cue as they are from a central stimulus.

A child with attention deficits may show erratic selective attention, tuning in and out of focus unpredictably throughout a school day. For this reason, teachers often report extreme *variability of performance* and wide shifts in the degree of concentration from moment to moment, hour to hour, or day to day. A cardinal feature of poor selective attention is its highly erratic and seemingly fortuitous flux.

Children with weak selective attention can show some improvement when the motivation for attention is increased (see Chap. 5, Fig. 1). What is important clinically, however, is the pattern of weak attention observed at normal, everyday levels of motivation. Rare moments of focus should never be used to rule out the presence of an attention deficit.

Distractibility

Related to poor selective attention is the phenomenon of distractibility. Children with attention deficits may be predisposed to specific modalities of distraction. In some cases, youngsters demonstrate a high level of visual distractibility. Their eyes seem constantly in motion, revealing their reluctance to commit themselves to visual choices. They may be insensitive to fine visual detail in reading, spelling, or drawing. Such children may lose their place when trying to read. In the classroom their heads may move erratically, in perpetual jerky, scanning movements.

Other children show predominantly auditory distractibility. They may have particular trouble attending in a bustling classroom. Their behavior may deteriorate in the cafeteria or in the corridors, where noise levels are especially high. Such youngsters may cover their ears with their hands (particularly in kindergarten or first grade) during periods of auditory distraction. Sometimes they complain or become irritable in the presence of background noises. At night, such children may have difficulty falling asleep because of auditory distractibility, rendering them susceptible to arousal by comparitively inconspicuous sounds. Many youngsters will give anecdotal reports of their own "hyperacusis," lamenting their inability to choose among competing auditory stimuli.

Some children appear to be distracted by their own thoughts. They engage readily in the free flight of ideas. For example, a teacher tells a class something about a dog. The child thinks of his friend's dog and, of course, of his friend. Then he thinks of how he and his friend played at the beach last summer. He then thinks about beaches and oceans. This leads to some thoughts about sharks. He decides that, when he grows up, he is going to go fishing for sharks in the ocean. While he is out there, he will stop off in Africa to go on a safari looking for elephants. Such free flight occurs while other more salient activities transpire in the classroom. This form of distractibility is common and can be devastating for a child. Such a youngster is often described as a dreamer.

Impulsivity

Many children with attention deficits are impulsive; this behavior contaminates their academic performance, social interaction, and decision making (Douglas

1972, Kagan 1965). They show little sustained, reflective behavior. They may be able to achieve proficiency only in tasks that can be accomplished quickly and with little planning or reflection. When required to pursue assignments that demand reflection, such children have difficulty monitoring the quality of their work, and they make careless mistakes.

Impulsivity may masquerade as a fine-motor handicap. A youngster's handwriting may be quite illegible, *not* because of poor pencil control, but because of the rate at which the child attempts to write. Such children may show improved performance in many areas when they are "decelerated," or asked to verbalize a plan before lunging at a task. Impulsivity may also lead to social embarassment. Impulsive children often commit *faux pas* through lack of forethought. Many of their acts may be offensive to peers or adults. It is not uncommon to hear the impulsive child express dismay because "nobody likes me." Often such youngsters are ostracized by their peers. (See Chapter 9.)

Inappropriate Activity Modulation

Not all children with attention deficits are overactive, and not all overactive children manifest attentional difficulties. Some underactive or normally active children display inattentive, impulsive behaviors: they have been called *hypoactive-hyperactive children*. A child may be overactive and difficult to manage, but the overactivity may be efficient and productive and the attention appropriately selective. Such a fervent youth may be mislabeled as hyperkinetic when, in fact, the child is displaying strengths and the potential for strong leadership in later childhood or as an adult. It is best not to control or "cure" such individuals! On the other hand, a child with *diminished* activity levels may be impulsive, inefficient, and inattentive. Therefore, the clinician must consider not just the amount of a child's activity but also its *quality, efficiency,* and *purposefulness* along with associated patterns of attention. Clinical tools, such as a dynamometer, cannot measure the appropriateness of activity. The qualitative assessment of a child's motor output depends more on prolonged, trained observation, careful consideration of efficiency, and judgment of the goal-directedness of activity selection from moment to moment.

Task Impersistence

Children with attention deficits often have great difficulty finishing tasks. Sometimes, because of their impulsivity, they complete only those actions that can be consummated quickly. The widely applied concept of "attention span" is not always useful in this context, since some children with attention deficits are masterful perseverators, such as the child who heard the air conditioning and not his doctor. A child with attention deficits may not develop durable, strong areas of interest. Such a youngster often shows only a superficial commitment to and interest in the surrounding world. Parents and teachers may note that as soon as the child arrives at the threshold of depth in an area, he "loses interest." Such a child may leave behind a record of dabbling in pursuits few or none of which were ever carried to completion.

Fatigability and Sleep-Arousal Imbalance

It has been observed that many children with attention deficits appear to fatigue easily. Satterfield (1972) has proposed that a subgroup of inattentive children are actually "underaroused." Such children may appear to have this dysfunction localized in the reticular activating system of the brain stem. Studies based on potentials evoked by auditory signals, on galvanic skin stimulation, and on reaction times have all suggested that some children with attention deficits are in a suboptimal state of alertness or arousal during their waking hours. In a sense, such youngsters may be less than fully awake during the day. Empirically, teachers and investigators have observed that some children with attention deficits appear fatigued. One frequently observes an overactive and inattentive youngster yawning. As one mother commented: "It's as if he's racing around all day trying to stay awake." Fidgetiness, distractibility, and weak attentional focus might be viewed in some cases as signs of fatigue or underarousal. In certain instances, beneficial effects of stimulant medication may be explained as helping to arouse the underaroused child (see Chapter 7). Conversely, the paradoxical effect of barbiturates might be accounted for in this manner. Such children often have a history of difficulty falling asleep at night. A subgroup of children with attention deficits seem to demonstrate an imbalance between sleep and arousal: not properly somnolent at night, nor fully alert during the day. In fact, a relationship has been noted between "hyperactivity" and the symptoms of narcolepsy (Navelet et al. 1976). The final word on the underarousal hypothesis is not yet available. Indeed, many investigators have argued that children with attention difficulties may be overaroused (Sroufe 1975). Such children are said to be too receptive to too many stimuli, or too arousable. There remains considerable controversy in this area. It may be that some youngsters with attention deficits are underaroused while others are overaroused. The bottom line may be a difficulty in regulating the processes underlying arousal.

Insatiability

A cardinal feature in many inattentive children is insatiability, (Wender 1971). Such youngsters have difficulty finding contentment. Their perpetual appetite, meets little satisfaction. The more that is given, the more is sought. Such young people seem in perpetual need of stimulation and attention. They are on a constant quest for some ever-elusive gratification. They may become whiny, restless, and chronically anxious. These traits are noticeable particularly in the preschool and early elementary-school youngster. The restlessness may become a lifelong theme, persisting through high school and into adult life. Under optimum conditions insatiability may evolve ultimately into ambition. At its worse, the trait of insatiability may lead to chronic unemployment, marital instability, and serious antisocial behavior.

Poor Reinforceability

Relative immunity to the effects of punishment and reward is common among youngsters with attention deficits. This may be related to insatiability, a trait that certainly limits the benefits of positive reinforcement. Parents will comment frequently on such a youngster's apparent insensitivity to punishment and on their inability to influence the child's future behavior through either threats or incentives.

Impaired Forgetting

The capacity to forget selectively is important for learning and survival. Many youngsters with poor selective attention also reveal impaired forgetting. Their minds tend to be cluttered with irrelevant detail, with accumulated trivia, and with incidental data that often stuns parents and other adults. Such a child may remember what color blouse Aunt Minnie wore last Christmas but be unable to recall a telephone message taken within the last 15 minutes. Children with this characteristic pattern may have a store of knowledge equal to or far greater than that of their peers, but the data base is irrelevant, inapplicable, and unrewarding in the conventional world.

Associated Learning Handicaps

Any discrete learning handicap or cluster of deficits may be encountered in association with attention weakness. Some youngsters with attention deficits apparently have no associated "specific learning disabilities." When a youngster has both learning handicaps and attention deficits, there is always some question as to whether inattention is secondary to the learning handicap or vice versa. Alternatively, an attention deficit and a learning handicap may coexist as independent but highly interacting variables. Inattention can impair the development of prerequisite learning skills, and cognitive handicaps can result in profound feelings of futility, which, in turn, may erode attention.

Attention deficits can be ranked under four general categories, as summarized in Table 2. Some children manifest *primary attention deficits.* They demonstrate (perhaps on a neurologic, genetic, or biochemical basis) a fundamental inefficiency and ineffectiveness in selecting foci for attention and activity. Specific manifestations as described earlier in this chapter may be present to varying degrees. Such youngsters may not be appropriately aroused, alert, or organized in their selectivity.

Other children can be said to have *secondary attention deficits.* As noted earlier, attention is a self-perpetuating process; an attentional focus needs to have a payoff if it is to continue. When concentration is rewarded with retainable and useful information, it is more likely to be sustained. A child with a secondary attention deficit may become inattentive because of specific handicaps in one or more areas of information processing. For example, a youngster with an auditory-sequential memory deficit may derive no attention-fixing reinforcement in the classroom because what is heard is so often poorly decoded or rapidly forgotten. If a child cannot process and store what has been heard, he is likely (secondarily) to become chronically inattentive or susceptible to competing, less complex stimuli. It is thus likely that many perceptual and cognitive handicaps, if they are sufficiently severe and relevant to learning, may engender secondary inattention.

Another form of secondary attention deficit is precipitated by emotional "drainage." Children who harbor psychosocial preoccupations may become chronically anxious, depressed, or affectively dysfunctional. Such concerns can drain a child's attentional reserve, producing a clinical picture similar to that associated with a primary attention deficit. Thus, chronic anxiety may masquerade as inattention.

The third major category is that of *situational inattention.* In this case there is no functional difficulty within the child but rather a discrepancy in the classroom, at

Table 2. A General Classification of Chronic Inattention in School-Age Children

Subtypes	Description	Some Common Associations	Common Denominators
Primary attention deficit	Intrinsic inefficiencies of selective attention	Early onset of temperamental dysfunction; Perinatal stress events; Signs of neuromaturational delay; Inattention in multiple settings and situations; Sleep disorders	Purposeless selection of stimuli; Weak resistance to distraction; Impersistence; Inefficiencies of motor activity; Insatiability; Impulsivity; Academic failure; Social failure; Performance inconsistency; Diminished self-esteem
Secondary attention deficit	Inattention secondary to deficits in information processing	Visual perceptual motor problems; Developmental language disabilities; Deficits of sequential organization and short-term memory; Signs of neuromaturational delay	
	Inattention secondary to pyschosocial and emotional disturbances	Family problems; Emotional disturbance in other family members; Primary depression and anxiety	
Situational inattention	Apparent inattention resulting from inappropriate expectations, perceptions, or educational circumstances extrinsic to the child	Tendency toward inattention only in specific settings or situations; Strong foci of interest and competence; Discrepant perceptions of child by adults	
Intended inattention	Inattention as a conscious strategy	Task-specific attention weakness—"designed" to avoid humiliation	
Mixed forms	Two or more subtypes	Relevent to subtypes	

home, or elsewhere. This comprises a variety of mismatching situations: inappropriate curriculum materials, inadequate teaching, discrepancies between a child's cognitive style and expectations in the school or home, discord between the child and the educational system, and misapplied academic pressures at home. Such phenomena of inattentive behavior may be confined to specific situations (e.g., one classroom) and are likely to be less pervasive or global than those seen with other forms of attention deficit.

One may encounter *mixed forms* of chronic inattention. A youngster's primary attention deficit may be aggravated by specific learning handicaps and emotional factors. The problem becomes particularly complex when this child's school setting is inappropriate. In such a case, a primary deficiency of attention is worsened by learning handicaps and anxiety and is strained further by situational mismatching.

A fourth category is *inattention by intention*. This may be noted particularly with older children who have been overdosed with failure throughout the years. Students have a limited tolerance for failure and humiliation. As the setbacks accumulate, a youngster may voluntarily "tune out" stimuli that are likely to lead to renewed feelings of inadequacy and social disapproval. In time, intentional inattention can become so well integrated in a child's strategic armamentarium that he is unaware of "tuning out."

The concept of intentional inattention is overdiagnosed. Often, it is far too easy to say that a child is intentionally inattentive, thereby neglecting the very real needs of youngsters with primary or secondary attention deficits, or of those languishing in inappropriate learning situations. The notion of intentional inattention has a moral cast to it. As such, it can perpetuate retribution rather than remediation for a struggling child. Intentional inattention should not be invoked glibly or without diligent investigation of other possible causes of chronic inattention.

Screening and Assessment

During a one-to-one encounter within the confines of a physician's office, a child with attention deficits may perform very well, and it may be difficult for the clinician to appreciate or sympathize with the anguish of parents and teachers. As a result, the clinician may offer inappropriate reassurance and mistakenly allocate blame to home or school. Very careful history taking, the use of questionnaires for parents and teachers, and direct observation of developmentally appropriate performance are essential for a valid assessment of a child's selective attention. Scales developed by Connors (1973) may be helpful. The Boston Children's Hospital Parent and Teacher Questionnaires included in Appendix C contain activity-attention scales designed to measure and account for much of the clinical phenomenology described earlier in this chapter. Although a total score may be useful, it is more important to focus on individual traits, their severity, and their specificity in various settings.

As discussed in more detail in Chapter 5, a neurodevelopmental examination can elicit or provoke attention weaknesses that are not apparent during a routine history and physical examination in the pediatrician's office. When the clinician proceeds through an assessment of neurological maturation and various devel-

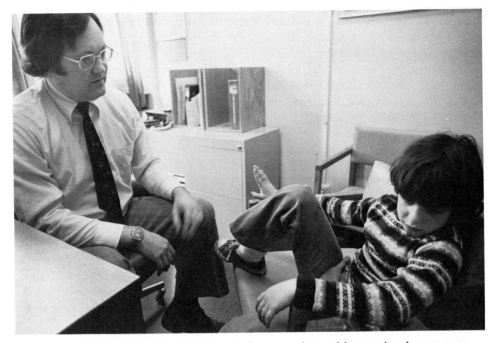

Frequently a child who is said to be chronically overactive and inattentive does not appear so in the physician's office. It is common, however, for such a youngster to become increasingly fidgety and inattentive during a neurodevelopmental examination. In this case, the child has been given developmentally appropriate tasks to perform and can be seen to "writhe," lose eye contact, and become impersistent. The neurodevelopmental examination can be a provocative test for attention deficits, enabling a physician to sample a child's concentration patterns.

opmental areas, a seemingly attentive child may become increasingly distractible, impulsive, fatigable, and fidgety. During a neurodevelopmental examination, the clinician can also look carefully at which types of activities elicit the greatest degree of inattention. For example, one might note that a child becomes impulsive when given complicated verbal directions. Alternatively, a child might tire easily at tasks involving fine motor output or the integration of a visual input with a fine motor response. Such empirical findings can be useful in educational planning and in counseling parents and children. The physician must integrate his or her own observations of the child's attention patterns with those perceived by parents, teachers, and other professionals.

Ultimately a description of a child's patterns of inattention is important in management of the problem. The nature of distractibility, the extent of impulsiveness, and the qualities of a child's poorly selective attention may have clear implications for regular classroom management and for special educational intervention. Symptoms such as insatiability, poor reinforceability, and inappropriate activity modulation all have direct implications for the counseling of parents and of children themselves (see Chapter 9). In short, painstaking description must form the basis for prescription.

VISUAL-SPATIAL AND GESTALT PROCESSING

One commonly hears of children who have difficulties with "spatial relations." A parent or teacher may comment on a child's visual perception, attributing to it either weakness or strength. Catching a ball, parking a car, using a road map, and decoding the written word all require an appreciation of the properties of space. The development of increasing discrimination in this area is an important process for the school-age child, having implications for both skill acquisition and self-esteem.

The nearly instantaneous appreciation of configuration, pattern, shape, or Gestalt is critical for comprehending the physical world. Shortly after birth, infants begin to explore spatial relations by moving their bodies and obtaining instant feedback from visual, tactile, and somesthetic (muscle and joint) sensory pathways. These circuits become integrated. Ultimately, a system of constancies and predictabilities evolves, during a period which Piaget has called the developmental stage of sensorimotor intelligence (Piaget and Inhelder 1969).

Perception is a process through which the central nervous system organizes sensory data. Visual-perceptual function refers to the ability to appreciate or discriminate between patterns and relationships in space. Keen visual perception helps academic progress, particularly in the earliest grades. A young child's judgment of spatial relationships potentiates an understanding of physical properties. Appreciation of position, size, contour, and whole-part relationships forms a basis for future academic progress. The ability to differentiate visually between various symbols or letters is a critical prerequisite for reading, writing, spelling, and arithmetic.

Visual perception is part of a broader central nervous system operation that instantaneously processes Gestalt or simultaneously presented data. This is in contrast to the processing of sequentially (or segmentally) presented stimuli (as covered in the next section). Although vision is the most common sensory modality through which holistic patterns and configurations are appreciated, our eyes do not have a monopoly on the collection of such information! Form appreciation can derive from proprioceptive and kinesthetic as well as other input channels. The perception of an overall shape or form is a precursor to its storage and eventual recognition or retrieval. Thus, a youngster who has difficulty with the appreciation of spatial attributes may have problems with visual memory for configurations and consequently with the recognition and retrieval of words, shapes, and even faces.

In the literature and according to traditional wisdom about the development of the school-age child, visual perception is often associated with visual-motor coordination (Kephart 1960). The latter depends, in part, upon the adequacy of spatial perception and the constant monitoring of visual feedback. Consequently, some children with a poor appreciation of spatial relationships may have difficulty interpreting data needed to produce a motor response. For many tasks a child must obtain information through seeing and then use this input to plan and execute a motor movement (praxis): catching a ball, tying shoelaces, copying words or geometric forms, and buttoning shirts are examples of complex activities that depend upon (among other things) visual-motor integration. In evaluating the so-called clumsy child, one should consider the adequacy of visual-spatial input. This will be discussed further in the section on voluntary motor output.

Clinical Phenomenology

The early identification of children with specific delays in the development of holistic or visual-spatial processing can be difficult. Developmental assessments in infancy and the early preschool years often are insensitive to subtle dysfunctions in this area. Initial clinical manifestations may include difficulty learning how to tie shoelaces, problems with discrimination between left and right, confusion and anxiety over the recognition of letters or other symbols, trouble catching a ball or riding a bicycle, and problems acquiring skills in drawing or copying. It is essential to recognize, however, that each of these symptoms individually suggests a differential diagnosis that is broader than a visual-perceptual handicap. Only by analyzing multiple tasks and using standardized observational data can one make a strong case for a visual-spatial disability.

A child with severe visual-spatial deficits is likely to encounter problems in learning to read. Initially, this might involve confusion between similar letters, such as *b* and *d* or *p* and *g*. The normal immature tendency toward letter reversals may persist beyond the expected age (this, too, having other "causes"). Concurrently, the child may experience difficulty recognizing certain words despite repeated exposures, or developing stable associations between sounds and visual symbols. What begins as visual-spatial confusion may progress to difficulties with visual recognition and concomitant struggles with the recall of visual configurations (words, faces, pictures) from memory stores. These problems then affect spelling and other processes demanding the revisualization of stored imagery. Visual-spatial disorientation can further interfere with writing, as the child may have difficulty with the visual planning of a page, with arranging words in sentences, and with spacing of letters and words. Such youngsters often have trouble copying from a blackboard or drawing.

There is considerable controversy about the extent to which visual perceptual handicaps have a lasting impact on learning. It had been thought that virtually all learning disorders were associated with confusion about direction, form appreciation, and the like (Strauss and Kephart 1955, Vernon 1960). Recently the pendulum has swung back; it is now believed that many such disabilities may be relatively trivial and self-limited and that deficits in language, attention, and memory may have longer-lasting impact. It is known that many highly successful adults continue to have problems discriminating between left and right, tying shoelaces, or parking a car. Moreover, many youngsters are able, independently or with assistance, to develop strong compensatory strategies that enable them to succeed in learning despite visual processing handicaps. On the other hand, it is certainly true that youngsters with severe visual-spatial disorientation may endure frustration and humiliation in their quest for skills.

The likelihood of a child's succeeding despite relative visual-spatial disorientation depends upon a number of factors. A youngster is most likely to experience failure secondary to visual-spatial problems if he does not have significant compensatory strengths in other areas (e.g., language or sequential-analytic abilities). Other predisposing factors might include experiential deprivation, inability to "find" compensatory strategies, low preacademic motivation, low overall intelligence, negative early academic experience leading to learning inhibition, emotional problems, and the rare case in which visual-spatial disorientation is so severe that it can be neither bypassed nor ameliorated.

Screening and Assessment

Many historical clues, as summarized in Table 3, might suggest that a child has visual-spatial or Gestalt processing problems. Visual-spatial orientation often is assessed by asking children to copy geometric forms that are standardized for age. Typical examples are illustrated in Figure 3. Regrettably, these tasks are highly contaminated: factors such as fine-motor ability, pencil control, experience and visual attention are some of the variables operating in form copying. A child who is delayed in such copying does not necessarily have a visual perceptual, problem, although this finding might be taken as one bit of evidence for such a deficit, suggesting the need for further evaluation. Tasks involving the search for hidden figures in a picture, and those requiring matching of similar patterns, are examples of visual-perceptual activities that are not contaminated by significant motor output.

Support for the diagnosis of a visual-perceptual problem may be derived from certain subtests of the Wechsler Intelligence Scale for Children (WISC). In particular, depressed scores may be seen in object assembly, picture completion,

---

Table 3. The Screening Assessment of Visual-Spatial Processing Deficits

Clinical Clues from the History

Delay in learning directionality concepts, telling left from right, mastering visual-spatial-directed tasks (e.g., tying shoelaces, putting on socks, catching a ball).

General motor awkwardness in some cases. (*N.B.* Some children may be "well coordinated" and yet have visual-spatial confusion.)

Excessive visual distractibility, problems with visual figure-ground relationships, difficulty with visual pursuit or tracking.

Difficulty learning to recognize and discriminate between visual symbols (e.g., letters, numbers), leading to later slowness or awkwardness with symbol formation (writing).

Problems with drawing, tracing, using scissors, fixing things.

N.B. Most of the above are influenced strongly by motor output, experience, memory, and the capacity to *integrate* a visual or somesthetic input with a motor response.

Some Screening Tasks

Form Copying
    Approximate Standards: See Figure 3 for specific forms.
    Comments: Form copying also measures fine motor and/or pencil control, experience or practice, visual attention, and eye-hand coordination.
Dressing-Undressing, Writing, Catching a Ball
    These are difficult to standardize, but may yield some fragmentary evidence for visual-spatial confusion.
    Visual-motor *integrative* function plays a critical role in these tasks.

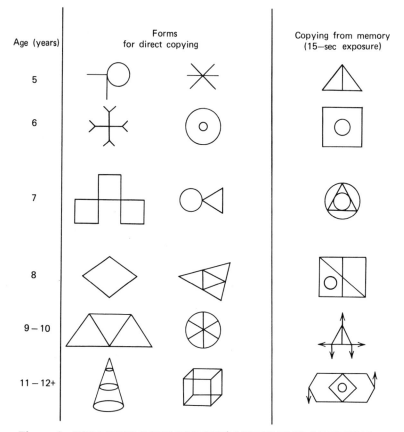

Figure 3. FORMS TO COPY FOR THE SCREENING OF VISUAL PERCEPTUAL-MOTOR FUNCTION
These forms may be used by the physician in the process of screening. The child should be asked to copy them, using a sharp pencil and unlined paper. Immature performance may reflect any of a variety of problems, including visual-spatial disorientation, inexperience, fine motor weakness, impulsivity, and difficulty with visual-fine motor integration. *This screen should never be used as a definitive diagnostic test.* Suspicious findings should be validated through the history and more comprehensive standardized examinations.

and block design. Again, these subtests also measure other functions and therefore require careful interpretation. More formal tests of form copying include the Developmental Test of Visual Motor Integration and the Bender-Gestalt Test. Other standardized tests, such as the Frostig Developmental Test of Visual Perception and Ravens Progressive Matrices, are said to be more direct measures of visual perceptual development. These tests have been well standardized and have a long track record (see Appendix A).

TEMPORAL-SEQUENTIAL ORGANIZATION AND SEGMENTAL PROCESSING

Learning and communication depend, to a great extent, upon getting things in the right order. To communicate efficiently with words, a speaker must arrange syllables in a meaningful sequence; for sentences, individual words have to be organized in proper serial order. Following directions, counting, telling time, using a calendar, and arranging a schedule all involve the manipulation of time segments. As noted in the previous section, children progressively collect information about relative size, position, shape, and whole-part relationships as they develop their visual-spatial orientation. A similar growth process is seen as youngsters acquire knowledge that organizes their universe based on information that comes in "packages" in which the *order* of stimuli is important. To learn how to tie shoelaces, the sequence of the steps must be perceived, stored, and applied to the task. Success depends upon performing the steps in the proper order. A well-developed ability to understand and store sequences of information is a critical prerequisite for academic success.

Early in life, children acquire experience with time and sequence. Many of the data they are expected to assimilate are delivered in a serial order that is crucial to meaning. Remembering requires an ability to store information in the correct sequence. Much of a child's daily routine depends upon sequential organization; wrist watches, calendars, class schedules, meal times, and even a variety of normal body routines testify to the importance of time sequences. Young children acquire a progressive appreciation of order as they master routine rhythms, days of the week, and months of the year, and as they begin to comprehend time-oriented vocabulary such as *before* and *after, today* and *tomorrow*, and *now* and *later*.

As children progress through the school years, their capacity to deal with sequences is essential for learning to read, for spelling, and for mastering many basic concepts of numerical order. In later elementary school, when the demands for written output increase, effective sequencing becomes an important part of the organization of written reports. The arrangement of ideas in an essay clearly calls for good sequencing abilities.

Sequential organization is critical for learning (Bryden 1972, Hurwitz et al. 1972, Rudel and Denckla 1976). The child must retain sequentially-presented information to follow instructions in school and at home. Sequencing ability pervades many sensory, perceptual, and motor processes. There are visual sequences (e.g., of objects or letter symbols), auditory sequences (e.g., of numbers, words, or musical notes), and sequences for the execution of complex motor activities.

Clinical Phenomenology

Children confused about sequential organization may have serious problems with short-term and intermediate storage and retrieval of information. Parents and teachers may describe a child as one who seldom follows instructions, seems unable to retain what has just been said, and gets overloaded or bewildered when a series of directions is presented.

During the preschool years, a child with temporal-sequential "disorganization" may appear to struggle when learning time-oriented prepositions, such as *before* and *after*. Time relationships in general may be a source of constant indecision. As one young child said: "Daddy, I sure hope you come home late tonight, so we can play before it gets dark." Such children often have difficulty learning the days of the week, the months of the year, and the order of school or home routines. Parents and kindergarten teachers have observed such youngsters harping constantly on questions such as: "Did we eat lunch yet, or is lunch before?" Such temporal confusion is particularly blatant in children in the preschool and early elementary grades. Ultimately, these youngsters master temporal prepositions and show steady improvement in their time orientation. Many youngsters with temporal-sequential problems are delayed in learning to tell time. As they progress through school, they may experience problems with spelling because of difficulty remembering the order of letters in words. Their errors in both reading and spelling may reflect confusion about sequence (e.g., *saw* for *was*). Children with sequencing difficulties may also be somewhat delayed in the acquisition of basic number concepts and overall mathematical skills. Many have problems mastering the multiplication tables.

Some youngsters with sequencing problems appear to be chronically inattentive. According to their teachers, they tune in and out during classroom instruction. In many cases the reason is difficulty with multistep directions. For example, a teacher may tell the class: "Open your books and turn to page 14. Answer the questions at the top of the page. Then turn to the next page and copy those new words. When you're all finished, close your books and put down your pencils and sit up straight, so I will know you are done." A child who has difficulty retaining sequential information may have registered only something about a pencil! He may react by becoming disruptive or secondarily inattentive; he may be chastised for copying his neighbor's work.

As we have noted earlier in this chapter, attention demands reinforcement. If information is presented in complex sequences and a child cannot process these, his attention is unlikely to be rewarded, and so there will be a tendency to tune out. Thus, temporal-sequential disorganization can be an important cause of a secondary attention deficit. Such children may show maladaptive classroom behaviors, partly as protective strategies or as manifestations of frustration and anxiety secondary to their disabilities.

We noted earlier that sequential organization is also important for spoken and written output. Children with sequencing problems may have difficulty organizing narrative in an appropriate order. Their parents may comment that is agonizing for them to tell a joke or relate an experience. In the later elementary schools years, as the demand for written output increases, such youngsters may have particular problems with the organizational aspects of written expression.

Some children with sequencing difficulties have problems with complicated athletic activities. They may be weak at motor sequential organization, or they may become confused over rules in such sequentially sophisticated team sports as baseball, football, and basketball. In the early years, they may experience some delay in surmounting such motor-sequential challenges as shoelace tying and bicycle riding.

Children with deficiencies in sequential and segmental processing may be relatively inattentive to the fine detail of written words. Their rather superficial, segmental processing may result in careless reading mistakes and in a tendency to overgeneralize from context, since they favor more of a holistic than an analytic approach to decoding. The acquisition of good reading and spelling skills is enhanced by a child's capacity to dissect the component sound units in a word and then to resynthesize words utilizing correct sequences of these units. Children who have difficulties with sequential organization may experience considerable frustration with word segmentation and reblending processes. They may rely too heavily upon Gestalt or holistic-configurational cues to word recognition and retrieval. Early reading and spelling ability depends, in part, upon a synergism between holistic-Gestalt processing and sequential organization.

Screening and Assessment

Many clues from a child's history can suggest the possibility of a problem with sequential organization. Subtle early developmental confusions, as already noted in this section, can be used as presumptive evidence for such a problem (clues from the history are summarized in Table 4).

Table 4. The Screening Assessment of Temporal-Sequential-Analytic Deficits*

Clinical Clues from the History

Lateness in mastering time-laden language e.g., sooner, later, before, next, etc.) sequence of days of the week, serial order of months.

Delay in learning how to tell time.

Confusion over number concepts, problems with multiplication tables.

Sequential errors in narrative organization, syntax, spelling, reading.

Deficit of short-term memory: problems following multistep directions, retaining telephone messages, complying with sequential instructions at home.

Tendency to accomplish tasks (e.g., getting dressed) in the wrong order.

Problems learning to segment and blend words for analysis.

Difficulty with complex sequential motor activities.

Some Screening Tasks

Digit spans: The clinician recites a list of numbers at one per second without intonation. Child repeats in same order:

Approximate Standards: Ages 4 to 6: four numbers; ages 6 to 8: five numbers; ages 9 to 12: six numbers forward, four to five numbers repeated by child in reverse order.

Comments: This task also reflects attention, meaningfulness of numbers, and the rate of processing. It is affected adversely by anxiety.

Object Span and Block Tapping: Examiner points in various sequences to a series objects or blank squares on a desk. The child then repeats them in the same order.

Approximate Standards: Ages 4 to 6: four objects (or squares); ages 7 to 9: five objects; ages 9 to 12: six objects.

Comments: Success also depends upon sustained visual attention. The object span is affected by the meaningfulness of the objects to the child.

Table 4. (Continued)

Serial Commands: Examiner gives a sequence of simple commands. Child carries out the commands in the appropriate order. Example: "Put the pencil on the chair. Open the door. Put the pencil in the drawer and sit down."

Approximate Standards: Ages 4 to 6: three commands; ages 6 to 8: four commands; ages 8 to 10: five commands; ages 10 to 12: six commands.

Comments: Several sets of commands should be given. Look for omissions and sequencing errors. Children with receptive language problems may also perform poorly in serial commands.

Sequential Knowledge:

Ages 4–5:	Count forward 0–10
	Which comes first, lunch or breakfast
Ages 5–6:	Count backward 10–0
	Days of week forward
	Letters of alphabet
Ages 7–8:	Days of week backward from Thursday
	Seasons of year
	Spell out "was" and "dog" backward
	Able to tell time
Ages 8–10:	Months of year forward
	Count backward from 30 by 5's
	Spell "live" and "dial" backward
Ages 10–12:	Months of year backward from April
	Count backward from 50 by 7's

Comments: The above "acquisitions" are influenced by cultural and educational factors, such that failure may *not necessarily* indicate sequencing deficits (nor does success necessarily rule out such problems).

* Clinical clues and screening observations should suggest formulation hypotheses to be confirmed by additional evidence. Children with sequencing deficits may *not* show problems in *all* areas listed. Some of these historical hints and task weaknesses may indicate problems in areas other than sequencing (e.g., memory, rate of processing, attention, segmenting ability, anxiety). Standards of performance may vary somewhat, especially under the influence of cultural differences.

Having a child repeat a series of numbers in the correct order (digit span) taps into the immediate retrieval of a sequence and often is interpreted as a measure of auditory-sequential memory. Although there is considerable contamination by other functions such as the weaknesses of a child's number concept, concurrent anxieties, or attention deficits. Children with slow rates of processing may also fail in digit spans. Nevertheless, in screening for sequencing problems a digit span can be useful. A child's appreciation of visual order and his capacity to retain and integrate a visual sequence with a visual-motor output can be assessed through the use of an object span, in which the child is asked to point to a series of items in a particular order, as demonstrated by the examiner. A block-tapping exercise is performed in the same manner, using squares instead of recognizable objects, thus eliminating perceptual and meaningful cues. Tasks of visual-sequential memory are influenced by the strength of a child's visual attention.

Problems with sequential organization are common in a population of youngsters with learning difficulties. The pediatrician can screen for some forms of sequencing weaknesses. Here he has pointed to the objects on the desk in a particular order; the child is expected to point to them in the same order. By varying the number of objects, the examiner can adjust the difficulty of the task.

One can also administer serial commands that involve a sequence of instructions, observing the child's ability to integrate an auditory sequence with an appropriate series of gross motor responses. Pure motor sequencing involves imitation of physical activities, as demonstrated by the examiner. Screening observations for sequential organization are summarized in Table 4. Such tasks are currently being standardized for use in clinical settings.

Well-established, standardized tests can screen for a suspected problem with sequential organization. Assessments of visual sequencing and auditory sequential memory are included in the Illinois Test of Psycholinguistic Abilities. In addition, the Digit Span and Picture Arrangement subtests of the WISC may suggest sequencing problems. The Detroit Tests of Learning Aptitude include subtests which are said to measure attention span but also have implications for a youngster's sequencing ability, since they involve memory for serial order (see Appendix A).

Clinicians evaluating sequential organization should be aware that a generalized "slowness" of processing can mimic a sequencing problem. A child

RECEPTIVE LANGUAGE FUNCTION

Receptive language function involves the interpretation of auditory stimuli and the extraction of meanings from words and sentences. The capacity to decode language accurately promotes a child's understanding and mastery of his surroundings. Language acquisition enhances self-awareness, interactions with others, and attainment of academic skills. The accumulation of a usable vocabulary coincides with a child's struggle to find meaning and establish symbolic associations, while the discovery of syntax, or a sense of the rules and grammar by which words are linked, helps to facilitate meaningful communication.

The tight bonding of academic readiness to language development has been appreciated increasingly in recent years. An understanding of the progression of normal language acquisition can be helpful in dealing with the language aspects of learning problems. Five stages have been described by Menyuk (1975) and are summarized below.

Before babbling. During the earliest weeks of infancy, babies utter both crying and noncrying sounds. The nature of these sounds is conditioned somewhat by the mother's responsiveness to them. From these vocalizations the earliest antecedents of conversation emerge. By two months infants show increased competence in discriminating between various speech sounds, rhythms, and intonations. Young infants vary considerably in their "linguistic behavior." In particular there are wide differences in the degree to which babies use communication to manipulate the environment.

Babbling. In this stage the infant's repertoire of speech sounds grows, as does the frequency of such utterances. Repetitive consonant as well as vowel sounds are produced. It is possible to begin to discern what are called prosodic features (intonations and stresses) of the babbled utterances. The infant begins to respond differently to different voices and to use his utterances for specific purposes. There is increasing vocalized interaction with the mother. At this stage there are considerable individual differences in the rate of acquisition of new speech sounds. These differences have been found to depend on constitutional variations, socioeconomic status, and sex.

One word. The one-word stage of language development is the beginning of what has been termed true language. At first infants begin to notice and produce word-length utterances. They acquire the concept that any phonological (i.e., sound) sequence "can stand for or represent an object or action in the environment" (Menyuk, 1975). The infant can then associate the sounds he hears with particular objects and events. Ultimately, he begins to relate what he hears to what he produces. The young child begins to recognize that sequences of sounds represent something. By 15 to 24 months of age, most children have passed the 50-word level. The rate of acquisition of this vocabulary varies considerably, as does the content. It has been noted that at this stage some children use language mainly to categorize extrinsic phenomena, while others use it to express and manipulate. Maternal feedback and individual experiences are influential factors.

Two words. During this stage two-word utterances emerge, and the beginnings of semantic relationships are expressed. This is also a stage at which the earliest development of syntax begins. Children begin to establish the importance of word order, as well as prosody (rhythm and intonation), in communication.

Acquisition of the grammar of language. In this late-toddler and preschool stage, the language of the child can be increasingly understood apart from the context in which it appears and the gestures that accompany it. Markers of tense and number appear. There is modification of noun and verb phrases and sentences. The child begins to determine the rules used in generating sentences. Menyuk cites the following example: "The child begins by generating negative sentences through adding the negative word to the topic of the sentence ('No go'). The child then specifies in each utterance who is not going ('Me no go,' or 'Daddy no go'). He then specifies the time or mode of action ('Daddy no can go'; 'Daddy no going'). He finally applies the negative attachment rule in the appropriate way and generates the complete negative ('Daddy isn't going'; 'Daddy can't go')."During this stage children also acquire rules for expressing relationships between sentences, as well as within sentences. They learn to conjoin sentences and to embed sentences, utilizing various relationships expressed by words such as *and, but, because, when,* and *where.*

A child who reaches school age is able to produce utterances that are, for the most part, grammatically and semantically appropriate. Through experience the child has acquired a strong sense of the rules of language. Future development will enhace this facility. In addition, during the school years children will experience a continuing growth in vocabulary, as well as an increase in the versatility and depth of their comprehension of individual words. Certain aspects of language development may parallel the growth of higher conceptual abilities, whereas other components of language may relate more closely to perceptual development. Children who are particularly agile or adept in the processing and use of language are likely to find it easier to acquire basic skills in all areas.

Psycholinguists have characterized a child's innate sense of the rules of structures and systems of cues in verbal communication as *metalinguistic awareness.* This critical strength portends a potentially redeemable cognitive style in a youngster with learning deficits in other functional areas.

As a child's education progresses, language expectations become increasingly complex and germane. This shift may be contrasted to that noted for visual-spatial skills, which are emphasized during the first three elementary grades.

Clinical Phenomenology

The language of psycholinguists becomes increasingly complex each year. Nevertheless, a number of clinically applicable conceptual models have emerged in recent reviews of the relationships between language and learning (Wiig and Semel 1976, Johnson 1968). The phenomenology described in this section is derived from these and other models of language processing. A simplified scheme is illustrated in Figure 4. An overlapping though nonexhaustive listing of observable language underpinnings in the school-age child is provided below. Children with language-based learning disorders may have difficulty in one or more of these general areas of function:

who often misses the last steps of a serial instruction may do so because he is taking too long to interpret and store the initial segments.

Further evidence for sequential disorganization may be harvested from an analysis of a youngster's errors in spelling and reading. As children enter secondary school, a basic disorder of sequencing can be more difficult to document with standardized tests. For older children, the clinician may need to place a great deal of importance upon a re-creation of the history, including the kinds of difficulties the child has had throughout his school career (see Chapter 5).

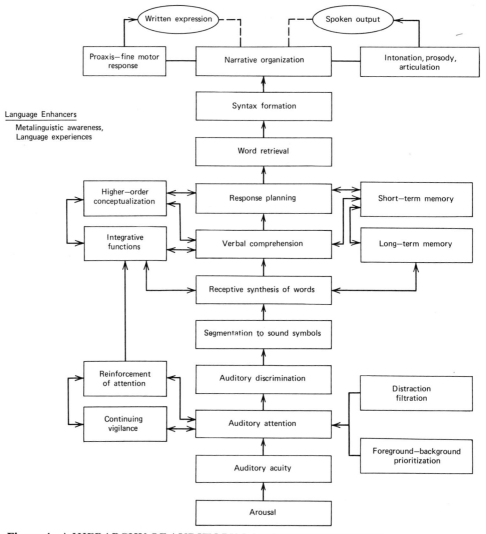

Figure 4. A HIERARCHY OF AUDITORY-LANGUAGE FUNCTION
This highly simplified diagram may help the clinician to conceptualize some steps involved in the reception, decoding, and expressive use of language. Children with developmental problems in this area characteristically may reveal deficits at one or more of the points illustrated in this figure.

Auditory acuity. Sensorineural hearing losses, or pathology of the ear canal, tympanic membranes, or the peripheral anatomical structures can interfere with the passage of sound to the cerebral cortex, thereby causing symptoms that may mimic a problem with central auditory processing. Chronic serous otitis media may be an antecedent of hearing deficit and later language disability (Ingram 1976). Such sensory losses must be ruled out in the evaluation of all children with possible or actual language impairment.

Auditory attention. Selective attention to human speech sounds is necessary for optimum language function. Children with weak auditory attention may have difficulty suppressing extraneous background noise. Such an auditory figure-ground problem may present clinically as a behavior disorder, as overactivity, or as a type of "hypercusis." Kindergarten or first-grade children so affected may cup their hands over their ears in order to "turn down the volume" of extraneous auditory input. Such children may avoid noisy places. As with other aspects of attention, weak auditory focus may be either a result or a cause of language impairment; in some cases it may represent both. Children with auditory inattention may manifest impulsivity when presented with highly verbal tasks and appear far more reflective and attentive when confronted with visually based instructions.

Speech-sound discrimination. The capacity to tell the difference between similar auditory signals obviously is crucial for optimum language processing. Confusion between phonemes (sound units) can create significant problems when a child attempts reading, which necessitates the establishment of firm sound-symbol associations; when the sounds are not perceived as distinct, the associations are weak (Popp 1978, Jonson 1968). The significance of auditory discrimination handicaps is a matter of some controversy. Their existence in isolation is dubious.

The assessment of auditory discrimination, particularly in older children, is difficult. Nevertheless, occasionally such handicaps declare themselves. One 14-year-old boy boasted to his physician: "You know, doctor, I think I am reading much more *fluidly* now." The physician corrected him: "I think you mean you mean you are reading more *fluently* now." "Yes, that's what I said," the child responded, "I am reading more *fluidly* now." The youngster had great difficulty analyzing the phonetic content of words. Decoding unfamiliar words was particularly puzzling, and he experienced a significant delay in learning to read. Oral reading was especially difficult.

Segmentation and blending of words. This involves a "sense" that words consist of combinations of sounds that can be broken down and reassembled. Sequential organization and the ability to analyze the sound fragments of a word without losing their serial order are necessary decoding abilities. Word-analysis skills in reading are particularly dependent on this aspect of language.

Syntax mastery. An appreciation of the rules of syntax is a critical aspect of language processing (Chomsky 1969). The syntactical structure of sentences in itself provides major cues to meaning. The capacity to decode and utilize complex sentences is a major academic facilitator. Many youngsters with language processing problems tune out, as their circuits become overloaded in the presence of syntactically complex sentences. They have particular difficulty retaining and attributing full meaning to such communication. Both reading and writing skills depend to a large extent upon the mastery of syntax.

Language memory. The capacity to store and retrieve spoken language is crucial for learning. Some children have a far greater storage capacity for visually presented materials. So-called auditory memory depends upon a number of factors, including the meaningfulness of the input, the motivation to retain, intrinsic storage and retrieval capacity, cultural factors, and the strength of auditory attention. One can distinguish between short- and long-term auditory memory, and between auditory recognition ("I've heard that word before") and auditory recall or retrieval ("That's called a unicorn"). Auditory memory also serves to integrate verbal input with various forms of output. A child, for example, who has difficulty transforming an auditory input into a fine motor response (e.g., writing from dictation) might be having trouble retaining the auditory "trace" long enough to "blueprint" the appropriate fine motor response. The efficient integration of auditory-motor activities is highly dependent upon the ability to retain and "read from" a verbal program. Children who struggle with a weak auditory memory may reveal a high level of impulsivity when presented with verbal instructions. This may, in fact, be compensatory, as they perform quickly to avoid losing the instruction.

Receptive vocabulary. The school-age child expands his receptive vocabulary (the store of words he understands) exponentially with age. The rate of this growth is determined by sociocultural factors as well as developmental and neurological correlates. A diminished receptive vocabulary may indicate generalized developmental delay, deprivation or inexperience, or isolated language problems. A child with a reduced receptive vocabulary is likely to show concomitant limitations in expressive vocabulary. The converse in not true, however, as some youngsters with excellent receptive word stores have difficulty with the rapid retrieval of words for use in verbal communication.

Auditory comprehension. Attribution of meaning to spoken words and sentences and rapid association between one's past experiences and current communication from others, are necessary prerequisites for efficient understanding of language. Auditory attention, vocabulary, speech-sound discrimination, and syntax mastery are some of the many feeder lines contributing to auditory comprehension. Difficulty understanding spoken language can thus represent a "disconnection" in one or more of many auditory-language circuits.

Metalinguistic awareness. The capacity to infer meaning from structural clues, from intonations, and from semantic contexts is an important aspect of receptive language (Hook and Johnson 1978). Children who do *not* need to attend to every individual phoneme in a sentence in order to understand its literal or implied meaning may have well-developed metalinguistic awareness. Their sensitivity to accessory cues greatly facilitates rapid and effortless comprehension. Students with language disorders and diminished metalinguistic awareness may require more time for processing complex or rapidly delivered verbal communication.

Rate of language processing. The rate or efficiency of decoding is a critical and often neglected area of language processing. A child may comprehend verbal data adequately but process language at a rate considerably below that of a peer group. Such a youngster may be a chronic auditory straggler, forever striving to catch up with the rapid onslaught of verbal communication. Prolonged latencies of response to language input may constitute serious obstacles in the classroom. This is particularly true in the late elementary-school grades, as the complexity, quantity, and rate of verbal delivery from the teacher increase markedly. Many affected youngsters become secondarily inattentive. An older elementary-school student who showed good attention strength at earlier ages may deteriorate in the face of the ever-increasing complexity and volume of language. In view of the behavioral and academic devastation that such inefficiencies of language processing can leave in their wake, it is ironic that very few language tests involve timed tasks, while so many assessments of visual-motor function record the rate of performance.

Developmental language disabilities often are subtle. Children with such handicaps may experience considerable maladjustment, emotional difficulty, and social failure. Their secondary psychic turmoil is often misdiagnosed as the primary cause of school failure; desperate strategies to cover up a language disability may be mislabeled as psychosocial illness. Some children with these problems become confused or panic-stricken as they decode verbal information in the classroom as if through a bad telephone connection or a poorly tuned-in radio. A clinician can make an extraordinary contribution to the quality of a child's life by suspecting or identifying a possible receptive language disorder that presents itself as a problem with behavior and/or learning.

Screening and Assessment

Disorders of receptive language can be elusive clinically. A child with a handicap in this area may be referred for a WISC and a Bender-Gestalt Test to "rule out learning disabilities," yet such instruments often fail to uncover developmental language impairments. Although traditional wisdom has indicated that children with language problems ought to show a large discrepancy between their WISC performance and verbal subtest scores, a relatively "normal" verbal score may be achieved by a child with significant language impairment. When a depression of subtest scores is seen, it may be suggest a language disorder, but its absence does not rule out such problems.

Any consideration of a possible language disorder needs to begin with an assessment of auditory acuity. Routine screening in the physician's office is useful. Clinicians should be aware, however, of the high rate of false-positive and false-negative results with screening audiometers in settings where soundproof facilities are not available (see Chapter 5). When there is a strong historical suspicion of hearing loss, it is essential that formal audiometric testing be sought and that it be provided by a trained audiologist.

Although an association between chronic or recurrent serous otitis media and language disability has been postulated, the definitive word has not yet been heard. Nevertheless, it is worth considering the possibility that the presence of serous middle-ear fluid, at periods of most rapid language acquisition, may impair language development significantly. A transient hearing loss secondary to serous otitis media may also affect auditory attention and retention in older children. At any rate, careful audiologic examination is an indispensable part of the pediatric evaluation of a learning problem.

Screening for speech and language disabilities demands a carefully assembled history and sensitive, direct, meaningful interaction with the child. Table 5 lists some historical clues that might trigger the clinical suspicion of a receptive language disability. The level of suspicion rises in the presence of a cluster of these factors.

Table 5. Clinical Clues to Suggest the Possibility of a Receptive Language Deficit

---

Early History:

Well-documented history of recurrent otitis media during the first four years of life

Known transient or permanent hearing impairment

Delayed acquisition of intelligible speech

Delayed utilization of word phrases, full sentences, and appropriate syntax

Family history of language-processing handicaps

Current History:

Weaknesses of attention, especially in settings where there is a high "verbal loading" (e.g., school).

Limited vocabulary (receptive or expressive) for age

WISC performance subtests considerably higher than verbal

Difficulties associating sounds with symbols for reading

Confusion over words that sound alike (e.g., bowl and ball)

Frequent need to have instructions repeated (utterances such as: "Huh?", "What d'ya mean?", "What d'ya say?")

Spelling errors that are phonetically poor approximations (e.g., "lag" for "laugh")

Problems with verbal comprehension

Difficulty processing rapid speech

Articulation difficulties or other problems with expressive language

---

A number of formal tests of language function in young children have been developed (see Appendix A). Some of these instruments "ceiling out" in early elementary school, however, making them relatively insensitive to subtle language problems in older age groups. Valid screening tests for language disorders in late elementary school are rare. The Illinois Test of Psycholinguistic Abilities is commonly used by language specialists and includes subtests that assess auditory sequential memory, sound blending, auditory closure (the capacity to generalize from incomplete auditory cues), basic auditory reception, and auditory association (the ability to visualize auditory information meaningfully). The Detroit Tests of Learning Aptitude also include subtests dealing with auditory sequencing, auditory memory, and selective attention. Several subtests of the WISC may be sensitive to language disabilities, particularly the Information, Vocabulary, Similarities, and Comprehension sections. The Goldman-Fristoe-Woodcock Auditory Skills Test Battery is designed to assess a child's ability to screen out background interference (in this case, cafeteria noise).

In some instances an expressive language problem may be a clue to the existence of associated deficits in receptive language processing. Thus, children with difficulties in articulation, word finding (retrieving familiar words), and/or narration (ability to tell a story) also may have underlying auditory perceptual problems, weaknesses of auditory memory, or other receptive language deficits. Such children may have shown a delay in the acquisition of intelligible speech. There may also be a history of concomitant weaknesses in the acquisition of expressive syntax.

EXPRESSIVE LANGUAGE FUNCTION

Competent spoken language depends on a number of factors, including the capacity to retrieve relevant words from memory, the arrangement of these words in phrases and/or sentences that conform to linguistic rules, the development of ideas in a meaningful sequence or narrative, and the planning and execution of the highly complex motor act of speech. Ultimately, this entire process transpires within a time frame that is rapid enough to satisfy demands in academic and social settings. During the school years, written and spoken language come to occupy center stage in the educational arena. Such skills are essential for self-monitoring, for successful social interaction, for dealing with an understanding of one's own feelings, and for demonstrating competence to the outside world.

Normal expressive language depends upon developmental and cultural factors. As children progress through the toddler and preschool years, their verbal facility helps them to build relationships and probe their world. In early elementary school, expressive language ability is associated with the acquisition of basic academic skills. Verbal fluency becomes increasingly important as children approach the late elementary-school years, when the highest form of expressive language—writing—becomes of paramount importance in the drive toward academic success.

Clinical Phenomenology

The various disorders of expressive language can be classified as follows:

1. *Deficits of resonance.* These disorders are characterized by abnormal oronasal sound balance. Deficits most commonly present as hypernasality (as in cleft palate) or hyponasality (as in adenoid hypertrophy).
2. *Voice disorders.* These problems are manifested as deviations in the quality, pitch, or volume of sound production. Such impairments have either psychological or physiological bases.
3. *Fluency disorders.* These disorders reflect disruption in the natural flow of connected speech. The most common type of fluency disorder is stuttering.
4. *Articulation disorders.* Such disorders include a large group of problems often encountered by the physician. They are characterized by imprecise production of speech sounds. Most articulation "problems" are common at certain ages and are, in fact, normal. However, their persistence often requires intervention.
5. *Language disorders.* Language disorders comprise problems in the manipulation and expression of the symbol system of language.

In this volume we shall not deal at length with resonance and voice disorders, although they are common, and physicians should be on alert for them; otolaryngological evaluation is often indicated. In addition, most such children require the assistance of a speech therapist in order to avoid secondary emotional problems and social stigmata. These disabilities are not generally associated with other learning disorders.

Problems with speech fluency are often encountered in pediatric practice. During the course of normal language development, all children display some nonfluent speech or disruption in the natural flow of words. This may occur at any time during the second to fifth years of life. A fluency problem may consist of pauses, repetitions of sounds, revisions of sentences, lapses in responding, or sound prolongations. One explanation offered for stuttering is that it represents the listener's inaccurate assessment of normal developmental dysfluency. Through negative feedback, the child begins to feel inadequate about speech, expects to have problems with speech, and perceives himself as an ineffective speaker. Consequently, an underlying natural propensity to dysfluency becomes exaggerated because of adult overconcern or disapprobation.

Most stuttering children are identified as such between the third and fourth years of life. However, dysfluency may appear later, when a child first enters school or as he approaches adolescence.

Stuttering most likely is a symptom with multiple causes. Its association with underlying neurological dysfunction is rare. It may occur in families but is not generally regarded as genetic. Nor is stuttering thought to be learned by imitation. Family attitudes toward nonfluency may well explain its occurrence in more than one child. The possibility that some children derive secondary gain from stuttering deserves consideration. School-age children who stutter require early and sensitive psychological assessment, as well as an evaluation of speech and language. In most cases they should be referred to a speech and language pathologist.

Poor articulation is the most common speech problem in children. Typical errors include (1) *substitutions,* involving replacement of one sound with another (e.g., *gwite* for *bite*); (2) *omissions,* presenting as a failure to produce certain speech sounds (e.g., *ca* for *cat*); and (3) *distortions,* manifesting themselves as inappropriate sound replacements. There is wide variability in the number of consonants and vowels that are misarticulated. A child's errors may vary from only a few inappropriate sounds to only a few appropriate ones. In severe cases, speech can be virtually unintelligible. Some causes of poor articulation are structural abnormalities within the oral cavity, dental irregularities, and anatomic defects of the palate. Paralysis or weakness of the tongue also affects speech output. Poor articulation may be a symptom of underlying hearing loss. As noted earlier, articulation deficits may accompany developmental receptive language disabilities. Environmental factors and psychological stresses may predispose to or potentiate poor speech-sound production. There is evidence suggesting that some children and adults with articulation problems have difficulty with sensory feedback (buccal, somesthetic, and kinesthetic) from their mouths, with resultant "oral dyspraxia." Such an articulation disorder may, in fact, be analogous to other perceptual-motor problems.

Disabilities of expressive language are manifest in a wide range of impairments. Some children cannot use the rules of syntax in a manner commensurate with their developmental ages. Often they are shy. In extreme cases, children overrely on gestures or communication through single words or phrases. They may appear to speak in a telegraphic style, often deleting words. These children may have a history of delay in the acquisition of language or a long time interval between the use of single words and the formation of word combinations. Children with severe deficits in expressive language must be evaluated for generalized developmental delay, hearing impairment, environmental problems, oral motor problems, and elective (selective) mutism.

In the discussion of receptive language disorders, the importance of processing efficiency was emphasized. This is equally germane to expressive language. Some youngsters express themselves appropriately, but the process requires a great deal of time and effort. They have difficulty keeping pace with conversation and become reluctant to use narrative because of the time needed for its construction.

Word-finding disorders (dysnomias) constitute another group of expressive language handicaps. They are more common than has been recognized generally. The parents of an affected child may report that "He can't say what he wants," or "It's as if it is just at the tip of his tongue." Characteristically, the child may be unable momentarily to recall the name of an object or event that he knows well. There is often an increased latency of response when such a child is asked to name pictures or objects, an observation that has been associated with serious reading delays (Denckla 1972, 1976). Gestures or pantomime that conform closely to the object may be used. Such children may speak in definitions or approximations rather than specific words. A boy who was asked what he had received for Christmas, for example, responded, "A stick you hit a round thing with." Other children with word-finding problems label objects by associations (e.g., *rain* for *umbrella*, or *tobacco* for *pipe*). Sometimes a word is substituted that sounds like the word sought (e.g., *slow* for *low*). Word-finding deficits often occur with other language handicaps, such as difficulties with syntax or auditory memory. Some children who have word-finding problems are verbose. Such a youngster may have difficulty finding precise words but may be fluent and talkative, utilizing an abundance of definitions, circumlocutions, and immature constructs. He may use a limited expressive vocabulary. In such a case, an eight-year-old may speak fluent five-year-old English!

An expressive language deficit may also involve problems with narrative organization. Some children have an inability to comment on content. They may have reduced storytelling skills. They may describe events only in the most concrete and primitive terms. Many have difficulty maintaining the organization of a narrative; they tend to ramble and build incoherent structures. The possibility of problems with sequential organization has already been discussed.

Expressive language impairments may disrupt social relationships within a family or with peer groups. Secondary behavioral or affective changes can ensue, and a significant degree of disorganization or maladaptive coping may follow. Some children with expressive language problems have difficulty learning to read. Their disabilities have even greater impact when, as students, they are expected to produce a great deal of written material in late elementary and junior high school. Early detection, anticipatory guidance, and intervention are particularly helpful in minimizing their early adolescent plights.

Screening and Assessment

The evaluation of expressive language function requires consideration of the child's ability to find words, to formulate sentences, and to narrate. A picture- or object-naming task can be used for clinical screening. The child can also be asked to describe recent experiences, while the listener assesses his ability to organize narrative, to find the right words, and to use grammar appropriately. In addition, one should gauge the child's capacity to produce language at an adequate rate and to articulate in a manner commensurate with age level. The clinician should be aware of the child's *mean length of utterance* (abbreviated *mlu* by psycholinguists), since parsimonious language production may conceal underlying expressive deficits. Well-standardized tests for articulation, such as the

This photograph shows a pediatrician administering the Boston Naming Test. It consists of a series of pictures, which the child is asked to identify rapidly; one screens such functions as word finding, visual recognition ability, retrieval memory, and expressive vocabulary. This kind of assessment also may suggest either a slow rate of processing or excessive impulsivity. The nature of errors (e.g., circumlocutions, use of definitions instead of words, identification mistakes) is often revealing.

Denver Articulation Screening Test, are available for office use. The Boston Naming Test has been developed as one indicator of a child's word-finding ability. Some youngsters who perform well on this test may have no difficulty finding words when presented with a visual stimulus (a picture or object) but have more difficulty when the input is auditory or conceptual (e.g., "Name as many animals as you can").

A child's capacity to narrate and describe experiences is difficult to measure with a test. The Mykelbust Picture Story Language Test is one such attempt. However, its standardization and validation are questionable. The physician can attempt to use a picture stimulus as an informal means of obtaining a sample of narration.

Historical clues should always be sought, as delineated in Table 6. The indicators in this table might suggest the need for consideration of a problem with expressive language in a child with learning problems. One's clinical suspicions should grow in the presence of a cluster or clusters of these factors. The Boston Children's Hospital Parent and School Questionnaires (Appendix C) contain items that screen a child's expressive language abilities.

MEMORY

Developmental growth is cumulative and, therefore, relies on the storage of data, experience, and acquired skill. Retention and smooth retrieval of such

Table 6. Clinical Clues to Suggest the Possibility of an Expressive Language Deficit

Early History:

Well documented history of recurrent otitis media during the first four years of life

Known transient or permanent hearing impairment

Delayed acquisition of intelligible speech

Delayed utilization of word phrases, full sentences, and appropriate syntax

Family history of language impairment

Current History:

Immature articulation patterns

Unusual economy of language (diminished mean length of utterances), problems with fluency

Difficulty "finding" the right words to describe experiences; problems applying syntactical rules and organizing narrative

Excessive reliance on circumlocutions ("whatchamacallits") and definitions ("a thing with a lot of legs" for "octupus")

Verbal hesitancy ("uh, um . . .").

Social passivity (shyness) and excessively taciturn behavior in school; reluctance to volunteer known answers

Inordinate difficulties with written expression (sometimes beginning in late elementary grades).

Poor story- and joke-telling ability.

Relatively limited or immature expressive vocabulary for age (*N.B.* Such a child may still be quite "verbal"—or verbose—despite limited expressive language development)

Problems or hesitancy naming pictures and objects (a good screening assessment for pediatricians)

material are fundamental to the learning process. Three basic stages of memory have been described: the reception or registration of information (including attention and decoding), its storage, and its retrieval. In learning, children must be able to select appropriate data for retention, "file" these for possible later use, and, when the occasion arises, recall with ease and speed that which has been stored.

Many investigators have made a distinction between recognition and retrieval, long-term and short-term memory, and short-term memory and immediate recall (parroting). Instant memory clearly isn't as critical for learning as the capacity to select a stimulus, store it, and recognize or retrieve it, as needed. In most instances an individual's recognition skills are superior to his retrieval abilities. If the discrepancy is particularly wide, academic difficulties may ensue. For example, a child may be able to select a correctly spelled word from a list that includes misspelled ones (recognition) but be unable to spell spontaneously (retrieval). In some cases, recognition abilities may *also* be significantly depressed.

Recognition and retrieval both depend upon the meaningfulness of data. It is clearly more difficult to retain a nonsense word than to remember one associated with specific visual imagery, meaning, or prior experience. There is, however, considerable variation among children with regard to what is most meaningful and thereby least perishable in memory. Often it is difficult to separate retention from attention. A child with attention deficits may appear to forget or not recognize data to which he has been exposed. In such instances, a seeming short-term memory deficit may only reflect an initial failure to register data in the memory store. Conversely, strongly focused initial attention to a stimulus increases the likelihood of easy recognition and retrieval.

Clinical Phenomenology

Children handicapped by memory deficits often show impairments that are part of a broader clinical picture of dysfunction (Ring 1975, McSpadden and Strain 1977). They may experience considerable academic and behavioral anguish. In particular, those with reduced short-term memories may have difficulty retaining instructions and may be unfairly labeled as poorly motivated or lazy. Children with weaknesses of visual memory may retain only vague impressions of the configurations of words and therefore may be slow to acquire a normal rate of reading or an adequate sight vocabulary (Weaver 1978).

Clinical analysis of a possible memory deficit involves a number of considerations. First, one must distinguish among immediate recall, short-term memory, and long-term memory. Second, it is essential to distinguish between recognition and retrieval. Third, one must always ask, "Memory for what?" Some children have an excellent memory for numbers but a relatively weak memory for words. Some have a superb memory for faces, while others struggle to recognize people and, even more, to remember their names! A memory for jokes is another skill that is highly variable. Finally, it is common to evaluate auditory and visual memory as relatively separate functional abilities. Considerable discussion of so-called auditory learners or visual learners has been based on the belief that retentive abilities may depend upon the sensory modalities through which information is received. It has been suggested that such phenomena have major educational implications for handicapped children.

Does one teach to the ears or to the eyes in an individual case? There is considerable disagreement about the validity of such observations (Arter and Jenkins 1977). Furthermore, there is no conclusive evidence that teaching through a stronger modality necessarily enhances learning. Well-controlled research is critically needed to resolve this pedagogic controversy.

Many other components of memory have been described. Paired-associate learning problems or reduced capacity to preserve relationships between two sets of data, is a proposed model that has been associated with reading failure (Rudel et al. 1976, Gascon and Goodglass 1970). The capacity to retain, retrieve, and apply rules (e.g., grammatical, spelling, mathematical, scientific) is another essential memory function that becomes particularly germane in late elementary and in secondary school.

Screening and Assessment

As part of a comprehensive developmental history, the pediatrician should inquire about various aspects of a child's memory. The questionnaires in Appendix C include items that explore this element.

For office screening, a variety of measures can be utilized to assess short-term memory. These measures, some of which have already been described, include such tasks as recall of a digit span, copying forms from memory (see Fig. 3), repetition of increasingly complex sentences, and the various assessments described for sequencing abilities (see Table 4).

Long-term memory can be evaluated, to some extent, by gauging a child's general store of information. The need for standardized questions is obvious. Moreover, this type of assessment must be undertaken with full recognition of possible cultural and social biases.

Many well-standardized intelligence and "readiness" tests include items relating to short- or long-term memory. It is essential that the clinician be aware of the multitude of "contaminants" in such evaluations, particularly with regard to the meaningfulness of the stimuli for an individual child (often based on previous experience or cultural factors), the youngster's perceptual abilities, and variations in attentional strength. Table 7 provides a summary of some of the specific forms of memory deficit that might be encountered clinically, with representative standardized tests that can elicit or demonstrate these phenomena.

VOLUNTARY MOTOR FUNCTION

"When the gym teacher tells us to do something, I understand exactly what he means; I even know how to do it, I think. But, my body just never seems to do the job." This statement by a nine-year-old boy typifies the plight of the youngster with gross motor deficiencies. The following statement reveals similar despair: "They always pick me last. This morning they were all fighting over which team had to have me. One guy was shouting about it. He said it isn't fair because his team had me twice last week. Another kid said they would only take me if his team could be spotted four runs. Later, on the bus, they were all making fun of me, calling me a 'fag' and a 'spaz'. There are a few good kids, I mean kids who aren't mean, but they don't want to play with me. I guess it could hurt their reputation."

Table 7. Some Features of Memory and Their Observation

Phenomenon	Observation Procedure(s)	Comments on Observations
Auditory sequential memory	Forward and reverse digit spans; *Detroit Tests* of "auditory attention span"	May also reflect attention weakness, anxiety, slow processing.
Visual sequential memory	Block tapping; object spans; Picture Arrangement subtest of WISC-R	Picture Arrangement also reflects social perception and experience
Sensorimotor sequential memory	Imitative rhythm tapping; motor sequencing tasks (see Table 4)	Sensitivity to rhythm cues and motor abilities may influence performance
Visual memory for pattern of Gestalt	Form copying from memory; Benton Test of Visual Memory; matching designs from memory	May involve either retrieval or recognition
Sentence memory	Tests of sentence repetition; serial commands	May also reflect a child's appreciation of grammar and syntax
Associative memory	Tests of paired-associate learning	Not generally tested clinically
Long-term memory	Tests of general knowledge; Information subtest of WISC-R	"Contaminated" by cultural and language factors
Recognition memory	Selection of pictures or words encountered earlier	May be affected by variation in visual attention
Retrieval memory	Tests of revisualization or reauditorization of previously encountered stimuli	May be reflected in spelling and word-finding abilities
Motor memory	Observation of ability to reenact a newly acquired motor skill	May be affected by gross motor ability

Such statements exude a pathos that may pervade the life of a youngster who has subtle deficiencies in motor output. Comments such as these are easily elicited by the sensitive clinician. They highlight the tight bond between motor output effectiveness, self-image, and social interaction.

Gross and fine motor control are elements of organization of the central nervous system. The constant feedback of somesthetic cues from muscles and joints contributes to a sense of body position, to maintenance of static posture, and to sustenance of dynamic motor acts. Other facets of gross motor function include the facilitation and inhibition of appropriate muscle groups during activity, the planning and execution of a motor "product," and the coordination or integration of muscle activity with sensory feedback and memory.

There has been a prolonged and turbulent romance between motor function and academic performance. In the field of learning disabilities, zealous voices, backed by varying degrees of conviction and scientific support, have proposed a close relationship between gross motor function and reading ability. Some observers have insisted that remediation of gross motor delays is a necessary prerequisite to optimal intervention in a host of learning problems. This continues to be an area of controversy in pediatrics and education. It is fair to say that the clinician is likely to encounter children with gross motor delays who have no reading problems, as well as youngsters with reading deficiencies and extraordinary athletic abilities. Although there may be an association between gross motor deficits and learning disorders or attention deficits in some children, the association is anything but inviolate (Denckla 1978). It is likely that physicians and educators are standing on much firmer ground when they see gross motor problems as having an impact on self-image and personality, rather than as a primary cause or necessary concomitant of so-called learning disabilities.

Up until this point, we have focused mainly on gross motor function or a child's utilization of large muscle groups and total body awareness. It is equally common for the developmentalist to consider fine motor output. Although small motor function can be expressed through movements of the tongue, eyelids, or toes, for the most part clinicians and investigators conceive of fine motor production as an activity of the hands and fingers. As with gross motor function, fine motor output depends upon adequate sensory information, working to inform, plan, execute, and monitor an output response. Although fine motor function is often thought to be related to eye-hand coordination, other types of sensory cues contribute to finger gnosia (the awareness of digit locations). Kinesthetic, proprioceptive, and haptic (touch) sensory inputs are among the important afferent pathways linked to fine motor output.

Early in infancy babies begin to show visually directed reaching, as well as additional evidence of coordination between sensory and motor pathways. As young children grow older, they become increasingly capable of more selective fine motor activities; progressively distal precision is achieved.

For the school-age child effective fine motor function is the basis for many manipulative activities. The use of eating utensils, participation in crafts activities, and the manipulation of scissors, buttons, and zippers all stress the fine motor "system." Learning to tie one's shoelaces is a major motor triumph, although, as we have noted earlier, this task also involves a variety of other functional elements (e.g., attention, experience, motor sequencing, and visual-spatial orientation). In academic settings pencil control is the most important fine motor task. Letter formation and legibility depend upon relatively intact output and feedback pathways for graphomotor function (motor aspects of writing). As children progress through elementary school and into secondary levels of education, the *rate* of fine motor and graphomotor output is especially important. The effectiveness of a child's pencil grip and the capacity to thwart "writer's cramp" are ingredients of academic success at the secondary level.

Clinical Phenomenology

Gross Motor Function

As noted above, children with gross motor deficits may or may not have associated learning disorders. Children with delays in gross motor development may display diminished self-esteem, tendencies toward social withdrawal, and, in extreme cases, depression. Such secondary emotional scars are most likely to occur in those children who have not been able to find and express compensatory strengths to earn parent and peer approval. When gross motor deficits are associated with specific learning problems, their impact on affect, behavior, and self-esteem are likely to be greatest.

Children with gross motor delays may be reluctant to participate in group sports activities. There may be a history of relative slowness learning to ride a bicycle or to catch a ball. The child may be clumsy at home. Often subtle problems with gross motor development are not apparent until the child reaches the school-age years. A youngster may have entirely normal motor milestones before the age of five or six. When complex motor activities are attempted, ineptness may become apparent. Often one can describe the phenomenology of a child's gross motor deficits by noting relative strengths and weaknesses in particular sporting events. By looking specifically at the sensory or perceptual input required for specific sports, certain phenomena can be explained: a youngster with visual-spatial confusion, for example, may have blatant gross motor problems when attempting to hit or throw a baseball. The same child may be exquisitely tuned for somesthetic, vestibular, proprioceptive, and kinesthetic feedback and therefore be adept at swimming, skiing, or gymnastics.

Some children may have problems with "inner space" (i.e., body-position sense, balance, and various somesthetic inputs), while others have relative weaknesses with the decoding of "outer space" (judging baseball trajectories, aiming at targets, etc.). Other forms of gross motor deficiency exist with respect to integrative-coordinating functions. A youngster may have difficulty in any or all of the following areas: motor planning, memory for motor skills, sequential-motor organization, the integration of sensory input with motor output in general, and the coordination and applied use of specific muscle groups. After describing a child's specific gross motor problems, it should be possible to prescribe a therapeutic program in which the child is more likely to achieve success and reap the dividends of a higher self-image and enhanced feelings of efficacy.

Another clinical phenomenon involves the child with relatively weak gross motor skills whose parents place a heavy emphasis upon success in this area. Values in a community may promote an obsessive interest in sports or athletic abilities. Those youngsters who cannot measure up perceive themselves as second-class citizens in a family or town. This effect may be devastating when a sibling, neighbor, or other close associate shows athletic prowess. This phenomenon raises philosophical issues: Should a child with relative weakness in gross motor function be pressured to participate in sports activities? Or should such a youngster be allowed to pursue his own interests, with every effort being made to excuse participation in humiliating sporting events? Some might argue that motor mastery is particularly important for a growing boy or girl, and that it is critical for every child to be exposed to such activities to promote both physical and mental health. Others might argue that it takes a variety of styles to make an ecology of people and that brains that were not built to participate in sports should not be compelled to do so. Regardless of how one feels about this issue, the clinician needs to be sensitive and responsive to the potential or actual suffering of a child with gross motor dysfunction. Parents, children, and teachers may need help in developing a management plan to assure that such a child does not endure excessive humiliation and feelings of inadequacy.

Fine Motor Function

School-age children with fine motor deficits usually do not present to the clinician with a well-packaged, vivid history of such handicaps. In most cases fine motor deficiencies are subtle. Youngsters with these impairments may have shown no deficits whatsoever on preschool developmental assessments such as the Denver Developmental Screening Test. It is only when more complex and sustained fine motor execution is required that such children reveal their shortcomings. In school, inefficiencies of fine motor performance may directly affect the ability to write, to copy from the blackboard, to draw, and to cut with scissors. Pencil control in particular may be adversely affected. To compensate for inadequate pencil manipulation, a child in early elementary school may develop an awkward, maladaptive grip. The normal tripod grasp may be replaced by one that is too proximal or too distal on the pencil. Alternatively, a child may over-rely on the webbing between the first and second fingers, or he may engage in one of a number of bizarre improvisations. Such ineffective pencil

Table 8. Gross Motor Screening

Some Clues from the History

Reluctance to participate in competitive physical activities; apprehension over physical education classes

Difficulty catching or throwing a ball, skipping, jumping, balancing

Delayed mastery of bicycle riding, other learned motor tasks

Clumsiness, motor disorganization at home

N.B. Some children with visual-motor integration problems may have particular difficulty with motor activities requiring considerable visual input and feedback (e.g., baseball, volleyball), but may perform better if the inputs are largely proprioceptive or kinesthetic (e.g., swimming, skiing, gymnastics)

Some Tasks for Direct Screening*

Stressed Gait: These provide an opportunity to observe incoordination of gait, particularly in younger children. One should look at overall performance, upper limb posturing, and asymmetries.

    Ages 4–5:   Skipping, hopping, walking on heels

    Ages 5–8:   Tandem gaits (forward and backward)

    Ages 9–10: Sidewise tandem gait, walking on sides of feet

Eye-Upper Limb Coordination: This can be observed by having a child toss a ball or beanbag at a target and catch a ball thrown by the examiner. In children under 9, a ball should be caught with both hands. In older children, a tennis ball should be caught with one hand.

Body Position Sense and Regulation: This parameter is observed by having a child sustain balance or stance.

    Age 5–6:   Stand on one foot, eyes open (10 seconds)

    Age 7–9:   Stand heel to toe, eyes closed (15 seconds)

    Age 9–12:   Stand on tip toes, eyes closed (15 seconds)

Complex Motor Organization: Planning, sequencing, and coordinating of complex output should be observed.

    Ages 5–7:   Imitate examiner's gestures: clap twice over head, twice behind back; clap three times in front of chest, twice behind back, once in front of chest; clap twice in front of chest, once behind back, once in front of chest, once behind back.

    Ages 7–9:   Hop twice on each foot in succession in place (repeat four times without stopping).

    Ages 10–12: Jump and touch back of heels; jump and clap hands three times before coming down.

* Some of these tasks are described in detail in the Oseresky Examination of Motor Proficiency (see Appendix).

grips may work well for a child in the early elementary-school grades, when a relatively small volume of written output is required. However, as the child approaches late elementary and junior high school, a sustainable and supple pencil grasp becomes important; at this point a youngster with a maladaptive grasp may experience great anguish over long assignments and over tasks involving timed writing output (e.g., examinations). Problems in this area may not be revealed until fairly late in a child's academic career.

It is not uncommon for professionals to assume that a child who has an illegible handwriting must also have fine motor problems. This is not necessarily the case. Illegibility can result from a variety of other factors, including impulsiveness, relative inexperience, improper teaching, or difficulties with visual-spatial orientation.

One parameter that is frequently overlooked but is critically important is the rate and/or efficiency of fine motor (and graphomotor) output. Children generally dislike tasks that are prolonged, laborious, or awkward. The youngster who writes slowly may become "writing inhibited." Those children who write too slowly to keep up with the flow of their ideas often become nonproductive with regard to written output. From the point of view of academic productivity, "speed writing" may be equally as important as "speed reading."

Screening and Assessment

The direct observation of a child's gross and fine motor performance requires the presentation of developmentally appropriate tasks. It is important to recognize, however, that most tests of motor performance are poorly standardized for older children. There are broad experiential differences and a considerable degree of normal variation. The items listed in Tables 8 and 9 provide rough, approximate screening guidelines for the clinician. The *quality* of a child's performance may be more important than simply whether or not he can perform a task. Is a motor act accomplished efficiently, or with multiple extraneous movements or unusual postures? How smoothly are instructions translated into motor acts? How easily does the child master a relatively unfamiliar motor task? What happens to a youngster's affect when he is asked to undertake a gross motor challenge?

While observing gross motor performance, the clinician should take note of the following: (a) overall coordination; (b) balance; (c) visual-motor integration; (d) the capacity to inhibit specific muscle groups while facilitating the activity of others; and (e) motor sequential organization. At times it is useful to have a child express in words the motor activity that is about to be undertaken. This can give some indication of the child's capacity for motor planning.

If a clinician is to observe gross motor performance, developmentally appropriate tasks must be used. Referral to a pediatrician for evaluation of clumsiness and school problems is common. In such cases, the pediatrician might have the child hop back and forth across the room to assess motor function. If the child is 11 years old, this would be particularly nondiscriminating, as hopping is a three- to four-year-old developmental task! Relatively subtle, but significant gross motor deficits could be missed by using developmentally inappropriate tasks.

In describing and formulating a youngster's gross motor strengths and weaknesses, the physician needs to supplement his own direct observations with

Table 9. The Screening Assessment of Fine Motor Function

Some clues from the History:

Reluctance to engage in or complete small motor tasks—model building, tracing, drawing, cutting with scissors

Relative slowness or incompetence in the above tasks

Delay in learning to use eating utensils, continuing awkwardness in this activity

Illegible handwriting (*N.B.* One must be aware of other causes of poor writing—see text), problems with letter formation

Tremulousness of fingers

Awkward pencil grasp

Some Tasks for Direct Screening:

General Observations: In screening fine motor function the clinician should be alert to the following factors that can enrich clinical observations:

    Effectiveness of pincer grasp

Use of most distal muscle groups (as opposed to overreliance on more proximal musculature)

Adequacy of eye-hand coordination

Possible overreliance on visual feedback (e.g., eyes kept very close to activity)

Presence of associated movements (e.g., of contralateral digits, tongue, lips)

Use of verbal reinforcers (i.e., subvocalizations of various types: sounds, rhythms, melodies, words)

Continuous performance patterns: Does the quality of output remain consistent, improve, or deteriorate with time (and practice)?

Level of impulsivity (a trait commonly mistaken for fine motor weakness)

Self-monitoring (i.e., quality control, detection of own errors)

Speed, efficiency, and accuracy of execution

*Nonpencil Tasks:**

Ages 5–6:	Direct imitation of constructions using 1-inch cube blocks; eight-block tower, ten-block pyramid, three-block bridge
	Observations of buttoning, use of zippers
Ages 7–9:	Put half-inch square beads on a shoelace (8 beads in 45 seconds)
	Observe child tying shoelaces
	Finger-to-nose test
	Sequential rapid finger opposition
Ages 10–12:	Put pennies in a box with one hand, one at a time, without sliding them (preferred hand—10 pennies in less than 25 seconds)
	Bead stringing may be used also (see above)

Pencil Tasks:

Form Copying: Age-appropriate forms (see Figure 3) can be used to observe pencil control. One needs to discriminate between visual-spatial and fine motor performance (sometimes difficult). Poorly executed angles, intersections, wavy lines may suggest pencil control weaknesses (or poor planning)

Mazes, Road Tracks, Connecting Dots: Various pencil tracking tasks can be used to observe rate and accuracy of pencil movement as well as factors listed under Observations of Pencil Grasp below

---

* Standardization and further description of some similar tasks can be found in the Oseresky Tests of Motor Proficiency (see Appendix).

Table 9. (Continued)

Observations of Writing (letter formation, spatial planning, spacing, legibility, speed, accuracy):
　Ages 4–5:　Write name; write some letters
　Ages 6–7:　Write alphabet; write some numbers
　Ages 8+:　Copy and dictate sentences
　Ages 9+:　Describe a scene or picture in writing; sample cursive writing
　Ages 10+:　Describe an event in writing
Observations of Pencil Grasp-Note the following:
　Proximity to efficient tripod grasp
　Finger location on pencil (not too distal or proximal)
　Tightness of grip
　Pressure application to paper
　Apparent comfort
　Hand position (presence or absence of "hook")
　Eye distance from page

---

historical data from the child, from the school, and from parents. The questionnaires in Appendix C contain items that help to evaluate gross motor function in the school-age child.

Table 9 lists examples of historical clues from fine motor tasks that might be used for observing children. In evaluating fine motor function one needs to assess the quality of eye-hand coordination, as well as the rate and efficiency of fine motor output. One indicator of fine motor inefficiency is the prevalence of a variety of associated movements when a child undertakes a task. Excessive mouthing, foot tapping, or suggestive mirror movements during fine motor activities in older children may be indications of relative immaturity in this area.

Deficits in finger awareness or localization may also be associated with fine motor inefficiency. The tests for finger differentiation and/or finger agnosia presented in the section on neurological indicators may be helpful in this regard (see Chapter 5). A youngster with severe finger agnosia might be expected to have difficulty with fine motor output. One might observe that such a youngster overrelies on visual feedback during fine motor and writing activities. Such a child may hold his head excessively close to the page. He may have to *see* the pencil at the top of an *h* to know when to begin its descent.

The constant need to monitor finger activity visually may sharply decrease the rate of written and other fine motor outputs.

In the evaluation of fine motor function, children of all ages should be observed using a pencil. Careful attention should be paid to the strength and effectiveness of the grasp and the ability to control the pencil's movement. In the formation of angles and intersections during form copying (as part of a visual-perceptual assessment), one can also obtain some indication of fine motor ability. One cautiously differentiates impulsivity from fine motor difficulties.

A number of standardized examinations can be used to evaluate motor function. The Lincoln-Oseresky Motor Development Scale is designed to assess both gross and fine motor abilities. Although the Coding subtest of the WISC may reveal problems with eye-hand coordination or fine motor output in general, it is somewhat contaminated by the need for an ability to appreciate and

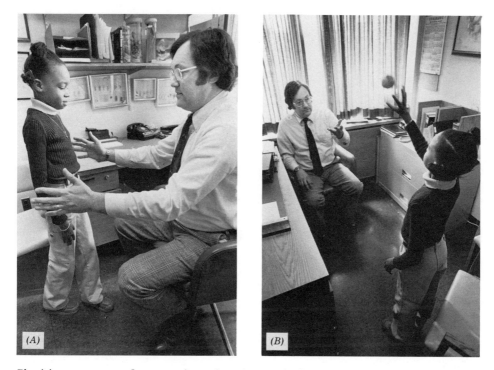

Physicians can screen for strengths and weaknesses in the area of gross motor function. In doing so, it is important to provide developmentally appropriate tasks that tap several aspects of gross motor ability. *(A)* The physician is asking the child to place the heel of one foot in contact with the toe of the other and to sustain that tandem position with eyes closed. This entails body position sense, proprioceptive feedback, balance, the ability to self-correct when swaying, and motor persistence. *(B)* The illustration on the right shows a child catching a tennis ball with one hand. This allows one to sample visually-directed gross motor activity. The ability to respond to a visual input is observed along with her timing and her judgment of an outer-space trajectory. Such direct observations, along with historical data, can help physicians "prescribe" gross motor experiences that are likely to be successful.

retain visual associations. When available, the services of an occupational or physical therapist can be helpful in assessing both gross and fine motor output. In addition, such professionals can help prepare a plan for improving function and helping a child feel better about motor effectiveness.

DEVELOPMENTAL FACILITATION

The final sections of this chapter describe four elements of development that function as facilitators of performance in the school-age child. They include:

- Higher-order integration and conceptualization
- Cognitive strategy formation
- Working capacity
- Social cognition and adaptation

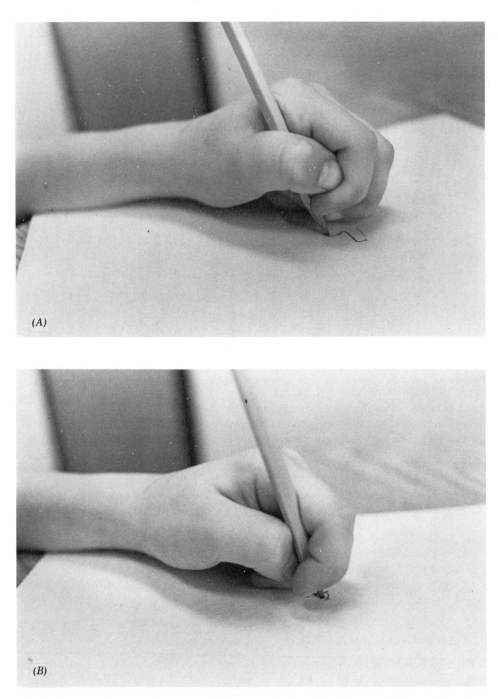

(A)

(B)

Maladaptive pencil grasps in young children can lead to significant problems with written output as volume demands and time constraints increase through late elementary school and the junior high years. These two photographs illustrate examples of such grips. It can be instructive for a pediatrician to observe a child writing and to scrutinize the quality, consistency, and overall efficiency of graphomotor function.

Children whose daily performance suggests "hypertrophy" in any of these areas may be able to compensate for relative deficiencies in perception, language, memory, attention, or other elemental functions. Such redeeming characteristics may promote academic success and help to sustain self-esteem in a child with specific learning disorders. In general, these developmental facilitators do not lend themselves easily to standardized clinical measurement. Consequently the following sections contain no explicit discussion of clinical phenomenology or screening and assessment. Nevertheless, in the evaluation of a failing child, these four elements of development must be scrutinized.

Higher-Order Integration and Conceptualization

So far we have said little about the elusive notion of intelligence. It has been the subject of a vast and controversial literature, with little or no consensus even on its definition. Overreliance on intelligence quotients can lead to unjustified complacency or fatalism when dealing with a failing child. Nevertheless, it is obvious that "high-order" functions exist and regulate information processing and cognitive abilities. As Torgesen (1977) has noted: "Poor performance in many different task settings may be due to the child's failure to actively engage the task through the use of efficient strategies and other techniques of intelligence."

This section and the one that follows (on cognitive strategy formation) offer a discussion of factors that probably relate to "intelligence."

At the higest levels of cognitive function there exist complex processes that have fascinated neurobehavioral scientists for centuries. Theoretical frameworks have been constructed for the description, classification, and developmental staging of such abilities. For clinical purposes some higher-order processes that appear particularly germane to children with learning disorders can be catalogued. They include:

- The capacity to reason on an abstract or symbolic level
- The ability to develop and apply generalizations, classifications, or rules that facilitate further adaptive behavior and learning
- The capacity to manipulate ideas in new orders or positions (i.e., creativity and imagination)
- The ability to identify discrepancies as well as consistencies within complex materials
- The capacity for transfer of skills and/or knowledge from one context to another
- The ability to integrate data coming from more than one sensory input and/or memory store in such a way as to discover new relationships that are constant in the universe
- The capacity to perform well-integrated but separate simultaneous functions
- The ability to *infer* broader meanings from literal contexts.

Relatively weak higher-order integration and conceptual abilities may be found in some children with learning disorders. This may result from a failure to understand, assimilate, store, or attend meaningfully to accumulated experience. In other cases, however, problems with higher-order conceptual activity may represent primary disabilities in themselves.

Many youngsters have difficulties operating on abstract or symbolic levels. Often described as "concrete," such children may be bound to the most basic perceptual properties of data. When asked what apples and oranges have in common, such a child may note that they are "both round" rather than indicating a more abstract categorical relationship such as that both are fruits.

Some children have difficulty assimilating generalizations, classifications, or rules about the universe. These youngsters, too, may appear "concrete" and may constantly need to renew their experiences. On the other hand, some youngsters with underlying perceptual problems and other types of learning disorders become quite adept at using rules as compensatory mechanisms to aid in their learning.

The phenomenon of intersensory integration has recently been the object of renewed interest. Many children who previously were felt to have visual-perceptual-motor problems are now recognized as having difficulty rather with the integration of input and output. For some youngsters the *simultaneous utilization* of multiple functions of the brain presents the greatest challenge (Ayres 1972).

When asked to read aloud from the Gray Oral Reading Test, one student responded: "Would you like me to read this or understand it?" One can hypothesize that some youngsters like these have problems with the crossover connections between discrete functional pathways.

Cognitive Strategy Formation

To know how to cope effectively, to be able to develop strategies that promote success, and to be deft at avoiding humiliation are ingredients for success in childhood. The clinician interested in the school-age child will encounter a wide array of coping styles and strategy patterns. For some children these methods of coping may be highly effective; for others the maneuvers are chronically self-destructive.

The capacity to cope with adversity, with feelings of inadequacy, and with the threat of peer humiliation is crucial for the school-age child with learning disorders. Those who cannot cope show a variety of secondary maladaptive behaviors including social withdrawal, nonproductive passivity, acting-out behavior, or somatic dysfunction (see Chapter 9). In some cases it is thought that serious antisocial behavior and delinquency may be end-stage coping behaviors in children chronically deprived of academic success and adult approval.

As children grow, their capacity to devise and apply adaptive strategies grows with them. They learn how to circumvent awkward situations in order to save face. They develop strategies to deal with failure, to derive secondary gain, and to control social relationships. In the learning process, strategy application is particularly crucial. Children need to discover and mobilize their strengths while bypassing their weaknesses. They need to invoke appropriate problem-solving strategies at the right times for the right tasks. Finally, they need to be able to evaluate and incorporate previously successful strategies and apply them readily in analogous situations.

The clinician will encounter children who cannot or do not cope well with academic frustration. Such a child may present with symptoms that relate more to poor coping than to the specific learning problem. For example, a child may be referred for an evaluation because he is the class clown and highly disruptive. In actuality such behavior may be a strategy for preventing embarrassment ("the best defense is a good offense").

Children who use counterproductive cognitive strategies present a challenge to educators and clinicians. A thorough evaluation often will demonstrate that the child is employing strategies that are inappropriate for his particular profile of abilities. A student with strengths in sequential processing, for example, may be using a Gestalt or configurational approach to spelling. The suggestion of alternative cognitive and behavioral strategies for such a youngster can be most helpful (see Chapter 9).

The assessment of strategies depends upon careful history taking and direct observation of a child. For example, when presenting a child with a digit span, one might observe that the child whispers the numbers to himself in the correct order, adding one number to the subvocalized sequence each time the examiner recites a digit. This productive strategy is commonly seen in children after the age of nine years. Specific coping strategies can also be detected during reading and writing exercises. Generalizing from the context of reading material when one cannot decode a particular word would be another example of strategy.

During the process of building a working alliance with a child, it is possible to develop an idea of the array of strategies the youngster uses to deal with potential humiliation and to overcome specific learning deficits. Many children are able to articulate these and will openly share them with a sympathetic clinician.

Working Capacity

It is widely assumed that students vary in their learning capacities; some can learn more quickly and effectively than others. On the other hand, it may be presumed erroneously that all children are equal with regard to the amount of work that they can accomplish. Variable "working capacity" has not received much experimental or educational scrutiny. Yet the clinician is likely to encounter children who have good learning abilities but limited working capacities. There are also children who have strong working capacities and limited learning abilities. Some appear to have neither; and, of course, a large number of children have no difficulty with either working or learning.

It is possible to "factor-analyze" the concept of working capacity to understand why some children are able to complete large chunks of academic work, while others find the load insurmountable and excessively fatiguing. One of the clearest examples of work output is the act of writing, an activity that will be discussed in more detail in the next chapter. As components of working capacity are reviewed, however, it is useful to consider the ways in which they contribute to written output in older children (see page 116). Factors that contribute to working capacity include:

1. Sustained selective attention
2. Capacity to thwart fatigue

3. Motor stamina and efficiency (e.g., for writing)
4. Ease of retrieval from memory stores
5. Organizational ability
6. Capacity to delay gratification
7. Motivation and incentives (belief in the likelihood of success)
8. Ability to perform rapidly enough so as not to deplete attention reserves

Many of the impairments described earlier in this chapter can result in a diminished working capacity. Chronically inattentive, distractible children may become increasingly ineffective academically as the demands change from predominantly receptive and retentive tasks to assignments requiring large amounts of productivity or output, a transition characteristic of the late elementary-school grades. We have applied the term *developmental high-output failure* to describe those children who decompensate in late elementary or early junior high school because of the increased demands for work output. Many such youngsters have difficulty with attention, a tendency toward fatigability and impersistence, particular problems with rapid word finding and graphamotor weaknesses. These traits make written assignments extremely difficult and can result in serious learning inhibitions and, in some cases, antisocial behaviors.

There are no formal tests of working capacity. It is essential that the clinician be sensitive to the possibility that a failing junior-high-school student may really be experiencing the characteristic late onset of this developmental dysfunction. Earlier signs of failure may not have been evident because the demands for output did not exceed the child's threshold for productivity. On the other hand, book reports and other lengthy assignments may be beyond the ability of children with limited output capacities. Such youngsters often are mislabeled as poorly motivated or lazy. Like most labels, these become self-fulfilling prophecies. The alert clinician who identifies a child with developmental high output failure can perform a great service by helping schools to modify the student's work load and by counselling the parents, the child, and school personnel about the need to strive for increased efficiency, a greater capacity for output, and enhanced organizational skills. The most critical intervention on behalf of such children involves their release from the shackles of moral condemnation by the adult world!

Social Cognition and Adaptation

A major area of performance for the school-age child is social interaction. Each school day stresses social skills as much as, if not more than, academic abilities. When a youngster has had a "hard day," there may have been far more trouble with other children than with books and pencils. During school hours there is a perpetual process of peer judging, labeling, social ranking, and scapegoating. Most youngsters become acutely aware of this type of social pressure and of the need to "prepare a face to meet the faces" that they encounter.

Teachers, parents, and physicians need to be aware of the loci of social pressures within a school. The bus stop, the school bus, the corridors, the bathrooms, the playground, the gymnasium, and the cafeteria can be far more stressful than the classroom. In evaluating social performance, often it is helpful to review these particular "scenes" with the child. A youngster can describe vividly typical scenarios that unfold at these sites. The sensitive listener can discern nuances of tone and word choice that lucidly reflect a child's social experiences and the degree of "success" he is having on the interactional scene. It is useful to have a child relate (with some prompting) the current terminology that is employed by peers. It is helpful for the clinician to know if and how a child is being labeled by other children; such information has direct implications for counselling (see Chapter 9).

Many children with developmental dysfunctions and learning problems are beleaguered with social burdens. They experience much of their greatest sense of failure in their peer relationships. Frequently they are forced to associate either with older or with younger children. Some feel more comfortable with or act like children of the opposite sex. Others withdraw into the safety of their own homes, relating mainly to their mothers, younger siblings, junk foods, and television sets!

There may be many reasons for an association between social failure and a disorder of learning and development. The following factors are often found in varying degees in such children:

Impaired feedback. Some children with learning disorders have difficulty attending to, perceiving, and interpreting social cues. They appear to be socially "tone deaf." Their feedback from social contact is nonexistent or distorted. They may have trouble decoding facial expressions, making it difficult to know when they have said or done something that has offended someone else. There may also be an auditory component wherein such youngsters may not process or appreciate intonations of disapproval or verbal reactions to their *faux pas.*

Difficulty predicting social consequences. Some children with interactional difficulties appear unable to predict the social consequences of their actions. They perform acts that result in progressive alienation from peers. At times they attempt to compensate by behaving in an even more bizarre and socially maladaptive manner. One eight-year-old boy complained that no one in his class liked him. To overcome ostracism, he went to the playground and kissed all the other boys, hoping that they would then approve of him! Despite reflective planning, this child had no sense of the potential consequences of his strategy. Thus, he sank further into disrepute. Such children can induce great heartache in their parents as well as their teachers and physicians. The torment of having no friends often is acknowledged, but such children who are friendless insist (usually accurately) that they do not know why this is so.

Gross motor problems. Some children who have gross motor weaknesses in addition to learning disorders may be isolated because of their inability or reluctance to participate in team sports and other competitive physical activities. Such youngsters may be labeled fags. They often experience peer rejection and, in some cases, may withdraw on their own. These children frequently impose inhibitions on their underlying developmental deficits, culminating in a lifelong series of retreats to avoid motoric humiliation.

Behavioral disorganization. Children with significant attention deficits may be offensive to their peers. Their impulsivity can lead to destructive acts that, in turn, result in significant unpopularity and social outcasting. Such children may not understand the reasons for their rejection. In some cases an impulsive child may not reflect on relationships enough to understand the virtues of sharing and praising. The capacity to sustain relationships may be as depleted as the ability to sustain cognitive activities or efforts. Moreover, the trait of insatiability may actually cause relationships to suffer exhaustion!

Physical unattractiveness. Some youngsters with developmental dysfunction and/or learning disorders may have phenotypic features that are physically unattractive. Obviously, some children without developmental problems may have the same difficulty. However, the combined effects of physical unattractiveness and dysfunction may lead to particular problems for the school-age child. Such a youngster is quite likely to be shunned by peers.

Stigmatization and bad reputation. Children with developmental problems may falter socially simply because of the services they are receiving or the deficits they harbor. A child who has been retained in a grade or goes to a resource room or learning center several times a week may be shunned by other youngsters, as if they fear contagion or guilt by association. Concern about potential stigmatization is often used as justification for *not* offering specialized services to a child. A better alternative is to work with the child as well as his classmates to minimize this form of social abuse. The peer group needs to be educated to refrain from the use of devastating labels such as "retard," "mental" (used as a noun), and "hypomental spaz." One 13-year-old youngster attending a special school for learning disabilities was the target of considerable abuse from other children in his neighborhood; they labeled the van that picked him up each morning "the mental bus." Such social stress can cause significant conflict in a youngster who is told by the adult world that he "needs help" and yet is cruelly branded by his peers for accepting it. It may also impose on a student a bad reputation that lingers long after the learning problem has been resolved.

The sensitive clinician dealing with children who have learning disorders needs to be sensitive to the insidious social stresses in a child's life. Data from the Parent and Teacher Questionnaires can be helpful (see Appendix C). A sympathetic and confidential discussion with a child can corroborate and document the extent or impact of peer abuse. Specific counseling in and around such concerns can be redemptive (see Chapter 9).

4

Arenas of Academic Attainment

If the pupil's knees are not well-formed, or inclined upwards,
he must be taught to keep his legs at as great a distance as
possible, and to incline his body so much to that side, on
which the arm is extended, as to oblige him to rest the opposite
leg upon the toes; and this will in a great measure hide the
defect of his make. In the same manner if the arm be too long,
or the elbow inclined upwards, it will be proper to make him
turn the palm of his hand downwards, so as to make it perfectly
horizontal.This will infallibly incline the elbow outwards, and
prevent the worse position the arm can possibly fall into,
which is that of inclining the elbow to the body. The position of
the hand so necessary keeps the elbow out, that it would not be
improper to make the pupil sometimes practice it, though he
may have no defect in his make; as an occasional use of the
former position to this may often be necessary both for the sake
of justness and variety.

> *William Scott,* Lessons in Elocution for the Improvement
> of Youth In Reading and Speaking, to which
> are Prefixed Elements of Gesture and Rules
> for Expressing with Propriety the Various
> Passions of the Mind.
> *Plymouth, Massachusetts (1825)*

Chapter 3 reviewed some prerequisite functions for general academic achievement. This chapter will focus on five areas of performance in which the school-age child may or may not demonstrate competence. The five principal performance areas considered herein were chosen for their relevance to success in school. They include reading, writing, spelling, arithmetic, and overall knowledge acquisition. These discussions of basic academic areas are intended as an introduction. The interested reader is directed to more detailed textbooks describing learing disorders affecting individual academic areas (Lerner 1976, Johnson and Mykelbust 1967, Robeck and Wilson 1974, Gearheart 1973, Money 1966).

The reader may find Table 1 useful as a normative frame of reference. This table summarizes the sequences and *approximate* grade levels of skill aquisition in elementary school. Dr. Terrell Clark was a major contributor to the development of this schema.

Table 1. A Model of the Progressive Acquisition of Academic Skills

A. Reading (Kindergarten through Sixth Grade)*

Level	1. Decoding Skills	2. Reading Level	3. Related Functions
Kindergarten	Recognizes some letteres; recognizes own name in print	Not applicable	Orientation to left —→right progression
First grade	a. Simple consonants (b, m, t, s) and short vowels (hat, get) b. Long vowels (cake, mule) c. Difficult consonants (z, j, soft g) and silent letters (knife, walk)	a. Preprimer (50–75 words) b. Primer (100–175 words) c. First reader (250–350 words)	Comprehension: Story titles; interpretation of pictures, locating information
Second grade	d. Consonant blends and diagraphs (ng, sh, th, ck, ch) e. Phonograms (ight, eep, est, ich) f. Vowel diagraphs (pail, reach) g. "R"-controlled vowels (car, bird)	2^1 and 2^2 level readers (950–1700 words)	Comprehension: Main idea, sequence of events, inference, judgment
Third grade		3^1 and 3^2 level readers (1900–3300 words)	Early emphasis on silent reading
Fourth grade	h. Structural analysis (prefixes, suffixes, roots) i. Multisyllabic, compound words	Fourth grade basal (2800–3500 words) Emphasis on Silent Reading Begins	Comprehension: Comparison Prediction; Drawing Conclusions, character descriptions
Fifth grade	Continuing automatization of above. Enhanced rate.	Fifth grade basal (4500–6000 words)	Study Skills: Outlining, summarizing, note taking
Sixth grade	Continuing automatization of above. Enhanced rate.	Sixth grade basal (6000–8500 words)	Skimming; Using reference materials

Kindergarten	First and last name aloud	Print own name; form numbers to 9	Counts 1–10; identifies 1–9	Forms sets up to 5	Size and shape recognition and identification	Concept of $\frac{1}{2}$	Identify clock, specific coins
First grade	Incidental instruction;	Print all upper- and lower-case letters	Counts 1–20; identifies up to 20	Simple addition and subtraction	Continuation of above	$\frac{1}{2}, \frac{1}{3}, \frac{1}{4}$	Tell time by hours; tell value of coins
Second grade	Start of formal instruction use of picture dictionary	Continuation of above	Counts by 2's; counts to 100; identifies two-digit numbers	Column addition and subtraction; place value	Concepts of point, line, line segment	$\frac{2}{3}, \frac{5}{8}$, etc.	Use calendar; tell time by $\frac{1}{2}$ hour
Third grade	Rules (plurals, tenses, etc.); use of dictionary	Introduction of "cursive" writing; transition from printing	Counts by 5's, 10's; identifies three- and four-digit numbers	Complex addition, subtraction; simple multiplication	Angles; bisecting lines; making segments	Lowest common denominator	Add money and make change
Fourth grade	Approximately 2000 words mastered by end of year	Continuation of above; volume demand growing	Roman numerals; decimals	Simple division; two-digit multiplication	Diameter; circumference; work with ruler, compass	Fractions, mixed numbers (adding)	Linear and liquid measurements

Table 1. (Continued)

Level	B. Spelling	C. Writing	D. Math: Numbers	D. Math: Operations	D. Math: Geometry	D. Math: Rational	D. Math: Applications
Fifth grade	Continuing growth in mastery	Nearly exclusive use of cursive writing; increased volume expectations; book reports, essays	Rounding off	Division with remainders	Polyhedrons; measuring areas	Other operations with fractions	Facts: years in a decade; days in a year; equivalents, conversions
Sixth grade	More than 3000 words mastered	Continuation with short stories, poems, note-taking; increasing speed demands	Refining above skills	Division with two to three digit divisors	Measuring angles, complex areas; constructing shapes	Continuing above	Expanding money concepts; measurement skills

*Grade levels are approximations; there is some variation among schools.

READING

In accordance with the nonlabeling philosophy of this book, the term *dyslexia* will not be applied in this section. This omission is supported by the National Advisory Committee on Dyslexia and Related Reading Disorders, which recommended that: "In view of these divergencies of opinion the Committee believes that the use of the term 'dyslexia' serves no useful purpose" (cited in Lerner 1976). Such a label implies a homogeneity of etiology, pathophysiology, clinical manifestations, and treatment that simply does not exist among a population of children with deficient reading skills.

Epidemiologic studies have investigated the prevalence of reading retardation (Minskoff 1973). In one such study, 28% of children in a major urban school system were reported to be delayed more than two years in reading, while only 3% were comparably deficient in a suburban community (Eisenberg 1966). In an independent school setting, none of the youngsters was more than two years delayed. Thus, it has been suggested that demographic factors can have a major impact on reading achievement, and any statement regarding the prevalence of reading disabilities must therefore take into account the socioeconomic status of the population surveyed.

Several problems associated with this analysis have been examined in recent years. Black children, for example, often reorder "standard English" into the speech patterns of "standard Black English." Thus, their performance on diagnostic tests for such skills as oral reading, auditory discrimination, and spelling may be inappropriately labeled as "poor," when in fact it may reflect perfect competence in a different dialect. The effect of such linguistic differences has received increasing attention (Baratz 1973, Bartel et al. 1973, Smith 1975). Preliminary evidence suggests that dialect differences do not interfere with learning to read. Teachers' attitudes about such distinctions, however, may affect the children and impair the reading process (Weaver and Shonkoff 1978).

Multiple studies of elementary-school students have shown a much higher prevalence of reading problems in boys than in girls, with ratios varying from 4–1 to 8–1. Countless other factors have been examined in an effort to describe the epidemiology of reading retardation. Inconsistent data have been collected with regard to such diverse variables as birth order, left-handedness, colorblindness, group IQ, and hair color!

It is probably fair to say that the symptom of reading retardation represents a "final common pathway" from such diverse origins as educational experience, preacademic motivation, neurological integrity, linguistic competence, general health, developmental readiness, emotional stability, and cultural milieu. An astute clinician should consider all possible contributing factors, for several predispositions often act synergistically in the development of a reading disability.

In order to understand and collaborate productively in the management of a child with reading problems, one needs a conceptual model of the developmental progression toward reading competency. The following sections offer a *simplified* but clinically useful schema.

Early Life Experiences Affecting Reading

Long before children begin to acquire actual reading skills, precursor sensitivities and behaviors unfold.

Development of speech and language. The early recognition of the association between speech sounds and objects or actions constitutes an important aspect of preparedness for reading. Increasing abilities in receptive and expressive oral language form the foundation upon which written language is later built (see Chapter 3). During the late preschool years, an exponential growth in vocabulary and a greater facility with more sophisticated syntax complement the child's expanding metalinguistic awareness, which provides the basis for reading (Cazden 1976).

Development of visual-spatial and temporal-sequential skills. The importance of visual-spatial and temporal-sequential organization as reading-readiness capabilities has been discussed in Chapter 3. An evolving sensitivity to these organizing systems so vital to human data processing begins in early infancy. Their ultimate role in potentiating the acquisition of word-recognition and analysis skills appears to be critical. Recent research has emphasized the relatively greater importance of early auditory abilities ("auditory perceptual skills") for later reading, as compared to the less critical visual skills (Weaver and Shonkoff 1978).

Environmental models and home influences. In the preschool years, young children become aware of the existence of written communication. They begin to appreciate that writing is associated with speech sounds, and they recognize the difference between pictures and written symbols. The importance of the bedtime story is a testimonial to the significance of this phenomenon. In recent years, considerable attention has been given to young children's "motivation" to acquire academic abilities. Strong inclinations toward skill development are viewed as positive prognostic signs for ultimate learning. A young child might be noticed pretending to write or read. One might discern an early infatuation with books, magazines, and other reading materials. Such academic warming-up rituals are generally encouraged by other family members and may be traced to some or all of the following origins: a romantic attraction to school and learning processes; an orientation toward achievement and recognition; a desire to shape or model oneself after an adult, a friend, or an older sibling; or a response to perceived rewards or incentives created at home or in a preschool setting. Although much preacademic behavior has been stimulated by educational television programs such as *Sesame Street* and *The Electric Company* (Gibbon et al. 1975), the attitudes and actions of family members are the most crucial influences on the development of readiness skills (Durkin 1966).

Beginning to Read

The earliest ventures into reading represent a complex process, whose understanding has consumed the life work of many a scholar and has been a major focus of several disciplines. In our simplified representation, several early steps can be described. Their precise sequence depends largely on the teaching methods employed and, to some extent, on the cognitive style of the child.

Early associations between sounds and visual symbols. When a child enters the educational system, he may have already developed some basic familiarity with the names of letters and, more importantly, with the sounds with which they are associated. Although investigators have detected a high correlation between letter naming in the preschool child and later success in reading (deHirsch et al. 1966), the relationship may not be causal. In fact, the common denominator may be the home environment itself. Beyond the simple naming of letters, however, sound-symbol associations are crucial in learning to read, and they may present troublesome hurdles for a dysfunctioning child (Venezsky 1976).

Sequential organization of the sound-symbol system. Early in the reading process, children begin to appreciate the importance of letter order. They recognize that specific letter combinations represent definite speech sounds. This becomes a critical requisite for the phonic analysis of unfamiliar words (Chall 1967).

Structural analysis. As part of their early academic experience, children learn that they can take apart and reassemble words as if they were jigsaw puzzles. This process of segmentation and reblending (analysis and synthesis) is often used in the teaching of reading. Difficulties with sound blending have often been noted in youngsters with delayed acquisition of reading skills.

Sight-word recognition. The appreciation of whole words as Gestalt patterns or configurations is another way in which beginners may learn to approach reading. Sight-word recognition, or "sight vocabulary," refers to the instantaneous recognition of words based on their overall visual form and detail. Some children develop sight-word recognition skills before they are able to analyze unfamiliar words, while others first develop the process of phonic analysis. To a large extent, this depends upon the teaching methods that are employed. Thus, in the evaluation of an early elementary school student's reading skills, some familiarity with the methods applied is essential.

Integration of component subskills. For the reading process to function smoothly, the child ultimately must combine the component skills by which tasks such as decoding and comprehension are mastered. According to the model presented above, this would include the integration of sight-word recognition and structural (Phonic) analysis skills. This concept of reading assumes the presence of subskills. This is a controversial issue among reading theorists, some of whom insist that reading is a holistic process that cannot be subdivided into components (Guthrie 1973, Samuels 1976).

Comprehension. Reading involves the translation of visual symbols into meaningful language. The precursor subskills discussed above (e.g., sound-symbol associations, structural analysis) are therefore critical but not sufficient aspects of the process, because a person must have comprehension of the reading matter in order to be said to be able to read.

Reading to Expand Knowledge

As children progress through the middle and late elementary-school years, reading becomes their most important tool for the acquisition of knowledge. Success in such subjects as history, social studies, science, and mathematics presupposes efficient, nonfatiguing reading skills. Educators often refer to "functional reading level" to describe a youngster's competency when reading to extract knowledge or content. This functional level may differ from reading levels measured by standardized achievement tests. Several characteristics of functional reading capacity are discussed below.

Use of syntactic cues. As children begin to extract syntactic cues that reinforce the meanings of words, they read in a less labored manner. They can derive meaning from the structure, tense, suffixes, prefixes, and oral flow of a sentence rather than depending on painstaking word-by-word decoding. The ability to generalize from context and use grammatical structure to make inferences about meaning promotes more mature reading skills.

Expanded comprehension and retention. Increasing vocabulary, automatic word recognition, text organization, and prior knowledge are some of the feeder lines that interconnect to facilitate comprehension. In the early elementary grades, relatively more attention is devoted to recognizing words than to understanding the simple text. In the later elementary grades the mechanical skills of reading are automatized, so that attention can be focused primarily on comprehension. When automaticity is not fully achieved, some attention is drained by decoding tasks; this process interferes with the capacity of short-term memory to retain data for optimal comprehension (LaBerge and Samuels 1974).

Development of a reading style. As children become increasingly involved in the reading process, individual propensities for reliance on particular cues may emerge. Teaching techniques often influence the choice of style. Many children, however, clearly develop reading styles that exploit their own strengths. Some youngsters may rely more on visual cues and configurational appreciation of words, while others tend to be "splitters" rather than "lumpers." Inefficient or possibly maladaptive styles may also supervene, including excessive finger pointing, overreliance on context, or subvocalization. In many cases, however, these behaviors are compensatory and actually enhance a youngster's reading comfort.

Reading for a purpose. Ultimately, children benefit from reading by extracting information that they can apply to a task. The written word can help with airplane model building or automobile repair, providing an enticing link between reading for school and reading for oneself. In the late elementary and early secondary school years, children are attracted increasingly to reading materials with intrinsic appeal. At best, such reading may include biographies, great novels, and newspaper articles. As one strays toward the outer boundaries of adult acceptability, high-motivational reading may include excursions into pinup magazines, comic books, and a sibling's confidential diary! At any rate, within reasonably broad limits, high-motivational reading is to be encouraged, especially for youngsters whose reading skills are somewhat delayed.

The capacity to limit televiewing. As children's reading skills progress to the point where the extraction of useful information and entertainment is easy, the competing force of television looms as an increasingly important detractor from reading experience. The television set serves up information and knowledge with considerably less effort than that required for decoding the written word. Youngsters who have difficulty delaying gratification, especially those with attention deficits (see Chapter 3), are particularly vulnerable to the passive receipt of stimulation, delivered via the pulsating rhythm of television communication. In secondary school and beyond, reading facility relates to reading experience. Those who have largely substituted television watching for reading are likely to become reading-inefficient because of their limited experience with the printed word.

Reading Sophistication

The finishing touches in the acquisition of reading skills continue to be applied throughout secondary schools and into higher education and later life. Three basic aspects are noted below.

Critical analysis. The capacity to analyze and criticize written material develops during the late elementary-school years and continues throughout adolescence and adult life. When the developmental trend begins, the child has difficulty separating his own ideas from those of the writer. The youngster progresses to a stage where he is able to extract themes, separate personal ideas from those on the page, and become critical of the disparity. In high school this capacity is strengthened. Although many youngsters fall short of becoming talented literary critics, most can, at least, integrate the skeptical admonition, "Don't believe everything you read!"

Syntheses of divergent sources. The capacity to bring together various reading sources and assemble an integrated exposition or argument is another form of reading maturity. Reports or projects requiring such syntheses become particularly challenging in junior high school, with sophisticated reading becoming the foundation of advanced expository writing.

Reading between the lines. This capacity involves detecting irony, extracting subtle inferences, recognizing analogy, metaphor, and symbolism, and detecting recurrent *leitmotifs* that suggest an overall theme or meaning. Such reading is necessary for grasping the significance of literary works such as poetry and novels.

Deficient Reading: Signs and Observations

Delay in the acquisition of reading skills is the most frequent complaint among children with learning disorders. Early diagnosis is most important, since initial frustration in reading may lead to learning inhibitions and intransigent, negative feelings about education. It is helpful for the clinician to be aware of the descriptors that are used to examine the problems of such youngsters.

An evaluation team needs to analyze a youngster's reading carefully and to review the findings against a backdrop of neurodevelopmental and psychosocial data. As noted earlier, so-called reading disabilities subsume a heterogeneous group of children, any one of whom may present with any combination of deficits (and strengths) in the elements discussed in Chapter 3. Team members must, therefore, engage in the arduous task of determining which associated neurodevelopmental and psychosocial factors contribute significantly to a child's reading failure. The entire team must heed the warning that not all associations are causal! A youngster may come from a depriving, disorganized home

CHECKLIST FOR THE OBSERVATION
OF ORAL PARAGRAPH READING

	PERFORMANCE COMPONENTS			
01	OVERALL GRADE LEVEL:	>2 Yrs. DELAY	0-2 Yrs. DELAY	NO DELAY
02	RATE	SLOW	UNEVEN	FAST
03	COMPREHENSION	POOR	FAIR	GOOD
04	PRONUNCIATION	POOR	FAIR	GOOD
05	OMISSIONS OF WORDS/LETTERS	MANY	FEW	NONE
06	INSERTIONS OF WORDS/LETTERS	MANY	FEW	NONE
07	FINGER POINTING	MARKED	SLIGHT	NONE
08	LOSS OF PLACE	FREQUENT	RARE	NONE
09	WORD GUESSING	FREQUENT	RARE	NONE
10	ATTENTION TO DETAIL	POOR	FAIR	GOOD
11	SELF-CORRECTION	POOR	FAIR	GOOD
12	OVERRELIANCE ON CONTEXT	MARKED	SLIGHT	NONE
13	WORD-BY-WORD READING	MARKED	SLIGHT	NONE
14	EYE DISTANCE TO PAGE	< 3 INCHES	3-5 INCHES	>5 INCHES
15	VOWEL SUBSTITUTIONS	FREQUENT	RARE	NONE
16	SEQUENCING PROBLEMS	FREQUENT	RARE	NONE
17	LETTER REVERSALS	FREQUENT	OCCASSIONAL	NONE
18	OVERDEPENDENCE ON PHONICS	MARKED	SLIGHT	NONE
19	DISREGARD OF PUNCTUATION	FREQUENT	RARE	NONE
20	LACK OF EXPRESSION	MARKED	SLIGHT	NONE

Figure 1. CHECKLIST FOR THE OBSERVATION OF ORAL PARAGRAPH READING

environment and yet such circumstances may not be the cause (or, at least, the primary cause) of his reading failure. The developmental diagnostician must prepare a tight case for formulation, carrying out a process somewhat analogous to an attorney's preparation of a brief for court: any isolated bit of evidence represents circumstantial but not definitive proof. Only by constructing the total case, and attempting to demonstrate convincing causality, can one feel confident about approaching the truth. The neurodevelopmental examination, along with standardized test data and parent-teacher observations, generally suggest consistent themes of dysfunction that help explain the reasons for a child's reading problems. It is such consistency that should be sought in the diagnostic-formulation process (see Chapter 5).

Although a definitive diagnostic formulation and remediation plan requires expertise that the physician does not have, he or she can also make relevant observations by watching and listening to a youngster read. A sampling tool such as the Gray Oral Reading Test or the Gilmore Oral Reading Test (see Appendix A) is easy to incorporate into an office assessment. From such instruments, one may derive a performance grade level while simultaneously assessing the accuracy, error pattern, rate, style, and comprehension of a child's oral reading (see Fig. 1).

Since simple scoring of a test such as the Gray Oral does not describe the nature of a child's difficulties, qualitative analysis of performance is most important. Informal graded word lists, such as those described in the appendix, can also be used. Physicians who employ such methods to screen reading skills must be aware that they are looking only at oral reading, for many children show a significant discrepancy between their oral and silent reading abilities. A variety of achievement tests are available to evaluate the latter (see Appendix A).

Parameters of Assessment

Several factors should be considered in a screening description of a child's reading abilities.

Word recognition. Many standardized reading tests yield a specific grade level for word-recognition skills. Such data are only approximations, however, and children may show a significant degree of variation, depending upon the test used to sample reading performance. Many youngsters with attention deficits tend to score higher on a one-to-one administered oral reading test than on the group achievement tests commonly given in school.

Word-analysis skills. Beyond specific grade level, consideration should be given to the quality of a child's sight vocabulary and word-analysis skills. As noted above, the former is reflected in the instantaneous recognition of a word. Analytic abilities, on the other hand, can be assessed by presenting a nonsense word or one that the youngster has not previously encountered and observing how it is decoded. It is often revealing to request the analysis of a word the child claims *not* to know. After suggesting, "Why don't you try to sound that one out?" the clinician can then observe the child's capacity to attribute sounds to symbols, to segment words into their component elements, and to resynthesize or blend fragments back into words. A number of the development elements discussed in Chapter 3 may be tapped by this process, including sequencing abilities, short-term memory, and auditory discrimination. The physician must remember, however, that a child's word-analysis skills may be determined to some extent by the method used for teaching reading. A student who has been instructed through a sight method, for example, may not be as adept at word analysis as one who has been taught through a predominantly linguistic or phonic approach (see Chapter 6).

Reading rate. Both the Gilmore and the Gray Oral Reading tests are timed tests. A youngster's overall grade level may thus be affected by the calculated rate of reading. Children with relatively small sight vocabularies may score poorly on this type of evaluation. When trying to read rapidly, some children fail to comprehend the material. A few will plunge into an atypical speed-reading display at the very sight of a stopwatch! It is sometimes helpful to suggest that a child slow down in the interest of improved comprehension.

Comprehension. Understanding what has been read is the essence of reading. Comprehension may differ substantially on tests of oral versus silent reading. Some reading-disabled youngsters have difficulty with the simultaneous oral recital of words and their association with meaning. Others become engaged in a frenetic struggle to transform visual symbols into sounds that leaves little cognitive residuum or time for comprehension. The psychology of reading comprehension has been studied extensively (Gibson and Levin 1975, Davis 1967, Caroll 1976). It depends on many factors, including the abilities to associate meaning with a graphic symbol; understand words in context and select the meaning that fits that context; read in "thought units"; draw inferences; understand the writer's organization; evaluate subtleties of tone, mood, and intent; and retain and apply ideas derived from reading. In screening a youngster's reading comprehension, clinicians should recognize that by asking questions about the content of a particular paragraph, they are also assessing a child's short-term memory and oral comprehension.

Patterns of Dysfunction
The developmental diagnostician needs to characterize consistent tendencies with regard to reading dificits. Figure 1 outlines a simplified model for documenting specific dysfunctional patterns. Some youngsters have a propensity for skips or *omissions.* They may pass over words, phrases, or entire lines. Sometimes this behavior results from difficulties with visual tracking, sometimes from inadequate visual attention to detail, as in many young children with primary attention deficits. Other youngsters have difficulties with *sequencing,* which may be reflected in confusion about letter order (e.g., *was* for *saw*) or in problems with the sequence of words in a phrase or sentence. *Insertions* or *substitutions,* another common form of error, may be seen in youngsters who have poor word-analysis skills or who tend to be impulsive. Letter reversals also may be due to impulsivity, or they may be secondary to perceptual problems affecting directional sense.

The basic rhythm of reading also may be impaired. As children progress through elementary school, one anticipates continued development with regard to intonation and expression. Some children with incompletely integrated reading skills, however, have a tendency to indulge in *word-by-word* reading. Such reading is monotonous, expressionless, hesitant, and often apparently oblivious to punctuation. The increasing inefficiency of such a pattern of dysfunction becomes evident in later grades.

Compensatory Styles
The mechanisms a child uses to aid in reading can often have diagnostic significance. Some youngsters, for example, tend to overrely on clues from the context, picking out one or two key words and "filling the cracks" with self-generated vocabulary. Thus, "The boy chased the cat who climbed up a tree"

may be read as "The boy chased the cat down the street." Such overreliance on context impairs comprehension. Dependence upon contextual "crutches" may reflect attention difficulties, poor reading skills in general, or a relatively limited sight vocabulary.

Finger pointing is another commonly observed compensatory strategy. Some children use this mechanism to counteract problems with visual attention to detail, figure-ground discrimination, or visual pursuit (i.e., tracking difficulties). For youngsters who have difficulties reading a mass of print in a paragraph but show excellent word-recognition skills when presented with flash cards or reading-word lists, finger pointing can often be a good strategy.

Another common compensatory mechanism is subvocalization (the semiaudible mouthing of words while reading "silently"). Subvocalizers apparently are unable to extract meaning directly from a visual symbol, and therefore, they interpose a step by transforming the visual symbol into a speech sound. In the past, this strategy was said to be particularly characteristic of "auditory learners" during the early stages of silent reading. Such children could reportedly retain information better if it passed through their ears.

A less rewarding but common maneuver is to acknowledge one or two initial letters and then guess at the rest of the word (or the entire sentence). Impulsive youngsters, those with difficulties sustaining visual attention to detail, and those whose word analysis skills are rusty may pilot-test such strategies.

A final compensatory mechanism is seen in youngsters who read with their eyes two inches or less from the page. Such behavior may suggest underlying refractory errors (such as myopia or astigmatism), amblyopia, poor visual attention to detail, excessive distractibility, or chronic fatigue.

An observation of reading, particularly in the early grades, can serve as a reprise following a neurodevelopmental examination. Many of the *leitmotifs* discerned during the observation of developmental function may reappear as a grand finale in the reading process.

Reading is central to learning, owing not only to its critical role in the acquisition of knowledge and skill but also to its intimate relationship to writing, spelling, and arithmetic. Skill in one of these areas can serve to reinforce and enhance facility in the others.

SPELLING

It is unlikely that a child would be referred to a medical setting for evaluation of an isolated spelling problem. Although specific "dysorthographia" exists, it is unusual for it to be brought into a medical setting when all other aspects of learning and life are said to be healthy. On the other hand, deficient spelling is often a manifestation of broader developmental dysfunction. Children with reading disorders frequently have serious spelling problems. Difficulties with spelling can result from a variety of developmental deficits. From a neurodevelopmental point of view, spelling is important because of what it might suggest about a child's memory.

Accurate spelling relies heavily upon the integration of visual memory for Gestalt, visual-sequential competence, and retention. Letter order and the visual configuration of a word provide essential cues for spelling. In addition, a strong

Table 2. A classification of Spelling Error Propensities*

Error Propensity	Examples	Some Possible Associations
Extraneous letters (insertions)	"beflore" for "before" "alfter" for "after"	Impulsivity; poor revisualization; poorly integrated sight vocabulary; language—phonics problems
Missing letters (omissions)	"bicyle for "bicycle" "whel" for "wheel"	Impulsivity; poor revisualization; poorly integrated sight vocabulary; language—phonics problems
Sequential confusion	"rigde" for "ridge" "dog" for "god"	Impulsivity; problems with sequential organization
Visual errors with phonetic resemblance	"lite" for "light" "grate" for "great"	Overreliance on phonics; problems with visual memory—revisualization
Phonetic errors with visual resemblance	"goase" for "goose" "crowl" for "crawl"	Impulsivity; overreliance on visual cues; poor sound-symbol associations; problems with auditory discrimination
Letter reversal	"bog" for "dog" "pig" for "big"	Impulsivity; problems with directionality (visual-spatial orientation); inattention
Spelling without resemblance (neither visual nor phonetic)	"ritt" for "right" "citzen" for "kitchen"	Language disability; problems with visual memory; poor sound-symbol associations; limited exposure

*These types of errors (when they occur consistently) *may* suggest underlying areas of deficit.

sense of sound-symbol association, or phonics is crucial for spelling accuracy. A youngster who has difficulty with auditory discrimination, or has not developed well-established associations between oral sound units (phonemes) and written symbols (graphemes), is likely to have particular trouble with the task of spelling.

A graded spelling list can be used to screen a child's abilities. In evaluating spelling performance, it is particularly important that the examiner observe error patterns (see Table 2). Three basic patterns of misspellings have been described: phonetically correct errors, visually approximate mistakes, and what might be called "errors without rationale." A phonetically correct error is one in which the pronunciation of the misspelling is close to the actual word (e.g., *laff* for *laugh*). Such children may have problems with visual retrieval memory. A visually approximate error looks similar to the actual word but does not make sense phonetically (e.g., *lagh* for *laugh*). In some instances, such errors may result from difficulty with sequencing (e.g., *gald* for *glad*). An "irrational" error is one that approximates neither the phonetic nor the visual characteristics of the actual word (e.g., *lift* for *laugh*). Some children present clinically with a preponderance of one or another of the three types of error. Those who demonstrate one of the first two patterns are said to have a better prognosis for both spelling and reading than the youngsters whose errors are without apparent rationale. There are also children with mixed patterns of errors. In some cases, misspellings may result from chronic impulsivity and weak visual attention to detail. Such children may show markedly inconsistent performance on spelling tests.

In screening a child's spelling, it is helpful to differentiate between recognition and retrieval word memory. Some youngsters are able to recognize a correctly (or incorrectly) spelled word but are unable to retrieve the accurate spelling when asked to write the word themselves. Such a child may perform very well on a test that requires selection of the correctly spelled word from a list of misspellings (e.g., Stanford Achievement Test) yet have great difficulty on a test that requires writing words from dictation (e.g., Wide Range Achievement Test). The Boder Diagnostic Spelling and Reading Test, on the other hand, requires a youngster to spell words that are definitely part of his sight vocabulary; this provides an assessment of the ability to *revisualize* or retrieve the detail of words that are known to be recognizable to the child. Having a youngster proofread his own spelling words can also be helpful in this regard. A child who has difficulty retrieving (revisualizing) words may have little or no problem recognizing a word he has misspelled.

Another factor in spelling relates to a child's capacity to understand, incorporate, and apply rules. Relative strength or weakness in assimilating consistencies and established spelling rules can have a profound influence on performance. Children with rule-use problems may also have difficulty with rules of grammar, syntax, and mathematical operations.

As children progress through the late elementary and early secondary school years, spelling becomes increasingly useful as a diagnostic test. In particular, the characterization of error types can have significant prognostic value (see above) and can provide clues about possible underlying neurodevelopmental weaknesses that may be more difficult to elicit directly.

WRITTEN LANGUAGE

In the middle and upper elementary-school grades, an earlier emphasis on input functions such as attention, perception, recognition, and discrimination gives way to a spiraling demand for output (commonly called "work"). The most critical academic output skill for the older child is written language. Most youngsters survive the transition to demands for high written output and, to varying degrees, welcome the opportunity to express themselves. Writing becomes a critical tool for thought and expression, providing a display case for acquired skills and knowledge.

Some children have particular difficulties with written expression (Mykelbust 1973). Writing, perhaps the most sophisticated application of language, and therefore the last to be mastered, may be a late-onset obstacle for the dysfunctioning child (Bain 1976). It is not unusual for children at the late elementary or early junior high school level to become seriously discouraged because of an inability to write comfortably, quickly, and effectively. Many of these youngsters may have experienced little or no difficulty learning to read. For some, writing becomes a chore to be avoided whenever possible. The ripple effects from this strategic retreat can lead to progressive disenchantment with the learning process and, in some cases, to social alienation.

Components of Written-Language Disorders

A broad array of developmental dysfunctions may underlie disorders of writing (see list below). Some children may have difficulty writing because of multiple disabilities, while others have isolated or discrete deficits. The common underpinnings of writing deficits include lags in motor and visual-motor skills and expressive language function, and issues of efficiency, attention, and retention.

Written Output: Common Underpinnings

The list below summarizes factors that need consideration in older children with inhibitions or deficiencies of written output. The act of writing entails the convergence of multiple developmental pathways. Children with writing problems may need help in one or more of these areas:

1. Fine motor function
2. Pencil control—comfort, effectiveness, speed
3. Visual and auditory memory—for spelling and planning
4. Well-integrated simultaneous rule application (spelling, punctuation, grammar, syntax, etc.)
5. Spatial planning and utilization of page
6. Effective visual-motor integration
7. Rapid and effective word finding
8. Strength of attention—delay of gratification, stamina, reflectivity, task persistence, focus
9. Narrative and sequential organizational ability
10. Reading skills
11. Experience, training, and practice
12. Incentives—cultural factors, likelihood of success, role modeling, expectations (and responses to expectations), and prior results (i.e., earlier positive reinforcement)
13. Risk taking—willingness to commit or "expose" oneself in a written (i.e., permanent or semipermanent) record
14. Interest in content

Motor and Visual-Motor Components

Fine motor weakness. Some children with eye-hand coordination problems experience difficulty executing the motor patterns needed to form letters, numbers, or words. Early in their educational experience, many of these youngsters develop awkward or abnormal pencil grips (see Chapter 3). Their maladaptive grips may become a serious liability, as they have a lowered threshold for fatigue and writer's cramp when required to produce a relatively large amount of written material (e.g., a book report or an essay). "Speed writing" may also present difficulties. At the secondary level, the capacity to write rapidly is often more crucial than legibility. A youngster at this stage needs to be able to adjust the mechanics of writing to a rate that can keep pace with a flow of thoughts, a rate that can be in concert with his attention patterns and strengths, thus thwarting the ever-present threat of fatigue!

Disorders of visual-motor integration. Children who have problems perceiving visual configurations and transferring them to paper are at serious risk for writing inefficiencies. Early in their academic careers such youngsters may demonstrate problems with letter formation. They may appear to do things the hard way; their writing is encumbered by excessive disconnections, confusion over directionality, and highly unusual (and sometimes uncomfortable) execution. Despite well-developed abilities to spell, narrate, and read with fluency, some youngsters may encounter problems with the visual-motor-integrative aspects of writing. This condition has been called *dysgraphia.*

Deficits of visual memory and revisualization. Some youngsters can competently recognize and copy letters, words, or shapes but are unable to retain visual images for retrieval and reproduction from memory (see the section on spelling). Such children may have particular difficulty when writing from dictation. Although less trouble may be encountered when the child can select his own words, the ultimate product often reflects an impoverished vocabulary content.

Spatial planning. Some children with visual-spatial confusion may have particular difficulty arranging letters, words, or sentences in an orderly manner on a page. Problems in planning when and where to begin or end individual words may be considerable, and the use of margins or lines may appear haphazard. This is true particularly in younger children.

Expressive Language Components

Word-finding difficulties (dysnomia). Some children have difficulty with written expression because of concomitant problems with oral language. Such youngsters may be slow in finding the proper words to express ideas either in speech or in writing. During the early school years they often have problems in naming pictures or objects or in rapidly naming examples within categories (e.g., animals, plants, foods). Many of these youngsters are unable to retrieve words from their vocabulary stores rapidly enough for fluent writing. A prolonged latency of response renders written output excessively tedious and labored, thereby exhausting a child's attention reserve and depleting his motivation.

Deficiencies in Narrative Organization and Syntax

Some youngsters can speak fluently, copy well, and spell without difficulty, but must struggle to arrange thoughts in an organized exposition for writing. Organization deficits are often detected in the narrative speech of these youngsters. Some of these children have underlying difficulties with sequential organization. In older youngsters, problems with sequencing and segmentation may be difficult to demonstrate (except by taking a careful history), and disorganization of written output may be the major manifestation of sequential disorganization. Poor production of written matter can also reflect difficulty using the rules of syntax and grammar.

Efficiency, Attention, and Retention Components

Diminished rate of processing. Some children have acquired all the readiness skills for writing, but when they attempt to organize and integrate the various processes, the ultimate outcome is tediously slow and labored. For these youngsters, writing becomes increasingly discouraging and time consuming. They often become writing-inhibited.

Attention deficit. As children with chronic attention problems mature, some show progressive improvement in their capacity to regulate their activity and focus their concentration. A late manifestation of weak attention, however, may be diminished work output. For such youngsters, lengthy written assignments often result in increasing fatigue, impulsivity, and poor self-monitoring. Such children are frequently labeled as "poorly motivated," "lazy," or "absent-minded."

Memory. An efficient short-term memory system is essential for a smooth flow of written output. A youngster who repeatedly "loses his train of thought" or forgets the point he was about to make can have a great deal of difficulty with written output. His productions often turn out to be disjointed and "free-associative." It is important to emphasize that the act of writing represents the confluence of multiple memory functions.

The Impact and Context of Written-Language Failure

Students of learning disorders and child development have traditionally underestimated the importance of written language. While deficits in decoding skills have received a great deal of attention, both in research and service, the capacity to encode efficiently (i.e., to produce output) has received far less scrutiny. As a result, children with encoding problems tend to be a maligned and misunderstood minority. Typically, they are likely to reach the depths of despair in junior high school, as the following drama often is played out:

Mom: "George, do you have any homework tonight?"

George: "No, Mom, I did it in school."

Mom: "You did it all in school today?"

George: "Ya, I did it all in school today."

Mom: "How come you never have any homework?"

George: "Bug off, I'm goin' out."

After months of repetition of this script, a note arrives from school, stating that George owes 26 book reports, and they are due right before Christmas vacation! Everything has caved in around George, for whom writing is excruciating. Like those of most 14-year-olds, George's powers of rationalization exceed his attentional strength. He has assumed that if he ignored the book reports they would somehow be taken care of. For some reason this did not occur. George is now desperate. At this point, there is not much he can do—except to go out!

Children who have difficulty writing often hate to write. Ultimately, they write very little, and thus they superimpose relative writing inexperience on their underlying developmental deficiencies. Several complicating aspects of this problem are particularly serious. First, these difficulties often become manifest at the onset of puberty, at a time when there are significant concerns about body image and competence. Most youngsters at this age are coping with an inordinately high level of peer tyranny. The coercive pressure to conform is overwhelming. The early adolescent must adhere to a dress code, remain "cool" at all times, demonstrate no "rough edges," and show little reliance on the adult world. It is, therefore, difficult for a child with writing disorders to acknowledge the problem, confess to needing help, and, ultimately, to accept assistance. Second, junior high school students attend junior high schools. At this level there may be less remedial service available, and perhaps less sensitivity to special needs, than in the elementary school. Particularly if a child can read adequately, a handicap affecting writing may not be acknowledged or "serviced." Thus, there may be a tendency for children with writing problems to be condemned morally and convicted of attitudinal crimes with little regard for possible underlying developmental inefficiencies. Finally, writing problems may be complicated by family difficulties. Adolescence imposes a stress on all family members, and sometimes it coincides with parental midlife crises. Agonizing reevaluations of work, of marriage, and of family often produce domestic turmoil at a time when the communication gap between parents and child is widening.

The danger is that a child with a written-output problem may have nowhere to turn. He may find little sympathy or understanding at home (where other problems may be paramount). In school, the student may encounter only criticism and may be made to feel inadequate. Often the only gratification such a child can achieve comes from peers. In many communities, it is common for all the failing 13-and14-year-old adolescents to find each other! They may meet in front of the corner drugstore each Friday night. They may form a strong coalition, bonded through collaboration in vaguely antisocial acts (such as drugs, alcohol, abusive language). That coalition may be considered their only trail toward "success." In extreme cases they may substitute this "omnipotent" peer group for family and for community.

Early adolescence can be a critical turning point with regard to future pathways. The emergence of delinquent behavior and other maladaptive strategies of social survival are a major societal threat. Such a complex network of factors makes a comprehensive view of a youngster essential. One should never tell an adolescent that he can do better, unless one is sure that he can!

Screening Written Language

In screening a child with learning difficulties, a writing sample may be revealing. If possible, it is useful to observe at least three levels of written output: copying sentences or words, writing from dictation, and writing an original paragraph on a particular subject. The clinician can attend to such components as pencil grasp and fine motor control, word finding, organizational skill, and visual-motor integration. Standardized tests of writing are rare. The Myklebust Picture Story Language Test is one that presents a picture stimulus about which the child is expected to write. Writing tests are particularly vulnerable to problems of standardization and cultural biases.

MATHEMATICS

Difficulties with mathematics include a group of frequently encountered, but poorly understood, cognitive styles and disorders, as well as a variety of specific syndromes such as the Developmental Gerstmann syndrome, Leonhard's syndrome, and various forms of "dyscalculia." In the neurological literature, the association between arithmetic disability and finger agnosia has received some attention, although the significance of this relationship remains obscure. As with reading, mathematics involves a broad range of readiness skills and competencies, and a wide variety of deficits have been described in dysfunctioning children (Friedus 1966).

The symptoms of mathematics failure can be divided into subgroups. A distinction is often made between children who fail in arithmetic because of language or reading problems and those who have true deficits in quantitative thinking or visual-spatial orientation (McLeod and Crump 1978). An inability to revisualize numbers, difficulty in forming written numerals, and problems in assimilating instructions all can thwart the acquisition of arithmetic skills. Many children with developmental language disabilities have difficulty because they cannot use words to decode and describe mathematical processes. Others have trouble recalling specific numbers.

While all children with math disabilities do not necessarily have other academic problems, there may be some association among deficit areas. Problems with revisualization, for example, can impair both spelling and arithmetic. Many children with writing disorders have difficulty arranging numbers correctly on a page. Others have fundamental problems with number formation. In the early grades, a child's need to concentrate heavily on the motor aspects of writing numbers may interfere with the acquisition of basic mathematics operational skills.

Components of Mathematics Disorders

Different combinations of discrete dysfunctions are found in association with arithmetic underachievement. Some have prompted attempts at classification (Kosc 1974). No consistent taxonomy has achieved widespread acceptance, however, because of the recognition that individual cases are often exhibit unique clusters of deficits. A number of the possible components of a mathematics disorder are described below.

Verbal mathematics expression. Children with difficulties in this area may have problems using words to express mathematical terms, concepts, and relationships.

Concrete mathematical manipulations. Youngsters with difficulties in this area may have problems with relative size or number and the hands-on manipulation of quantitative materials, such as sticks, cubes, or other objects.

Establishment of one-to-one correspondence. Difficulty in this area may be related to problems dealing with constant mathematical proportions. When setting a table, for example, such a child may have difficulty recognizing that four place settings are needed for four people.

Auditory-visual associations. Some children have difficulty with the visual identification of numbers, despite the fact that they can count verbally. Such sound-symbol disassociation can also be seen with the act of naming letters.

The clustering phenomenon. Some children with arithmetic disabilities have problems discerning or identifying specific clusters; they always have to count objects individually.

Graphic representation of numbers. Many children have difficulty writing numbers. This may result from revisualization problems, as noted above.

Mathematical comprehension. Deficits in mathematical comprehension can impair a child's capacity to reason mathematically or to perform mental calculations. Some youngsters are able to read or write numbers but are unable to understand what they have read or written. One such child may know that the numeral he has written is called "six", but he may not realize that it comes before seven!

Operational functions. Children with disturbances of mathematics operational function often can understand, read, and write numbers and may have no difficulty establishing numerical relationships. Basic mathematical operations such as addition, subtraction, multiplication, and division, however, may present major challenges. Youngsters with this type of problem often overrely on finger counting for simple computation. Some go so far as to develop their own rule system for calculations.

Conservation. Some children have difficulty with this Piagetian concept that a quantity does not change if its shape or arrangement is altered. The equivalent volume of a tall, thin 8-ounce glass and a short, fat 8-ounce container is one example used in the classic demonstration of this phenomenon.

Sequential organization. Many youngsters with sequencing problems have particular difficulty in establishing numerical order and learning basic operations such as mastery of the multiplication tables.

Interpreting process signs. Some children have difficulty with the rapid interpretation of the specific signs for mathematical processes (such as +, -, ×).

The selection process. Some youngsters are unable to choose the correct process in order to solve a mathematics problem. They can perform perfectly well when they are told to add, subtract, multiply, or divide, but they cannot make this decision themselves when given a word problem.

Confusion over geometric-spatial relationships. Problems with geometrical relationships and spatial representation can result in difficulties with such tasks as reading maps and interpreting graphs. The principles of geometry may be particularly obscure for such children.

Sequential memory. A child with sequential memory problems may have difficulty retrieving the order of operations to solve a problem. Many such youngsters perform much better when given a visual demonstration model to copy.

Difficulty with measurements. A child may have basic problems with concepts involved in measurement, which may interfere seriously with a variety of secondary applications of mathematics.

Abstract symbolization. Youngsters with deficits in this area may have particular difficulties with the symbolic aspects of mathematics. Algebra and other aspects of mathematics in which there is a symbolic representation of quantities may be difficult to master.

Assessment

Some of the components of a math disability can be elicited through a careful history. Neurodevelopmental examinations and standardized tests can also help define the contributing factors and boundaries of a child's mathematical dysfunction. When there are serious concerns about mathematical performance, however, a comprehensive educational assessment should be performed. The Key Math Diagnostic Arithmetic Test, the arithmetic subtest of the Wide Range Achievement Test (WRAT), and the Peabody Individual Achievement Test (PIAT) are among the standardized diagnostic and achievement tests that are available to a psychoeducational specialist.

THE ACQUISITION OF KNOWLEDGE

There is a vast literature in psychology and child development about the ways in which children harvest information about the universe. Reading is a prime information source but by no means the only one. Deficits in acquiring knowledge are more difficult to document and study than are problems of specific skill acquisition. It is thus important to distinguish between the phenomena: a child may have great difficulty acquiring the basic skills of reading, writing, spelling, and arithmetic, for example, but be quite adept at acquiring factual information. Youngsters with attention deficits may be veritable sponges for facts. Some become experts in a discrete area such as prehistoric animals or sports. Others show a general infatuation with encyclopedias, atlases, or particular magazines. The magnetic attraction of a specific sphere of knowledge for an individual child can be a profound mystery. At times, the desire to acquire knowledge in a particular area stems from cultural or familial influences. At other times, the romantic lure of a subject is totally inscrutable.

In dealing with children with impaired learning, it is essential to separate the process of knowledge accumulation from that of skill acquisition. As youngsters grow older, if serious learning disorders persist, they must be encouraged to absorb knowledge through any means possible, such as oral discussions, tapes, and (even) television. Every effort should be made by parents and teachers to continue to impart information and stimulate intellectual curiosity.

5

The Assessment Process: Systematic Formulation

Here are the very people of the streets whom he passes every
day, here they are coming to him, to him of all men, telling him
all about it, how it happened, what it feels like, why they did it:
Looking to him, right away, for advice and physic. They are no
two of them alike: And their records, laid before him, range
through every intermediate shade. . . . He begins to see that
he has more to learn than the use of a stethoscope: He must
learn lives.

Confessio Medici

THE FORMULATION PROCESS

A comprehensive and systematic formulation of a school-age child's developmental health is the major product of the assessment process. Intrinsically,
this is an interdisciplinary procedure. The team composition can vary considerably and might include any or all of the following: professionals from the
child's school, a psychoeducational specialist (e.g., learning disabilities teacher,
special educator, or clinical psychologist), a physician (and/or nurse), one or
more parents, and (even) the child. Additional participating personnel are likely
to vary with local resources and the needs of an individual child. Such staff might
include a social worker, a child psychiatrist, a pediatric neurologist, an occupational therapist, an audiologist, a speech and language pathologist, a physical
therapist, or a vocational educational specialist. In a primary health care setting,
such an array of personnel is unlikely to exist. Many of these resources, however,
may be available within a public school system.

A report from a health professional is a major part of the formulation process.
This chapter suggests an expanded medical contribution to evaluation. Some
practitioners may find this model too extensive or time consuming. Some
physicians or nurses may wish to extract aspects that are most relevant or suitable
to their own routines and the needs of their community. In some cases, the
physician may serve as a coordinator of an extensive evaluation in a primary care
setting, a medical center, or a school health program.

121

THE DEVELOPMENTAL HEALTH HISTORY

A carefully mined history yields a rich lode of clues for case formulation. By retracing the origins and pathways of developmental phenomena and their interactions with environmental and health factors, consistencies and apparent paradoxes in a child's functioning can be discerned. The process of comprehensive history-taking is arduous and expensive. It can be made easier through the use of parent and teacher questionnaires. The forms in the appendix of this book, which are used at the Children's Hospital Medical Center in Boston, can help elicit a thorough history with some economy of time. A dialogue between the clinician and parents can be based on an elaboration of issues raised in the forms. Subsequently, the questionnaires can be used for writing reports.

Some parents may have difficulty interpreting or responding to the questions. It is important that they understand that confusing sections may be omitted, or, if they prefer, they needn't complete the forms at all! This proviso can prevent embarrassment for those parents who, because of learning problems of their own, language barriers, or phobic reactions to questionnaires in general (a defensible stance) are likely to be intimidated.

A school questionnaire should be dispatched before an evaluation. It usually is completed by the classroom teacher. In some cases, schools prefer to duplicate forms and have them filled out by several professionals. This is necessary particularly at the secondary level. Teachers usually are cooperative, and often they find such questionnaires useful in generating their own formulations.

The clinician who uses questionnaires must recognize that they may contain unreliable information. Recall of early developmental events may be vague, and interpretations of questions vary greatly. Despite these limitations, questionnaire data can be a useful clinical starting point as one attempts to assemble a history. Questionnaires can also be used to educate medical trainees about the content of a complete developmental health history. The relevant subject areas of a developmental health history are discussed below.

Relevant Areas

Definition of the problem. The chief complaint(s), as expressed (possibly disparately) by each parent, the school, and, if possible, by the child, should be defined precisely. Is the problem perceived as primarily academic, medical, "emotional," motivational (i.e., "moral"), or imaginary? Interobserver discrepancies can be particularly revealing and laden with counseling implications.

The developmental course. It is essential to acquire a picture of the natural history of a youngster's dysfunction. When was it first noted? By whom? How did the problem find expression at various ages? What were the early symptoms of dysfunction? It is helpful to document a child's responses to any initial educational experiences. Knowledge of how the youngster functioned in preschool, kindergarten, and the earliest grades should contribute to an expanded developmental history. Positive and negative reactions to particular types of teachers are revealing and may have had a profound influence on the child's current educational strategies, inhibitions, and attitudes. The results of previous assessments and interventions (e.g., medications, psychotherapy, social services, or educational supports) should be carefully analyzed.

Perceived strengths and weaknesses. A survey of the child's various strengths and weaknesses as perceived by parents and school personnel is most helpful. This should include an account of strengths and weaknesses in all of the elements discussed in Chapter 3 as well as academic performance areas reveiwed in Chapter 4. Contradiction and agreement between parent and teacher questionnaire ratings should be analyzed. When school personnel perceive a child functioning very well in a particular academic subject, and the parents see him failing in the same area, one should consider the possibilities of unrealistic parental standards, or the effects of internal school policies leading to denial by the school. An inventory of a child's perceived strengths and weaknesses can be useful when the physician seeks validation (or refutation) of suggestive findings from a neurodevelopmental examination or standardized tests. The results of such assessments should be consistent with perceived performance. If they are not, one needs to justify the disqualification of some piece(s) of evidence!

Parameters of activity and attention. The importance of activity and attention was emphasized in Chapter 3. The concomitants of poor selective attention were noted to be nonspecific symptoms of a variety of developmental dysfunctions, as well as possible primary disabilities in themselves. Because of their pivotal position in school-age function, no historical account is complete without a systematic analysis of the parameters of activity and attention. The Connors Teaching Rating Scale has been used widely (Connors 1973). Some prefer scales that include a broader range of associated symptoms. The Children's Hospital Teacher Questionnaire contains an Activity-Attention Scale that parallels the one in the Parent Questionnaire. These ratings can be helpful in determining the extent to which attention problems are situational. They also highlight specific clinical manifestations as summarized in Chapter 3. Observations of attention and activity elicited during the performance of developmentally appropriate tasks can be compared to the perceptions documented in the questionnaires.

Associated behavioral phenomena. It is useful to determine how a child behaves in three basic settings: home, school, and the neighborhood. The Parent and Teacher Questionnaires include inventories of associated behaviors divided into four categories: social-withdrawal behaviors; social-aggressive behaviors; somatic manifestations of dysfunction; and affective-dependent behaviors. This systematic inventory teases out relevant emotional factors and reactions to chronic success deprivation. Moreover, these behaviors, which are commonly associated with learning disorders, have direct implications for planning counseling strategies (see Chapter 9).

The Teacher Questionnaire contains a section that allows school personnel to check off possible "redeeming features" involving attitude, motivation, sense of humor, imagination, and creativity. There should be serious concern about a teacher-child relationship if all of these are checked as deficient! The perception of "no redeeming features" often reflects only the eyesight of the beholder. The Parent Questionnaire also concludes with an inventory of associated strengths. From a therapeutic point of view, it may be more helpful to identify and capitalize on a child's assets than to focus on his shortcomings. This inventory may help in the search for strengths. Emphasizing the positive aspects of performance can minimize the risk that iatrogenic child demoralization will result from the evaluation process.

Perinatal health events. A careful review of pregnancy, labor, delivery, and the immediate newborn period will identify specific perinatal stresses that may predispose to later learning disorders. Although such associations have been suggested in large populations of children (Caputo and Mandell 1970), it must be emphasized that a clear causal relationship between a perinatal problem (such as prematurity or hyperbilirubinemia) and a learning disorder can never be proved in an individual case. Several longitudinal studies have found that clusters of stresses are more predictive than any single perinatal event. There is abundant evidence that perinatal stress superimposed on a substrate of economic deprivation or social disorganization is more likely to lead to later academic difficulties than when comparable perinatal problems occur under optimal environmental conditions (Rutter 1970, Davis et al. 1972). A physician may need to deal with parental feelings of guilt or confusion as a result of misconceptions about the etiological implications of early stresses.

Early temperament. Temperament has been the subject of a great deal of study (Carey et al. 1977, Thomas and Chess 1977). Feeding, sleeping, and crying represent early performance areas—the reading, writing, and arithmetic of the first months of life. Colic, irritability, poor consolability, slowness to "warm up," excessive activity, and poor rhythmicity of function are examples of temperamental "dysfunction" in early life. It is important, therefore, to document these aspects of a child's function in early childhood. The inventory of temperament in the Parent Questionnaire attempts to elicit information about such early characteristics. Most difficult babies do not develop later behavioral or learning problems. Some youngsters with attention problems during the elementary-school years, however, present a history of early temperamental dysfunction; heavy loadings of such factors may represent the earliest indicators of central nervous system disorganization. The difficult baby may engender unnatural parenting styles, establishing patterns of interaction that ultimately lead to chronic conflict and inconsistent nurturing. At its worst, such parent-offspring mismatching may lead to child abuse and neglect. More common manifestations include chronic feelings of parental guilt and inadequacy, and the inadvertent potentiation of a child's intrinsic behavioral disorganization. Early intervention and understanding in infancy can be preventive and therapeutic.

Early developmental attainment. Retrospective accounts of developmental milestones tend to be unreliable. This is particularly true in families where the child has precipitated a great deal of stress, where there are many siblings, or where no records were kept. For children with learning disorders, a survey of early developmental milestones has a low yield; major delays are rarely detected. It is particularly useful, however, to learn about language acquisition and the development of verbal intelligibility, which may have implications for later learning abilities. The histories of children with significant perceptual-motor problems generally reveal normal gross and fine motor milestones during the infant and toddler years and the early preschool period. Later developmental events such as learning to tie shoelaces and ride a bicycle may be more sensitive indicators of problems in this area.

General health history. The Parent Questionnaire includes a health inventory during the first five years of life. Health events that are most likely to have later educational impact are stressed. Chronic illnesses, allergies, recurrent ear infections, meningitis, lead intoxication, and prolonged hospitalizations are examples of health setbacks that may significantly affect later function.

The health history includes a traditional "review of systems," recording recent and current medical problems. It is important to note the use of medications that may have educational implications. A youngster who is taking antihistamines chronically, for example, may be easily fatigued and consequently may have a diminished capacity to sustain attention. Also relevant are recurrent symptoms such as abdominal pain, enuresis, encopresis, headaches, and sleep problems, which often accompany school dysfunction.

Family history. A systematic review of the developmental histories of immediate family members sometimes can reveal patterns of learning and behavioral disorder. Family histories of "hyperactivity," specific academic problems, behavioral disorganization, or retention in school for parents, grandparents, or siblings are relevant. When formulating counseling strategies, it is important to document the academic performance of siblings. If another child in the family is perceived as the academic superstar (and often in other areas as well), this can complicate life for a youngster with learning disorders. Appropriate management of this situation is critical (see Chapter 9).

A detailed family history will sometimes suggest a possible genetic basis for specific developmental disabilities. This hypothesis can be risky and nearly impossible to prove, as one attempts to weight the inputs of nature and nurture or the likelihood of fortuitous occurrences of similar learning disorders within the same family. Any conclusions based on a genetic link to such disabilities should be pondered carefully because of their potential adverse effects on family dynamics.

Sociodemographic factors. It is important to form a picture of "roots," of a neighborhood, and of a community as part of a child's evaluation. Environmental stresses or hazards as well as positive neighborhood supports should be identified. Parental occupations, nuclear family composition, the role of any extended family, and housing arrangements need to be elucidated. Cultural gaps between home and school, home and neighborhood, or neighborhood and school must be ascertained. Major discrepancies at any of these interfaces may substantially affect a child's school performance. In some cases, inadequacies of resource in a local public school system may relate directly to a child's academic failure.

A sense of the organization of home routines may be useful. Are there consistent mealtimes? Does the family eat together? Is there a predictable pattern to daily events? A child from a chaotic home, for example, may have difficulty adjusting to structured classroom expectations. Critical events in the life of a family, such as death, separation or divorce, frequent change of residence, a fire, or an automobile accident also can exert a lasting influence on a child's development.

THE GENERAL HEALTH EXAMINATION

In the zeal to describe and assess functional health, it is essential *not* to overlook physical factors that may contribute to a child's dysfunction. A complete physical examination is part of the evaluation of a youngster with learning problems. Diagnostic findings may help to explain current dysfunction or may reveal "aggravating factors" compounding the child's life struggles. Health stresses have both physical and psychological implications.

General Appearance

A youngster's overall appearance ("Gestalt") is often revealing. Pediatricians have often demonstrated uncanny sensitivity to the appearance of an acutely ill youngster. Whether the patient "looks sick" is often a crucial observation in deciding the need for further study or therapy. Assessing the general appearance of a healthy child, however, is not a well-defined pediatric procedure. Nevertheless, physiognomy can be a revealing reflection of competence and success; it is therefore helpful in the evaluation of the failing student. The following are some observations that can be made by stepping back and forming a general impression a child.

1. Does this child project physical features, aspects of deportment, body habitus, posture, or mannerism that may be inviting verbal abuse by peers? Is the youngster unusually obese, small for age, or fragile-appearing? Many dysfunctioning children are preoccupied with an exaggerated sense of body grotesqueness or a perceived lack of muscular development. For example, a school-age boy may display an appearance that his peers judge to be different from (unfortunately) established male stereotypes. Consequently, he may be labeled a "fag." Other children may be ridiculed for atypical physical features such as lop ears, a large nose, a conspicuous birthmark, or some minor congenital anomaly. The clinician needs to notice these "indicators" and provide the youngster with an opportunity to discuss their social impact. In particular, it is useful for the physician to deal with those "defacing lesions" that may be correctable. In many cases a school-age child is too embarrassed to mention cosmetic concerns; it is sometimes incumbent upon the clinician to take the initiative and express an interest in these "unmentionable" defects.

2. Research in recent years has suggested a relationship between certain phenotypic signs and developmental dysfunctions or behavioral disorganization (Quinn and Rappaport 1974). Studies of Waldrop et al. (1971) have elaborated upon these associations. While the search for minor-anomaly findings offers little therapeutic promise, it may be helpful in case formulation, particularly when one is considering genetic or prenatal effects that predispose to learning or behavioral disorders. Some clinicians now include minor-anomaly descriptions in their diagnostic evaluations. It is important that such descriptions not stigmatize a youngster and that clinicians acknowledge that the majority of children with such "defects" function appropriately for their age. Indeed it would be unfortunate if a youngster grew up feeling he wore the cloak of "brain damage" in the form of a crooked finger, an extra eye fold, or two whorls in the back of his scalp!

3. What can one conclude about the relationship between a child's personal hygienic status, general care, and self-image? Some youngsters appear to be chronically unkempt, troubled, and poorly nourished. These kinds of subjective

observations need to be interpreted with some caution: isolated observations may be fortuitous, but extremes in either direction may be revealing. The immaculately groomed, obsessive-compulsive child may have significant preoccupations with body image. Conversely, a malodorous youngster who enters an examining room with his nose running, fly open, socks of two different colors, torn trousers, and a shirt whose label is prominently displayed above his manubrium may be demonstrating underlying behavioral disorganization and inattention, or chronic neglect! The ultimate interpretation of such sartorial features, however, must take into account the constantly changing wide range of "normal" stylistic variation among school-age children.

The Standard Physical Examination

The physical assessment of a school-age child with learning disorders includes careful measurement of blood pressure, as well as a percentile documentation of height, weight, and head circumference. An attempt should be made to evaluate overall maturational status. For adolescents, the assessment of the development of secondary sexual characteristics is vital. Youngsters with delayed sexual maturation may be carrying an enormous psychological burden, for which reassuring counseling can be liberating. Dentition is another physical parameter that may be useful in assessing physical maturity. Significantly short stature often suggests the need for an x-ray study of the wrist for bone age. A child with short stature and learning problems may need further evaluation to rule out an endocrinopathy or chromosomal abnormality. Although associations between delayed bone age, dental immaturity, and neuromaturational lags have not yet been clarified, their clinical coincidence may be suggestive of delay.

Examination of structures about the head should be meticulous. Lesions in the hard or soft palate may have led to recurrent ear infections. Serous otitis media or chronic scarring of the tympanic membranes, especially in conjunction with a history of possible hearing loss, suggests the need for audiometry and/or tympanometry. Anatomical abnormalities of the buccal cavity may be associated with difficulties in sound production and articulation, which will require further evaluation by a speech and language pathologist. Skin lesions on the face (or trunk and limbs) may be diagnostic of phakomatoses, such as neurofibromatosis or Sturge-Weber Syndrome; these are relatively rare. Signs of chronic conditions such as allergic rhinitis, recurrent laryngitis, and chronic sinusitis overlie phenomena that can drain attentional strength and cause excess fatigability and school absenteeism. Careful fundoscopic examination should be performed, as well as an assessment of oculomotor function, to rule out strabismus or amblyopia.

Examination of the neck should include palpation of thyroid tissue. Although previously undiagnosed congenital hypothyroidism is unlikely to present as a subtle learning disorder in the school-age child, acquired hypothyroidism secondary to subacute thyroiditis may be a rare unsuspected cause of underachievement. Thyrotoxicosis or other hyperthyroid conditions can be associated with school problems and "hyperactivity." While this is possible, it is certainly a *rare* phenomenon within a dysfunctioning school population.

Examination of the chest should include cardiac auscultation and pulmonary evaluation. In this age group, the yield for previously undetected cardiac findings will be very small. Wheezing or diminished respiratory exchange may indicate chronic pulmonary obstruction with resultant increased fatigability. Precocious, delayed, or asymmetric breast development in adolescent girls and gynecomastia in pubescent boys can be sources of considerable anxiety. When these benign conditions are detected, reassurance regarding their normalcy can be helpful.

The examination of the abdomen does not offer abundant educationally relevant data. The physician should be alert for evidence of retained feces. Stool retention and encopresis have been common concomitants of learning disorders observed in the learning clinics at the Children's Hospital Medical Center. Youngsters with attention deficits appear to have a particular propensity for bowel dysfunction, perhaps because their lack of persistence on the toilet parallels their lack of closure in other activities!

The genitalia should be examined, particularly with regard to maturational status during early adolescence. The examination of this "private area" may occasionally elicit concerns that have counseling implications. Older children should be asked directly whether they have any questions about sexual development or anatomic normalcy. Menarchal girls, for example, may have unsettling fantasies about this natural function. Some obese boys worry that their genitalia are too small, when, actually, they are embedded in a sizable prepubic fat pad. The clinician should occasionally take the initiative with regard to potentially embarrassing issues. The child should be reassured that confidentiality will be respected.

Examination of the extremities should include noting any orthopedic deformities that may impair gross or fine motor function. Significant muscle asymmetry should also be noted. In addition, any discrepancies or asymmetries in muscle tone should be included.

Specific somatic complaints should be investigated in the apparently healthy child with a school problem. Recurrent abdominal pain may be related to severe constipation and stool retention rather than a wish to avoid school work. Occasionally, the linkage between a learning disorder and a medical symptom can be critically important. A youngster with a learning disorder and recurrent localized headaches, for example, may have an arteriovenous malformation in the brain. Although such pains are more likely to represent migraine or tension headaches, it would be tragic to overlook a more serious etiology.

Laboratory Studies

In the evaluation of a child with learning disorders, parents and schools often are interested in having laboratory tests performed. They may be disappointed to learn of the low yields of such procedures. Nonmedical professionals and parents sometimes have a heavy investment in finding "metabolic causes" of learning disorders. They may be convinced that abnormalities of blood sugar, calcium, zinc, and various "enzymes" are common sources of most dysfunctions. The intense consumer demand for these tests has been encouraged by a variety of popular programs and books based on hypotheses for which there is not yet any scientific evidence (see Chapter 7).

Parents and teachers are often interested in having the physician perform "tests of nutrition." Specific blood tests to evaluate a child's nutritional status are unavailable in most clinical settings. Moreover, their yield is likely to be negligible. A nutritional history and a thorough physical examination are more likely to provide meaningful nutritional data than any specific laboratory studies.

The dark cloud of hypoglycemia may loom omniously over the evaluation of a youngster with attentional difficulties; the clinician may have to yield to an overwhelming parental hunger for a glucose tolerance test! It is highly unlikely, however, that any significant carbohydrate metabolic disorders will be uncovered.

Electroencephalograms and skull x-ray films are sometimes included in a comprehensive developmental evaluation. Again, the yield of clinically useful data tends to be low. Some studies have suggested that there are characteristic EEG findings in children with learning disorders or attentional difficulties. Millichap (1977) reported 7 to 8% with seizure discharges, 20% with moderate disturbances suggestive of seizures, and a large number with borderline abnormalities in studies of children with so-called minimal brain damage. Posterior slow waves have been reported most frequently, although studies in this area are inconclusive. Most of the positive tracings reported do not appear to have therapeutic implications and may, in fact, only add the stigma of "brain damage" to the burdens of an already preoccupied family. When a seizure disorder is suspected or there is an extremely episodic pattern of attentional lapses, an EEG (with a sleep tracing) is useful. When petit mal is suspected, hyperventilation may bring out the characteristic pattern of three spikes and waves per second. Specialized studies with auditory or visual evoked potentials offer promise for elucidating the electrophysiologic concomitants of an attention deficit. However, the therapeutic implications of such procedures are minimal at present.

When there are any indications of a "hard neurologic disorder," extensive investigation, including a brain scan and radiological studies, is justified. In such cases, the primary clinician is likely to seek a neurological or neurosurgical consultation. Clear-cut localizing or lateralizing findings on the neurological examination (see below) further indicate the need for more detailed diagnostic procedures. Moreover, when a history reveals an abrupt or recent deterioration in learning and personality a detailed neurological investigation is strongly suggested.

In very young children with attention problems, laboratory determinations for lead intoxication are important. Youngsters with a history of pica must be investigated. In those with a past record of possible lead intoxication, x-ray films of bone (especially of the knees) may reveal lead lines. Examinations of tooth lead levels (from decidous teeth) have been promising and have been linked to school dysfunctions (Needleman et al. 1979). Studies of mild to moderate lead intoxication have shown associations with later learning and attentional difficulties (Burdé and Choate 1975).

Physical findings occasionally suggest the possibility of a chromosomal abnormality. For example, learning disorders have beeen associated with Turner's Syndrome. Children who present with the phenotypic characteristics of this condition should have (at least) a buccal smear determination. More extensive chromosomal analysis may be appropriate for children with multiple phenotypic abnormalities or with the typical signs of a known chromosomal disorder.

Sensory Assessments

Evaluation of vision and hearing must be included in the assessment of a child with learning disorders.

The visual assessment is generally performed using the Snellen Charts. Allen Cards can be used for preschool children. Although visual defects alone rarely lead to learning problems, myopia or astigmatism can contribute to visual inattention and poor visual discrimination in the classroom. A student is often unaware of difficulty focusing on the blackboard or a written paragraph, making direct assessment crucial. In addition to screening for acuity, the clinician should look for evidence of oculomotor problems such as strabismus. Assessment of color vision may be revealing, and youngsters with red-green color blindness (protanopia or deuteranopia) should be made aware of their disability. Studies have not demonstrated a significant association between color blindness and learning disorders. Any child with suspected visual abnormalities should be referred to an ophthalmologist for further evaluation and management.

Audiological assessment can be more complex. Many primary care physicians are able to conduct screening tests with office audiometers. Such procedures, however, have a high rate of both false-positive and false-negative results, often because of testing rooms that are not truly soundproofed and poorly calibrated instruments. If a child is thought to be at high risk for a hearing loss, referral to a university hospital or a speech and language center is essential. Table 1 lists criteria that have been developed for the selective prescreening of children at risk for hearing loss. These historical criteria were found to be sensitive in identifying those who could benefit from more complete audiological assessment (Palfrey et al. 1978b). School-age children with articulation problems, as well as those with apparent language disabilities and auditory attention deficits, should be studied carefully to detect possible mild to moderate hearing loss.

NEUROLOGICAL EXAMINATIONS

There is considerable misunderstanding about the utility of neurological examinations in the evaluation of children with learning disorders. Parents and schools often have unrealistic expectations about the yield of useful information. They may expect the neurological examination to help in labeling. They may believe it will answer "once and for all" the question of whether a child's problems are "organic" or "emotional." Despite the potential for abuse, a carefully performed and judiciously interpreted neurological examination can contribute to understanding a child's functional status.

The neurological examination of a child has two distinct components: the standard neurological assessment and the examination for minor neurological signs or indicators. The standard neurological examination can uncover localized central nervous system deficits. In rare instances, actual lesions or pathological processes may be suspected. In most cases, however, a precise pathologic process is *not* identified. The examination for minor neurological signs, on the other hand, is less oriented to space and more related to time. That is to say, a significant portion of this assessment is concerned with specific

Table 1. Selective Prescreening of Young Children for Audiological Examinations*

1. Family history of hearing loss
2. Prematurity
3. Rh incompatability
4. History of treatment with kanomycin and/or streptomycin
5. Orofacial, cardiac or renal anomalies
6. History of meningitis
7. History of congenital rubella
8. History of recurrent otitis media (more than two episodes in a year)
9. Failure of screening test in school
10. Parent or teacher concern about consistent inattention or apparently poor hearing
11. Problems with receptive or expressive language function

* Adapted from Palfrey et al. (1978).

changes in the fine tuning of the central nervous system, adjustments which occur with advancing age in all children. Its purpose is to document maturational delays or persistent inefficiencies as reflected in certain of the "minor" neurological indicators. These two phases of the neurological examination will be considered separately.

The Standard Neurological Examination

The neurological examination should include measurement of head circumference and a careful inspection of the optic fundi. A detailed examination of the cranial nerves is unlikely to provide useful data. The greatest emphasis is placed on the assessment of II and VIII (i.e., vision and hearing). Extraocular movements (III,IV, and VI) are also important (for visual tracking).The quality of binocular fusion should be examined, and the presence or absence of strabismus or nystagmus should be recorded. Rapid tongue movements (XII) should be observed for impairment of rate or mobility. Any asymmetry of the facial musculature (VII) should be noted.

A detailed examination of sensation to light touch and pain is unlikely to yield clues in the evaluation of a learning disorder. Such an assessment is probably necessary only in the presence of specific symptomatic indications.

Assessment of cerebellar function includes finger-to-nose and heel-knee-shin tests, as well as evaluation of the Romberg Sign.

Abnormalities or asymmetries of muscle strength or tone must be noted.

An evaluation of deep tendon reflexes can be helpful, particularly with regard to their symmetry. The biceps and brachioradialis reflexes in the upper extremities, and the Achilles tendon and patella reflexes in the lower limbs should be assessed. The presence of clonus should be documented, as well as any pathological reflexes, such as the Babinski response.

Although this volume seeks to deemphasize the search for syndromes, neurological and neuropsychological investigators have suggested two possibly relevant *hemisyndromes.* These have been described by Denckla (1978). The right hemisyndrome consists of three or more right-side-of-body signs, such as distal weakness, hypotonia, and increased reflexes, which imply that the left cerebral hemisphere may be dysfunctional or dysgenetic. It is suggested that such youngsters may have a "left-hemisphere style." They are said to "behave to a striking degree like mild or subtle versions of adult aphasia and/or related disorders." According to Denckla, "They respond in the holistic, big configuration, simultaneous-sensitive manner of the 'strong right brain,' relatively speaking, and have difficulty balancing this style with the detail-attentive, sequential, analytic, linguistic style of the left brain that is so important academically."

Analogously, a left hemisyndrome is said to be characterized by left-sided distal weakness, hypotonia, and increased reflexes. Such youngsters are said to have problems with "higher order verbal skills, spatial orientation skills, mathematical understanding, and normal give and take of social-emotional expressions." Such hemisyndromes are still at an early investigative stage. Their diagnosis does not, as yet, have any direct therapeutic implications, but it does encourage the careful documentation of reflex symmetry, muscle tone, and strength.

A careful neurological examination can rule out such relatively low-prevalence disorders as muscular dystrophies, space-occupying lesions, and progressive demyelinating diseases that might present as learning problems. A child with mild cerebral palsy might be similarly detected. In fact, there may be a fine line between so-called mild CP and the signs of developmental dysfunction described in this book. Since the therapeutic interventions are similar, the "benefit" of a cerebral palsy label in such instances is dubious.

Observation of Minor Neurological Indicators

Indicators of central nervous system efficiency and maturation have been referred to traditionally as *soft neurologic signs.*

The systematic search for such indicators has been useful clinically (Peters et al. 1975). As noted, two types have been described—those whose clinical significance is determined by the child's chronological age, and those that represent mild, borderline versions of neurological signs that are abnormal *at any age.* The former, which include such phenomena as synkinesias, can generally be determined with fairly good interobserver reliability. The latter, on the other hand, include findings such as equivocal hypertonia (which may elicit less consistent agreement between examiners). Although the literature has not differentiated consistently between those two types of soft signs, the second would appear to be more reflective of a localized neurological deficit, whereas the first type suggests the possibility of "immaturity." Such distinctions, however remain tentative hypotheses, given the present state of knowledge (or ignorance) surrounding brain function.

Age-dependent minor neurological indicators are nearly universal in young children and become progressively rare during the later elementary-school years. Whether by myelinization or increasing dendritic connections (or by yet undiscovered mechanisms), these findings appear to be linked to central nervous system maturation. Many of them reappear during old age or senescence. The persistence of these neuromaturational markers beyond the age levels at which they generally disappear has been associated with learning disorders, behavior

As part of an examination for minor neurological indicators, the physician is attempting to elicit synkinetic movements. Rapid apposition of the first and second fingers is demonstrated; the child imitates the examiner. In this photograph the patient exhibits a mirror movement, mimicking the posture of his right hand on the contralateral side. Such synkinetic movements become increasingly rare beyond age seven. Their persistence often is attributed to "neuromaturational delay."

problems, and other manifestations of developmental dysfunction.

Neurological soft signs are subject to misinterpretation in several respects. First, a single sign, in isolation, may not be meaningful. Highly successful children may show one or more of these indicators, whereas other youngsters with significant developmental dysfunction may have *no* evidence of neuromaturational delay or minor indicators. Clusters appear to be more accurate discriminators than any single isolated sign. Efforts are being made currently to quantify these findings, a process which should make them more useful. Second, it is inappropriate to interpret neuromaturational indicators as evidence that a child will catch up eventually. The word "maturation" is misused widely in children with learning disorders. A so-called maturational lag in no way implies that there will be a spontaneous developmental remission. Evidence of immaturity, therefore, should not be used as justification for therapeutic inaction. Instead, such evidence can suggest a constitutional component in a child's learning or behavioral problems. Finally, one must always relate the presence of neuromaturational indicators to a child's age. A six-year-old with many such indicators, for example, is not nearly as likely to be "dysfunctional" as a youngster with the same cluster at age 11 or 12.

The most commonly elicited minor neurological indicators include the following (see also Table 2):

Table 2. Summary of Minor Neurological Indicators

	Indicators Associated with Neurological Immaturity	
Task	*Immature response*	*Norms (references)*
Rapid alternating hand movements (pronation-supination)	Dysdiadochokinesis	Mature by 7 years (progresses over 4–8 years) (Grant et al., 1973)
	Synkinesia	Markedly decreased after 9 years (Cohen et. al., 1967)
Repeated finger-to-thumb apposition	Awkward execution	Mature after 8 years (Grant et al., 1973)
	Synkinesia	Markedly decreased after 9 years (Cohen et al., 1967)
Sequential apposition of thumb to each of the fingers, forward and backward	Synkinesia	Markedly decreased after 9 years (Cohen et al., 1967)
Alternate squeezing and relaxing single hand grip of rubber toy	Synkinesia	Markedly decreased after 9 years (Cohen et al., 1967)
Walking on sides of feet	Posturing of the upper extremities	Passed by $>20\%$ but $<80\%$ between 8–13 years (Connolly and Stratton, 1968)
Separation of third and fourth fingers only	Movement involving separation of other fingers (overflow)	Passed by $>20\%$ but $<80\%$ between 10–16 years (Connolly and Stratton, 1968)
Lifting of third finger on dominant hand and fourth finger on non-dominant hand	Lifting of other fingers (overflow)	Passed by $>20\%$, but $<80\%$ from 5 years upward, depending upon finger examined (Connolly and Stratton, 1968)
Finger localization (identification of stimulated fingers)	Inability to respond correctly	Mature level reached at 11–12 years (progressive development beginning before 6 years) (Benton, 1955b)
Finger differentiation (discrimination of simultaneous stimulation of two fingers of one hand)	Inability to discriminate	Mature response by 95% at 7 years (Kinsbourne and Warrington, 1963)
Double simultaneous stimulation of face and hand	Extinction of distal stimulus (rostral dominance)	5 years—14% mature 6 years—54% mature 7 years—88% mature (Kraft, 1968)
Identification of right and left on self (laterality)	Incorrect response	7 years (Belmont and Birch, 1963)

N	*Age (years)*	*Percent correct*
82	4	32
92	5	59
65	6	73
25	77	92
20	8	95

(Berges and Lezine, 1965)

134

Table 2. (Continued)

	Indicators Associated with Neurological Immaturity			
Task	*Immature response*		*Norms (references)*	

Task	Immature response	Norms (references)		
Identification of right and left on the examiner	Incorrect response	*N*	*Age (years)*	*Percent correct*
		82	4	7
		92	5	15
		65	6	27
		25	7	48
		20	8	70
		(Berges and Lezine, 1965)		
Execution of crossed commands on self (e.g., "Touch your left knee with your right hand")	Incorrect response	*N*	*Age (years)*	*Percent correct*
		82	4	7
		92	5	32
		65	6	61
		25	7	84
		20	8	90
		(Berges and Lezine, 1965)		
Consistent hand preference (hand dominance)	Inconsistent preference	Established by 9 years (Belmont and Birch, 1963)		
Stablization of ipsilateral eye and hand preference)	Mixed preference ("mixed dominance")	Established by 10 years (Belmont and Birch, 1963)		

Indicators Associated with Classic Abnormalities ("Equivocal Hard Signs")

Motor impersistence (Garfield, 1964)
Choreiform syndrome (Prechtl and Stemmer, 1962; Wolff and Hurwitz, 1966)
Slight asymmetry of deep tendon reflexes
"Hyperactive" deep tendon reflexes
Awkward postures or gait
Mild tremors
Mild ataxia
Nystagmus
Strabismus
Borderline abnormalities or asymmetry of muscle tone
Equivocal abnormal reflexes (e.g., Babinski)

Synkenetic ("mirror") movements. In these motor phenomena one side of the body mimics an activity carried out on the contralateral side. When a child is asked to oppose his thumb and forefinger repeatedly, for example, the other hand mirrors the action. Synkinesias are very common in preschool children, but less prevalent and less mirrorlike as children mature through the elementary school grades. In older school children, synkinetic movements may be elicited by more complex unilateral acts. Persistence of true mirror movements beyond the age of eight years is unusual; it tends to occur commonly in children with learning and behavioral disorders (Cohen et al. 1967).

Other associated movements ("overflow"). Other forms of extraneous or inefficient movement also may be interpreted as evidence of a neuromaturational lag in older children (Touwen and Precht 1970). For example, a child may consistently show rhythmic mouth movements, or head bobbing, in conjunction with another activity occurring in a more caudad anatomical region. While rapidly apposing the thumb and forefinger, or even while writing, a child may exhibit rhythmic tongue movements. Most associated moements tend to proceed caudocranially in direction. Thus, whereas rapid finger movements may elicit associated mouth movements, having a child move his tongue rapidly is unlikely to be associated with movements in the fingers. In assessing gross and fine motor function, the physician should be alert for associated movements as an indication of immature and inefficient performance.

Imitative finger movement is one technique for eliciting finger agnosia. The examiner apposes one finger at a time against the thumb of each hand. The child imitates, using his own corresponding finger. Some youngsters may be inaccurate performing this task or may require close visual monitoring of their own fingers. Ordinarily they should be able to imitate without close visual scrutiny of their own digits. Finger agnosia may be associated with impaired writing and fine motor deficits.

Dysdiodochokinesis. The ability to perform rapid alternating movements can be tested by sequential pronation and supination of the hands. Some children seem unable to suppress activity in proximal muscle groups, exhibiting excessive flailing of the limbs (Touwen and Precht 1970). When a child is asked to pretend to turn a door knob back and forth rapidly, whether or not the elbows deviate markedly from the flanks is of interest. This phenomenon is normal and common in preschool children but is associated with dysfunction in older children.

Finger agnosia. A child's ability to perceive and name the locations of fingers in the absence of visual cues can be tested by asking him, with eyes closed, how many digits the examiner is touching. Alternatively (and more usefully in older children), one can ask how many of the child's fingers are held between two of the examiner's fingers (Kinsbourne and Warrington 1964). Reduced finger awareness may have some predictability for educational readiness in young children. There is also some indication that difficulties with finger localization may reflect poor feedback from the digits and consequently may be associated with inefficient writing and other fine motor deficits.

Stimulus extinction. Young children have difficulty perceiving simultaneously presented sensory stimuli (Kraft 1968). In some cases, more proximal stimuli are noticed over distal ones, or two-point discrimination in general may be poor. For example, a child with eyes closed may be touched simultaneously on the hand and face but report only the touch on the face (sometimes referred to as *rostral dominance*). This response pattern is common in younger children but generally is not encountered after the age of seven. Its persistence may be associated with dysfunction. Recent studies, however, have indicated that poor performance may be related to expectations, "mind sets," or conceptual presumptions (involving interpretation of the instructions) rather than neuromaturational delay (Nolan and Kagan 1978).

Motor impersistence. The inability to maintain a fixed motor stance with arms extended, mouth open, and tongue protruding is a sign originally described in association with known "brain damage" (Garfield 1964). It is observed commonly in children with primary attention deficits.

Choreiform movements. Involuntary rotatory and rhythmic movements, when present, are most commonly seen in the outstretched fingers or protruded tongue when a child is asked to close his eyes, extend both arms, spread his fingers, open his mouth, protrude his tongue, and sustain this posture for at least 30 seconds. A number of studies in older children have correlated such involuntary movements with school failure and behavior problems (Wolff and Hurwitz 1966). Prechtl and Stemmer (1962) originally described "the choreiform syndrome" to characterize children with this finding and a history of hyperactivity, impulsivity, emotional lability, poor frustration tolerance, and difficulties with reading and social interaction. Since such symptoms are common in children with learning disorders of all types; however, the existence of this particular "syndrome" has been questioned.

Lateral preference. The propensity toward preferential use of one side of the body may reflect the development of one hemisphere of the brain for a particular set of functions (Benson and Geschwind 1968). Hand preference is

By observing a child with arms outstretched, fingers spread, eyes closed, mouth open, and tongue protruding, the physician may elicit several minor neurological indicators, including motor impersistence, chorieform twitches of the fingers or tongue, or excessive spooning of the hands. In this case, after a short time, downward deviation of the arms was noticed (suggestive of motor impersistence).

usually well established between four and six years. Eye preference often is established by age 2. Ear and foot preference can also be evaluated, but less is known about their clinical significance. Ear preference may be helpful in determining which hemisphere of the brain is predominantly language oriented. Children with delays in establishing lateral preferences may have problems in other developmental areas. This has been a controversial subject in the child-development, psychological, and neurological literature. Mixed preference (e.g., a tendency to be lefthanded and right-eyed) has been associated in some studies with an increased incidence of reading disabilities (Corballis and Beale, 1976). Contradictory findings also have been reported. There have been no consistent documented associations between left-handedness and learning disorders (Vernon 1960, Belmont and Birch 1965).

Left-right discrimination. It is important to distinguish between a sense of laterality and the ability to respond to left and right commands; the latter involves a high degree of language efficiency. As children grow older, they become progressively competent in this area, but in some cases delayed left-right differentiation may be part of a developmental lag (Benton 1968). By age six most children can tell left from right on their own bodies. Before their eighth birthdays, they are usually able to cross the midline (e.g., "Touch your right ear with your left hand"). By age nine or 10 they usually can identify right and left on the examiner (e.g., "Touch my right knee with your left hand"). By early adolescence, children are competent at rapidly distinguishing left and right, starting from new bases in space (e.g., "right face, left face," as in military commands). Problems with left-right discrimination may result from complex manifestations of maturational, developmental, or basic processing problems. Such deficits may be associated with learning disorders (Croxen and Lytton 1971). Left-right reversals of letters and consequent reading retardation were described in the early and influential studies of Samuel Orton (1937). Such confusion was attributed to incomplete cerebral lateralization (dominance).

The minor neurological indicators described in this section are examined in the evaluation of dysfunctioning children. Although they do not have direct implications for intervention, they may suggest strong "constitutional loadings," which may have relevance for direct counseling and for feedback to teachers or parents. In some cases, delay in neuromaturation is accompanied by other forms of maturational lag, such as in skeletal age, dentition, emotional or social sophistication, onset of puberty, or physical stature. Studies showing strong correlations between these areas are not yet available. There have been some associations, however, between neuromaturational delay and functional conditions such as enuresis. Evidence of neuromaturational delay is of little value out of context. When combined with environmental, developmental, health, emotional, and educational performance issues, however, it may complement the clinical formulation of a child's problems.

The Neurodevelopmental Examination

In addition to a standard physical and neurological examination and a search for minor neurological signs, the medical evaluation should include a systematic screening of the elements of development, including age-appropriate tasks of

In this illustration the pediatrician is administering a version of the Token Test. This can serve as a screening tool for receptive language abilities. It provides an opportunity to observe a child's ability to transform succinct verbal directions into specific fine motor responses. Children who have difficulty comprehending, retaining, integrating, or responding to verbal input may perform poorly on this assessment. Such youngsters might then be referred for more extensive language evaluations.

gross motor function, fine motor output, Gestalt and visual-spatial orientation, temporal-sequential organization, memory, and language. At the Children's Hospital Medical Center we have been compiling comprehensive neuro-developmental screening assessments, some parts of which are described in the tables in Chapter 3. Figure 1 is a reproduction of the cover page of this examination. In order to maximize its contribution to the multidisciplinary evaluation process, a pediatric neurodevelopmental battery should adhere to a descriptive rather than a psychometric model. That is to say, an overall "score" is inappropriate and likely to be misleading. Instead, a neurodevelopmental assessment (in combination with historic data and input from other disciplines) should generate a narrative description of a youngster's strengths and deficits. Such a description can be especially rich if the clinician is alert to strategies, attention patterns, styles, reactions to success and failure and other *leitmotifs* in the child's performance during the examination process.

The neurodevelopmental assessment can become an active process for the patient, the parent(s), and the physician. Behavior patterns elicited by asking a child to perform developmentally appropriate tasks offer revealing insights into function, style, and coping. The following observations should be a part of one's empirical analysis:

1. How well does the child deal with positive and negative reinforcement? Does he respond appropriately to praise? How does he deal with criticism or negative feedback?

2. Does the youngster appear to use good cognitive strategies? For example, if the child has difficulty remembering digits, does he attempt to subvocalize (i.e., whisper the numbers to himself)?

3. What patterns of selective attention and activity emerge during the neurodevelopmental examination? Is the child impulsive? Does he fatigue easily? Does performance tend to deteriorate or improve over time? Is he particularly fidgety or overactive? Are certain kinds of tasks more likely to lead to impulsivity and inattention than others?

4. Is the child anxious or defensive about his performance? How does he deal with frustration or failure?

5. If the parents observe, how does the child relate to them during the examination? How do they support or pressure him? How do the parents react to the child's successes and frustrations?

6. What kind of an alliance forms between the physician and the child during the neurodevelopmental examination? Is he "slow to warm up"? Is he able to make eye contact with the examiner? Is he trusting or is he defiant? Can he be coaxed to take risks, or is he inordinately cautious about his performance?

7. What happens when the examiner suggests strategies to the child? Can he adapt these to his own needs? For example, if a child is very impulsive in copying a geometric form, and the examiner asks him to describe in words what he is going to do before beginning the drawing, is the child able to integrate this smoothly and without undue anxiety? Does an externally offered strategy work for the child? How easy is it to teach the child a new approach?

8. Is this child easy or difficult for the examiner to like? It is helpful for the physician to try to understand why a particular child may come across as either amicable or unpleasant.

```
PEDIATRIC DEVELOPMENTAL EXAMINATION
       FOR SCHOOL AGE CHILDREN

   The Children's Hospital Medical Center
            Boston, Massachusetts

EXAMINER: _____

CHILD'S AGE:  Years _____  Months _____

GRADE IN SCHOOL:  Year _____  Month _____    SCHOOL: _____

DATE OF EXAMINATION: _____         _____

TIME:  Began _____  Completed _____         _____
```

SUMMARY OF SCREENING EXAMINATION

AREA OF ASSESSMENT	#	AREA OF FUNCTION	SUMMARY RATING				SCORE (Optional)
			Delayed	Appropriate	Advanced	Variable	
AREAS OF DEVELOPMENT	01	Gross Motor					
	02	Fine Motor					
	03	Sequencing - Retentive					
	04	Visual-Perceptual-Motor					
	05	Auditory-Language					
ACADEMIC SCREEN	06	Reading					
	07	Math					
	08	Spelling					
	09	Writing					
NEURO-BEHAVIORAL ASSESSMENT	10	Neuromaturation					
	11	Attention-Activity					
SUMMARY	12	Overall					

```
SUMMARY COMMENTS: _____

_____

_____

_____
```

[M. D. Levine, M.D., Irving Hurwitz, Ph.D., Craig B. Liden, M.D.]

Figure 1. COVER PAGE OF A NEURODEVELOPMENTAL SCREENING EXAMINATION, CHILDREN'S HOSPITAL MEDICAL CENTER, BOSTON

9. How does the child respond to humor? Does he react appropriately to lighter moments during the neurodevelopmental examination?

10. How much feedback does the child demand? Is he asking continually whether he was right or not? Does he demand to know how his performance compares to that of other children?

11. During the neurodevelopmental examination, are there certain recurrent patterns? Does the child have problems every time complex verbal directions

introduce a task? Are there difficulties integrating verbal directions with fine or gross motor output? Does the child's performance tend to deteriorate when a task involves relatively passive listening or observing? Does he seem to have problems with all challenges that require short-term memory? Does the child show consistent weaknesses in the retrieveal of information but not in recognition? Questions such as these cut across the boundaries between categories of developmental tasks. The observation of a child during a neurodevelopmental examination should be comparable to the careful reading of a fine novel; the identification of recurring themes is the most revealing way to understand what one has read (or observed).

Direct Sampling of Academic Performance

Following the neurodevelopmental assessment, the physician should sample a child's academic performance. Although few physicians have the necessary expertise to evaluate academic skills, it is difficult to participate in the management of a problem purely by hearsay. Therefore, a brief observation of a child's reading, spelling, writing, and arithmetic is useful. Portions of standardized achievement tests may be helpful (see the appendix). Specific forms can also be used to guide one's observations (see Figure 1, Chapter 4). It is important that the physician *not* confuse "academic sampling" with definitive psychoeducational evaluation. The latter falls within the domains of education and psychology.

Task Analysis

Since there is no functional purity in any task or activity, an important part of "developmental reasoning" is the process of task analysis (Cruickshank 1975). The accomplishment of any particular act, or the acquisition of a specific skill, entails the confluence of multiple functions. Systematic task analyses of a child's performance patterns will help to identify the common threads of disability or strength. Here the medical model becomes particularly useful. A child's inability to perform a given task suggests a differential diagnosis. Difficulty in tying shoelaces at age nine might be used as an example. What is involved in tying one's shoelaces? The task components might include previous exposure and experience (clearly affected by barefootedness or the lifelong occupancy of sandals or loafers); fine motor function and eye-hand coordination; motor sequencing; sustained and focused attention to the task; visual-spatial orientation; anatomic integrity (i.e., the existence of functional hands and feet); and adult expectations with regard to self-help skills. In an individual child, the clinician may be able to identify one or more specific functional "lesions" from this list. If a series of additional tasks are then analyzed, poor eye-hand coordination or a motor-sequencing problem may emerge as a recurrent theme. Corroboration of this "diagnosis" may be found in historical data and standardized testing.

The results of a neurodevelopmental examination must be weighted in the context of a child's presenting problems. Observations from neurodevelopmental assessment should never be interpreted in isolation, since they are subject to the biases of atypical or "bad" days and biased sampling of behavior and

It is useful for the pediatrician to observe a child in the act of oral reading. In this case the Gray Oral Reading Paragraphs are being used. This child is relying excessively on finger pointing and very close visual monitoring. One might suspect difficulties with visual attention, acuity, or tracking ability.

performance. In tandem with historical data and standardized psychoeducational evaluations, however, neurodevelopmental findings can be influential and therapeutically helpful.

ORCHESTRATING THE VISIT

Much of the information collected from discussions with parents and children is dependent upon the quality of the alliance between the clinician, the child, and the family.

It usually is a good idea for the clinician to see parents *alone first*. This provides them with the opportunity to voice concerns that they may be reluctant to articulate with the youngster present in the room. The clinician should develop an appreciation of why the parents are asking for an evaluation *at this time* and should attempt to uncover the breadth and depth of their concerns. Does this child remind them of someone else? What are their suspicions about the causes of this child's dysfunction? What is it that they are most afraid of (if anything) with this youngster? Is there a discrepancy in the degree of concern between the two parents? Are there any hidden "political" agendas in this evaluation? What kind of relationship exists between the parents and the school? What are the parents' expectations from this evaluation? Do they harbor a preconceived idea of what they will be taking home (e.g., pills, a diet, an educational plan)? How do they perceive the child's strengths and weaknesses? How do they articulate or conceptualize the reasons for the child's current problems? Are any recent or impending family changes likely to be complicating this child's current developmental problems? These and related questions will be considered in greater detail in the first sections of Chapter 8.

It is important to learn what the parents have told the child about the evaluation. It is not uncommon that a child who comes for an assessment of a learning disorder has been told that he is there for a regular "checkup."

Following an initial discussion with the parents, the physician should see the child alone. There should be some discussion about the nature of the visit and what is going to happen. It is important that the child be guaranteed that no secrets will be kept from him, although it will be acceptable to keep secrets *with* him. The establishment of a working alliance is crucial (see Chapter 8).

When speaking with the child alone, the pediatrician can explore the youngster's feelings about current school problems. Some gentle probing and reassurance may be necessary to elicit this kind of information. The child should be reminded that many other youngsters come for evaluations. Sometimes it is helpful to use the analogy of the clinician as "coach," an individual who offers advice so that the youngster can become more proficient in school. Daily scenarios (i.e., in school, at home, and in the neighborhood) should be explored to get a sense of the child's interests, performance standards, self-esteem, self-expectations, and aspirations.

The physical examination of a school-age child should be performed (whenever feasible) *without* the parents in the room. Many school-age children are embarrassed to undress for an examination in front of their mothers or fathers. Often they are more embarrassed about being embarrassed! That is to say, they may be reluctant even to voice their apprehensions, and they will appreciate the physician's suggestion that the parents *not* be in the room. If there is any significant protest from the parents or the patient, the doctor should obviously allow parental presence. In most cases, however, one will find them pleased that the child has a chance to relate exclusively to the physician.

A physical examination can help establish rapport, elicit somatic concerns from the child, and reassure the youngster about body integrity and health. The examination can also be useful for its informal developmental content. Observing a child dress and undress, for example, can provide valuable insights about behavioral organization and motor function. (Table 3 outlines a system of developmental observations that can be made during dressing and undressing. These observations have been used in working with preschool children in the Brookline Early Education Project.)

It is generally helpful to have the parents present during the neurodevelopmental examination. This enables the physician to observe some parent-child interaction, to make determinations about the degree of parental pressure to

Table 3. Observations on Undressing and Dressing for a Physical Examination

Clothing	Shoelaces
1 = light	1 = well done
2 = medium	2 = done poorly
3 = heavy	3 = unable to do
Sequence	Overall organization
1 = appropriate	1 = well organized
2 = inconsistent	2 = inconsistent
3 = disorganized	3 = disorganized
Monitoring	Independence
1 = good	1 = completely independent
2 = inconsistent	2 = somewhat dependent
3 = poor	3 = totally dependent
Intersensory integration	Rate
1 = good	1 = fast
2 = inconsistent	2 = appropriate
3 = poor	3 = slow
Shoe laterality	Parental History
1 = appropriate	0 = not applicable
2 = very hesitant	1 = observations confirmed
3 = incorrect	by parental history
Sock, shirt reversability	Comments: _____
1 = appropriate	_____
2 = very hesitant	_____
3 = incorrect	_____
Buttons, zippers	_____
1 = appropriate	_____
2 = very hesitant	_____
3 = incorrect	_____

which the child is exposed, and to acquire a sense of the ways a youngster uses parents as resources. In most cases the presence of the parent does not appear to impair neurodevelopmental "performance." If the clinician feels that parental presence will create too much tension, the child can be seen alone. An advantage of having parents observe the neurodevelopmental examination is that it makes later feedback more concrete. The clinician can point out shared examples of test performance rather than abstract descriptions as a basis for discussing the child's developmental style, strengths, and weaknesses.

In general, feedback sessions should take place in the child's presence. It is important for the clinician not to exclude the youngster, who might otherwise fantasize about what is being said. If private communication with parents is essential, this can take place on a subsequent visit or over the telephone. Excluding the child can often lead to apprehension, anxiety, and unhelpful mystification of the problem. In a hospital clinic, it is not unusual to see school-age children with their ears pressed against the doors of the examining rooms, wondering: "What are they saying about me? What is wrong with me? How come they can't tell me?"

In most cases, it is appropriate for the child to read (or be read) the final evaluation report. Many professionals are finding that children can handle and have a right to this kind of feedback. Many youngsters are willing and able to discuss their strengths and weaknesses, as revealed in the evaluation process. In some instances, children are encouraged to attend the formal meeting at which their individual educational plans are being formulated. This is true particularly at the secondary-school level.

THE ADOLESCENT: A SPECIAL CASE

The assessment of adolescents with learning disorders presents special challenges. Many confounding factors emerge. The following observations should be borne in mind:

1. Normative data on adolescent development is relatively sparse. Most standardized tests for learning disabilities have a tendency to ceiling out at younger ages. Specific tests for learning disabilities in adolescents generally are unavailable.

2. Most neuromaturational assessments have a negligible yield in this age group. A youngster with signs of neuromaturational delay at an earlier age is unlikely to continue to reveal these at age 16 or 17.

3. Children generally have little tolerance for chronic failure. An adolescent who has waged a long, losing battle against learning in school is likely to superimpose a dense web of academic inhibitions, defenses, and maladaptive coping methods over underlying constitutional deficiencies. Such overlay may appear to be "the whole problem," thereby suggesting a purely emotional, attitudinal, or motivational formulation. The assessment process must unravel such intertwined secondary effects in an effort to understand and sympathize with a history of coping with disabilities. Particularly in the early adolescent years, there may be strident denial of underlying weaknesses, an effort to appear "normal," "cool," and "regular." Penetrating this veneer can be difficult.

4. Teachers and other school personnel are less apt to be sensitive to learning disorders in older children and adolescents. On the secondary-school level, teachers tend to be oriented toward subject matter and somewhat less nurturant toward children than their elementary-school counterparts.

5. It can be difficult for a physician to establish trust and rapport with older children (especially during early adolescence, from about the ages of 11 to 15). Young people at this age often feel self-conscious about visiting a physician. They may be reluctant to discuss any "rough edges" or shortcomings. Their enormous desire to be inconspicuous and "supernormal" can make a doctor's office or a clinic setting particularly threatening. A physician who has had continuity with a child for many years, however, may be in the best position to coordinate a diagnostic evaluation.

6. Because adolescents do not like to pursue activities in which they are deficient, they often have their learning disorders aggravated by a relative lack of practice or experience. For example, if a child writes poorly, by the age of 16 it is likely that he has written far less than his "easy-writer" peers. Ironically, the less competent a child feels, the less opportunity he will give himself to improve! The cumulative effect of such inexperience is strikingly conspicuous in adolescence.

7. It may be very difficult to separate out developmental strengths and weaknesses to determine whether shortcomings are primary or secondary in a dysfunctioning adolescent. For example, in younger children it is commonly said that difficulty naming objects and pictures is often associated with reading problems. It is thought that problems in recall may affect word recognition. As a person grows older, however, the act of naming words (reading) becomes a mechanism for developing good recognition skills. Thus by the age of 16 a child may have relatively poor naming abilities (compared to peers) secondary to deficits in reading ability.

8. Some adolescents make remarkable progress in dealing with learning disorders because of an increasing capacity for abstract reasoning and what Piaget has called "formal operations" (Piaget and Inhelder 1969). This capability might help compensate for persistent disabilities of perception, attention, and retention. (See the section on developmental facilitation in Chapter 3.)

9. The diagnosis and management of adolescents with learning disorders has been impaired further by misconceptions about the natural history of developmental dysfunction. Many clinicians have been taught that "hyperactivity" ends at puberty. On the contrary, children with processing disorders and attention deficits are likely to have increasing trouble during adolescent years, if they are not managed properly. The association of underlying disabilities with the later development of antisocial behavior has been well established (Bachara and Zaba 1978, Hogenson 1974, Mauser 1974). Affective disorders and sociopathy may be late complications of chronic academic failure. Although some children show remarkable developmental resiliency, others persist in their failure spirals throughout junior and senior high school. The clinical phenomenology may evolve with age (see Chapter 3). As maturation and heightened expectations supervene, earlier problems with reading may evolve into struggles with writing or work organization.

10. The evaluation process in adolescence requires a particularly meticulous

review of the history. Developmental and academic problems encountered during early elementary school years must be reconstructed from historical information and previous test data. Hypotheses about specific disabilities during the early school years must be traced to the present. The process of task analysis, which is critical in any developmental assessment, is particularly germane in the evaluation of adolescent function.

11. Much of the formulating process in older children depends upon the direct observation of performance. The clinician should review samples of an adolescent's spelling, writing, and arithmetic output and listen to him reading and speaking. From these data, along with past history, the clinician may piece together a natural history of a learning disorder.

12. Children in late adolescence tend to be more inclined toward introspection than those from 12 to 16 years of age. With the right kind of encouragement, it is possible for such young adults to depict in vivid detail the specific learning tasks they find most difficult. Creative educational planning that combines continued academic skill development with individualized vocational instruction should be negotiated jointly by the adolescent and involved professionals.

THE BILINGUAL CHILD

The child from a bilingual family presents another set of challenges for the assessment process (Ogbu 1978). Although basic intelligence tests are available in many languages, they must be administered by someone with a good understanding of the relevant tongue. Standardized tests for the evaluation of learning disorders, on the other hand, have not yet been extensively translated.

In the evaluation of bilingual children, it is essential to consider developmental factors in a cultural context. Does the child have the same kinds of learning problems in his native tongue as in English? Are cultural discrepancies as great as or greater than the language barriers? To what extent are social adjustment problems potentiating or aggravating deficient learning in school? What kinds of resources does the school have to deal with the special problems of bilingualism?

It is critically important, whenever possible, to have an assessment conducted by personnel who are familiar with the child's language and culture, preferably from personal experience. Informed advocacy for a bilingual child is critically important in the search for services, especially when language barriers prevent the parents from maneuvering deftly within the educational or political system.

THE TRUE LIKENESS

When all the returns are in from various sources, there will often be contradictions and perplexing inconsistencies, with no consensus regarding formulation. The clinician then asks: What is the true picture of this child? What portions of the assessment represent a reliable and valid sampling? Which of the findings are atypical, coincidental, or artifacts of the assessment process? A child's need to be evaluated may be exceeded only by the need to evaluate the evaluation! It is essential that child assessors understand potential pitfalls in the description process. The evaluations of certain children are likely to be more hazardous than those of others. The ways in which an assessment can acknowledge and cope with these dangers will determine its intellectual honesty, thoroughness, and ultimate helpfulness. Some evaluation pitfalls are summarized below.

Time-related sampling biases. Children who have difficulties with attention are especially challenging to evaluate. Some may have taken three WISCs, and the raw scores and subtest patterns seem to describe *three* different children; the physician needs to be aware that most diagnostic instruments were not standardized on "hyperactive kids." Test-retest reliability coefficients were not culled from youngsters as functionally erratic as many of those commonly encountered in a pediatrician's office. The Children's Hospital Teacher Questionnaire (see the appendix) inquires about "typical" academic performance as well as a child's variability in each area. The clinician often encounters children who are disorganized, inattentive, and best described as "inconsistent." Their individual test scores may depend on a host of unknown factors including the time of the day, rapport with the examiner, last night's sleep, this morning's breakfast, or current distractibility. For such children, overreliance on scores from one evaluation session may be misleading.

Judging from peaks of performance. Sometimes a teacher or parent displays a child's truly excellent work and proclaims: "See, he can do it when he really wants to. It's just a matter of motivation or attitude." This kind of sampling can be dangerous and can lead to withholding services from a truly disabled child. It must be recognized that every youngster with deficits occasionally can produce atypically competent work. The interpretation of *typical performance* rather than those rare *tours de force* is the goal of the evaluation process. Several years ago one of the authors happened to turn on a television set just in time to see a particular second baseman hit a 420-foot home run. This was the ball-player's only home run of the season and the fourth in his very long career. One might have turned off the television set at that point and said, "I saw him hit a home run. I know he can do it when he really wants to. He could be leading the league in home runs! It's just a matter of attitude." Clearly such reasoning is fallacious. Day-in and day-out performance is a better indication of function than the isolated moment of excellence. The child who once was "caught" drawing a straight line can still have problems with fine motor control. The converse is also true; an occasional slump should not in itself constitute grounds for special education!

Motivational determinism. Several sections of this book have referred to the overuse of the word *motivation*. This is particularly true about children who have difficulties with attention. Clearly, when motivation is increased, there is often a remarkable improvement in attention. As noted earlier, a child who is chronically inattentive during arithmetic classes may show remarkable concentration during the showing of the movie *Dracula* or *Star Wars*. Such high-motivation settings, however, are not appropriate milieux in which to measure attention strength. Figure 2 illustrates this: the vertical axis presents a qualitative rating of attention; the horizontal axis contains a similarly derived rating of a situation's motivation content. It can be seen that, at minimal motivation input, a "normal" child (i.e., lines C and D) displays a moderate amount of attention while a chronically inattentive child (lines E and F) shows little concentration. In the moderate range, there is a wide variety of attention strength. At high and super levels of motivation, the attention of all children shows relative strength. If attention is measured at high and super motivation levels, there is a tendency to deny the existence of attention problems. This is clearly inappropriate, since it is more relevant to assess attention in the context of the moderate motivational force of school and every day life. The converse is also true; if the class is dull enough, even those students capable of tenacious attention will drift off dramatically!

Evaluationmanship. Some youngsters are great test-takers. They may excel on standardized examinations yet decompensate in regular classrooms. One always

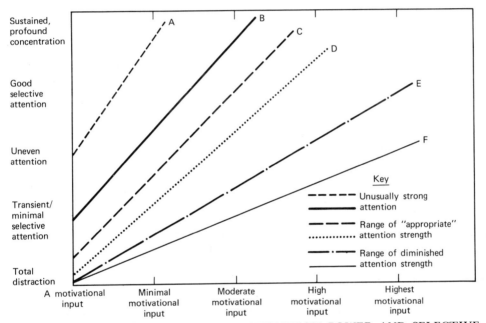

Figure 2. RELATIONSHIP BETWEEN MOTIVATION POWER AND SELECTIVE FOCUS IN CHILDREN WITH VARYING DEGREES OF ATTENTION STRENGTH
This graph is illustrates the relationship between the level of motivation associated with a particular task or setting and the attention strength of a child. The vertical axis shows a gradation of levels of attention, while the horizontal axis describes varying levels of motivational input. Rote drill, for example, may represent a low-incentive input at the left extreme of the horizontal axis, while a football game or horror story on television may constitute a high-motivation input. The lines (A through F) illustrate attention strength of six different children. For certain children (e.g., child A) very little high-motivational input is required to elicit sustained, effective attention. For other children (e.g., E and F), relatively high levels of motivation are needed to attain moderate degrees of selective attention. This hypothetical graph illustrates the principle that with high enough levels of extrinsically provided motivation, almost any child can attend. It is most helpful to evaluate a child's attention patterns at moderate or usual levels, rather than under exceptionally high motivational circumstances (see text).

needs to balance the two perspectives. It has been noted that many inefficient, disorganized, or inattentive youngsters perform particularly well on a one-to-one basis. Such children may appear competent in a physician's office. A pediatrician can do a disservice by providing reassurance on the basis of this atypical sample of behavior. The following is a common scenario: The teacher states that Michael is disruptive and disorganized in the classroom and may be "hyperactive." Michael is taken to his pediatrician. During ten minutes in the physician's office he smiles, exchanges pleasantries, sits very still, acts appealingly, and cooperates enthusiastically. The pediatrician points to the child and says: "How can they say he's 'hyperactive?' Michael could never sit still this long if he had real problems." The mother returns home and calls the school principal to report that she has seen her pediatrician, and he has reassured her that there is "nothing wrong with Michael." The implication is that the problem is with the school. This can lead to a needless delay in obtaining appropriate services. Several years may be wasted for a youngster who is hopelessly deficient in all subject areas and totally disenchanted with the process of learning. Such erroneous assessments can be prevented by more thorough evaluation by the pediatrician (incorporating age-appropriate neurodevelopmental tasks), more careful and systematic consideration of data from the school system, and more open communication between the physician and the school. There should be a delay in offering reassurance until contradictory findings are thoroughly analyzed.

Professional perseverations. Behavioral and cognitive phenomena may often be in the mind of the observer. In many diagnostic processes there tends to be very little attention to interobserver reliability. Each examiner may have his pet diagnoses, which can be custom fitted to any child. Some diagnosticians may lean toward "brain damage"; others may prefer attention deficits. Some are prone to say that children have troubles because they "can't handle their feelings" or because they harbor deeply repressed hostility. There may be a tendency to see reflected in a child one's own disciplinary inclinations or the contents of an article one has just read. When there is a plethora of observational data, each diagnostician can highlight or deemphasize particular findings to make a case for the kind of formulation he finds most appealing.

This pitfall can never be eliminated completely. It is therefore essential that each diagnostician be aware of personal formulation habits, tendencies, and perseverative propensities. In addition, professionals working with each other must be sensitive to such inclinations in colleagues, so that checks and balances can occur. The mutually respectful collaboration of professionals with a variety of professional biases can help guard against such perseveration. Whenever most of the reports from a team or an individual evaluator sound alike, there may be reason for some concern about the formulation process. Regrettably, findings may correlate more with the evaluator(s) than with the needs of the evaluee!

If these hazards are borne in mind, misleading formulations may be minimized. The reliability of findings should be constantly questioned. The child and the parents should be involved; it is often helpful to have them critically scrutinize final reports, so that they too may contribute to what must be the final step in systematic formulation, the assessment of the assessment.

6

Education
and Intervention
in School

A proper and effectual remedy for this wandering of the
thoughts I would be glad to find. He that will observe such
children will find that even when they endeavor their utmost,
they cannot keep their minds from straggling. The way to cure
it, I am satisfied, is not angry shouting or beating, for that
presently fills their heads with all the ideas that fear, dread or
confusion can offer to them. To bring back gently their
wandering thoughts by leading them into the path and going
before them in the train they would pursue, without any rebuke
or so much as taking notice (where it can be avoided) of their
roving, I suppose would sooner reconcile and inure them to
attention.

John Locke, *On The Conduct of The Understanding*, Section XXX (1762)

This book does not attempt to catalog and evaluate the ever-expanding arsenal
of educational weapons to combat learning disorders. Sophisticated treatises,
research projects, demonstration models, and commercial packages testify to
high activity levels in this area. Research in educational intervention has had to
traverse a scientific obstacle course. Carefully controlled studies of new curriculum approaches, with attention to sample selection, randomization, and blind
measurement of outcome, have been sparsely represented in the literature.
Instead, there exists a surplus of uncontrolled reports, testimonials, and triumphant anecdotes! Truly rigorous studies of remediation are expensive and
difficult to design. In the "treatment" of learning disorders, it sometimes seems
as if everything works, since it is difficult to sort out the specific remedial effects
of an intervention from its inevitable by-products: pedagogic placebo effects, the
nonspecific influence of increased attention to a child, and the magical healing
properties of time.

Notwithstanding the current state of the art, clinical choices must be made.
The interested reader is referred to several excellent texts that describe specific
educational interventions for children with learning disorders (Lerner 1976,
Johnson and Mykelbust 1967, Robeck and Wilson 1974, Gearhegart 1973, Money
1966).

This chapter will survey and sample some of the educational options for children with learning disorders. It includes consideration of medical participation in the educational process. The first section describes the physician as a sensitizer and demystifier at the interface between physiological and educational issues. It is followed by a discussion of "special education" and alternatives for children with learning problems. The next section explores issues relevant to the regular classroom learning of such children. The chapter concludes with some discussion about "moving on or staying back" and a section on early education and prevention.

THE SENSITIZATION PROCESS

Whether the health professional is serving as a source of primary care or as a member of an independent interdisciplinary evaluation team (or both), he or she may play an essential role in promoting sensitivity to a child's special needs. By communicating with a child's teachers and school administrators, the clinician can depict the struggle in sympathetic terms. In some cases, the educational institution may have labeled a difficult youngster as "emotionally disturbed," "poorly motivated," or "improperly reared." In some circumstances such relatively glib formulations may, in fact, constitute convenient justifications for withholding special services. It is certainly more economical and less burdensome to declare that a child has a "terrible attitude" than to entertain the possibility that the student may have significant difficulties with (for example) receptive language, which would call for a complete evaluation, possible language therapy, regular classroom modifications, and the services of a learning center or resource room for part of each day. Such attitudes (often derived from economic pressures on the school budget) are becoming increasingly rare, as there is widespread sensitization to the plight of the dysfunctioning child.

In a report, at a conference, or even in a telephone conversation, health care professionals can help to explicate neurological, constitutional, developmental, and psychosocial influences at work in a failing child. In particular, the clinician can sensitize school personnel to the complexity of a student's problems, the relevant nature-nurture interaction issues, the consequences of his unusual or discordant learning style, and any maladaptive coping methods that have been appropriated to deal with failure (see Chapter 9). In offering this opinion, the physician should be careful not to establish an adversary relationship with the school. In individual cases, it is important to demonstrate an awareness of the school's predicament. It is also essential that the clinician recognize the administrative influence of the person with whom he is communicating. The classroom teacher, for example, may not be in a position to obtain special services for a particular child. Even the principal or director of special education in the community may be relatively impotent with regard to control of the purse strings and the allocation of resources needed for special educational intervention. In fact, the school board itself may be at the mercy of certain community groups who may or may not be committed to children with special educational needs (see Chapter 8). Current legislation (Public Law 94–142) strengthens the hand of special education within the community (see Table 1). An understanding of this law and its local ramifications is therefore vitally important (Palfrey et al. 1978).

SPECIAL EDUCATION

In constructing an individualized educational plan, parents and professionals are faced with multiple options. They may confront a physician with some of the alternatives, seeking advice based on the doctor's knowledge of the student, family, and school system.

General Service Prototypes

General service prototypes for children with learning disorders are compiled below.

The Full-Time Private School for "Learning Disabilities"

Full-time private institutions have continued to propagate throughout the country. They tend to offer smaller classes, individualized educational-prescriptive programs, and a high level of sensitivity to children with special needs. As with all institutions, their quality, price tags, and levels of accountability vary. Some private shcools are wedded to a particular philosophy or curriculum system. Certain programs, for example, may be based on the Orton-Gillingham reading method. Others may place a heavy emphasis on other models of multisensorial learning. Some private schools have embraced specific dietary, optometric, and/or motor-patterning programs. Before electing to send a child to a particular school, the parents and the physician, as advisor, should be certain that they understand its priorities, philosophical commitments, therapeutic tenets, and educational techniques. The physician can be helpful in assisting parents to evaluate any "quasi-medical" content of a program.

Private schools may or may not be residential. Multiple counseling issues enter into the decision of whether a child should remain at home or go to a boarding school. Conditions at home, family values, and psychodynamic realities are likely to influence this choice.

The Full-Time Special Class

In this prototype a child is given full-time instruction in a special classroom. Often the child is "matched" with other youngsters who have similar difficulties. In other cases a more "generic" model involves a heterogeneous mix of handicapped children. Ideally, this kind of intervention features small classes conducted by specifcally trained professionals. It is critical for the consumer-advocate to have a clear understanding of what is being offered. With what kinds of problems do the other children in the classroom present? What types of curriculum materials will be used? What is the size of the class? What is the staff-student ratio? What are the academic qualifications of the teacher(s)? What are the relative proportions of specific educational intervention and social-supportive help? Will the child be spending any portion of the day in a more regular classroom setting (e.g. physical education, recess, industrial arts)? The physician might advise the child's parents to talk with mothers and fathers of other youngsters who have been in this setting.

At present there is a strong movement toward "generic" special education. Full-time classrooms for special-needs children are being replaced, in many areas, by part-time resource rooms or learning centers (see below). There is considerable concern about the rigid labeling of classrooms. It is hoped that the reader of this book will become increasingly aware of the absurdity of specific titles on the door, such as "E.D. Room" (class for emotionally disturbed children), "L.D. Room," and "Slow Learners Room." Since students seldom fit neatly into rigid categories, such pigeonholing represents a dangerous oversimplication. To place an overactive, inattentive child in a room for emotionally disturbed children often communicates that the primary problem is related to psychodynamic issues (usually at home). Such an implication can be harmful to a child and his family especially if the youngster's problems are largely constitutional. Moreover, the label can define the mission of the classroom in such a way that the emphasis is behavioral manageability, with little stress on special educational needs. For these reasons it seems more appropriate to offer special help within emotionally supportive and educationally potent facilities that do not require a potentially misleading label as a ticket for admission. In some areas, however, such labeling is the key to services. A child cannot get special help unless he has been diagnostically categorized. In such cases it is obvious that the clinician must go along with the system, while still playing an important role in minimizing its effects and sensitizing everyone to the injustice of the label.

The Resource Room
This facility, also referred to as the learning center, is a room reserved for specialized part-time help for children with learning disorders. In some schools it is a converted broom closet! In newer facilities appropriate space is allocated for learning centers. A child may attend the learning center once or twice a week or as often as several periods per day. Small-group or one-to-one help may be offered. The actual content of activities in the resource room can vary considerably (as described below). Children who participate in a learning center or resource room spend the remainder of their time "mainstreamed" in regular classes. Some youngsters occasionally feel stigmatized by having to go to the learning center. This becomes an important counseling issue for the clinician and parents. One should help the child to save face and to recognize the benefits of individualized attention.

Tutoring
Remedial reading and other forms of specific tutoring may be offered to a child. In most cases this help is on a one-to-one or small-group basis. It tends to be subject-oriented, with an emphasis on practice or drill. It may be offered within the school, or parents may wish to seek tutoring outside of the regular school day. They may ask their physician whether it is appropriate for them to serve as tutors for their own children. This decision depends largely on family dynamics. If too much home-based pressure is exerted or if such domestic tutelage will alter the natural spontaneity of family life, then it is contraindicated. Ideally, a child should receive all of his formal education during the school day.

Modified Regular Education
In this prototype, a child receives no particular special help, but the classroom teacher is aware of his particular needs. Certain modifications in teaching and expectations can be implemented. Sometimes a volunteer or a teacher's aide may

provide help within the regular classroom. Occasionally, specific individualized curriculum changes are needed. This format should be reserved for children with minimal academic lag.

Public Law 94-142 (see Table 1) mandates that the ideal special educational program is one which is "least restrictive" (i.e., closest to normal integration in the community). The overall intent of the law is to guarantee the availability of a free appropriate public education for all handicapped children. In an effort to mainstream handicapped children, a student is helped to become as regular a citizen as possible within the community (insofar as this is feasible without neglecting special educational needs). The clinician can help to maintain the balance between normalization and special services for children with learning disorders.

In advising parents to participate actively in the selection of a service prototype, the physician should review the specific educational objectives delineated in the *individualized educational plan* (the IEP). Such objectives should

Table 1. A Legislative Mandate: The Education for All Handicapped Children Act (Public Law 94-142)*

1. All children with handicaps are entitled to an interdisplinary evaluation.
2. An individualized educational plan (IEP) is developed for each handicapped child. It specifies goals and objectives as well as services. A full range of services must be available.
3. A program is developed that is in the "least restrictive" setting; i.e., the child spends as much time as is appropriate in a regular classroom ("mainstreaming").
4. An independent outside evaluation or second opinion may be obtained when indicated.
5. Parents are notified and involved in the evaluation process and must approve the individualized educational plan. They have the right to appeal a child's plan. All information and communication must be in the native language of the child and parents.
6. There is a provision for vigorous child identification activities. The age range is from three through twenty-one, except where state law limits are from five through eighteen.
7. There is an annual review of each child's program and progress as well as state and local monitoring processes.
8. All testing is supposed to be nondiscriminatory with regard to cultural and socioeconomic background.
9. The medical or pediatric involvement varies from state to state (Twarog and Levine, 1979).
10. The rights of handicapped children and their parents are protected through confidentiality and due process requirements.
11. Each state and each local school district must submit an annual program plan which includes their policies and procedures for providing special education.
12. Federal funds are available to assist state and local school districts in implementing the law.

* This table was prepared by Mrs. Bambi Levine.

These two views depict resource-room or learning-center settings for children with special needs. *(A)* Youngsters are getting help with numerical concepts through the use of a specific teaching aid. *(B)* Several children are being helped with basic shape recognition. They are learning to use proprioceptive and kinesthetic cues to develop more effective intersensory integration. Such activities may help children in such areas as visual discrimination, reading recognition, and retrieval skills in general. The use of small-group educational settings remains an important part of special educational intervention for children with learning problems.

158

document clearly the amount of progress anticipated in specific deficit areas. The clinician can then collaborate with others to monitor a child's growth, to reevaluate the educational plan at specific intervals and to note whether or not educational objectives have been met. Stating and meeting such objectives is never an easy undertaking. One of the most difficult questions of all remains: "How much progress is enough progress?" Since the state of the art does not allow us a clear indication of a child's "potential," the determination of the adequacy of progress is hazardous.

Additional Special Education Services

A variety of specialized services may need to be incorporated into a child's educational plan. Details of the "menu" may differ from school to school and from town to town. Common individualized services that one might request for a student are listed below.

Speech and/or language therapy. The services of a speech and language pathologist are critical in helping children with deficits in either receptive or expressive language. These professionals serve a wide range of youngsters who have problems with stuttering, vocabulary, word finding, articulation, sound sequencing, auditory attention, narrative organization, comprehension, and the processing of complex language. Speech and language therapists can also serve as consultants to classroom teachers, offering suggestions about the presentation of materials to language-impaired youngsters.

Occupational therapy. Many schools employ occupational therapists to help children with visual-spatial, motor, and general sensory-integration problems. Although the efficacy of such therapy has not yet been established for the treatment of learning disorders, such programs can help nurture a child's sense of competence and mastery over the physical-spatial universe.

Counseling services. Most school systems now have school adjustment or guidance counselors. Such professionals can offer valuable support and advice in the school setting. Some children feel comfortable dealing with school problems in situ. Specific academic troubles, social conflicts, and relevant affective issues can be explored during individual or group counseling sessions. In general, guidance personnel are trained in educational counseling and place more emphasis on helping youngsters select and cope with academic courses. School adjustment counselors are often social workers who deal with a wide range of family and school dynamics.

School psychology. Besides taking an important diagnostic role, the school psychologist can offer psychological counseling to students and can help plan classroom management strategies in collaboration with a youngster's teachers.

Adaptive physical education. Many schools are beginning to develop adaptive physical education programs for children with gross motor deficits and other physical problems. These programs can be quite helpful for a youngster who has problems with motor incoordination and self-image. When conducted properly, such classes are nonstigmatizing.

Special activities programs. Some schools are developing special activities programs for children with learning problems. These may focus on one particular area, such as art, music, nature study, dance, drama, or sports. Well-designed activity-oriented groups help the child develop greater personal insights, increased self-confidence, and expanded social skills.

Tutoring. Individualized tutoring is another special service. In some schools it has been merged into the resource room or learning center. Several times a week the reading or math specialist may offer supplemental assistance to a child who is struggling in a particular subject area.

All of these services are increasingly available in schools throughout the United States. When specific components are lacking, referral to appropriate community resources may be needed. It is important for the entire evaluation team to be aware of existing private and state-run local agencies where such services may be found.

The Facilitation of Development: Some Philosophical Issues

In assisting a child with a learning disorder, the clinician needs to consider some basic philosophical objectives. Should one aim strictly toward the improvement of academic performance? This would require specific help with reading, writing, arithmetic, and spelling. Should one, instead, set aside academic performance and concentrate on improving those areas of developmental dysfunction that are causing or aggravating academic failure? For example, one might work on memory, fine motor control, or sequential organization, with academic skills being taught in a separate setting or postponed (especially with younger children). Alternatively, should one bypass entirely a child's weak developmental areas and concentrate on augmenting strengths? One could, for example, focus on a child's strong visual memory and strive to make it even stronger. Another option might be the ultimate bypass, circumventing virtually all developmental weaknesses and academic shortcomings. Instead, vocationally oriented elective courses might be designed around skills that are relevant to the youngster's career goals.

There is no simple formula to select among the above alternatives for a particular child. There is a general tendency to try to remediate developmental weaknesses in young children, while bypass strategies are invoked increasingly in secondary school and beyond. In general, very severe disabilities might be bypassed, while milder deficits may be more amenable to enhancement. In between, a combined effort aimed at improving performance, strengthening weaknesses, using strengths, and including some bypass allowances (for the sake of mental health) is perhaps most justifiable. Such a combined approach should probably be the objective in educating most children at all levels. Developmental fatalism in secondary school is unnecessary. It is ironic that medical science is willing to help retrain the brain of a 70-year-old stroke victim, while a 16-year-old's "learning disabilities" are deemed too intransigent to correct!

It is important to include parents and children in some discussion of the philosophy and goals of an intervention plan. For some children, an analogy such as the following may be useful:

Suppose you were a baseball player. Suppose you were a very good base runner, an excellent fielder, and a good hitter, as long as the pitcher was throwing fast balls. However, whenever the pitcher threw you a curve ball, you would swing and miss. Does this mean that you are a bad baseball player? No! On the contrary, you have a very specific dysfunction in one area of baseball: curve balls. We have several options for helping you: First, we could have you go out and keep swinging at curve balls during practice (a drill approach based on performance). Or, we could have you practice hitting fast balls, so that some day you might become one of the best fast-ball hitters who ever lived (strengthening strengths). Another possibility is for you to quit baseball and go into some other field. After all, you may as well do things you are good at, and in which you can be successful (vocational education). Another possibility would be for us to take slow-motion movies of the way in which you swing at curve balls. We might find that there is one aspect of your eye-hand coordination or spatial perception that is prevent-ing you from hitting curve balls. Then, instead of practicing your hitting, we could give you some specific exercises to strengthen these weaknesses (a "learning disabilities" approach). This kind of demystification can be enlightening to a youngster who is groping with the abstract techniques that are being mobilized to help him.

Examples of Development-Enhancing Activities

Discussed below are some developmental-strengthening techniques that might be utilized in a resource room or learning center for a variety of specific dysfunctions.

Visual-Spatial Processing

Exercises to enhance visual-spatial orientation might include copying forms, working with form boards and puzzles, matching shapes or detailed pictures, finding discrepancies or errors in designs or drawings, working with mazes and road maps, and involving the whole body in movements through space. Tasks requiring complicated tracing, eye-tracking exercises, and work with scissors have also been used. Many of the activities appropriated to enhance visual-spatial orientation may have additional benefits with regard to eye-hand coordination and fine motor function.

Fine Motor Function

Children with difficulties in fine motor control are often helped by the use of form boards, tracing exercises, scissors, and copying tasks. Building model airplanes and working on specific crafts may be both highly motivating and helpful with regard to fine motor output.

A controversial area of fine motor intervention has to do with pencil grasp. Children with fine motor difficulties and maladaptive pencil grips probably should be helped to alter their technique to facilitate more efficient writing output. A well-established but awkward hold on the pencil can be altered to a well-positioned tripod grasp, which initially should be expected to be used only for a small portion of each day (hopefully gradually increasing over time). Use of an auxiliary rubber or plastic grip on the pencil can be helpful.

Children with both fine motor and visual-spatial problems can benefit from writing on a grid or practicing letter formation within the squares on a sheet of graph paper. This can help with spatial planning and also strengthen pencil control to some extent. Some children benefit from writing on a variety of surfaces and using an assortment of writing implements (felt-tip pen, ballpoint, pencil, crayon, etc.). In the early grades, affected children may derive help from mastering specific fine motor skills, such as tying shoelaces and manipulating buttons.

Sequential Organization

Children who have problems with analytic-sequential processing may benefit from specialized activities to strengthen concepts of time, serial order, segmentation, and synthesis of parts. Imitative tapping, rhythmic activities, the arrangement of pictures in an order that tells a story, work with diaries, calendars, or clocks, and the mastery of progressively complex serial commands are examples of such activities. Practice in segmenting and reblending words can be helpful, as can informational quiz games having to do with serial order (e.g., which comes first—April or February?). Tasks involving seriation according to size, volume, or weight illustrate specific principles of ordering. Some children may benefit from arranging anecdotal events and incidents in a logical narrative sequence. In some instances, complex motor sequencing exercises may be useful.

Memory

As noted in Chapter 3, memory is an extraordinarily complex function, and exercises designed to enhance retention need to be aimed at specific demonstrated weaknesses. Some youngsters have difficulties with memory of words, for example, but have no problems with memory for numbers, faces, or events. Children with deficits in visual memory for configurations (perhaps affecting spelling and sight vocabulary) might be encouraged to draw pictures from memory, answer questions about a picture after studying it for a short time, perform tasks of visual closure (finding missing parts, completing incomplete drawings), or tell what is missing from a series of objects previously encountered. The game of "Concentration" is another example of a potentially memory-enhancing activity.

Auditory memory can be "exercised" by recalling the details of taped stories, repeating sentences, following serial commands, and complying with increasingly complex instructions. The same tasks that reinforce auditory and visual memory can be utilized to strengthen selective attention in these modalities.

Receptive Language

Children with developmental language disabilities are often helped by the use of tapes and vocabulary-building exercises. Practice in sound discrimination and blending, a variety of word games, and storytelling followed by questions can be utilized. Often such exercises are supervised by a speech and language pathologist, who may work in collaboration with the classroom teacher or resource-room coordinator.

Expressive Language

Specialized language therapy may be offered to children who have difficulty with verbal encoding. In older youngsters, exercises involving synonyms, antonyms, and word games can help develop word finding and other aspects of oral expression. Children can also receive specific help with syntax formation, narrative organization, and storytelling abilities. As noted in Chapter 4, many children with writing difficulties also have subtle problems with oral language. Helping such students overcome their expressive handicaps may also facilitate more competent written output.

Organization

Many children with learning disorders need supervised instruction in what might be termed "organizational skills." Within the learning center, they can be assisted to develop strategies, articulate problem-solving approaches, be more reflective, pace their work appropriately, prepare outlines, take notes, and proofread or monitor their productions. The resource-room teacher can help a child establish an appropriate "cognitive tempo" or work rhythm. Some children with learning disorders have problems with the allocation of time to tasks. A youngster may respond in a highly impulsive manner when confronted with a situation that must be thought out carefully. The same child may perseverate and spend far too much time on another kind of problem. Children who have difficulty working within a time limit may need explicit guidance and practice in pacing themselves (perhaps even with the help of a stopwatch or clock). A learning-center teacher, in collaboration with parents, can help formulate recommendations about home study habits (see Chapter 9).

Attention

The child with attention deficits can usually achieve focus in a resource room. The organizational issues described in the previous paragraph are particularly important for such youngsters. They can often benefit from the negotiation of tasks and from an explicit verbal understanding with the resource room teacher about the nature of their attention problems. For example, the teacher might suggest to an impulsive child: "Let me see you take a *long* time to solve this problem." The attempt to induce reflective behavior in a child unaccustomed to contemplative effort may be productive. Similar challenges can be constructed for students with excessive distractibility, task impersistence, figetiness, and overactivity. In attempting to make the child conscious of, and therefore potentially in control of, these tendencies, it is important that the teacher not overshoot or create an attention hypochondriac! Within the resource-room setting, a child with attention problems can receive one-to-one teaching of basic academic skills. For such youngsters, a relatively short one-to-one educational interaction is generally more productive than considerably longer, less closely monitored periods in a regular classroom.

Higher-Order Conceptualization

Resource-room activities tailored to deal with higher-order conceptual abilities are less well established than those geared to perceptual issues. Children who appear to have difficulties with abstract reasoning, rule application, and complex integrative functions may not be particularly amenable to remedial intervention. Games of object sorting, work with riddles, attribute blocks, paradoxes or analogies, and story interpretations are examples of activities that might be undertaken by students who have difficulty with conceptualization, or whose thinking tends to be too concrete.

The Supportive Role

The "psychotherapeutic" value of the resource-room teacher cannot be overemphasized. Such a person can become an important "friend," "admirer," and "co-conspirator." Special educators are recognizing the critical role that they play in the lives of children with learning disorders. Optimal communication between an interested physician and resource-room teacher no doubt facilitates a struggling child's academic and social survival.

Costs and Benefits

Highly individualized special educational services for children with learning disorders can become a major community or family expense. The physician can help in sensitizing communities to the need for such interventions. Children with developmental dysfunctions traditionally have been "expensive" members of our society. One can argue, however, that preventing the nonproductive and perhaps antisocial consequences of chronic failure is, in the long run, cost-effective. Allocations for therapeutic and preventive educational services in childhood and adolescence are clearly more economical than long-term outlays, such as unemployment benefits, prison terms, and chronic psychiatric care. In the past, parents have had to lobby for the rightful service claims of their disabled children (Budoff 1975). In the future, it will be the responsibility of professionals working in this field to demonstrate the benefits of special education and to tease out those services that can be shown to make a difference.

THE REGULAR CLASSROOM EDUCATION OF A CHILD WITH A LEARNING DISORDER

The child with a learning disorder raises many questions with regard to mainstreaming in the regular classroom. Frequently, modifications are needed in teacher expectations, curriculum materials, and discipline. As increasing numbers of children are mainstreamed, misunderstandings in the regular classroom are likely to burgeon.

The Teacher–Student "Match"

Teachers vary widely in personality, pedagogic style, and tolerance for children's individual behaviors. In many schools a conscious effort is made to match particular types of special-needs students with specific classroom teachers. The physician in a community may learn which teachers in a particular school are most (and least) suitable for particular special needs.

Ideally, the physician and the classroom teacher should form a productive alliance (see Chapter 8). They should collaborate in the diagnostic process as well as in management and follow-up. The classroom teacher can provide observational data that often are more valid than any test scores.

When fully sensitized to a child's special needs, the classroom teacher can establish a close bond with the student based on tacit understandings. It is important for the regular classroom teacher to spend time alone talking with a child who has a learning disorder. The teacher should reassure the student that his struggles are understood. A balance should be achieved between allowances that the teacher will make for the child's shortcomings and the student's level of accountability for his own actions. The child should feel that the teacher is sympathetic and will do everything possible to prevent embarrassment in front of peers. If the teacher needs to repeat instructions slowly for a particular child, this must be done in such a way that other students are unaware of the target of these repetitions. The classroom teacher must constantly be sensitive to the lingering fear of humiliation or potential embarrassment. A secret signal system can be developed whereby a dysfunctioning student has a private way of indicating to the teacher something is not understood. Conversely, the teacher should signal disapproval or criticism in a way that does not lead to blatant exposure. This does not mean that the regular classroom teacher must treat the child as an educational cripple. There should be clear-cut, relatively nonnegotiable expectations. What is expected from the child should not far exceed his current levels of performance and behavior. Realistic increments of growth or progress should be sought.

The classroom teacher should strive to avoid becoming angry with a child who has learning disorders. On the other hand, the student needs to remember that the teacher is not a saint. Physicians and other professionals involved in evaluating and monitoring a child's progress also need to be sympathetic to the classroom teacher whose exposure is prolonged and potentially agonizing.

When a child has a learning disorder, the regular classroom teacher may need to adjust both the difficulty of the work and its amount in order to accommodate to the child's current functional level. It is essential that the classroom teacher have a quantitative sense of a child's capacities in a variety of areas; the overloading of central nervous system circuits must be avoided. Both the rate and volume of input and output are critical variables. Instructions should not be given too quickly or in multiple sequential steps if a child appears to have difficulties with such processing. Analogously, expectations of the rate of output (e.g., writing, oral reading) should be scaled down appropriately. For both input and output, certain children may require multiple small units of data rather than single large ones. A student may respond best to one-step instructions followed (after completion of the initial task) by further input. Hopefully, with time, children can grow in their capacity to handle multiple-step loadings. On the output side, it is sometimes better to ask a child to solve three problems, hand them in, take three more problems, and then submit those, rather than tackling six at once. Such special considerations are particularly helpful to children with difficulties in behavioral organization, attention, memory, and language. Those who have a great deal of trouble processing verbal instructions may benefit from visual demonstration models.

When a child is taking medication, it is helpful for the student and teacher to have an understanding about its use. It is usually inappropriate to conceal such treatment from school personnel. The classroom teacher can be an indispensable source of feedback to the clinician about the efficacy and side-effects of stimulant medication. This process is made easier when there is a general ambiance of full disclosure, within which the parents, the child, the teacher, and the clinician are all communicating freely.

A serious mismatch between child and teacher may generate an "educational emergency." A child with a learning disorder can have the grief compounded by a personality clash. This situation should lead promptly to a conference, during which alternative options can be considered in a nonaccusatory, nonthreatening manner. Occasionally the pediatrician may serve as a mediator in such disputes.

Classroom Structure

Rules and regulations, rhythmic tempo, and degrees of freedom become issues in selecting a regular classroom for a child with learning disorders. The so-called open or relatively unstructured classroom may be appropriate for highly imaginative, creative children who have little difficulty acquiring academic skills. Some children revel in the opportunity to proceed at their own rate. On the other hand, many children with attention deficits and other kinds of learning problems require a structured classroom, in which there is a high level of accountability, predictability, and routinization. Between the extremes of openness and tight confinement is a spectrum of options. In surveying the scene, it is important not to accept descriptions at face value. Many an open classroom harbors stringent predictability and accountability, while traditional settings can be loosely organized. Above all, there must be an appropriate admixture of consistency and flexibility.

The overactive child may need to be mobile from time to time and to change pursuits with some frequency. Accompanying this elasticity, however, should be regularity, rather than random shifts in the extent of freedom.

Another structural issue concerns the self-contained classroom, as opposed to frequent changes in teachers during the school day. This, too, depends very much upon the child and his unique pattern of strengths and weaknesses. Many children with chronic learning disorders have difficulty adjusting to multiple teachers and/or sites at the early secondary school level. They strain at trying to accommodate to differing teaching and disciplinary styles. They may need to develop a strong identification with one teacher. Close coordination may be needed among members of the educational cast to offer a consistent approach to such a child's difficulties.

Curriculum Options: The Example of Reading

Within the regular classroom it may be possible to offer some curriculum options. One might consider matching a teaching method to a child's cognitive strengths (Popp 1978). To illustrate this strategy, some methods that might be used to teach reading in the early grades are surveyed below. This brief outline can provide the physician with a simplified introduction to a complex subject:

Linguistic methods. A linguistic reading method is based upon the supposition that young children have well-integrated oral language skills. It emphasizes sounds (phonology) and works toward the establishment of sound-symbol associations. Reading is taught initially by using words that have a consistent and regular spelling pattern. Words with a consonant-vowel-consonant (CVC) sequence are offered as whole words. Children learn to decode by making generalizations about families of words that contrast only minimally (e.g., can, tan, ran). There are many linguistic curricula. Examples include *Merrill Linguistic Readers, SRA Basic Skills Series, Let's Read, Programmed Reading,* and *Palo Alto.*

Phonics approaches. Phonics methods differ from linguistic strategies in that the latter present sound-symbol equivalence in whole words, while the phonics system presents letters and units of sound in isolation for blending into meaningful words (e.g., /b/-/a/-/t/=*bat*). One might surmise that such a system would be particularly difficult for a child who has deficiencies in auditory discrimination, sequencing, or central auditory processing. Among the commercial packages for the phonics approach are *Phonovisual Program, New Phonics Skill Text, Phonics We Use, Open Court Basic Readers, Lippincott's Basic Reading,* and *Structural Reading.*

Embellishing the alphabet. A number of reading approaches depend on *alterations* in the traditional alphabet. Some, such as the *initial teaching alphabet* (i.t.a.) and the *REBUS System,* actually alter the symbol system to make it more understandable to children. The *DISTAR Reading System* uses modifications of the traditional printing system and emphasizes early letter recognition. There is also a strong behavioral approach, utilizing symbol-action games, blending tasks, and rhyming activities. *Words in color* is another approach in which a given phoneme is consistently represented by a particular color, thereby providing an additional visual cue.

Language-experience approaches. These systems use a child's direct experience to enhance reading. For example, a student may begin by telling a story to a teacher, who, in turn, writes it down and then teaches the child how to read it. Each day the child may choose a word or two to learn how to read. There is a strong emphasis on reading materials that emerge directly from a child's own experience, in order to enhance motivation. Visual processing is stressed, with relative deemphasis on phonic decoding skills.

Multisensory methods. A variety of multisensory curricula have been advanced. Their use has been particularly widespread for children with learning disorders. Some depend heavily upon kinesthetic and tactile processing, using tracing as a major means of learning sound symbols. These are often referred to as *V-A-K-T* (visual-auditory-kinesthetic-tactual) techniques. Others depend on large motor movements to accomplish tracing activities, or employ a variety of textures (e.g., sandpaper, sandboxes, finger paints). A child might be asked to look at a word and then hear the word, repeat it, feel muscle movements while tracing it, and sense a tactile surface under the fingertips. The *Fernald* and the *Gillingham-*

Stillman methods are examples of reading approaches that emphasize such tactile and kinesthetic inputs. With the Fernald method, the child learns the word as a total Gestalt, while the Gillingham-Stillman method emphasizes tracing to teach individual letters or sound units. Ultimately, individual sounds are blended into larger groupings and then short word units. One feature of the Gillingham-Stillman method is the simultaneous mastering of spelling and reading. In some cases, actual independent reading may be postponed until most of the phonics program has been covered and mastered.

Conventional basal approach. Basal readers are a series of curriculum packages that have an eclectic approach. They combine phonics, vocabulary building, study skills, comprehension exercises, and other techniques. They emphasize a "look-say" method of teaching, beginning the reading process in a "meaning-oriented" program. Children are presented with a series of books of increasing difficulty. Among the common conventional basal series are *Ginn Reading 720, Harper & Row Readers, Houghton-Mifflin Series, Scott Foresman Reading System,* and the *Holt, Rinehart and Winston* series.

Other reading methods. Highly individualized approaches have been employed in which youngsters are allowed to proceed at their own pace, using mainly high-motivational materials. More recently, computers and programmed reading instruction have been used in the context of teaching machines, elaborate reading laboratories, and behavior-modification approaches. So-called total reading systems now offer multimedia materials such as books, puzzles, games, and tape cassettes.

Traditional wisdom has dictated that children with learning problems be taught either through multisensory approaches or by using their own specific strengths (e.g., sight methods for those with strong visual processing). The efficacy of such strategies has not been proved. Matching strong modalities with particular reading approaches may or may not be successful (Arter and Jenkins 1977). Nevertheless, there is some justification for giving careful thought to the ways in which a reading approach is in harmony with a youngster's cognitive style.

Analogously, one might consider customized approaches to teaching other academic skills in order to select appropriate curriculum materials. A diagnostic team requires the services of a special educator who can help to translate developmental and biomedical findings into appropriate curriculum recommendations in all skill areas.

Behavioral Management

A major issue for the regular classroom teacher concerns the behavioral management of disorganized, inattentive, overactive, disruptive, or otherwise difficult-to-control children. Here again, close cooperation between diagnosticians, therapists, and teachers is essential. Communication channels between the classroom and the home must be wide open, with consistency around levels of expectation. Often the physician can act as a liaison to promote optimal coordination.

The physician and other diagnostic personnel can help the teacher separate behaviors that are likely to be a primary manifestation of a child's handicap (e.g., impulsivity) from those that represent strategies to save face (e.g., class clowning) and those that may constitute significant psychopathology (e.g., self-deprecatory behaviors). Chapter 9 offers examples of specific strategies that teachers might use in dealing with certain behaviors.

Attention deficits present a special challenge to the classroom teacher. Children whose attention is highly unpredictable make exasperating students or classmates. Various techniques have been tried to reinforce attention. Some children with significant visual inattention have been confined to a carrel, or small booth, in which there are few, if any, competing visual stimuli. Preferential seating in the classroom and systems of reward and punishment (behavior-modification techniques) have also been employed with variable success. The pediatrician may want to suggest certain guidelines (some of which already may have been tried) to aid in the classroom management of an inattentive child:

1. Begin and end each day with praise for the child. Many children with attention deficits have a significantly diminished self-image and feel as if there is no chance for success in school.

2. Break up work into small units (as described above). Avoid lengthy instructions and assignments whose persistence far exceeds the child's demonstrated working capacity.

3. Have a secret way of signaling a child who is inattentive to the task at hand. It is not helpful to call on a chronically inattentive child who is caught staring out the window. This may be humiliating and is likely to increase anxiety, which will further drain attention.

4. Whenever possible such children should be in small classrooms, and the teacher should try to offer individual attention. There should be an awareness that such children may learn more on a one-to-one basis in ten minutes than they do during two hours in a large classroom!

5. A minimum of background noise and visual stimulation is helpful. A classroom with 200 different pictures on the wall, a fish tank, a gerbil cage, four terrariums, and a multicolored mobile may offer more sensory data than an inattentive child can filter!

6. A high level of consistency in scheduling can help provide organization for such a child. Children with attention deficits generally do not adapt well to major shifts in program content or order.

7. The teacher needs to be sensitive to peer abuse. Its impact can be minimized by helping the vulnerable child to save face.

8. Participation in tasks that have high intrinsic motivational properties and require reflective behaviors should be encouraged. Puzzles, finding mistakes in other people's work, and games of concentration might be tried. The child should be helped to plan his work and to articulate problem-solving strategies.

9. Regular meetings with the child to discuss behavioral and academic progress are important. Offer very concrete methods for feedback and monitoring (e.g., graphs, scoring systems, diaries).

10. After an understanding is reached between teacher and child with regard to the attention deficit, discussion should center around whether or not the child was "tuned in" or "in control of his attention" rather than whether he was "bad" or "good." The concern here is that if a child is called "bad" often enough, this will constitute a self-fullfilling prophesy!

Bypass Strategies: The Example of Writing

An important alternative in the regular education of a child with learning problems entails the modification of teacher expectations. A classroom teacher must face the issue of whether or not to permit a child to bypass—entirely or partially—a deficient skill. While avoiding what is termed a cop-out, the teacher and the physician sometimes must rescue a youngster from inevitable failure situations. Bypass maneuvers are critical in managing writing problems. In view of the complexity and importance of this skill, it may be necessary to modify expectations for written output. The following are examples of such compromises:

Reduced expectations for volume output. When the class is expected to submit book reports of from five to six pages, a youngster with a writing disorder might be allowed to hand in two to three pages. Student privacy should be honored here.

Increased time for completion of written examinations. Some children with writing difficulties have particular problems completing timed tests. In such cases, the number of items should be reduced or the time allowance increased. Students with output-processing problems are now being permitted to take untimed college entrance examinations.

The use of a typewriter. Some (but not all) children with writing problems appear to benefit from typing lessons. It is difficult to predict which youngsters will show gains with typing. Teachers should be willing to allow students with writing problems to submit typed assignments—at least some of the time.

Abandonment of writing requirements. When a child is feeling overwhelmed, it might be appropriate to eliminate written output requirements, at least temporarily. Such a student might be required to read one extra book, instead of writing a book report. The youngster could confer with the teacher and offer an oral interpretation.

Printing (manuscript) instead of cursive writing. Some youngsters find cursive writing difficult and manuscript (printing) relatively easy. Interchange between the two should be acceptable. The discontinuity of printing may, however, decelerate the rate of written output. Some children may thus need to be encouraged to write cursively to improve their speed (even if there is some sacrifice of legibility) for certain tasks.

Use of tape recordings. Some students should be allowed (some of the time) to utilize a tape recorder and submit a cassette as a report. This can be particularly useful for children with writing problems based on motor impairment.

Omission of one or more criteria for evaluation. Some youngsters have great difficulty with the integrative aspects of writing; the simultaneous application of multiple prerequisite skills can be an insurmountable challenge. A teacher may wish to give such a youngster an assignment that will be graded only for the quality of ideas, with relative disregard for punctuation, capitalization, spelling, and "calligraphy." Ultimately, the child can be helped to put it all together, but in the meantime, an insistence upon perfect integrative facility may not be realistic and may destroy incentive.

These modifications in expectations are relevant to other areas of learning. The use of a calculator for arithmetic is another example of a temporary (or permanent) bypass maneuver. Optimal education and adjustment always depend upon a balance between intervention and circumvention.

Promotion or Retention

The pediatrician involved in the management of children with learning disorders is likely to become embroiled in a recurring seasonal controversy—namely, promotion or retention. There is considerable disagreement about the wisdom of retaining children in a particular grade because of slow learning or "immaturity"; there is a dearth of data to substantiate most of the arguments. As a result, one can only present some rough guidelines and precautions.

The term "immaturity" sometimes is applied recklessly and with little critical scrutiny. A youngster with significant developmental dysfunction, attention deficits, and secondary maladaptive coping methods commonly gets labeled as "immature." The implication is that somehow, ultimately, the child will "catch up" if kept in a holding pattern. When such a consensus is reached, the youngster is often retained and allowed to mark time at the current grade level. Unfortunately, such designs may constitute thinly disguised mandates for inaction. The wait-and-see attitude may replace needed individualized, direct intervention.

On the surface, such a decision can be very appealing, if for no other reason than its economy. If one does argue for the retention of a young child because of immaturity, however, there needs to be substantial evidence of a maturational lag. Such data as a retarded bone age, delayed dentition, and short stature (especially if other family members are taller) might be advanced to suggest a diagnosis of maturational delay. These factors, combined with significant findings on the neuromaturational assessment (see Chapter 5), might be used to make an argument for "true developmental immaturity." One might predict that such a youngster will be unable to keep up with peers and will reach puberty late. In such a case, and where there is a clear lag in the acquisition of academic skills, the argument for retention *might* be strengthened.

Criteria for social and emotional immaturity are poorly established. It is all too easy to state that a child is emotionally immature or socially young, when one is really describing a series of maladaptive behaviors that are *unlikely* to undergo spontaneous remission with maturation and that may be associated with underlying disabilities.

The following guidelines are advanced to help in the decision-making process with regard to retention or promotion:

1. One's threshold for retaining a child should be lowest at the two ends of education. Retentions in kindergarten or first grade, or in eleventh or twelfth grades, are probably more justified and less traumatic than during the in-between years.

2. It is critical to include the child as part of the decision-making process when considering retention.

3. Retention should never be used instead of intervention. If a child is to be retained, then special educational services in all likelihood should be expanded, rather than eliminated!

4. A child should never be threatened with retention. When a student needs to repeat a grade, a prior threat makes it difficult to interpret retention as anything but retribution. This, in turn, tinges a child's learning struggles with implications of moral turpitude.

5. Alternatives must always be considered. These include summer school, additional special help, a new special educational prototype, a "transitional" class, and a complete change in school or classroom structure.

6. Parents and professionals need to deal directly with the child's burden of stigmatization when retention occurs. One needs to collaborate with the child in developing coping methods to deal with potential (or actual) peer ridicule. It is essential that the child *not* be reassured about such criticism, but rather be equipped to handle it. If a child is vulnerable to social abuse, and has low self-esteem, then the threshold for repeating a grade should be elevated considerably.

7. The concept of "social promotion" can be as much of an excuse for inaction as can retention. Once again, it should be emphasized that the decision of whether to retain or promote a youngster should have little or no bearing on the quantity or quality of services offered to deal with his learning disorders.

If it looks as if the child is only "marginally ready" for first grade, it is sometimes helpful before the year begins to let the youngster know that he may be spending two years at that grade level. This lessens the academic pressure during the year and also "softens the blow" when retention ultimately is deemed necessary. In the event that it is decided to promote the child, this can serve as a pleasant surprise.

A closely related issue concerns the age of entry into school. At present countercurrents are flowing in diverse directions, ranging from early education to late entry for "unready" children to the delayed initiation of education for youngsters. As usual there exists a vast and contradictory literature. The best safeguard against educational failure and humiliation is teacher sensitivity and the capability for individualized education. The so-called unready or marginally ready child might spend more than one year in kindergarten or in first grade. This alternative may prove beneficial, as long as the youngster does not develop strong feelings of inadequacy in comparison with peers. Consistent teacher support and parental praise can minimize this phenomenon.

The assessment of educational readiness is an important function for the pediatrician. A comprehensive preschool examination can be extremely useful in screening for and anticipating potential slow starts. Careful attention to development and behavioral organization at age three can also be critical; a possibly vulnerable child can be enrolled in a nursery or other preschool program. A variety of assessment tools have been developed to help pediatricians and other health care professionals screen for possible manifestations of potential learning disorders (Dworkin and Levine 1980, Satz et al. 1975).

THE PREVENTION OF FAILURE

A number of programs have been established to provide early diagnosis and intervention for children who are "at risk" for academic failure. Some have been effective in the early grades (Arnold et al. 1977, Belmont and Birch 1974). Project Headstart has offered comprehensive health services for preschool children with socioeconomic vulnerabilities. Other programs have offered close supervision of the health and development of infants who have endured significant perinatal stresses. The systematic evaluation of outcomes and cost-benefit ratios for early diagnostic and educational services has been complicated.

The Brookline Early Educational Project (BEEP) is an attempt by a public school system to enroll children in a program three months before they are born (Levine et al. 1977)! All youngsters, regardless of degree of developmental risk, are monitored carefully for early signs of dysfunction. Comprehensive physical, developmental, and neurological assessments are performed regularly. During infancy, early educators offer ongoing support at the homes of participants. Parents are helped to become the earliest teachers of their children. As the children grow older, center-based preschool programs are offered. Curriculum is individualized for those youngsters who appear to be manifesting early signs of developmental dysfunction or behavioral disorganization.

From work within the Brookline Early Education Project, it was concluded that the concept of risk is a dynamic one. As one determined risk at various chronologic checkpoints, it became clear that the composition of the list changed from examination to examination. That is to say, some of the youngsters who appear to be developmentally vulnerable at four months looked fine at 14½ months, while a previously low-risk group were showing signs of dysfunction. The instability of risk factors has been advanced as justification for mainstreaming all youngsters in early education programs, rather than offering such services only to those who appear to be in need at an arbitrary age.

Early education programs have yet to demonstrate conclusively their efficacy (Bronfenbrenner 1974). Basic questions remain: Given the current state of the art, how accurately and at what ages can one predict subtle deficiencies in specific developmental elements, such as those outlined in Chapter 3? What proportion of identified handicaps will undergo spontaneous remission without any intervention at all? With the current availability of diagnostic instrumentation, how many false-negative (or false-positive) findings would result from early screening for potential learning disorders? If one can, in fact, uncover specific deficiencies before they become a problem for a child, can their natural history be altered through early educational input?

Regardless of the growth rate or propagation of early screening and intervention programs, the pediatrician remains an important figure in the early surveillance of young children, as well as in the provision of health and developmental counseling services. It is likely that well-supervised health care represents an important factor in the prevention of learning failure. The treatment of predisposing health disorders (e.g., recurrent otitis media), the prevention of central nervous system stresses (e.g., lead intoxication), and appropriate health maintenance and developmental anticipatory guidance, all contribute to the prevention of learning failure.

7

Medical Therapies
and Interventions

This is the story of Gerald McCoy
And the strange thing that happened to that little boy.
They say it all started when Gerald was two.
That's the age kids start talking (least most of them do).

But when he started talking, you know what he said?
He didn't say words, he said BOING BOING instead.
"What's that?" cried his father (his hair turning gray).
"That's a very odd thing for a young boy to say."

So poor Gerald's father rushed to the phone.
And quick dialed the number of Dr. Malone.
"I see," said the doctor, "it's just as you said.
"He doesn't say words, he goes BOING BOING instead.
"I have no cure for this; I can't handle the case."
So, he packed up his bags and walked out of the place.

From Public School 7 to Mrs. McCoy:
"Your little son Gerald's a most helpless boy.
"He'll go BOING BOING BOING all his life, I'm afraid.
"Sincerely yours, Fannie Schultz, Teacher, First Grade."

From Ronald McClaren, Gerald McBoing Boing

The physician's role in the formulation and implementation of a treatment plan for academic or behavioral problems is complex. In a field where no single mode of intervention has proved consistently effective for all children, and where anecdotal reports of dramatic successes often appear in the mass media, the ability to provide objective rational advice challenges even the most skilled clinicians. Despite extensive experience with stimulant drugs for the treatment of "hyperactive" children, guidelines for the appropriate use of such medication are not definitely established. Moreover, with the proliferation of many new management schemes that have not been subjected to rigorous evaluation, the physician often is asked to recommend a therapeutic program that he knows very little about. This chapter will provide an overview of current knowledge about a broad array of alternative interventions for behavioral and learning disorders. All are currently being prescribed in a variety of settings. Whereas some may be demonstrated ultimately to be effective therapies, it is likely that others will be relegated to the status of historical curiosity.

DRUG TREATMENT

Medication has been used for centuries to modify the behavior of children (Ross and Ross 1976). Galen, the ancient Greek physician, prescribed opium for colicky infants. Alcohol preparations, bromides, and barbituates were used for many years to treat irritability and restlessness. Although first noted to be effective in the treatment of hyperactive children in the 1930s, psychostimulants were not used extensively in pediatric practice in the United States until the late 1950s. After a period of general acceptance (in conjunction with the enthusiastic advertising of its merits by the pharmaceutical industry), a backlash against psychopharmacology for children developed in the late 1960s and extended into the next decade. When the *Washington Post* erroneously reported that 5 to 10% of school children in Omaha were being treated with "behavior" drugs, a public outcry was raised against "mind control" and the excessive dependence on drugs in American society (Maynard 1970).

During the past decade the use of drugs for the treatment of behavioral disorders in school children has continued to play a role in comprehensive management plans. Krager and Safer (1974) conducted a study in Baltimore County, Maryland, in which they surveyed school nurses in 1971 and 1973 to determine the number of children receiving medication for hyperactivity. They found that between 1% and 2% of the public school population, and less than 1% of the parochial school population, were being so treated. There was a 62% increase in the use of drugs in the public schools over the two-year study period, and a 77% increase in the parochial school system. Of the agents prescribed, the percentage of psychostimulants increased from 76% to 88%, with a greater use of methylphenidate over dextroamphetamine. The remainder of the children were reported as being treated with thioridazine (Mellaril), chlorpromazine (Thorazine), hydroxyzine (Atarax), diphenhydramine (Benadryl), and a variety of other medications.

Eisenberg (1971) remarked, "Pharmacologic methods provide neither the passport to a brave new world, nor the gateway to the inferno." In order to maximize the likelihood of appropriate clinical practice, the following basic principles should be followed (see Table 1):

1. Selection of candidates for medication must be based upon the results of an objective, comprehensive evaluation. This should include information obtained directly from school personnel who know the child well (see the teacher questionnarie in Appendix C). The ultimate indications for drug treatment should be based upon the child's clinical status, and not be unduly influenced by the family's or school's desire for such therapy. Finally, the value of nonpharmacological alternative treatments should be carefully considered before a decision is made to prescribe a drug.

2. Choice of medication should be based upon a rational consideration of both the child's behavioral characteristics and the specific goals of the therapy. For example, if modification of simple motoric overactivity is desired, stimulant

Table 1. Principles of Drug Therapy for Learning or Behavioral Problems

Objective evaluation of candidate for medication
Rational choice of drug
Rapport with child
Rapport with family
Communication with School
Close monitoring
Periodic discontinuation and reassessment
Comprehensive intervention
Review of rationale for medication
Continuing professional education

medication is not indicated. Alternatively, these may be the agents of choice for the treatment of a short attention span secondary to constitutional problems with distractibility.

3. Close rapport with the child must be established and maintained. He should be given the name of the drug, the reasons for its use, and the clinical response that will be expected. It is important that the child be included as an active, willing participant in the therapy, rather than treated as a passive recipient of medication. In fact, informed consent from the youngster, as well as the parents, is crucial.

4. Close rapport with the family must be established and maintained. Because of the mythology and adverse publicity associated with drug treatment for "hyperactivity", family members must be given an opportunity to communicate whatever thoughts they may have about such therapy. Specific information should be shared regarding the medication selected, its therapeutic benefits, possible side-effects, and the consequences of long-term treatment.

5. Direct communication with school personnel is critically important. Their input is essential for the initial diagnostic assessment as well as for subsequent monitoring.

6. Close supervision of drug treatment is absolutely essential. Weekly assessment in the beginning of therapy can be conducted by telephone contact with family and school, in order to evaluate clinical response and possible side-effects. Once a therapeutic dosage has been well established, the child should be seen every four to six months for a reassessment of the need for medication.

7. Periodic discontinuation of medication is most important. "Drug holidays" on weekends and school vacations should be encouraged. Complete cessation of drug therapy over the summer vacation, with a return to school off medication, is usually desirable. When parental resistance to drug-free periods is high because of unmanageable behavior at home, compromise strategies may have to be negotiated. The decision to continue long-term therapy must be based on a periodic weighting of potential risks and demonstrated benefits.

8. Drug treatment of disordered behavior must never be prescribed in isolation. It must always be considered as one component of a comprehensive management plan. When used appropriately, medication can make a child more available to benefit from the educational interventions and other environmental manipulations that make up the core of a total treatment package. Consequently, drugs should be a late aspect of a program, and never the first.

9. Inattentive children should be treated with drugs for their own sake, and not for the convenience of others who may not like their personalities. The purpose of medication is to facilitate more productive behavior that will promote learning and enhance self-esteem.

10. The physician who prescribes medication for behavioral disorders in children has a responsibility to remain informed about the most recent research in that area. New information must be carefully analyzed to establish its reliability, validity, and relevance for one's clinical practice.

Stimulant Medications

Stimulant medications have been used for the treatment of "hyperactive" children for more than 40 years, since Bradley (1937) first described the beneficial effects of racemic amphetamine on 30 children with serious behavioral disturbances. After a long latent period following this initial report, the use of pharmacologic agents for school children with behavioral problems peaked in the 1960s. During the last ten years, drug therapy has become a more controversial issue (Schrag and Divoky 1975).

The stimulant medications have clearly been the most frequently employed and most extensively studied pediatric psychopharmacologic agents. Most of the available literature has focused on the use of methylphenidate and amphetamines, with relatively less work on magnesium pemoline and caffeine. Although the clinical efficacy of central nervous system stimulants for a subgroup of children with attention deficits is generally well accepted, methodological problems in the existing literature have contributed to persistent confusion and controversy about the criteria for appropriate use.

Research Methodological Issues

The literature on stimulant drug therapy for "hyperactive" children is extensive, but incontrovertible findings are relatively scarce. Much of this is a result of methodological weaknesses, which have been discussed by a number of investigators (Grant 1962, Sprague and Werry 1971, Wolraich 1978). Some major problems will be discussed below (see Table 2).

1. There is a need for consistent criteria for defining "hyperactivity" and selecting children for study. No uniform diagnostic criteria have been developed, and the task of assembling homogeneous, or even comparable, groups for investigation has been severely compromised. Moreover, published studies vary across significant dimensions, such as the referral source of subjects (schools,

Table 2. Methodological Issues Regarding Stimulant Drug Research

Criteria for definition and selection of children
Objective measures of behavioral characteristics
Criteria for measuring behavioral change
Sample size and statistical analysis
Dosage and duration of treatment
Experimental design

institutions, neurology clinics, psychiatric clinics, pediatric practices, etc.), age of the participants, and sex. Since interobserver reliability for making a clinical diagnosis of "hyperactivity" has been shown to be poor (Kenny et al. 1971) and since variables such as age may be highly relevant, comparisons across studies are futile.

2. There is a need for objective, reliable, and valid measures of the behavioral characteristics to be assessed. Behaviors such as attention span, impulsivity, and persistence are elusive phenomena. If measured by a specific standardized task, such as reaction time or a continuous performance test, the results may reflect situation-specific behavior with limited generalizability. If global behavior rating scales are employed, problems arise with subjectivity and interobserver unreliability. In many cases, investigators have used different instruments or idiosyncratic measurement techniques, which automatically preclude cross-study comparisons. In the absence of valid parameters that reliably measure the behaviors to be studied, experimental results cannot readily be verified and must therefore remain tentative.

3. There is a need for well-standardized, objective criteria to define responses to treatment. This problem is related to the difficulty of defining the behavioral characteristic to be studied. Thus, in order to document improved attention span and decreased impulsivity, criteria for defining increments in these behaviors must be devised and uniformly employed.

4. There is a need for sufficiently large study populations to achieve statistically significant results. Published studies often have been based on the evaluation of a specific treatment on small numbers of children.

5. There is a need for uniform use of specific drug dosage and duration of treatment. Possible effects of varying drug dosage and lengths of time the children take medication must be considered when cross-study comparisons are made. The degree to which these variables have been controlled has varied in the literature.

6. There is a need for rigorous experimental design with appropriate control groups. Besides the factors discussed above, a number of prerequisites have been defined as necessary for valid research in this area, many of which are not found in a great number of published studies. These requirements for an acceptable study design include a placebo group, random assignment of cases to drug or control groups, a double-blind method, and elimination or control of experimental contaminants such as changed environment or concurrent therapy for one of the groups.

Many of the studies cited in this chapter fail to meet these criteria for valid research in this area. For that reason, many of the data remain tentative or speculative. In some studies, such as those that fail to employ a double-blind design, the fault lies in poor choice of methods. For others, such as those that fail to use highly reliable and valid criteria for measuring changes in behavior, the reason may be more a function of limitations of knowledge. For both reasons, a great deal of research remains to be done before the definitive role of stimulant medication for "hyperactivity" is resolved. As Eisenberg (1972) warned, however: "Medical practice does not permit the physician the luxury of deferring decisions until knowledge is certain. His task is to weigh putative benefits against putative risks in a strategy designed to maximize the probability of improvement for a particular patient." Thus, in the absence of ultimate answers to many of the basic questions, the practicing physician must make decisions about which of his patients called "hyperactive" should be given a trial of medication, what drug should be used, and for how long.

Pharmacology

Much of the literature on the mode of action of central nervous system stimulants in children is based upon work with the amphetamines. These drugs are sympathomimetic phenylethylamines which exist as dextro- or levo-rotary forms determined by methyl group substitution at the alpha carbon of the side chain of the molecule. The amphetamines are rapidly absorbed after oral administration and distributed throughout the body, with particular concentration in kidney, lung, and brain tissue. The central nervous system effects of an oral dose are generally first noted within 30 minutes, peak at two hours, and have disappeared by four to six hours. The lack of appreciable drug accumulation in body tissues allows frequent changes in dosage without difficulty. From 60 to 70% of an amphetamine is metabolized, with the remainder excreted unchanged in the urine (Baldessarini 1972).

Methylphenidate is a piperidine derivative that is structurally related to amphetamine and has essentially the same pharmacological properties. Relatively little is known about the absorption, distribution, and metabolism of methylphenidate in children (Goodman and Gilman 1975). There is evidence to suggest that it acts as an inhibitor of hepatic microsomal enzymes and may therefore cause decreased breakdown of drugs that are normally metabolized through such mechanisms, such as diphenylhydantoin and the tricyclic antidepressants.

Some degree of controversy exists over the precise mechanism of action of the amphetamines in the central nervous system. Like all sympathomimetic agents, they increase the availability of neurotransmitter substances for postsynaptic receptor sites by facilitating the release and inhibiting the reuptake of catecholamines. Although the precise locus of action in the central nervous system has not been documented, the ascending reticular formation of the brain stem and structures in the midbrain-diencephalon have been suggested (Goodman and Gilman 1975).

Methylphenidate has been described as a milder central nervous system stimulant than the amphetamines. Among the latter group, the *d*-isomer (dextroamphetamine) has been shown to be approximately four times as potent as the *l*-isomer.

Magnesium pemoline is an oxazolidine that has a half-life of about 12 hours, during which psychostimulant activity persists without sympathomimetic cardiovascular effects. It has been reported to stimulate RNA synthesis in the brain, although its precise mechanism of action is not known. Although previous use of this medication was restricted to adults with symptoms relating to senility, anxiety, depression, and schizophrenia, it has been approved by the Food and Drug Administration for the treatment of "hyperactive" children.

Indications for Use

The proper selection of children for whom stimulant medication would be appropriate is a critical medical responsibility. The difficulty of this task, however, was underlined by the Council on Child Health of the American Academy of Pediatrics (1975), which noted that more confusion exists regarding diagnosis and criteria for use of medication than for choice of drug. The current state of the art is such that diagnostic laboratory studies or pathognomonic findings are not available to help in this decision. The physician's response therefore depends upon clinical judgment, based upon a critical analysis of historical information in conjunction with careful examination and observation of the child.

Barkley (1977) reviewed over 110 studies involving more than 4200 "hyperactive" children and found that approximately 75% "improved" after treatment with stimulant medication (dextroamphetamine, methylphenidate, or magnesium pemoline), while about 25% remained the same or deteriorated. A number of studies have been conducted to attempt to identify possible variables that might prospectively discriminate drug responders from those who do not demonstrate a beneficial response. In a useful review of 36 research reports involving more than 1400 children, a variety of categories of variables were analyzed for their predictive value (Barkley 1976).

Psychophysiological parameters have been carefully studied over the years in the search for a biological marker for stimulant drug responsiveness. Investigators have carefully scrutinized a number of variables that have been postulated to bear some relationship to attention span. These include electroencephalograms (looking for mild abnormalities) (Satterfield et al. 1973, Rapoport et al. 1974, Weiss et al. 1971, Schain and Reynard 1975), average evoked potentials for visual and auditory stimuli (to evaluate thresholds for response to stimuli) (Buchsbaum and Wender 1973, Satterfield et al. 1972), skin conductance responses (to evaluate autonomic arousal levels) (Satterfield et al. 1972, Zahn et al. 1975), baseline heart rates and decelerations (Zahn et al. 1975, Barkley and Jackson 1976, Porges et al. 1975), baseline respiratory rates (Barkley and Jackson 1976), electropupillograms (a measure of reaction to light which may reflect autonomic arousal level and possibly correlate with attention span) (Yoss and Mayers 1971, Knopp et al. 1973), and free amphetamine recovery from urine (to evaluate metabolic disposition of the drug) (Epstein et al. 1968). All of these variables have been reported to differentiate stimulant drug responders from nonresponders. For many, however, contradictory results have been reported by different investigators. None of these parameters has been conclusively demonstrated to be a reliable biological marker for drug-responsive "hyperactivity."

Neurological factors have been extensively studied, with particular emphasis on the demonstration of "soft signs" and the differentiation between "organic" and "nonorganic" hyperactivity. Reports on all counts have been contradictory. Whereas some investigators have reported a high correlation between the presence of soft signs and the degree of drug responsiveness, others have found no relationship (Satterfield et al. 1972, Satterfield et al. 1973, Weiss et al 1971). Attempts to categorize children on the basis of historical, developmental, cognitive, or neurological evidence of "organicity" have similarly yielded no consistent correlations with response to stimulant therapy (Knights and Hinton 1969, Rie et al. 1976).

Demographic and sociofamilial factors have been examined for their relationship to drug responsiveness, with little consistent positive yield. (Schleifer et al.

1975, Loney et al. 1975, Hoffman et al. 1974). Whereas no consistent correlations have been demonstrated for such variables as age, race, sex, or socioeconomic status, most (but not all) data seem to show that hyperactive children from families with stable and positive dynamics are more likely to show improvement on stimulant medication than children from families troubled by disorganization or marital discord.

Although the use of behavior rating scales has been widespread in both clinical and educational settings, research has not consistently demonstrated their value as predictors of drug response. Neither parent nor teacher reports, nor the behavioral ratings of medical or psychological clinicians, have been reported to show sufficient sensitivity to preselect a subgroup of hyperactive children who will show a dramatic improvement on medication (Rapoport et al. 1971, Rie et al. 1976, Zahn et al. 1975, Barcai 1971, Werry and Sprague 1974). Although the sophistication and judgment of the informant completing the behavior rating scale can vary significantly, the greatest limitation of these instruments is that they often do not specifically assess the constructs that they are intended to measure.

The presence or absence of specific emotional difficulties is another dimension that has been explored with regard to the usefulness of stimulant medication (Fish 1971, Conrad and Insel 1967, Arnold et al. 1973). Although diagnostic distinctions in this area have been traditionally difficult, experience suggests that highly anxious or aggressive children with "hyperactive behavior disorders" are less likely to show a dramatic response to drugs than children with hyperkinetic behavior associated primarily with inattention.

Perhaps the most extensive work in the area of drug research and "hyperactivity" has been focused on the relationship between performance on a variety of psychological instruments and drug responsiveness. Again, no single test has been found to be a highly sensitive indicator on a consistent basis. Of the broad spectrum of assessment tools reviewed by Barkley (1976), however, the greatest degree of predictability was found with those diagnostic techniques most dependent on attention, such as Porteus Mazes, Kagan's Matching Familiar Figures Test, reaction-time tasks, and the number of toy changes during an observed free-play period (Rapoport et al. 1971, Rapoport et al. 1974, Porges et al. 1975, Routh et al. 1974).

In summary, despite an extensive literature reflecting a broad scope of interdisciplinary investigation, no simple battery of instruments or laboratory studies has been developed to guide the physician in the determination of a child's suitability for stimulant medication. Although those variables most closely related to selective attention appear to be the most sensitive predictors (Conners 1972a), the methodological limitations of studies in this area preclude the simple translation of current knowledge into definitive clinical guidelines. Thus, the practicing physician is generally faced with the need to decide on the use of stimulant medication without the benefit of well-established indications. This has led to the phenomenon of the therapeutic trial as a diagnostic procedure.

A word of caution should be added about the use of such a therapeutic trial. Almost all children will show initial evidence of a positive drug response, characterized by increased alertness and greater selective attention (Rapoport et al. 1978). This observation may result from a placebo as well as a pharmacological effect. In either case, an initial clinical response cannot be considered confirmation of the indication for drug therapy. In children for whom medication may be most appropriate, the dysfunction should be significant, and the clinical response should be dramatic and unequivocal. Since pharmacologic therapy must always be considered as an adjunct to a comprehensive program of behavioral management and individualized academic experiences (see Chapters 6 and 9), it is rarely indicated if its effects are subtle. Thus, the proper selection of patients for continuous treatment is critical.

Most clinicians will consider stimulant medication only for children between the ages of 5 and 12 years. Under 5 years, drug responses are most unpredictable, and some children actually experience a worsening of symptoms. Drug treatment in this younger group, although not absolutely contraindicated, must be undertaken with caution and reserved for the most difficult cases. For children under 5, dextroamphetamine is the drug of choice. For the adolescent age group, the use of stimulants is highly controversial. Although certain situations clearly warrant such treatment, the response to the medication in this age group is less consistently dramatic, and the availability of such drugs is potentially problematic.

Generally speaking, the ultimate decision about prescribing stimulant medication can only be reached by the use of enlightened clinical judgment with careful monitoring and follow-up of the response. Possible risks must always be weighted against potential benefits.

Clinical Use of Specific Agents

Methylphenidate and Dextroamphetamine. Among the stimulant medications, methylphenidate hydrochloride and dextroamphetamine sulfate are those whose effectiveness is best documented (see Table 3).

Methylphenidate (Ritalin) is begun at a dosage of 5 mg per day, given before breakfast. If there is no significant clinical response, the dose may be raised 5 to 10 mg each week, until either a positive therapeutic effect is achieved, signs of toxicity are noted, or a maximal dosage of 60 mg per day has been reached. If the beneficial effects of medication tend to wear off by the afternoon, a lunchtime dose can be added, provided the maximum daily dosage of 60 mg is not surpassed. Similarly, for children who show significant deterioration during late afternoon and evening, a third dose can be added in midafternoon. Although tolerance to a previously effective level of medication is generally not a significant problem in children, it does occur, and it can be managed by either an increase in dosage, change to another medication (e.g., dextroamphetamine), or a discontinuation of drug therapy for two weeks followed by resumption at a lower dose. If no clear-cut response to medication is seen after one month of treatment at a maximal level, then the drug should be discontinued.

The data on dosage levels for methylphenidate suggest that careful titration may be important. Although some clinicians have suggested dosages as high as 2 mg/kg, Werry and Sprague (1974) reported comparable effectiveness with 0.3 mg/kg. Moreover, Sprague and Sleator (1977) discovered differential effects of methylphenidate on learning and social behavior. Their data demonstrated peak enhancement of performance in a short-term memory task (learning) at a dosage

Table 3. Stimulant Medications Used for Treatment of Attention Deficits

Generic Name	Brand Name	Preparations	Range of Daily Dose (average)	Onset of Action	Duration of Action	Comments
Methylphenidate	Ritalin	Tablets: 5; 10; 20 mg	5–60 mg (10–30) (0.3–1.0 mg/kg)	30 min	3–5 hr	Not recommended below 6 years
Dextroamphetamine	Dexedrine	Tablets: 5 mg; sustained re-lease capsules: 5; 10; 15 mg	5–40 mg (5–20)	30 min	3–5 hr	Not recommended below 3 years
Pemoline	Cylert	Tablets: 18.75; 37.5; 75 mg	18.75–112.5 mg (56.25–75)	2–4 hr (may not see clinical results until 3–4 weeks of therapy)	"Long-acting"	Not recommended below 6 years

of 0.3 mg/kg and peak improvement on the Conners Rating Scale (behavior) at a dosage of 1.0 mg/kg. Of further significance was the observation that performance in the memory test showed deterioration as the dosage was raised above 0.3 mg/kg. The implications of these data are most significant, suggesting that drug therapy can be prescribed to facilitate learning, apart from controlling social behavior as an end in itself.

Dextroamphetamine (Dexedrine) is begun at a dosage of 2.5 mg per day, given before breakfast. Midday doses may be indicated, and weekly incremental raises of 2.5 to 5 mg per dose can be prescribed to a maximum of 40 mg per day, or until therapeutic or toxic responses are seen. Tolerance to dextroamphetamine may be managed as described for methylphenidate. Specific data regarding the differential effects of varied dosages, as reported for methylphenidate, are not available for the amphetamines. Dextroamphetamine is also available in a sustained, time-release capsule form which allows for a single morning dose, without the need for a lunchtime pill.

The issue of "drug holidays" is somewhat controversial. Some clinicians prescribe medication for school days only, with no treatment on weekends and vacations. It has been suggested that tolerance to medication with the subsequent need for higher dosages can be minimized by such intermittent therapy. Others recommend continuous drug administration if attention problems and "hyperactivity" interfere with adjustment at home and in the neighborhood. Some children will request medication on nonschool days when attempting to complete homework or projects requiring sustained attention. In general, judicious management favors the restriction of medication to school days, with seven-day-a-week therapy reserved for children whose interpersonal and intrafamilial relationships are severly compromised without treatment.

All children receiving stimulant drugs should undergo periodic trials off medication. When there is an immediate and dramatic deterioration, treatment should be resumed. On the other hand, if, after two to three weeks of "drug holiday," the differences are perceived as less than substantial, serious consideration should be given to permanent discontination of medication. In most cases, pharmacotherapy can be stopped completely during a summer vacation. The child may return to school in the fall without resuming drug treatment unless impaired selective attention and overactivity significantly limit productivity and disrupt classroom adjustment. In extreme instances, an interruption of therapy may not be possible. The goal should always be to use drugs for the shortest possible duration in all cases.

Magnesium Pemoline. Magnesium pemoline (Cylert) is begun at a single daily dosage of 18.75 mg given before breakfast. This may be increased to 37.5 or 75 mg per day until a therapeutic response or toxic reaction is observed. Clinical use is identical to that described for methylphenidate and dextroamphetamine.

Deanol. Deanol (Deaner) is a central nervous system stimulant that has been used in a limited number of controlled studies and not found to be effective. It is rarely prescribed, and there appears to be no indication for its use clinically (Millichap 1973).

Therapeutic Results

Despite the methodological problems described above, a substantial body of experimental data has been accumulated to support the efficacy of CNS stimulants for carefully selected children with attention deficits and "hyperactivity." Misunderstandings about the specific therapeutic effects of such medication, however, have been a major source of controversy among the general population. Because of an emphasis on the most visible aspect of some children's behavior (i.e., motoric overactivity), many people have assumed that stimulant medication is intended to "sedate" and thereby facilitate better external control over a child's behavior. This interpretation was inadvertently supported by early explanations of the calming, "paradoxical effects" of stimulant medication on the behavior of hyperactive children.

Considerable experimental evidence has now been accumulated, however, to demonstrate that the essential effect of stimulant medication is hardly sedating. Rather, it is now fairly well accepted that CNS stimulants alter behavior primarily by strengthening a child's selective attention and by reducing distractibility and impulsivity. These conclusions are derived from a variety of investigations (Conners 1972b, Werry 1970, Weiss et al. 1971).

Perhaps the most convincing evidence comes from studies involving specific measures of attention. The most popular instruments employed for this type of assessment include continuous performance tests (vigilance test), Porteus Mazes, Kagan's Matching Familiar Figures Test, reaction-time tasks, and carefully monitored observations of the number of toys or activity changes made during a free-play session. In a majority of studies reported in the literature, improved performance was noted on medication (Schleifer et al. 1975, Sykes et al. 1972, Zahn 1975, Werry and Aman 1975, Rapoport et al. 1974). Although each of these instruments clearly measures a variety of variables, the ability to focus on a task and inhibit impulsive responses is a common demand made by them all (Barkley 1977).

The investigative use of standardized psychometric examinations has produced more equivocal data. Among intelligence tests, the Wechsler Intelligence Scale for Children has been employed most frequently. Various drug effects have been reported, including changes in verbal IQ, performance IQ, full-scale IQ, and individual subtest scores (Conners 1972a, Hoffman et al. 1974, Weiss et al. 1971). However, no consistent effects of medication have been shown. Most investigators have concluded from these results that stimulant medication has its effect on attention during test taking, rather than on information processing itself (Barkley 1977).

Studies of medication effects on drawing and copying skills (e.g., Bender Gestalt Test, Goodenough Test) have yielded similar results. No consistent drug effects have been demonstrated, and those changes that have been documented were presumed to be secondary to improved attention (Conners 1971, Weiss et al. 1971). A recent report of specific improvement in handwriting after treatment with methylphenidate suggests the need for further study in this area (Lerer et al. 1977).

Behavioral rating scales have been used extensively to monitor responses to medication. Among the most widely used instruments are the Conners Teacher Rating Scale (Conners 1969), the Conners Parent Symptom Questionnaire

(Conners et al. 1969) and the Werry-Weiss-Peters Activity Rating Scale (Werry 1968). Data from these instruments provide considerable support for the selective attention–impulsivity dimension of drug response (Barkley 1977). Problems of test validity and interobserver reliability, however, have not been adequately resolved.

Psychophysiological studies have attempted, with limited success, to provide an alternative means to quantify the response to medication. Measurements of change in respiratory rate, blood pressure, heart rate, basal skin conductance, and electroencephalogram patterns (including average evoked potentials) have all produced equivocal or frankly contradictory results (Barkley 1977). Objective measures of actual activity level have yielded similarly inconclusive data, with reported improvement in seat restlessness and ankle fidgeting, but no change in the number of times a child is out of his seat or away from his desk (Christensen and Sprague 1973, Schliefer 1975). The general results of these latter studies show changes in activity level to be less significant than changes in attention.

In summary, present data appear to support the conclusion that a majority of appropriately selected children are "stimulated" by methylphenidate and the amphetamines rather than sedated. The drug effects appear to improve attention and inhibit distractible and impulsive behavior. Changes in intellectual abilities, academic achievement, or sensorimotor skills may be seen, but they are likely to be secondary to the effect of improved attention, rather than actual changes in abilities themselves. By increasing alertness, the stimulant medications facilitate more organized and purposeful behavior, which, in turn, leads to improvement in social adjustment and academic productivity. This effect is strengthened if appropriate supportive services are made available. The need for a comprehensive management program for children who are treated with drugs is thus critical. Medication alone is unlikely to result in sustained, improved academic performance or dramatic enhancement of social adjustment. It will, however, make the child with primary attention deficits more available and receptive to individualized teaching and sensitive behavioral management. Thus, the prescription of stimulant medication should follow rather than precede the development and implementation of a carefully tailored educational plan (see Chapter 6).

Adverse Side-Effects

Amphetamines and methylphenidate are drugs of relatively low toxicity. Side effects are rarely serious enough to warrant discontinuing treatment. When they do occur, adverse reactions are somewhat unpredictable and not consistently related to dosage.

The most commonly reported side-effects (see Table 4) include anorexia and insomnia, both of which generally occur within the first few weeks of therapy. These symptoms are usually transient and tend to diminish as tolerance develops. Occasionally they disappear if the dosage of medication is decreased. Millichap (1977) reported that anorexia occurs in 50% of children taking methylphenidate, with a somewhat greater incidence with amphetamines. This effect can be minimized by giving the medication with meals. Insomnia is often avoided if drug administration is restricted to the morning hours, although isolated case studies have been reported in which previously erratic sleeping

Table 4. Side-Effects of Stimulant Medications

Common Side-Effects:
    insomnia (transient often)
    anorexia (transient often)
Rare Side-Effects:

growth problems (?)	hypersensitivity (rashes)
headaches	constipation
abdominal pains	nightmares
irritability	tremors
drowsiness	tics
nausea	tachycardia
dizziness	hypertension
anxiety	withdrawal
depression	dry mouth
euphoria	elevated liver enzymes
palpitations	(pemoline only)

    decrease threshold for seizures
    inhibit metabolism of phenobarbital,
        diphenylhydantoin, primidone (methylphenidate only)
Contraindications to Use:
    cardiovascular disease
    hypertension
    hyperthyroidism
    glaucoma
    known hypersensitivity
    marked anxiety or agitation
    concurrent use of MAO inhibitors

patterns in "hyperactive" children have been improved by stimulant medication, including a late-afternoon dose.

Growth suppression has prompted a great deal of concern regarding the chronic use of stimulant medication. Safer and Allen (1973) reported significant inhibition of growth in height and weight after long-term use of amphetamines, with eventual tolerance developing to the weight-suppressant effects, but not to the inhibition of height growth. Methylphenidate was shown to have no effect on growth when administered in daily dosages of less than 20 mg. For higher doses, the growth-suppressant effects were still less than that observed for amphetamines. In general, the degree of growth inhibition for both drugs was directly proportional to the amount and duration of treatment. In a follow-up study (Safer et al. 1975), cessation of stimulant medication over the summer was observed to be accompanied by a "rebound" phenomenon, with accelerated catch-up in weight and height. Other investigators have produced contradictory data that refute the existence of a statistically significant reduction in growth rate from long-term stimulant medication (Gross 1976). As long as this issue remains unresolved, the prudent clinician should monitor the growth of all children receiving drug therapy. If decelerated linear growth is documented, risk-benefit calculations should be made regarding reduction or termination of medication.

Less frequently encountered side-effects of dextroamphetamine and methyl-phenidate are listed in Table 4. Although data in this regard are not conclusive, periodic monitoring of pulse and blood pressure is recommended.

The side-effects associated with magnesium pemoline are similar to those reported for the amphetamines and methylphenidate. Insomnia and anorexia are most common, with the former sometimes posing greater problems because of the drug's longer duration of action. The effects of pemoline on linear growth are less well studied. Some side-effects may appear as "rebound" phenomena, occurring in the evening hours after the drug effects should have worn off. In some cases, simply switching medications may be most useful. Alternatively, a decrease in dosage or total cessation of therapy may be indicated, depending upon the clinical situation.

Long-Term Effects

The long term effects of stimulant medication must be examined from two perspectives. From a pharmacologic point of view, except for questions about linear growth, there have been no documented adverse consequences of extended drug therapy. Despite theoretical concerns, no cardiovascular sequelae, such as persistent tachycardia or hypertension, have been reported. There is very little evidence of physical habituation, and no difficulties have been noted in association with drug withdrawal after prolonged administration. Moreover, because treated children do not generally experience a euphoric response to the medication, problems of later drug abuse do not appear to be any more frequent than reported for children who receive other chronic medications (e.g., insulin, anticonvulsants, etc.). Thus, current evidence suggests that the risks of long-term medication are negligible (Weiss et al. 1971, Werry 1968).

The long-term benefits of stimulant drugs are not well substantiated. Although short-term effects have been dramatic, studies have not been able to document significant changes in ultimate outcome. Some investigations have reported high rates of continuing behavioral disturbance and social failure (Minde et al. 1972). Thus, although short-term management goals may be facilitated by stimulant medication, later social, academic, and psychological adjustment does not appear to be appreciably altered. This phenomenon still needs further study. Nevertheless, this somewhat discouraging observation serves to underline the need for a comprehensive management approach that goes beyond the simple administration of medication.

Caffeine: An Alternative Stimulant

Several years ago, a number of clinicians anecdotally observed that some inattentive children voluntarily drank coffee because they reported it calmed them down and helped them to do better in school. Others noted that "hyperactivity" seemed to be highly prevalent in countries where children are predominantly milk drinkers (United States, Canada, British Isles) as compared to an alleged lower prevalence in South American countries, where children begin drinking coffee at an early age. The resultant hypothesis that caffeine is an effective treatment for hyperactivity was tested by Schnackenberg (1973) by giving one cup of coffee at breakfast and one cup at lunch (150 mg. of caffeine per 6-ounce cup) to 11 children previously found to be responsive to methylphenidate. The results of this uncontrolled study were reported as demonstrating that caffeine was as effective as methylphenidate, with fewer side-effects. Other investigators questioned whether the observed therapeutic effects were produced by caffeine alone or by its combination with other constituents of coffee. Several subsequent studies have produced a variety of contradictory results, with some data showing no difference between caffeine and placebo, and others suggesting exacerbation of symptoms from two cups of coffee per day (Gross 1975, Garfinkel et al. 1975, Reichard and Elder 1977).

Caffeine is a methylated xanthine derivative that occurs in plants whose extracts are used to make such beverages as coffee, tea, and cola-flavored soft drinks. It is a powerful central nervous system stimulant that excites the brain at the cortical, medullary, and spinal-cord levels. It remains to be seen whether a subgroup of children with attention deficits respond favorably to such a simple and presumably low-risk prescription as one or two cups of coffee each day. Generally speaking, however, current evidence does not consistently support the efficacy of caffeinated coffee.

Major Tranquilizers

Phenothiazines

Phenothiazine medications have been used extensively for the treatment of psychiatric disorders in adults and children for almost 30 years. Early uncontrolled studies reported significant benefits in children with regard to the reduction of agitation and overactivity and the amelioration of learning difficulties (Grant 1962). These preliminary findings resulted in widespread use of these drugs for the treatment of a wide variety of behavior disorders and learning problems. More recent controlled investigations of major tranquilizers have generated data showing either no measurable benefits or actual adverse effects on learning and cognitive function (Werry 1970). As a result, there has been a decrease in pediatric clinical use, except for more severely disturbed or psychotic children.

Among the more than two dozen phenothiazine preparations that are currently used in adult medicine, chlorpromazine (Thorazine) and thioridazine (Mellaril) have been prescribed and studied most extensively in children. When used for the treatment of youngsters with attention deficits, both medications have been shown to be effective in reducing acitivity levels but appear to have no significant impact on the associated symptoms of distractibility and poorly selective attention (Werry et al. 1966, Gittleman-Klein 1976). Some clinicians have suggested that phenothiazines reduce activity through their sedative effect, which simultaneously results in impaired learning abilities. Other investigators have warned that prolonged use of phenothiazines can have sustained adverse effects on cognitive functions (Helper et al. 1963).

Dosages for the phenothiazines are summarized in Table 5. Side-effects are common, with thioridazine appearing to be somewhat less toxic than chlorpromazine (see Table 6). The most frequent symptoms include lassitude and drowsiness, which is generally a greater problem during the first few weeks of therapy. Extrapyramidal symptoms are less commonly encountered, but may

Table 5. Major Tranquilizers Used for Treatment of Severe Psychiatric Disorders

Generic Name	Brand Name	Preparations	Range of Daily Dose (average)	Comments
Chlorpromazine	Thorazine	Tablets: 10; 25; 50; 100 mg	10–100 mg (10–30) (1.0 mg/kg)	Not recommended below 6 years Maximum improvement may not be seen for several weeks or even months
Thioridazine	Mellaril	Tablets: 10; 15; 25; 50; 100 mg	20–200 mg (20–100) (0.5–3.0 mg/kg)	Not recommended below 2 years
Haloperidol	Haldol	Tablets: 0.5; 1; 2; 5 mg	Insufficient data available for children	Not recommended for pediatric use Suggested single morning dose 0.025 mg/kg (Werry et al. 1976)

range from mild tremors to severe Parkinsonism or tardive dyskinesia. Other adverse reactions include blood dyscrasias, hepatic damage, corneal and/or lenticular deposits, pigmentary retinopathy, photosensitivity reactions, endocrine dysfunction, weight gain as a result of increased appetite, and enuresis. Many of the serious side-effects are hypersensitivity responses and are therefore not dose-related. In such cases, discontinuation of medication is essential. In general,

Table 6. Side-Effects of Major Tranquilizers

Drowsiness
Extrapyramidal symptoms
Jaundice
Blood dyscrasias, especially agranulocytosis
Hypotensive effects
EKG changes
Seizures
Allergic reactions, including photosensitivity
Skin pigmentation
Ocular changes
Enuresis or urinary retention
Increased appetite
Gastrointestinal complaints
Endocrine disturbances, including gynecomastia or thyroid problems
Dry mouth

it is advisable to monitor liver function tests and complete blood counts in the early stages of therapy with the phenothiazines.

In summary, chlorpromazine and thioridazine have been demonstrated to be effective inhibitors of hyperactivity, agitation, tension, and anxiety in severely disturbed children. Clinical experience suggests that the use of these medications be restricted to such patients and not prescribed for children with primary attention deficits and less severe emotional maladjustment.

Butyrophenones

Haloperidol (Haldol), the most commonly prescribed butyrophenone, is an extremely potent antipsychotic agent that is closely related to the piperazine phenothiazines. It has been used effectively for the treatment of agitation, social disruptiveness, and assaultive behavior in emotionally disturbed youth, as well as for the control of tics in Gilles de La Tourette Syndrome (Werry et al. 1976, Werry and Aman 1975). The side-effects associated with haloperidol treatment are similar to those of the other major tranquilizers, with a greater incidence of extrapyramidal reactions, expecially in younger children. In addition, it has been shown to potentiate the toxic effects of imipramine and to lower the threshold for generalized seizures. As with the phenothiazines, the indications for the use of haloperidol appear to be restricted to psychotic or severely disturbed children. Dosage guidelines are shown in Table 5.

Minor Tranquilizers

Minor tranquilizers are prescribed with greater frequency in adult medicine than any other drugs. The benzodiazepine compounds have been used most commonly in pediatric practice, and include chlordiazepoxide (Librium) and diazepam (Valium). These medications are indicated for the relief of anxiety and are therefore not useful for the treatment of children whose attention deficits are secondary to constitutional problems. In clinical situations where such behavior is felt to be essentially secondary to anxiety, counseling and environmental manipulation should be extensively pursued before consideration is given to pharmacologic management.

Tricyclic Antidepressants

A number of controlled and partially controlled studies have been reported on the use of tricyclic antidepressants for the treatment of children with nocturnal enuresis, school phobia, and attention deficits (Rapoport et al. 1974, Gross 1973, Huessy and Wright 1970). Imipramine (Tofranil), a dibenzazepine derivative, has been the agent most extensively employed. Many clinicians regard it as the second drug of choice after stimulant medications for the treatment of "hyperactivity." Although not shown to be better than placebo, or as effective as methylphenidate, in improving performance on attention-requiring tasks (Spring et al. 1974), imipramine has been noted to produce improved behavioral ratings by parents, teachers, and clinicians (Waizer et al. 1974). Although its mechanism of action for reducing inattentive behavior is not well understood, it is of interest that, like the amphetamines, it may increase the relative amounts of norepinephrine in the central nervous system (Goodman and Gilman 1975).

In terms of its clinical use, imipramine has the advantage of longer duration of action than most stimulants; it can therefore be given on a twice-daily schedule, which does not require a midday school dose. Dosage guidelines are shown in Table 7. Because of the relative paucity of data on the range of safety and side-effects of imipramine in children, it must be used with caution, especially if chronic treatment is anticipated. Side-effects include personality changes, hypertension, anorexia, and drowsiness (although insomnia is occasionally observed). As with stimulants, height growth and blood pressure should be monitored, and "drug holidays" prescribed. Because tolerance to the effects of the medication may develop, higher, potentially cardiotoxic dosages might be required to achieve a continuing therapeutic response. Evidence of electrocardiographic abnormalities has been reported (Winsberg et al. 1975). Some investigators have suggested the further possibility that imipramine may lower the threshold for a clinical seizure disorder (Brown et al. 1973). The risk of severe cardiac arrhythmias with potentially fatal consequences, as a result of an overdose of imipramine, makes it dangerous medication, especially in a home with young children. Appropriate warning to family members is mandatory.

Anticonvulsants

Anticonvulsant medications have been prescribed for the treatment of behavioral and learning problems in children found to have abnormal electroencephalographic recordings without clinical evidence of seizures. Although phenobarbital will frequently exacerbate "hyperactive" behavior, and is therefore contraindicated, other medications such as diphenylhydantoin (Dilantin), primidone (Mysoline), and carbamazepine (Tegretal) have been used clinically with some reported, but inconsistently documented, success. Millichap et al.

Table 7. Tricyclic Antidepressant Sometimes Used for Treatment of "Attention Deficits"

Generic Name	Brand Name	Preparations	Range of Daily Dose (average)	Comments
Imipramine	Tofranil	Tablets: 10; 25; 50 mg	10–100 mg (10–50)	Generally not recommended for use in children other than for enuresis Not recommended for use below 6 years Adverse reactions include personality changes, cardiovascular problems, drowsiness, blood dyscrasias, gastrointestinal symptoms, seizures, anorexia, insomnia, dizziness

(1969) described the successful treatment of auditory perceptual deficits with diphenylhydantoin, and they suggested that improved learning may result from the use of such medication when auditory perceptual and memory deficits are associated with EEG abnormalities.

The indications for anticonvulsant therapy in this area are controversial. There is little conclusive evidence that it has any specific effect on either behavioral problems or learning ability. In children with documented convulsive disorders, no consistent relationship has been shown to exist between the degree of seizure control and the presence of behavioral disorders. In children without clinical seizures, who may have paroxysmal spikes and waves on their electroencephalogram, however, some clinicians recommend a therapeutic trial of diphenylhydantoin despite the lack of well-controlled data to support the efficacy of any such approach. In the absence of such data, the use of a potentially toxic medication such as diphenylhydantoin must be weighted against alternative management options.

Antihistamines

A variety of antihistamines have been used clinically to treat "hyperactive" children, with relatively little documented benefit. Diphenhydramine hydrochloride (Benadryl) has been tried for its sedative action in an attempt to produce a "calming effect," with no reported consistent success. Moreover, the resulting drowsiness often proves to be counterproductive with respect to the child's availability for optimal learning. Despite its ineffectiveness in modifying hyperactive behavior, diphenhydramine occasionally provides effective evening sedation when a bedtime dose is given to children who have trouble falling asleep. In some cases, however, paradoxical excitation may occur, which is not unlike the toxic reaction to an antihistamine overdose.

The use of antihistamines for their antiallergic actions is a highly controversial issue in the management of behavior disorders. The role of allergic factors in the etiology of "hyperactivity" is discussed in further detail later in this chapter.

Hydroxyzine hydrochloride (Atarax) and hydroxyzine pamoate (Vistaril), antihistaminic sedatives with anti-anxiety effects, have been prescribed for the daytime management and nighttime sedation of "hyperactive" children. They, too, have received the endorsement of many clinicians without the substantiation of controlled investigation. One private pediatric practice experience reported the successful use of hydroxyzine hydrochloride for 58 children between the ages of 2 and 16 years with a wide variety of behavior problems ranging from temper tantrums and irritability to marked excitability, discipline problems, and stuttering (Nathan and Andelman 1957). Limited data on clinical experience with these medications in children make current recommendations difficult to determine.

Hypnotics and Sedatives

Many children with primary attention disorders have difficulty falling asleep or staying asleep (see Chapter 3). In some cases this phenomenon can present major problems for the family, and the plea for a "sleeping pill" may become quite impassioned.

As noted above, barbiturates are contraindicated in such cases, but a bedtime dose of an antihistamine such as diphenhydramine or hydroxyzine may occasionally be helpful. Chloral hydrate, one of the oldest members of the hypnotic group of medications, is often an effective alternative. At a dosage of 500 mg or 1 gm h.s., chloral hydrate will usually facilitate a full night's sleep with no significant side-effects. "Hangover" appears infrequently, and occasional gastrointestinal upset can be alleviated by giving the oral medication after eating, or administering by rectal suppository. Habitual use should be avoided, as tolerance and physical dependence can occur.

The role of stimulant medication in altering the sleep-wakefulness balance of children with primary attention deficits remains somewhat controversial. It has been suggested that such youngsters are neither fully awake nor fully asleep at any time, and that stimulant medication helps to normalize that cycle. Despite the frequent problem of increasing insomnia when treatment with psychostimulant drugs is begun, some clinicians have reported success treating sleeping problems in a number of these children by adding an afternoon dose of medication. Although the efficacy of this approach has not been well substantiated, a therapeutic trial might be indicated in situations where other alternatives are not feasible or have previously failed.

Megavitamins

Vitamins are low-molecular-weight organic compounds, many of which are precursors of the coenzymes necessary for normal metabolism. A number of disease states (e.g., vitamin D-dependent rickets, steatorrheas, pyridoxine-dependent seizure disorders) have been described whose pathophysiology is directly related to relatively deficient supplies of these substances. Dietary supplementation, or substantially increased provision of vitamins, in such cases has been therapeutically successful. In otherwise healthy children, however, a normal diet supplies the recommended dietary allowances of the common vitamins, and the Committee on Nutrition of the American Academy of Pediatrics (1967) has consistently indicated that additional intake for such children is not necessary.

The use of massive dosages of vitamin preparations, known as megavitamin therapy, was first introduced into clinical medicine in the 1950s by practitioners who were experimenting with the effects of nicotinic acid and nicotinamide on adults with schizophrenia. Based upon the hypothesis that a mescaline like oxidation product of epinephrine is produced by a factor in the serum of schizophrenic patients, Hoffer and Osmond (1960) suggested that nicotinic acid would diminish the production of such a toxic substance by competing for methyl groups and thus prevent the conversion of norepinephrine to epinephrine. The clinical use of large doses of nicotinic acid along with vitamins C and B[6] was endorsed anecdotally, but no supportive control data were generated.

In the late 1960s Pauling lent prestigious support to the advocates of megavitamin therapy by postulating the concept of "orthomolecular medicine." Using a biochemical and genetic model, he argued that brain function is affected by its molecular environment and that the optimum concentrations of normally present substances for a given brain may differ substantially from those provided by normal diet and "metabolic machinery." Thus, it was hypothesized that an alteration of those concentrations might be an effective form of treatment for mental illness (Pauling 1968).

In the early 1970s, Cott (1971) introduced the use of orthomolecular techniques for the treatment of children with learning disabilities. Partly on the basis of his early work with autistic and schizophrenic youngsters, he annnounced that parent and teacher reports endorsed the efficacy of megavitamin therapy for children with a variety of learning and behavioral disorders.

Formal responses to these new therapies were prompt and emphatic. The American Psychiatric Association (1973) established a Task Force on Vitamin Therapy in Psychiatry which concluded that, in view of the lack of support for the theoretical basis of such treatment, and the absence of controlled studies demonstrating its efficacy, the current advocacy of orthomolecular treatment and megavitamin therapy through the mass media was "deplorable." The Committee on Nutrition of the American Academy of Pediatrics (1976) followed with a policy statement on the use of megavitamin therapy for childhood psychoses and learning disabilities. The committee reiterated the lack of evidence supporting the use of megavitamins in adult schizophrenics or in children with learning disabilities or psychoses and charged that such therapy "is not justified on the basis of documented clinical results."

Although some clinicians continue to prescribe massive doses of vitamins for a variety of developmental disorders, such an approach must be recognized as nonconventional and unproved. Beyond the lack of documented effectiveness, physicians must also consider the potential risks of toxicity, such as increased intracranial pressure with elevated levels of vitamin A, and potential hepatotoxicity from long-term administration of high doses of nicotinic acid (Winter and Boyer 1973).

Thyroid Medications

Although behavioral and academic difficulties are often among the presenting symptoms of hypothyroidism or hyperthyroidism in school-age children, the differential diagnosis is readily resolved through the recognition of the other characteristic manifestations of a thyroid disorder, which are generally quite distinctive. If such a diagnosis is made, appropriate treatment of the underlying disease will result in improved school performance. In the absence of documented thyroid dysfuntion, however, there is no evidence that thyroid hormone therapy will be of any benefit in the treatment of learning or behavioral problems.

A few isolated studies have been reported on the use of hormonal preparations. Because of observed mood elevation from thyrotropin-releasing-hormone (TRH) in depressed adults, and its reported calming effects on an emotionally labile, retarded adolescent, Tiwary et al. (1975) investigated its effect on two six-year-old children with normal intelligence and "minimal brain dysfunction." They reported a dramatic behavioral response within three or four hours of an intravenous dose, with improved "quality of task and play performance." In a related study of ten children using a double-blind crossover design, however, O'Tuama et al. (1977) could find no difference between TRH and placebo. In view of the currently available data, the potential risks of hormone therapy in clinical practice far outwiegh the unlikely possibility of any therapeutic effect.

Other Medications

Lithium carbonate is a salt that has essentially no psychotropic effect on normal adults but has been demonstrated to be therapeutically effective in the treatment of the manic phase of manic-depressive illness. It has been used to treat children with attention deficits and has been found to be of no benefit (Greenhill et al. 1973).

Levodopa (L-DOPA) is an intermediary metabolite in the enzymatic synthesis of catecholamines that is used to treat Parkinson's disease in adults. In a single case report, it was successfully used to treat a so-called "hyperactive" 14-year-old boy who did not respond favorably to dextroamphetamine, methylphenidate, imipramine, and a variety of other drugs (Gross 1977). No data are currently available to warrant its clinical use for youngsters with attention deficits.

DIETARY MANAGEMENT

In June 1973, Ben Feingold delivered an address at the annual meeting of the American Medical Association in New York in which he charged that "hyperactivity" was primarily associated with ingestion of low-molecular-weight chemicals such as salicylates and common food additives (Feingold et al. 1973). In September of that year in London he presented a similar paper, which was subsequently read into the *Congressional Record* of the United States Congress (Beal 1973)! These presentations marked the beginning of a rather controversial history whose final chapter has yet to be written.

Theory

Feingold, former director of the Allergy Clinic at the Kaiser-Permanente Medical Center in California, originally observed subjective behavioral improvement in an emotionally disturbed adult with known aspirin hypersensitivity who was placed on a diet free of salicylates and artificial flavors and colors. Because of the presumed cross-reactivity between salicylates and artificial colors, especially tartrazine (yellow FD&C number 5 dye), Feingold prescribed a comparable elimination diet for "hyperactive" children, with an additional caveat against the "natural salicylates" found in many fruits. He then wrote a popular book entitled *Why Your Child is Hyperactive* (1975). He reported that 30% to 50% of 25 "hyperactive" children in his clinical practice became essentially free of symptoms within four weeks after being placed on a strict diet that excluded all salicylates and artificial food colors and flavors. No statistical analysis of these results was provided. The theoretical explanation for this reported clinical phenomenon was said to be a genetic "variation" (i.e., not an "abnormality") that predisposes some children to an adverse reaction to synthetic additives. Feingold stressed that "the hyperactive disturbance is nonimmunologic" and that it is an inborn chemical response, affecting the central nervous system through an "innate releasing mechanism." It was noted specifically that this constitutional condition is toxic, not allergic, and that there is no natural body defense against it. Moreover, the theory postulates the need for lifelong abstinence from the offending agents.

Clinical Application

The so-called Feingold Diet (or K-P Diet, for Kaiser-Permanente) is based upon the elimination of two groups of foods: those containing natural salicylates, including a number of fruits and two vegetables (tomato and cucumber), and those containing a synthetic color or flavor (see Table 8). The former group was originally thought to include apples, apricots, almonds, berries, cherries, currants, grapes, raisins, nectarines, oranges, plums, prunes, and peaches. However, recent analyses have found little or no salicylate in some of the previously forbidden fruits (*Medical Letter,* 1978). The food-additive group

Table 8. The "K-P Diet"

Group I: Natural Salicylates

Fruits

Almonds	Currants
Apples	Grapes
Apricots	Raisins
Blackberries	Nectarines
Boysenberries	Oranges
Gooseberries	Peaches
Raspberries	Plums
Strawberries	Prunes
Cherries	

Vegetables

Tomatoes
Cucumbers

Group II: Artificial Colors and Flavors
(All foods containing synthetic colors or flavors are prohibited)

Common Items

Most cereals
Manufactured cakes, cookies, pastries, doughnuts, etc.
Luncheon meats (bologna, salami, frankfurters, sausages, most pork products)
Most manufactured ice creams, sherbets, ices, gelatins, puddings
Powdered puddings and dessert mixes
Flavored yogurt
All manufactured candies
Cider, wine, beer
All soft drinks (regular and diet)
All instant breakfast drinks
All powdered sweet drinks
Tea
Oleomargarine, colored butter
Mustard, ketchup, chili sauce
All mint-flavored items, cloves
Cider or wine vinegar
Commercial chocolate syrup
Most (almost all) pediatric medications and vitamins
All toothpastes and tooth powder
All mouthwashes, cough drops, throat lozenges

includes most cereals, desserts, cakes, cookies, luncheon meats, soft drinks, flavored yogurts, butter, margarine, gum, candy, vitamins, and toothpaste. Moreover, artificial colors and flavors are added to almost all pediatric medications, and many over-the-counter drugs contain salicylates.

The most obvious characteristic of the K-P Diet is the substantial demand it places on a child and family. In order to be effective, according to its advocates, the diet must be adhered to 100%! A single bite of a prohibited food reportedly will produce an undesired behavioral response which can persist for at least three days. Thus, even the slightest infraction committed once every three or four days can eliminate totally any detectable benefits from the diet, even if rigid compliance is otherwise maintained. This postulated high degree of sensitivity necessitates meticulous perusal of package labels; thus, considerably more effort is needed for shopping. Since the list of forbidden foods contains the most popular "junk foods" consumed by large numbers of children, enforcement presents a major challenge to children and their families. Proponents of the K-P Diet offer recipes for additive-free cookies, cakes, and candies that can be prepared at home, but this obviously requires a great deal more effort than simply buying the commercially prepared products.

When initiating the K-P Diet, parents are advised to keep a "diet diary" in which *everything* that the child puts in his mouth is recorded, along with a running description of behavior and school performance. A good response may be dramatic or gradual and is said to be noticeable anywhere from the first week to as long as seven weeks after the diet is begun. Once improved behavior is well established, a dietary infringement will reportedly produce symptoms within two to four hours, gradually disappearing over the following three days.

In general, advocates of the K-P Diet suggest that the greatest benefits are noted when the entire family adheres to it. This has the advantage of eliminating the temptation of outlawed foods in the house as well as providing the secondary gain of group support. Once the diet has been well established and shown to be effective, it is permissible to liberalize the regimen gradually, by reintroducing one new food at a time, no more frequently than every four days, while monitoring carefully for recurrence of symptoms. Because of the general prohibition on most citrus fruits, supplementation with *unflavored* vitamin C (40 mg per day) is recommended.

The relationship between the K-P Diet and stimulant medication is presently unresolved. Some clinicians have reported that the effects of diet appear to be most striking when children are not receiving medication (Williams et al. 1978). Others report maximal improvement when both are used simultaneously, while still others have noted increased activity levels when drugs and diet are combined. None of these assertions has been well documented.

Evaluation and Research

The Feingold hypothesis, and its reported successful application for the treatment of "hyperactive" children, precipitated two diverse reactions. Among the general public, the proliferation of "Feingold Associations" reflected the enthusiastic reception of frustrated parents who welcomed a "scientific" treatment plan that did not require medication and that conformed easily to the antitechnological cultural emphasis on "natural" therapeutics (Levine and Liden 1976). Among the scientific community, however, the predictable demand for supporting data led to a more cautious, if not cynical, response.

The initial criticism of Feingold's work focused on the fact that his claims were based on subjective, impressionistic data from anecdotal reports. The children selected for his original case studies were not chosen by any standardized or well-validated process, and no controls were used to compare to the treatment group. The observers were aware of the treatment being given, and the measures used to evaluate change were subjective. Because of the emphasis on family involvement (such as suggestions that Saturday afternoons be spent on family projects making "additive-free" candies and cakes), the effects of an increased family commitment to help the affected child were not controlled, nor was the factor of suggestibility or placebo effect. Moreover, because of the absence of rigid monitoring, the possibility of "cheating" by the participants could not be eliminated.

Several critics observed that the chemical basis for the determination of the offending foods was not well defined. The arbitrary indictment of flavors and colors has been criticized as too simplistic, in view of the widely differing chemical structures of these hundreds of substances. Moreover, the distinction between "naturally occurring" and "synthetic" foods is often misleading, referring merely to the origins of the products rather than their chemical properties.

The nutritional aspects of the diet, and the possible risks of strict adherence, have also been emphasized. Some have criticized the low-carbohydrate content, while others have underlined the risk of vitamin-C deficiency, unless supplements are given. Expert committees have been established to study the issue of dietary treatment for "hyperactivity." Through The Nutrition Foundation, the American food industry set up a blue-ribbon National Advisory Committee on Hyperkinesis and Food Additives (1975), which conducted a study of the available information and presented the following conclusions:

1. No controlled studies have demonstrated that hyperkinesia is related to the ingestion of food additives.
2. The claim that hyperactive children improve significantly on a diet that is free of salicylates and food additives has not been confirmed.
3. The nutritional qualities of the Feingold Diet have not been evaluated, and it may not meet the long-term nutrient needs of children.
4. The diet should not be used without competent medical supervision.

Later that same year, the United States Food and Drug Administration established an Interagency Collaborative Group on Hyperkinesis, which published a report with similar conclusions (1976). Each of these groups emphasized the need for well-defined research.

Recent literature on the efficacy of the K-P Diet has been inconclusive. Several studies have offered favorable endorsements based upon uncontrolled case reports (Cook and Woodhill 1976, Stine 1976, Salzman 1976). Subsequent investigations employing controlled clinical studies have generated inconsistent data (Conners et al. 1976, Hurley et al. 1978, Williams et al. 1978). On the basis of current information, it appears that the role of food additives as an aggravating agent for "hyperactivity" remains unclear. Although some evidence suggests that a subpopulation of children may be treated effectively by appropriate dietary restrictions, solid data are not available to either help identify this subgroup or substantiate the claim that it exists.

In the face of inadequate data, some physicians are reluctant to advise dietary therapy, while others encourage therapeutic trials. Many pediatricians assert that a reduction in the intake of food additives is a good idea, regardless of its effect on hyperactivity, and provide support for families who indicate a desire to try the diet. Until the results of a definitive evaluation of this treatment are available, the physician must weigh its potential benefits against its possible disadvantages.

Other Dietary Treatments

The role of hypoglycemia in the genesis or exacerbation of attention deficits and learning problems has been suggested but not well explored. A number of social critics have argued that poor dietary habits and frequently missed breakfasts result in periods of hypoglycemia that contribute to school difficulties. In his report on the use of megavitamin therapy for disorders of learning, Cott charged that learning and behaviorally disabled children consume a diet generally high in carbohydrates and foods prepared with sugar and have a higher incidence of hypoglycemia and "dysinsulinism." No data beyond anecdotal references were provided (Cott 1971). Although the manifestations of hypoglycemia can include some of the characteristics described in children with a variety of behavioral or learning problems, the absence of the more classic symptoms such as sweating, tachycardia, and fainting makes the diagnosis unlikely. Not a shred of objective evidence has been produced to link low or low-normal levels of blood glucose with the phenomenon of poor learning, and any possible relationship must be considered speculative. Silver (1975) suggests that a full 5- to 7-hour glucose tolerance test should be performed before a conclusion is reached about the role of hypoglycemia in a child with learning problems. Current evidence does not support the contention that this is a common cause of school dysfunction (Millichap 1977).

The issue of trace elements has also been raised by proponents of orthomolecular therapy. Zinc, copper, magnesium, manganese, chromium, and a host of other substances have been suggested as possible etiologic factors in children whose diets are deficient in such elements and in those who appear to require increased intake for normal function (Silver 1975). No objective data have been published either to substantiate a theoretical reason for such a model or to demonstrate any improvement as a result of such treatment.

ALLERGY MANAGEMENT

The role of allergy in the pathogenesis of attention deficits and learning disorders has been debated for several decades. It remains an area of unresolved controversy. One of the first attempts to link allergic phenomena with neurobehavioral symptoms was made by Shannon (1922), who reported "neuropathic manifestations in infants and children as a result of anaphylactic reactions to foods." Randolph (1947) presented a number of case reports to illustrate that allergy can be a causative factor in children with fatigue, irritability, and behavior problems. He noted that these youngsters had characteristic difficulties with concentration and memory and were often considered to be "nervous" instead of "allergic." Randolph postulated that chronic food allergy, especially to wheat and corn, was the usual culprit, and he urged that other contributing factors could be best evaluated after the allergic symptomatology was brought under control.

Speer (1958) elaborated on the "allergic-tension-fatigue syndrome" and described two clinical patterns: "allergic fatigue," characterized by "depressed neuropsychic activity," and "allergic tension," characterized by "exaggerated neuropsychic activity" with hyperkinesis and generalized heightened sensitivities. In view of the latter's similarity to the classic description of the "hyperactive child," the presumption of allergic etiology was felt to be supported. Other terms used in the literature include "cerebral allergy," "allergic toxemia," and "the allergic mental syndrome" (Speer 1954). In each of these cases a primary allergic effect on the central nervous system has been postulated. This model differs from the Feingold hypothesis, which suggests that the effect of food additives and natural salicylates is toxic rather than allergic.

Advocates of an allergic explanation for learning disorders and behavioral problems have interpreted a wide range of symptomatology within this framework. Thus, a history of early temperamental difficulties with "colic" has often been suggested as a manifestation of undiagnosed food allergy. Similarly, persistent enuresis, "tension headaches," and "psychogenic abdominal pain" have also been perceived as atopic phenomena by a number of clinicians. When these problems have been noted in children who present with none of the classic allergic conditions such as hayfever, eczema, or asthma, the presumption has been that "CNS" or "GI" allergy may be the only manifestation of atopy in such individuals.

Although the early literature on allergy and learning disorders was largely based on case reports, recent investigators have begun to produce group studies, many of which examine responses to dietary restriction and hyposensitization therapy based upon the results of extensive scratch and intradermal testing. Dramatic associations have been reported, including normalization of previously abnormal electroencephalograms (Kittler and Baldwin 1970) and improvements in IQ and achievement-test scores with alleviation of allergic symptoms (Millman et al. 1976). However, a number of major methodological weaknesses, including inadequate statistical analyses and the absence of sufficient controls, preclude any substantive conclusions.

Data are not available currently to support a primary etiologic role for allergic factors in the pathogenesis of attention deficits or other learning disorders. It is clear, however, that children can have their school problems exacerbated by conventional atopic symptomatology (as well as by many other symptoms of chronic disease). Upper respiratory congestion, persistent rhinitis, coughing, tearing, and itching all will interfere with a child's ability to sustain attention. Associated irritability and fatigue may be quite common. Moreover, increased illness and absence from school can contribute to a further deterioration in learning. The need to identify and provide appropriate treatment for children with symptomatic allergic problems is thus important for the facilitation of optimal school performance. In the face of significant behavioral or learning difficulties, however, the etiologic importance of allergic factors has not been substantiated. Until objective data can be produced to justify this approach, the identification and treatment of subclinical or cryptic atopy is never indicated.

PERCEPTUAL TRAINING PROGRAMS

A wide variety of perceptual training programs have been developed and recommended for the remediation of learning disorders. Although the physician often may be asked by parents for an opinion about the merits of a particular treatment program, he is generally not aware of the data regarding its efficacy. Keogh defined four major assumptions upon which all perceptual training programs are based:

1. Perceptual, motor, perceptual-motor, and sensory-motor abilities follow a well-defined predictable developmental course.
2. Planned experiences can affect the rate and nature of that developmental course.
3. Certain levels of perceptual-motor and sensory-motor maturity are necessary prerequisites for higher-order learning.
4. Remediation for children with learning disabilities should be focused on the underlying perceptual-motor skills rather than on specific academic or cognitive skills (Millichap 1977).

With these basic premises in mind, we shall review a selection of perceptual training programs.

Optometric Training

Optometric training for learning problems is based upon an assumption that learning, especially reading, is fundamentally a visual-perceptual task. Such intervention is generally prescribed on the basis of the findings of an elaborate optometric examination, which can take as long as one hour for a school-age child. Although many optometric programs include a broad array of perceptual-motor and direct academic remediation techniques, the unique aspect of these protocols involves specific eye exercises to improve visual tracking abilities, as well as a wide variety of binocular functions and visual-perceptual-motor skills.

When the Optometric Extension Program made available a standardized protocol for testing and treating school children with learning problems, many practicing optometrists became specialists in this area and offered specific intervention programs in their offices (Benton 1973). In response to the proliferation of such programs, the American Academy of Pediatrics, the American Academy of Ophthalmology and Otolaryngology, and the American Association of Ophthalmology issued a joint organizational statement, expressing considerable reservations about the appropriateness of such treatments.

Five conclusions were stated (American Academy of Pediatrics, 1972):

1. Learning disability and dyslexia . . . require a multidisciplinary approach . . . Eye care should never be instituted in isolation when a patient has a reading problem. Children with learning disabilities have the same incidence of ocular abnormalities . . . as children who are normal achievers and reading at grade level. These abnormalities should be corrected.

2. . . . Studies have shown that there is no peripheral eye defect which produces dyslexia and associated learning disabilities. Eye defects do not cause reversals of letters, words, or numbers.

3. No known scientific evidence supports claims for improving the academic abilities of learning disabled or dyslexic children with treatment based solely on: (a) visual training (muscle exercises, ocular pursuit, glasses); (b) neurologic organizational training (laterality training, balance board, perceptual training). Furthermore, such training has frequently resulted in unwarranted expense and has delayed proper instruction for the child.

4. Excluding correctible ocular defects, glasses have no value in the specific treatment of dyslexia or other learning problems. . . .

5. The teaching of learning disabled and dyslexic children is a problem of educational science. No one approach is applicable to all children.

Flax (1973) denounced the joint organizational statement and charged that its references were incorrectly documented. Benton (1973) responded to that criticism with a carefully worded defense of the group's conclusions. Although some literature supports the effectiveness of optometric training programs, the data are primarily based on poorly controlled studies or on interventions that included additional academic remediation (Keogh 1974). In the absence of conclusive documentation of the value of optometric training, most physicians hesitate to recommend it, preferring to rely on special educators for the remediation of those visual-perceptual or visual-motor problems that may be contributing to specific learning difficulties.

Patterning

Patterning is a method of treatment developed at the Institutes for the Achievement of Human Potential by Glen Doman, a physical therapist, and Carl Delacato, an educator. Their program is based upon the use of a variety of sensory and motor experiences designed to facilitate more efficient neurological organization. Based on the principle that "ontogeny recapitulates phylogeny," the afferent nervous system is bombarded with stimuli alleged to stimulate passage through a normal developmental sequence. Although the "patterning" label comes from the passive manipulation of the child's limbs and head to stimulate primitive motor patterns, a variety of other unsubstantiated, pseudo-scientific "therapeutic" methods may be incorporated into a treatment program. These include visual stimulation by flashing lights; tactile stimulation through contact with various textures; auditory stimulation by noises and sounds; rebreathing expired air in a face mask to increase carbon dioxide inhalation, which is believed to increase cerebral blood flow; reduction of fluid, salt, and sugar intake, supposedly to decrease cerebrospinal fluid production; and repetition of a variety of gross motor activities, such as creeping, crawling, rolling, and hanging upside-down. Its proponents claim that their treatment program can be prescribed appropriately for children with a wide range of neurologically based disabilities.

For the child with a communication disorder or learning problem, emphasis is placed on the critical importance of mature "dominance" (Delacato 1959). In fact, the achievement of unilateral eye, hand, and foot preference is considered a primary aim of treatment, in the belief that children with "learning disability" or "hyperactivity" can be cured if the appropriate "neurological organization" is promoted. Facilitation of such dominance is attempted by forced restriction of the nondominant (left) hand, active training of the dominant (right) hand, and unilateral patching to "strengthen" the dominant (right) eye. In addition, nonverbal music is actively discouraged because it is presumed to stimulate the "nondominant hemisphere."

A number of studies have been done on the effects of the Doman-Delacato program on children with learning disorders (Freeman 1967). Serious methodological problems, however, render the reported results questionable. In view of the high demands placed on parents in terms of time and commitment, the lack of conclusive data demonstrating its effectiveness, and the often grandiose claims of dramatic "cures," a number of organizations—including the American Academy of Pediatrics (1965) and the American Academy of Cerebral Palsy (1965)—have published statements expressing serious reservations about this form of therapy. Others, including the authors of this book, have gone further in their criticism and have condemned the program and its promotional tactics as a brand of charlatanism.

Sensory Integrative Therapy

Sensory integrative therapy was developed by A. Jean Ayres, an occupational therapist, who spent the early part of her career working with youngsters with cerebral palsy, and later adapted her formulations for learning-disabled children. On the basis of several factor analyses of perceptual, motor, and psycholinguistic test scores, in conjunction with basic neurophysiological data, Ayres hypothesized the existence of syndromes of sensory integration dysfunction. The original list of syndromes (Ayres 1965) involved disorders of:

1. Postural, ocular, and bilateral integration (including problems with right-left discrimination).
2. Praxis (including finger agnosia)
3. Functions of the left side of the body
4. Form and space perception
5. Auditory language function

Subsequent revisions of this taxonomy of disorders resulted in the description of new syndromes, such as "tactile defensiveness." This latter condition is characterized by a negative or withdrawal response to certain types of tactile stimulation, in conjunction with deficits in tactile perception, overactivity, and distractible behavior. Ayres emphasized that these syndromes rarely appear in "pure states" in any child and suggested that deficits in any of the specific functional areas should raise the possibility of problems in the other areas as well. Over the years these categories have been refined and elaborated upon. Many of the original test items have been standardized and incorporated into the Southern California Sensory Integration Test Battery (Ayres 1972b).

Like other perceptual-motor training programs, sensory integrative therapy is based upon the belief that higher cortical functions are dependent upon adequate neuro-organization at more primitive brain levels. Thus, research is cited that presumably demonstrates the necessary organization of auditory and visual processes by brain-stem structures, as well as the prerequisite normalization of postural mechanisms in the midbrain, in order for higher-order learning to proceed. Such a theory leads logically toward remedial techniques to facilitate improved integration and organization at brain-stem and midbrain levels, rather than intervention directed specifically toward higher cognitive processes, such as reading.

As a result of her studies of learning-disabled children, Ayres reported consistent observations of inadequate sensory integration at the brain-stem level, as suggested by the presence of "immature postural reactions, poor extraocular muscle control, poorly developed visual orientation to environmental space, difficulty in the processing of sound into percepts, and a tendency toward distractibility" (Ayres 1969). Intervention programs are individualized to address specifically each child's unique sensory integrative profile. Remediation techniques include carefully controlled vestibular and somatosensory stimulation (both passive and active), including such activities as spinning, riding a scooter-board down a ramp, and using a battery-operated brush for vibratory stimulation; and work with manipulatory puzzles. Each aspect of the total program is oriented toward a specific goal, based upon the theoretical model. Inhibition of primitive postural reflexes (such as symmetric and asymmetric tonic neck reflexes) and activation of equilibrium responses, for example, are presumed to affect midbrain organization, with reading skills being improved by enhanced cortical interhemispheral communication. Tactile stimulation is designed, in part, to "lower the level of excitation of the reticular arousal system" and thus to counteract the effect of distractibility and hyperactivity. Although "eye exercises" are not used, it is believed that the facilitation of visual processing in the brain stem produces overflow to the postural and ocular mechanisms at that level, with subsequent improvement in extraocular muscle control (Ayres 1972a).

Ayres has published data demonstrating greater academic gains from sensory integrative therapy than from academic tutoring (Ayres 1972a). Other studies have failed to confirm the efficacy of this type of treatment. As with all forms of perceptual-motor intervention, no definitive conclusions can be reached on the basis of currently available data.

The Physician's Role

The indications for perceptual-motor training for children with school problems are currently not clearly defined. As noted by Hallahan and Cruickshank (1973), well-designed research in this area has a very short history compared to the rather long tradition of enthusiastic clinical support. Most published studies have had serious methodological weaknesses, including vague criteria for subject selection, inadequate or nonexistent control groups, failure to control for placebo effects, and poor statistical analyses. Some critics have challenged the theoretical bases of such programs by questioning whether the remediation and evaluation techniques are actually dealing with the same abilities or functions (Mann 1971).

With data so limited, the practicing physician confronts a perplexing dilemma when asked by a parent or educator to endorse a specific perceptual-motor training program. Available evidence provides little support for the contention that perceptual training alone directly improves reading skills (Weaver and Shonkoff 1978). It does, however, seem to improve performance on those tasks that are practiced as part of the training program (so-called "splinter skills"). Thus, repetitive tracing of geometric forms tends to improve one's ability to trace geometric forms but has not been shown to have a significant effect on reading or writing skills. The decision about whether to prescribe a perceptual-motor training program thus depends upon the aim of the intervention. In some cases, especially for younger children, perceptually oriented activities might help facilitate more proficient performance in perceptual tasks. If, on the other hand, remediation of reading and writing is desired, then the available data do not seem to support the efficacy of perceptual-motor exercises.

Some advocates have suggested that perceptual-motor programs give children with learning disorders consistent, structured experiences that facilitate the development of better general organizational skills. Others respond that the same benefits can be achieved by structured, academic tutoring sessions, which simultaneously address the presenting problems more directly.

The issue of gross motor coordination programs, or modified physical education in the school, raises a host of new concerns (see Chapter 6). Although few data support the contention that the development of gross motor skills is related to general learning ability, it is certainly clear that a child's ability to master his body movements can enhance feelings of self-esteem and confidence (see Chapters 3 and 9). For many children with learning problems, gross motor incoordination is an additional burden that may affect their peer relationships and social adjustment. In such cases, supportive, noncompetitive athletic experiences can be important additions to the therapeutic arsenal.

The ultimate decision regarding the appropriateness of perceptual-motor training programs requires input from a variety of sources. The educator or therapist must describe the dysfunction(s) to be remediated and outline the specific goals of the treatment program. Careful consideration must be given to how the proposed therapy fits in with the remaining components (such as counseling and academic remediation) of the child's comprehensive educational-therapeutic plan. Issues such as hours spent, cost to the family, and the child's own reaction to the various treatments must be taken into consideration. Currently available data are inconclusive with regard to perceptual-motor training for children with learning disorders. Until the necessary studies are completed, physicians must help protect their patients from the grandiose promises of overzealous therapists, while demanding ongoing objective review and reevaluation of those programs that are implemented.

ACTIVITY GROUPS

Organized activity groups, both within and outside the formal school curriculum, can be useful adjuncts to a comprehensive plan of management for children with school problems. If properly supervised, they can provide opportunities for the development of productive peer relationships, as well as a forum for successful performance in an area of relative competence.

Art therapy has been employed in a variety of ways for children with developmental problems. In a program designed for "brain injured" and "hyperactive" children, Cruickshank et al. (1961) recommended the use of art as "one more way to practice skills and develop understandings." The goals of such activity included the development of perceptual and motor as well as socialization skills in a relatively nonacademic setting. Gonick-Barris (1976) challenged the use of art primarily for the promotion of structure and suggested its use for exploration, creation, and expression. Under properly organized conditions, she reported the successful use of clay, paint, and three-dimensional collage for expression of emotional impulses by children diagnosed as having "minimal brain dysfunction." Frame (1974) stated a somewhat similar philosophy in reporting the use of expressive art as a supplement to a remedial tutoring program. In this case study, the child's drawings provided the tutor with insight into his inner conflicts and anxieties, promoting an increased awareness of his emotional needs within the tutorial setting.

Music therapy has been shown to be beneficial. Steele (1973) reported the use of a preschool music program for promoting a wide variety of academic readiness skills, including attending behavior and sequencing abilities. In 1966, the Cleveland Music School Settlement became the first community-based music therapy department in the country designed for children with learning or behavior problems. Through the use of an individualized approach within small groups, children have been helped to develop a range of abilities and thus to enhance their self-esteem.

Dance and relaxation experiences have also been used with some success for children with behavioral-developmental problems. Klein and Deffenbacher (1977) reported the use of large-muscle exercise and relaxation training programs for "hyperactive," impulsive children. Both programs were found to have potential benefits, especially when employed just before testing sessions.

Generally speaking, activity groups can be of significant benefit to youngsters with a variety of adjustment problems. The efficacy of a given program, however, depends upon the talents and sensitivities of the adult coordinators, so that generalizations about program impact cannot be made. If such groups are available within a community, physicians should make an effort to evaluate their offerings and refer appropriate children for enrollment.

BIOFEEDBACK

The use of biofeedback techniques to alter brain-wave activity has reportedly had some success in the treatment of seizure disorders. This achievement has led a number of investigators to explore the possibility of such treatment for children with attention deficits or learning difficulties.

The focus of this method of treatment is the alpha wave, an 8- to 14-Hz brain sine wave whose production is often associated with a relaxed state of optimal mental and physical performance. Nall (1973) has suggested that children with learning disabilities have little or no alpha activity on their electroencephalograms, although this has not been studied sufficiently. The basic principle of treatment is to use biofeedback techniques to condition children to maximize the alpha activity in their electroencephalograms.

Work in this area is in a preliminary stage. Lubar and Shouse (1976) reported the results of EEG feedback training sessions with a "hyperactive" 11-year-old boy who had been shown to be responsive to methylphenidate. Presentations contingent on the production of 12- to 14-Hz activity in the absence of 4- to 7-Hz slow-wave activity were used. After several months of "treatment" a substantial increase in alpha activity was noted and was associated with enhanced motor inhibition, as measured by a chin electromyograph and a global classroom behavioral assessment. When the training was reversed, increased 4- to 7-Hz activity was produced, with associated decreased motor inhibition. The carryover effect was noted outside the laboratory setting in both cases. The results of this preliminary investigation showed that alpha conditioning through biofeedback techniques, in conjunction with methylphenidate, was much more effective for the management of "hyperactivity" than methylphenidate alone. Until more work is completed in this area, the use of such techniques must remain investigatory.

SUMMARY

The range of alternative treatment options for behavioral and learning disorders is broad, and the objective data necessary to evaluate the available choices are relatively limited. The clinical investigator enjoys the luxury of reserving all judgment until definitive evidence has been accumulated. A practicing physician, on the other hand, must face his learning and behaviorally troubled patients (and their families) with a plan for immediate intervention. One day in the future, perhaps, a treatment plan for a school problem will follow its diagnosis, as penicillin follows a streptococcal pharyngitis. In the meantime, one must choose carefully and monitor closely.

8

The Multiple Alliances

Life is short and Art is long;
the Crisis is fleeting, Experiment risky,
Decision difficult. Not only must the physician be ready to do
his duty, but the patients, the attendants, and the patient's
surroundings must conduce to the cure.

Hippocrates, Aphorisms

In all human service and health disciplines clinicians strive to establish working alliances (Frankl and Hellman 1962, Keith 1968, Meeks 1971). The concept of alliance implies trust and cooperation between patient and clinician, without which the work in which they are engaged would be compromised. While the concept of alliance has its roots in psychotherapy and counseling, it is equally relevant for the pediatrician or family physician's relationship with his patient.

Although the pediatrician should not be seen as a psychotherapist, he is nevertheless called upon for "developmental counseling." This task entails responsiveness to questions related to a child's development and the parent-child relationship. Given the brevity of most pediatric visits, the pediatrician must become a skilled interviewer and a keen observer of concerns (Delozier 1975). Korsch and Negrete (1972) found that the amount of time spent in a doctor-patient interview was not the major determinant of either the effectiveness of the session or the satisfaction of the patient; rather, it was the physician's empathy, understanding, and ability to respond and communicate. In certain instances the development of such a relationship may require additional interview time. For the child with a learning problem, the hours thus expended can yield important benefits, minimizing the parents' anxiety and preventing disruption in parent-child relationships.

The pediatrician's alliances extend beyond the child and the family. There are others with whom he must interact in order to assist the child with a school problem. Often each person involved has a unique agenda (open or hidden), and individual interests may conflict. At the very least, the interface includes the child, the parents (each of whom may have a different perspective on the problem and different feelings toward the child), other family members, and the school. The school is composed of a heterogeneous group, each member having

210

a personal agenda and responding to individual pressures. School personnel might include the director of special services, the school principal, the regular classroom teacher, the resource-room teacher, the school psychologist or counselor, the speech and language specialist, and the nurse.

Developing an optimal program for a child with learning problems may threaten relationships and produce frustration and anger. The pediatrician's role is not simply to be the child's advocate but to serve as a responsible professional who can help to balance, coordinate, and mediate (see Chapter 1), taking account of both the child's needs and the emotional, financial, and administrative burdens of all involved.

PEDIATRIC ALLIANCE WITH THE PARENTS

The pediatrician is, first of all, a child's physician, but a high priority is given to the alliance with parents. While it may be the mother who spends most of the time with the child, it is important for the pediatrician to meet the father as well, at the beginning of his contact with the family. All too often, the father is a figure whom pediatricians rarely (if ever) see, thereby omitting a vital component of the child's nurturing environment. Ongoing contact with the father, even by telephone, frequently serves as a strongly reinforcing intervention.

The cultivation of an alliance with the parents requires that a pediatrician be sensitive to their subtle or hidden concerns, build rapport and trust, and exchange ideas in a way that parents and children can understand and appreciate. Failure to comply with a physician's recommendations is frequently a reflection of communication breakdowns in the doctor-patient relationship (Korsch et al. 1968, Korsch and Negrete 1972).

In listening closely to what parents are saying, thinking, and feeling, the pediatrician must be aware that parenting is a very complicated process, and that even the "simplest" question from a parent may spring from a repository of feelings involving such components as:

· What the child represents to each parent
· Anxieties and insecurities, as well as feelings of incompetence, in the parenting role (especially with special-needs children)
· The parents' own experiences as children, and their relationships with their own parents
· Each parent's personality, and how it impinges upon the parenting role and matches that of the child
· The parents' relationship with each other

Of course, the pediatrician cannot assess, in detail, all of these factors, but he should be sensitive to their importance to avoid missing relevant insinuations in a parent's communication.

The development of a working relationship between the pediatrician and patient assumes even greater importance for those families where a child shows a learning style that is maladaptive, or a development progression that is uneven. When a child's abilities are deficient in particular areas, it is not surprising to find that parents often feel anxious and guilty about the youngster's problems and their inability to solve them. Disappointment, depression, frustration, anger, shame, and guilt may be revealed by the parents as they discuss their child with the pediatrician. The complexity of a child's problems may work against a precise diagnosis, definitive prognosis, or infallible intervention plan, thus adding to the parents' frustration and anxiety. In such instances, a family may go from one professional to another in an elusive quest for "the answer."

Given this climate of intense concern, the pediatrician must exercise skill in developing rapport and trust with the family, so that their relationship can withstand uncertainties. Maintenance of the alliance provides an opportunity for consistent care and monitoring of a child's progress and enhances the pediatrician's role as a consultant to parents in child-rearing practices.

A number of factors are operative in the pediatrician's formation and maintenance of an alliance with the parents of a child with learning problems. Some of these factors are discussed below.

Having empathy and understanding for the parents and for what it is like to have a child who is failing.   The pediatrician should attempt to place himself in the parents' position in order to comprehend what they are experiencing. While such parents are a heterogeneous group and react differently to the stress of their child's problems, there are some common affects which most experience at some point. Many will feel depressed at having a child with problems, in a sense mourning for the healthy child they do not have. Some parents will feel guilty, in some way assuming they are responsible for their child's problems (e.g., "He inherited it from me") or for their inability to solve them. Some parents often feel inadequate and helpless, as if there is nothing they can do any more. Others are filled with anger at the child, or school, or professionals with whom they have come in contact. Often this anger is a by-product of their feelings of helplessness and frustration. Some parents experience shame and avoid visiting relatives or friends, afraid to "display" their child's handicap and their own failure. Most parents experience anxiety, as they wonder about what their children will "turn into" as adults.

Without being oversolicitous, the pediatrician can acknowledge that parenting is a difficult venture that is made even more problematic when a child has developmental and learning problems, and that there is no easy nor necessarily correct answer for every problem. The physician can empathize with the parent's anxiety, frustration, and anger but must help to keep these feelings from interfering with effective parenting. For instance, unwarranted parental guilt can be neutralized by correcting distortions, such as when a parent feels that hitting a child on one occasion at two years of age caused brain damage and subsequent learning problems. Empathy need not originate in relation to major problems; empathy can be communicated by the pediatrician when he acknowledges to a harried mother with two flu-ridden children that she must be having a difficult time. This kind of statement goes a long way in demonstrating a pediatrician's concern.

Viewing the parents as active partners with the pediatrician in the child's care.   While a pediatrician possesses expertise, it is no substitute for the front-line observations provided by parents. The active involvement of the parents from the beginning of the pediatric contact increases their sense that they can do things to help their child, thereby diminishing their feelings of frustration, anger, and helplessness.

It is also important for the pediatrician to be able to acknowledge when he does not have an answer to a problem. One can discuss the complexity of the issue and communicate to the parents other possible approaches that may be attempted. It is the task of the pediatrician to collaborate with the parents in seeking the best interventions. In most cases, the greater the parent involvement, the stronger the alliance.

Respecting the parents' defenses and coping styles. Given the many affects that are aroused when they have a child with learning problems, even psychologically healthy parents may adopt less-than-successful methods to manage their emotions. For instance, some parents may handle their anxieties by denying the severity of the problem; others may become angry at the pediatrician for his care of the child and may withdraw or cancel appointments. The ability of the physician to understand parental behaviors and then to respond sensitively, and not defensively, is critical. An empathic stance often serves to lessen the parents' defenses in an appropriate way, permitting them to listen more easily and to follow the physician's recommendations.

Not being judgmental or accusatory. Some parents of children with developmental problems feel as if their parenting is being constantly judged. This attitude often is reinforced subtly (or blatantly) by professionals, family, and friends. An endless procession of childrearing advice is paraded before the parents, frequently resulting in confusion and doubt about their ability to nurture. Some parents eventually feel that they have failed.

It is all too easy to find fault with parenting practices in any household. If the pediatrician is to gain the parents' trust, and if they are to feel comfortable in sharing their feelings and doubts, he must convey a sensitive, nonjudgmental attitude. There must be recognition of the complex bond between a parent and a child and of the many dynamic variables that enter into the "fit" among the participants in this relationship (a relationship made more complex and taxing when the child is failing). To develop and strengthen the alliance, the pediatrician must help to eradicate the parents' image of themselves as bad or inadequate.

Stressing the strengths of the child and the parents, especially in relation to their parenting roles. Sometimes parents of developmentally and cognitively disabled children focus exclusively on what has gone wrong. It should not be a burdensome task for the pediatrician to find and point out areas of strength in the child and parents. They need to hear positive things about themselves, insofar as the message is honest. Such statements can serve to counteract any pessimism and defeatism that may exist, while nurturing the parents' sense of competence. Emphasizing the positive should begin early in the pediatrician's contact with the family and should remain a guiding principle in their transactions.

Being available and accessible. It is comforting and reassuring for a parent to perceive the pediatrician as reachable and available (even by phone) within a reasonable length of time. A pediatrician who projects an image of being too busy and unable to answer questions raised by the family will weaken the alliance. Within the busiest schedule, there should be a time (perhaps a call hour) when parents know that they can contact the physician and not feel rushed.

The pediatrician should recognize that seemingly irrelevant questions raised by parents may mask more important concerns, and consequently they deserve to be answered thoroughly. For example, a parent's anxiety about a youngster's not being able to run as fast as a neighbor's child may be linked to worries about the child's brain, since the mother recalls that the birth of the child was not as smooth as it should have been. A sensitive response to these "irrelevant" questions often permits the parents eventually to verbalize more important concerns that the pediatrician can discuss with them.

Minimizing medical jargon.   Medical terminology that most parents do not understand serves only to create an aura of mystery about the child's problems. When unfamiliar medical words are used, care should be taken to explain what they mean, and concrete examples should always be offered. It is helpful for the pediatrician to ask the parents to indicate if any words are used that they do not understand. The clearer the language, the better the parents will be able to assimilate the problem, so that they feel less helpless in trying to solve it.

Avoiding oppositional stances.   Increasingly it is common for parents to approach the physician with their own formulations of a child's problem and their own therapeutic inclinations or desires. For example, a parent may have a desperate desire to place a child on a particular diet for overactivity. Another parent may express considerable zeal for the initiation of drug therapy. The physician enters the encounter with his own set of propensities and, ultimately, his specific formulation of the child's needs. It is crucial, however, that in alliance formation, the clinician not diametrically oppose parental expectations unless the proposed intervention is harmful to the child. In some situations, the parent may be right! In a discipline with a relative paucity of scientific fact, parental formulations are not always less plausible than those of the clinician. While the physician needs to take a stand and be intellectually honest, a spirit of compromise and understanding should prevail. At the very least, the physician should be influenced by the desires and the diagnostic or therapeutic opinions of parents. A strong oppositional stance, on the other hand, can fracture an alliance and precipitate a "shopping expedition," as the parents seek a point of view that confirms their hypotheses. Such a search can be "successful," but it may lead families to the office of a profit-seeking, nonscientific, questionably professional "expert." It is inappropriate to assume that when a parent disagrees with the physician, that mother or father is being "resistant" or practicing "denial." Although the content of the physician's response should *not* be determined by parental biases, ultimately the clinician must find a way to "sell" ideas in a manner that parents will find acceptable.

In general, the development of a working alliance has ramifications that originate in trust between a pediatrician and parent(s). Comfort in the relationship permits a greater openness and willingness to communicate concerns and worries. It enables parents to deal with observations about their child without becoming defensive. Moreover, it enhances the preventive role of the pediatrician as a dispenser of anticipatory guidance.

PEDIATRIC ALLIANCE WITH THE CHILD

The pediatrician must also nurture a relationship with the child. Children have an array of fantasies, anxieties, and feelings when they visit a doctor. The pediatrician's task is to earn a child's trust and to help him feel as comfortable as possible. Children are sensitive to nonverbal communication—to a smile, a touch on the shoulder, or a soft tone of voice.

As in the relationship with parents, the conveyance of empathy to the child is essential in the formation and maintenance of an alliance. The pediatrician should assume a phenomenological approach in attempting to understand what the youngster is experiencing. The clinical challenge is to comprehend how a child's particular developmental problems are affecting learning and emotional status. One must recognize that these children typically have experienced many failure situations, which have eroded self-esteem, produced feelings of sadness and frustration, and sometimes prompted maladaptive coping styles appropriated to save face. Unfortunately, some strategies serve only to minimize success experiences, as the child increasingly retreats from difficult situations.

In addition to empathy, other ingredients help to foster and maintain an alliance with children:

Children should know what is going to happen to them, and why it is going to happen. Pediatricians should explain all procedures carefully and, when possible, should actively involve the child, such as in listening with a stethoscope or in examining other instruments. Children are typically less anxious when they feel more involved and in control of a situation. They should be helped to feel like partners with the pediatrician in the attempt to solve their problems.

Children should be told about the visit and the nature of their problems in language that they can easily understand.   An important way to establish rapport with a child is to reduce complex "magical" problems to understandable and manageable terminology that serves to demystify them. This includes communication of diagnosis, prognosis, and prescriptions. Often, explanations by the pediatrician to the child can be provided when the mother or father is in the room, thereby serving as a model for the parents in communicating in a natural or honest way. The use of analogies and illustrative examples can be helpful. A child who is having problems with attention or memory may fantasize about these difficulties. The best way to dissuade him of the belief that he is "mental" is to provide a developmentally suitable translation of the problem. If necessary, diagrams and specific examples may be supplied.

Children should hear about the areas in which they have grown and the strengths that they have.   The pediatrician should always find time to talk with the child about things that he does well, and about progress that the child has shown (however small), in order to counteract, in part, the child's feelings of inadequacy and helplessness. Every attempt should be made to promote the child's sense of competence and mastery and to minimize coping styles that lead to further problems.

Children should hear about problem areas in a nonjudgmental way and learn about ways in which these problems can be solved.   Children with learning problems often feel incompetent and perceive that others also see them in this way. It is important that the pediatrician recognize how even a neutral remark about a child's problems may be misinterpreted as critical and accusatory. Much sensitivity is demanded in communicating honestly and in a way that the child perceives as supportive. In addition, nonjudgmental communication about problem areas should address what can be done by the child and others to solve problems. The youngster must never be left with a feeling that nothing can be done.

Children should not feel that the pediatrician is intruding upon them.   The pediatrician should respect a child's defenses and coping styles. Often a child who is anxious and resistant can be engaged if the physician recognizes the youngster's anxiety and does not get involved in a struggle with him. For example, a child who handles anxiety by being oppositional or belligerent during a physical exam might be asked to help out and hold the stethoscope. In this way, he feels more a participant in the process than an unwilling victim who is being studied for defects.

Children should feel that no secrets are being kept from them.   The pediatrician may offer a child "full disclosure," whenever this is feasible. A child should be included as much as possible in discussions of formulation and treatment. Decisions about medication and other kinds of intervention should always include the child. The child should have some access to test scores, reports, and other aspects of a diagnostic evaluation.

Children should feel that the physician can honor confidentiality. As children approach the later elementary-school grades, they often need reassurance from the clinician (and sometimes the parents) that secrets can be kept. The child should feel free to confide in the physician. There should be reassurance that information will not be leaked to the parents unless the child feels it is appropriate.

Children should not be embarrassed.   Every effort should be made to help the child save face during the awkward and potentially embarrassing evaluation process. At first, "delicate" questions should be avoided. When and if the parents make a comment that is intimidating or demeaning, the clinician should hasten to add a neutralizing statement. As noted in an earlier chapter, physical examination of a child in front of the parents can be a source of embarrassment. The physician may need to take the initiative in this regard.

Children should not perceive the physician as an agent of the school or parents.   The clinician needs to establish a special relationship with the child, one in which he is not viewed as an agent of the institutions of education and parenthood! The child should feel able to communicate openly his feelings about individual teachers, the school, or even his parents.

Children should not be indulged excessively in reassurance, lecturing, or moralizing.   If a child discusses a possibly humiliating or embarrassing situation, the clinician should not rush to offer reassurance. Instead, there should be some discussion of possible strategies or techniques to deal with such situations. The tone should be empathic and supportive. Lecturing or excessive moralization should be avoided. The emphasis should be on commiseration and on collaborative planning to overtake adversity.

Children should be seen alone during part of the visit. This statement may seem superfluous. However, some physicians are unaccustomed to being alone with children, and they tend to relate to youngsters through parents (usually mothers). In dealing with developmental formulation and counseling, the physician may need to spend more time with the child than with the parents.

PEDIATRIC ALLIANCE WITH SIBLINGS

Children who have a sibling with developmental, learning, or affective problems need support to deal with their own feelings and thoughts that arise as a consequence of their sibling's disabilities. Many experience anger and frustration at a brother or sister who takes so long to do things, who demands and receives so much attention (especially from parents), who seems to be a pest, who gives the impression of getting away with many things, and who never seems to share equally in household chores. Siblings also experience guilt over the anger they feel, over how little they want to help, and even over how fortunate they feel not to be the one with the problem. Shame and embarrassment arise in response to hearing others calling their sibling "mental" or "retard," and then they must deal with their own feelings of hurt and anger; they must decide whether or not to defend their sibling or join in the condemnation.

The pediatrician is in a unique position to help in this situation, since, unlike most psychotherapists, he has ongoing contact with the siblings. The pediatrician thus has opportunities to win the siblings' trust, to assist them in managing their feelings, to advise them on how to deal with the affected brother or sister, and to offer suggestions about responding to what other children say. The pediatrician can explain a child's handicap(s), offer a possible prognosis, and exchange ideas with siblings about ways they can help. This approach can increase their sense of mastery and build greater understanding of the behavior of their less fortunate brother or sister.

PEDIATRIC ALLIANCES WITH SCHOOL PERSONNEL

The strength of a pediatrician's ties with schools can relate directly to the quality of services he is able to help obtain for a patient. Rapport with school personnel depends upon many subtle agendas and issues. These include the following:

1. The clinician needs to be sensitive to the often conflicting pressures exerted upon school administrators (directors of special education, superintendents, and principals). Each day they confront parents who want new and different services. At the same time, they must answer boards of education or school committees, who frequently place a high priority on austerity or belt-tightening. Concurrently, they need to confront teaching staffs with their own unique sets of needs, values, and expectations. Notwithstanding, the school administrator must live with his own conscience. When a new force, such as the pediatrician, enters the scene, yet another set of agendas become operative.

2. The physician should be aware of the school's need to establish priorities and rank-order service allocation. A physician may advocate strongly that a child receive intensive one-to-one services. In fact, the physician's influence may be necessary to obtain such a program. On the other hand, it is important to bear in mind what the school cannot ignore: namely, that services for one child may displace those for children who are more in need, but whose parents are not resourceful enough to seek medical influence. While the clinician cannot abandon advocacy for his own patient, service recommendations should be made with resource allocation in mind. At the least, the physician should indicate to school personnel that he is aware of these issues.

3. The physician must respect and incorporate the diagnostic observations made by educational personnel and be a good listener to such professionals. Their long-range observations may be more helpful than intermittent samples of performance obtained through pediatric assessments or formal, standardized tests.

4. The pediatrician should not develop an adversary relationship with a school. At times, parents approach their physician because they are angry at an individual teacher, a particular school, or an entire school system. They may wish to engage the pediatrician as an ally in a frontal assault against the educational institution. Such alliances are likely to be counterproductive and potentially damaging to the child. It is important for the pediatrician to form an appropriate balance between representation of the rights and needs of a child and support for the efforts of a school. In most cases in which the school appears not to be offering appropriate services or supports for a youngster, the clinician has to be careful to avoid blaming a low-level administrator or "condemning the messenger." The "lesion" may be at a much higher level (such as the school committee or the tax-paying citizenry). To affect change for a particular child, a nonadversary, cooperative approach is more likely to yield results. In addition, the pediatrician needs to be building a long-standing relationship with a school system, such that there can be a continuing exchange of ideas involving many children. A painful adversary relationship around a single case may destroy a potentially useful interchange for many years (or forever).

5. The physician should be careful not to make unrealistic demands upon the *school system*. While it is imperative that the physician help to obtain necessary services for a child, it is also critical to recognize the difference between optimal and adequate interventions. A school system may not have the community mandate to provide the *best possible* services for a particular problem. For example, a child with severe attentional problems, in the best of all possible worlds, might benefit from one-to-one teaching for six hours a day. Most school systems cannot afford to offer this. On the other hand, most systems should be able to provide up to one hour a day of one-to-one tutoring and three hours of small-group or resource-room programming. A spirit of compromise based on a knowledge of available resources, community mandates, and the needs and rights of the child must prevail.

6. The pediatrician needs to be aware of possible defensive postures in the school. When a school-age child is being evaluated outside of school, the school personnel may feel that they too are being assessed. If a sixth-grade child is having difficulty writing, the school may harbor some feelings of guilt. Some

defensiveness may be obvious. Teachers might react by insisting that the problem is entirely in the home, or that the child is unmotivated, lazy, or uninterested. The physician should be sensitive to such defenses. He may need to convince school personnel that a child's developmental problem is a difficult one and that any succession of teachers would have had "their hands full." Excessive defensiveness on the part of school personnel may be intensified by accusations from the parents. The heat can be diminished with some well-placed praise and support for the teachers from the physician. This can go a long way toward strengthening alliances, toward focusing specifically on the needs of the child, and toward eliminating the political static that can interfere with the education of a child who has learning problems.

7. A physician should not allow a school to place him in a position of ultimate authority. Sometimes physicians are given an inordinately important role to play by school personnel and parents, who may be inappropriately overwhelmed by medical credentials. Beneath the veneer of adulation and high respect, however, school personnel may harbor resentment, jealousy, and anger. To be optimally effective, and to have a constructive alliance with school personnel, the clinician must make it clear that his is but one of a number of inputs whose additive effect can be helpful. At a case conference, it is wise for the physician to decline the opportunity to offer both the first and the last word! He should be careful to solicit the opinions and formulations of other personnel. Every effort must be made to avoid climbing atop any pedestal that school personnel might provide.

8. The physician must respect disciplinary territories (to some extent). Although this entire book invites physicians to trespass on turfs often jealously guarded by other professions, we have endorsed a transdisciplinary approach. The pediatrician needs to make it clear to other professionals that they are likely to have the last word with regard to findings in their respective disciplines. Nevertheless, the clinician should not be afraid or reluctant to make observations or comments where they seem needed. In addition, the advocacy role of the generalist must be borne in mind. The primary care physician may help parents "seek another opinion" with regard to a particular discipline's findings or recommendations. When the physician recommends a second opinion, he should do so in a way that does not alienate the initial evaluators.

9. The physician needs to establish an ongoing professional relationship with school personnel that is somewhat independent of individual cases. Opportunities should be seized to discuss learning problems and other relevant issues with school personnel. Some of this can take place during in-service educational activities. Those clinicians fortunate enough to relate to a relatively small number of schools may become familiar with available personnel and resources. There should be an open and rich set of professional interactions that stop short at the point where the physician becomes "an agent of the school." It is crucial for pediatricians to avoid political entanglements with a particular school or school system. When a pediatrician is a school doctor, consultant, or on the payroll of a particular educational institution, there is the danger of conflict of interest. Thus, a physican must achieve an appropriate balance between being highly supportive of the needs of individual children, being willing and able to be a gadfly to the schools when necessary, and yet sustaining a positive, supportive relationship with administrators and teachers.

10. The pediatrician should generally refrain from recommending private school for a child. Under a recent law (Public Law 94-142), communities *may* be expected to pay for private school education for certain handicapped children (See Table 1, Chapter 6). This can lead to political strife. In most cases, this is an area from which the pediatrician ought to retreat. It is his job to evaluate the child rather than the town or the school system! The physician can recommend specific services for a child but should avoid suggesting *where* these services might be obtained; that should be a community and parent decision. The physician who repeatedly recommends private school for children is assuming the capability of assessing the quality of the public school system and often becomes a chronic adversary to school personnel.

REFERRING PATIENTS FOR MENTAL HEALTH SERVICES

The following contingencies should prompt a pediatrician to refer a child or family for help from a child psychiatrist, psychologist, or a social worker.

1. When the particular problems of the child and family require *more time* than the pediatrician has available.
2. When a clinical disorder is known to need intensive intervention, as in autism, psychosis, or severe depression.
3. When the child's adjustment difficulties persist despite a pediatrician's management. This can stem from a number of factors, including (a) strong internalization of conflicts by the child; (b) negative family dynamics that aggravate disabilities (e.g., when marital problems prevail and a child is caught in the middle, withstanding stress that works against a solution to his problems); and (c) pervasive needs in a parent that unconsciously nurture a child's weaknesses (e.g., when a mother has difficulty tolerating independence in her children and thus unwittingly sabotages independence and mastery).
4. When the pediatrician requires a more comprehensive elucidation of a child's affective functioning or underlying relevant issues of family dynamics.

Preparation of the Family

The preparation of a family for referral to a mental health clinician may require sensitivity and time. While some parents are desperately ready to visit a psychiatrist, psychologist, or social worker, others are reluctant. This may originate from several sources: for some it confronts them with the fact that there is a problem, a truth they may have been trying to minimize or deny; for others it conjures up thoughts of their child being "crazy"; for still others it ignites guilt, anger or anxiety.

The pediatrician's task is to focus on *why* the referral is being made *at this time,* reviewing what has been done thus far, and justifying the mental health intervention. The pediatrician must empathize with any difficulties the parents are having following through on such a referral, while correcting any misconceptions about the content of therapy. If they need time to think about such a recommendation, the process should not be rushed; it is better to manage such misgivings over time than to have parents refuse a referral outright or enter into it with undue ambivalence or wariness.

The pediatrician should convey that the referral to an outside professional does not imply abandonment of the family: that he will collaborate with the mental health specialist and continue to care for (and about) the child. Moreover, if the family do not want to follow through on the referral or if they terminate therapy, the pediatrician should continue to be available for counseling and support.

When a referral is made, it is appropriate for the pediatrician to inform the parents and child that if there is not a "good fit" (for whatever reason) between the particular mental health professional and the family, another referral can be made. Sometimes there is a genuine *lack* of rapport between a therapist and patient. The family might subsequently work much better with a different clinician. Difficulty relating to a psychiatrist, social worker, or psychologist should *not* automatically be interpreted as "resistance." When therapy is proceeding poorly, the family has a *right* to expect the pediatrician to consider the possibility that the therapist is not doing a good job or that there is a mismatch.

Selection of a Mental Health Professional

In recommending a mental health specialist for a family, the pediatrician should be guided by several general considerations and by the very specific needs of the family being referred. The following questions should be raised and addressed in selecting a psychologist, social worker, or psychiatrist:

Is it the custom of this mental health specialist to keep in touch, give feedback, and collaborate with the pediatrician? Children with learning and developmental problems, who often need years of monitoring and intervention, require such close and ongoing coordination.

Is the mental health specialist comfortable in working with and going into schools? Some clinicians still adhere to a style of intervention that minimizes their contact with the child's school. A student with learning problems *must* have a therapist who is prepared to maintain regular contact with the school and to assist in the planning of classroom management.

Is the therapist well versed not only in "emotional disorders" but also in neurodevelopmental and cognitive issues? Does he deal with the interface between cognition and affect? This is a critical variable, since many dysfunctioning children cannot use or benefit from a traditional child-psychotherapeutic approach. A child who shows subtle lags in receptive language, memory, or higher-order conceptualization may lack the prerequisites for many forms of play therapy. In the past such children may have been perceived as resistant to treatment.

The therapist working with such a child must assess and comprehend how the child's particular developmental dysfunctions affect all dimensions of his life, including affect and social interaction. An increasing number of therapists have written about the need to focus on both cognition and affect in therapy (e.g., Beck 1976, Brooks 1979, Meichenbaum 1977, Rie 1974, Santostefano 1975). There are many ways to accomplish this. Santostefano (1978) has developed a type of intervention that he calls cognitive control therapy. Deficits in such areas as gross motor control, selective attention, memory, and higher-order conceptualization are addressed by introducing specific cognitive tasks during a therapy session. As the child confronts these challenges, the therapist actively deals with feelings and coping styles that emerge. Such feelings may include anxiety, anger, and low self-esteem and a child may demonstrate a variety of avoidance techniques (e.g., saying that tasks are dumb, crying, becoming belligerent, acting silly). The therapist works toward strengthening cognitive functioning as well as promoting a sense of mastery in the child, reducing avoidance behaviors, and striving to replace learning inhibition with excitement about pursuing knowledge.

Is the mental health specialist comfortable in giving advice? There are still a number of therapists who do *not* include specific counseling in their therapeutic strategies. Advice-giving predicated on a thorough understanding of the family and transmitted in an honest, clear, and sensitive manner is essential when a child has learning problems or shows significant developmental lags. The mental health professional should also feel comfortable in saying "I don't know" and in helping families look for answers.

Does the therapist have a flexible approach to the overall management of the case? Having a disabled child in the family gives rise to many stresses, and it is often helpful for the child's therapist to provide "developmental counseling" for parents. At times it is important for the therapist to see siblings, or grandparents, or to attend school conferences, offering a flexible approach predicated on the clinical and educational needs of the family.

Is the therapist comfortable in not having a "true" termination date with a family? This question relates to the issue of flexibility, but it deserves separate attention since it touches upon the possible "lifetime" planning and developmental counseling that are required for children with developmental deficits. While the therapist may at first see the child once or twice a week, there is no "final" termination but rather a recognition that the child and parents require continued guidance and support as different developmental milestones (e.g., entering junior high school, reaching puberty, going to camp for the first time, planning for a vocation) raise new questions. In some families the therapist might see the child every few months and the parents every few months, and visit the school several times a year. In other cases, the child may rarely be seen after the scheduled weekly meetings have stopped, but the therapist maintains regular contact with the parents or school or both.

Is the gender of the therapist critical? In most instances the sex of the mental health professional is not a high-priority variable in a referral. However, some parents may state that it is easier for them to talk with a man, while others prefer a therapist who is a woman. Some adolescents are more comfortable with a same-sex mental health specialist, especially if issues of sexuality are likely to be prominent. Some children who have been abused or traumatized by a parent may find it almost impossible to enter into an alliance with a therapist of the same sex as the abusive parent.

Can the mental health specialist mesh his formulations with those of the pediatrician? It is important that a therapist and a pediatrician emit consistent messages to children and parents. If the pediatrician explains to a family that a child has a primary attention deficit, it is essential that the psychotherapist *not* turn this around and insist that the child is inattentive *exlusively* because of anxiety. Again, this requires a close working relationship, the collaboration of two professionals who have similar understandings of the phenomenology of nature-nurture interactions. If the pediatrician has worked long and hard to alleviate guilt, to be nonaccusatory, to offer constructive advice, it is clearly counterproductive for there to be a referral to a professional who blames the parents, who is nonadvice-giving, and who focuses exclusively on psychodynamic determinism!

It is hoped that with increasing emphasis on development of pediatric skill in this area, primary care physicians will become increasingly wise consumers of mental health consultations for families. As pediatricians develop increasing knowledge of the differential diagnoses and multifaceted sources of dysfunction, they will be able to read reports from mental health specialists in an appropriately critical manner. They will be able to offer suggestions to therapists. More than anything else, however, they will be able to "deliver" patients for psychotherapy in such a way that the psychotherapist is provided with a lucid understanding of the constitutional and environmental forces underlying a child's dysfunction.

9

Developmental Counseling

We can no longer recall the poignancy of that moment and
weep over it as we do over the remembered sufferings of five or
ten years ago. Every one of those keen moments has left its
trace and lives in us still, but such traces have blent themselves
irrevocably with the finer texture of our youth in manhood;
and so it comes to pass that we can look on at the troubles of
our children with a smiling disbelief in the reality of their pain.

George Eliot, The Mill on the Floss

THE CONCEPT OF DEVELOPMENTAL COUNSELING

Many children cope heroically with patterns of central nervous system function
that do not measure up to adult expectations. Some who are failing at school are
able to apply compensatory strengths and use adult supports to sustain feelings
of self-worth. It may be that some children are able to strengthen themselves as
they develop the determination to achieve despite a disability. There are
children with learning disorders, however, in whom repeated failure exacts a
high toll. Frustration, anger, guilt, shame, and sometimes depression may stem
from "battle fatigue," as such youngsters struggle repeatedly in vain (Buscaglia
1975).

For many families there is little refuge from the painful speculations that
preoccupy them as they strive to understand their child's learning problems.
Sometimes the pressures are intensified by the child's own methods of handling
his plight. These may involve avoidance reactions, somatic symptoms, or
antisocial acts. Such maladaptive coping methods may alienate adults, thereby
aborting the help children receive from professionals. In such situations, the
parent-child relationship may be strained, as all parties feel angry and at a loss.
The school frequently is brought into this tense arena, since the child's problems
relate directly to educational adjustment.

The pediatrician may be the first professional who becomes aware of the
broad impact of a child's learning difficulties. Continuing access provides a
unique opportunity for developmental counseling, a process that aims to
demystify a child's disability while offering advice for managing specific problems. The early and ongoing intervention of the pediatrician can serve to

224

prevent or minimize the long-range consequences of failure, helping to avoid family conflicts and undue anguish related to the child's difficulties. The emphasis is on prevention. Developmental counseling includes the anticipatory guidance that many families require to help prepare for difficult developmental predicaments and their potential complications.

The efficacy of developmental counseling depends in great part on the patient-doctor relationship (i.e., the alliance) and on the physician's formulation of the child's developmental "scenario." If the pediatrician is to offer developmental counseling, he may need to refine available behavioral information, as described in Chapter 5. To gather and utilize such historical data, the steps discussed below are helpful.

Refining the Chief Complaints

Parents may describe a child's problems in abstract, global terms. They might characterize their child as "hyper," "willful," or "slow." Such adjectives may not be useful in defining specific maladaptations. The pediatrician needs to find out precisely what the parents mean by a particular term. For example, if a child is described as "hyperactive," specific anecdotal accounts can help to determine the extent to which the youngster's drivenness is situational (e.g., limited to academic work) or pervasive. The pediatrician needs to ponder whether the degree and nature of overactivity is unusual or in fact physiological for a particular age (e.g., when a two-year-old is "hyperactive" because of the normal surge in exploratory motility at that age). The pediatrician must realize that examples offered by parents may indicate what aspects of the child's development are most important and of greatest concern to them.

Pursuing a History

When the pediatrician has been the primary health care provider, he will possess cumulative insight into the child's developmental history. However, a parent might not discuss early distress signals with a physician. Such difficulties may surface in later childhood. The failure of some parents to inform their child's pediatrician of certain problems may be tied to denial as an attempt to lessen anxiety. Denial, however, is not always the main determinant in this situation. For instance, a parent may see a withdrawn child as simply one who likes to entertain himself and may not recognize the significance of the problem until the child begins school. Crowded waiting rooms and the rapid rhythm of a pediatric office routine may also impair communication about behavioral concerns.

When the pediatrician does not already have a thorough history, he should attempt to obtain this information. A detailed chronology yields valuable data for determining whether a child's present developmental problems are of long standing, or whether they are a less-entrenched reaction to a recent situation. In some cases, there may be evidence to help make this determination. Thus, a five-year-old with an attention problem, who has been characteristically distractible since the age of two, raises different concerns from a fully trained four-year-old who starts to wet shortly after the birth of a sibling.

Some problems that appear reactive or new may have had earlier, more subtle manifestations. For example, a six-year-old boy's ritualistic behavior in needing everything in place and not wanting anything touched in his room might be related to his own destructive activity, which was noted at the age of three. In fact, the current compulsive pattern may represent an attempt to regain control of potentially overwhelming inner feelings of aggression.

While most historical data derives from a parent interview or questionnaires (see the appendix), the pediatrician should not neglect other important sources of information, including the observations of a grandparent or the often astute comments of an older sibling.

A Survey of Views

The Parents' Views. As described in Chapter 1, learning failure is likely to result from a complicated interplay of constitutional and environmental variables. The contributions of these factors to a child's past and current problems often are difficult to sort out. Even when there is an obvious indication of central nervous system impairment (such as a seizure disorder), the extent of the endogenous contribution is not always clear. Furthermore, a major determinant of a child's early difficulties may no longer play a role in perpetuating the disorder.

Many parents, confronted by a child with significant developmental problems, come to the pediatrician with their own explanatory hypotheses. These theories range from complex to simple and from relatively accurate to partially true or almost totally implausible. Each hypothesis embodies many implications, such as the parents' perception of their own contribution to the child's problems, how modifiable the dysfunction may be, and what "treatments" are needed. The specific hypotheses that parents formulate or embrace also may represent ways that they attempt to handle their own troubled feelings.

If parents perceive learning failure simply as a vitamin deficiency (presumably correctible by a "megavitamin" approach), they may not be disposed to explore how their interaction with the child helps or constrains development. Conversely, a parent who attributes all of the child's handicaps and failures to poor parenting and emotional problems may expend fortunes for psychotherapy and fail to discern significant constitutional factors (e.g., language deficits) that may have contributed both to learning problems and to the sense of failure.

The pediatrician should sort out each parent's individual understanding of a child's dysfunction and assess the rigidity or flexibilty of the hypotheses. Clarification of distortions and replacement of misconceptions with more realistic explanations comprise a significant part of developmental counseling.

The Child's View. The child's perception of problems must not be overlooked. Children often generate myths about their own learning failure. These explanations may be far from true and may work against the child's assimilating help or enhancing his self-esteem. Some feel they were born "dumb" or "stupid," that there is something wrong with their "brains," or that they are congenitally "bad" or "lazy." If so resigned, they may feel it is futile to engage in learning tasks, and these feelings will perpetuate failure.

If, on the other hand, children are taught about their problems and offered appropriate hope and protection from humiliation, they are more likely to cooperate enthusiastically with the professional in any interventions.

The School's View.   The pediatrician should learn how the child is perceived by the school. School personnel usually have their own hypotheses about a child's difficulties; occasionally these hypotheses limit educational support (e.g., "The problem is an overprotective mother," or "The child could learn if he wanted to, he's just a manipulator"). The school questionnaire can be helpful in gathering this information (see the appendix). Inaccurate or oversimplistic hypotheses generated by school personnel must be modified. This endeavor may require the active involvement of the pediatrician.

Reviewing Earlier Management

When parents bring their concerns to the attention of the pediatrician, they may not yet have begun any corrective measures. Sometimes, however, a variety of strategies have been tried. For example, parents may have responded to excessive aggression in their four-year-old son by spanking him, sending him to his room, removing television, or withdrawing privileges. Some strategies may have proven more effective than others, but if the problems persist, the parents may question the efficacy of all the techniques they have used.

The pediatrician should obtain an account of what strategies have been tried, including how consistently and for what length of time various methods were applied. For example, parents may report that the technique of sending their child to his room when he hits his younger sibling was ineffective. On questioning, the pediatrician might discover that this strategy was attempted only two or three times and discontinued because the child screamed excessively in his room. Few interventions work that quickly; some may have been abandoned too readily.

The pediatrician should also obtain a picture of differences in parental styles and of the modes of action with which each parent is most comfortable. Some approaches, while potentially effective, are difficult for particular parents, arousing feelings of unease and guilt. For example, some parents have difficulty setting limits or holding a child accountable for his actions, somehow feeling that they risk losing the child's love. Such parents may be helped by a pediatrician who can deal sensitively with their discomfort and encourage them to engage in new and different interactions with their child. Developmental counseling is facilitated when the pediatrician understands the ideas and feelings that different intervention strategies represent for each parent and for the child.

If the school has developed special programs for the child, it is important for the pediatrician to know their content and effectiveness. The pediatrician should look for areas in which previous interventions have been successful (even if only moderately so) in order to reinforce the efforts of the family and school.

Obtaining Additional Information and Recommending Further Evaluation
This step is discussed in Chapter 5.

Recommending Intervention Strategies: Joining the Search for Mastery
Once the pediatrician has obtained a picture of a child's disabilities and has analyzed the parents', child's, and school's responses, particular advice can be offered to help manage and, hopefully, resolve problems.

The pediatrician's recommendations should aim primarily at promoting a sense of mastery or competence in the parents, child, and school. This sense of effectiveness is crucial. In the fields of education and mental health, there is growing evidence that a critical dimension of any intervention is the reinforcement of an individual's belief that he is competent and has control over life events (e.g., Bandura and Adams 1977, Frank 1976, Stott 1978, White 1959). If the parents of a struggling child lack a sense of competence, they may feel and act helpless and pessimistic.

Developmental counseling, with its emphasis on positive intervention strategies, can promote mastery by teaching problem-solving skills and offering examples of techniques the family and school can employ. It can minimize defeatism and doubt by communicating that the failure of an intervention does not imply incompetence. So-called failures become situations from which to learn, rather than catastrophies to bemoan.

Establishing a sense of mastery requires the selection of specific goals that have a high probability of being achieved in a relatively brief period. Success begets success, so that it is critical for the pediatrician to promote techniques that work early in his contact with the family. Such early triumphs will serve to sustain the parents, child, and school over the long run, especially when they experience setbacks or slower progress in some areas.

Specific components of the recommendation process are discussed below.

Communicating the Pediatrician's Understanding of the Problem. The pediatrician should discuss with the parents, child, and school his understanding of the nature and mutual interaction of the youngster's learning and emotional problems. Concrete examples are helpful, especially if they are tied to observations the family and school have made. For instance, parents may report that their six-year-old daughter does not listen to directions, leading them to believe she is being stubborn; the pediatrician can share with them the findings of a speech and language evaluation that reveal significant auditory memory and sequencing deficits and explain that such deficits can present as a failure to follow directions. The parents can then be helped to comprehend the child's reluctance to go to school and her anger at other children because of feelings of frustration and inadequacy in the face of the typical demands made upon a six-year-old child. The pediatrician must also attempt to make these disabilities more understandable to the child (i.e., to demystify them). In essence, the pediatrician seeks to correct inaccurate perceptions of a child's deficits and to heighten the family's and school's comprehension of what the child is experiencing.

The pediatrician's communication of the nature of a problem should embody a developmental perspective. That is, the parents should be helped to understand the relevance of the child's disability at a particular age. It may be that some problems are age-expectable and transitory (e.g., separation anxiety in a two-year-old or nightmares in a four-year-old), while others are more dysfunctional and pervasive. The difference between a three-year-old and an eight-year-old starting to soil after the birth of a sibling is an obvious example.

Statement of the Goals. Once a problem is delineated for the family and school, specific treatment or intervention goals can be considered. The pediatrician should define short- and long-term goals that embrace both cognitive and affective function. These should include consideration of areas of development of greatest immediate concern to the parents, to the child, and to the school, as well as objectives that involve longer-range planning (a year or two). For instance, a pediatrician may state that the management of memory deficits in a nine-year-old is a critical immediate goal if the child is to become a more proficient learner. Longer-range goals might include specific school placement and the acquisition of appropriate vocational skills. For another family, the pediatrician might select, as an immediate goal, control over a child's destructive behavior, and might look toward improvement in peer relations as a longer-term objective.

It is helpful if goals are outlined as precisely as possible, so that those working with a child can coordinate their efforts, and so that criteria are provided for gauging progress or the need for reassessment.

Statement of General Strategies. After the pediatrician has discussed his understanding of the child's disabilities and suggested some goals for intervention, a discussion of general strategies should follow. Assisting the parents and school to define broad strategies provides a foundation upon which they may build specific techniques. For example, the pediatrician may recommend a general strategy to the parents of a highly distractible eight-year-old boy: begin to give him short directions and *slowly* move toward longer inputs. With this general strategy in mind, the parents can develop specific tasks or situations to enhance the child's selective attention, such as advancing from short commands with no one else in the room to longer directions in the presence of several siblings. Once the parents grasp a general approach to their child's disability and develop problem-solving attitudes, they, themselves, have taken a significant step toward an increased sense of competence and mastery.

While discussing general strategies with the parents, child, and school, the pediatrician might suggest the reasons past interventions have not been successful. Some interventions may have failed because there was no clear objective in mind, others because the specific techniques were not appropriate, still others because they were not applied either consistently or long enough. The pediatrician should help the family and school learn from past "mistakes" in a noncritical and nonaccusatory way.

Statement of Specific Strategies. The pediatrician's overview of a general intervention approach should be complemented by specific strategies that the parents and school can implement as soon as possible. These individualized recommendations should follow from the general strategy design and be tied to both short- and long-term goals. For example, if the general strategy to minimize a child's constant demand for parental attention is to help him learn to wait for increasingly longer periods for their undivided attention, the pediatrician might recommend a specific approach, whereby the parent reserves a "special" 15- or 30-minute period after school and after dinner for the child; this special, exclusive time with the parents would be contingent on whether the child is able to forego excessively demanding behavior at other times of the day.

It is important for the pediatrician to stress that not all techniques will prove effective and that the family and school should devise their own interventions, as long as the general goals remain consistent.

Just as a parent's defenses should be managed sensitively, so too must the parent's values and cultural systems be respected. There are noticeable differences among different American subcultures in parenting practices and expectations for children. In some households the major form of discipline is corporal, in others it is verbal, while others prefer privilege-withdrawal. There are also differences among families in how comfortable parents feel about hugging and demonstrating affection for their young children, or in how much physical and verbal aggression is tolerated. Marked variations among families concerning their aspirations for their children (such as the emphasis placed on a college education) are also common.

The value system of the family and the community must be understood and appreciated. Insofar as possible, the recommendations of the pediatrician should fall within the ground rules of these systems. The less one is at odds with these value systems, the better are the chances of affecting change. Those parts of the family value system that work against the child's growth and self-esteem should be explored. The questioning of values must be undertaken delicately so as not to rupture an alliance with the parents. Care should be taken to communicate that such values may be suitable for some children but should be modified for others. A child's needs may be at odds with parental values, for example, where a father prizes competition in sports but his son has a gross motor dysfunction and finds greater satisfaction and enhanced self-esteem in gardening, or where parents with advanced college backgrounds feel attendance at a trade school would inflict a family wound, while their language-impaired child would prefer specific vocational training.

Some parents require help to understand how certain cherished beliefs may result in inappropriate expectations for their child, and how such values add stress for youngsters with certain types of disabilities. The end result of such a situation could be the child's total renunciation of the parents' values.

Statement of Expectations. In order to avoid unrealistic expectations or distorted perceptions of a child's prognosis, the physician should help parents deal with their thoughts about the future. The following suggestions may be helpful:

1. The parents should be helped to understand that prognostication is speculative. We simply do not know enough about the natural history of disabilities or the effects of intervention to predict outcomes with confidence. For this reason, parents should be encouraged to live in the present, focus primarily on short-term goals, sustain a level of optimism, and avoid either gloomy or euphoric notions about their child's function as an adolescent or adult. It is important to assure parents that children are resilient in their development, although the timing and degree of improvement cannot be forecast.

2. Parents should recognize that, despite intervention, the child will have a long-range course of both triumphs and setbacks. If appropriate, they should be reassured that they can fully expect to "win the war," although they may lose a few battles along the way! It is critical to prepare parents for the chronicity of their child's learning problems.

3. The pediatrician should be careful not to pose as a miracle worker. Some parents may have a sense that "everything will be all right," now that the physician is involved in the case. It sometimes happens that parents become too optimistic after an evaluation. They may feel that the ability to describe a child's problem is somehow synonymous with a cure. Without dousing such optimism, the pediatrician should be careful not to make false claims or to exaggerate the potential efficacy of any treatment.

4. Some anticipatory guidance can be offered. Parents can be helped to be ready for the unique issues that will arise at particular ages and grade levels. As one follows a child with a learning problem, it can be most helpful to look ahead a year or two to deal with how that child will fit into a particular setting. For example, in working with a fifth-grade student, the pediatrician may want to engage in some discussion about the transition to junior high school, with its new set of challenges. Any consideration of the future should not be aimed much beyond the subsequent year or two. The pediatrician should discourage parents from expending enormous amounts of energy on long-range planning. Rather, they should be advised that by concentrating their efforts on the present and near future, they will be in the best position to facilitate long-range success and happiness.

The Need to Assess the Strategies. Besides communicating what might be expected after the initiation of a particular intervention, it is also critical that every strategy should be evaluated for its efficacy. The pediatrician should emphasize that failure of any one technique need not imply that every technique will fail or that the situation is hopeless. A climate in which the family and school feel themselves to be vital participants in the evaluation process is critically important.

Ongoing assessment and modification can help to free the family and school from a web of helplessness and failure—a web that in the past has often entrapped them, rendered their struggles futile, and deprived them of hope.

SPECIFIC BEHAVIORAL ISSUES

It has been emphasized throughout this book that children with developmental and learning problems are a heterogeneous group. Individual constellations of strengths and weaknesses, a family's responses and adaptations, successes and failures, all vary in infinite combinations. Many youngsters with learning problems display little, if any, maladaptive behavior. Those who do may be subject to abuse by accusatory professionals, who may not understand the bases of the child's misguided struggle.

The pediatrician is often asked for advice and direction in managing behavioral problems that accompany learning disorders. In this section we consider issues and behaviors that can appear as complications of a learning problem. These topics have been selected because of their relatively high prevalence among children with learning problems. We cannot be exhaustive here about counseling techniques for individual behaviors; instead, issues are described and some management suggestions are offered. Hopefully, the strategies outlined will provide a launching pad for the developmentally oriented pediatrician, whose own developmental progress may show an increasing armamentarium of counseling options.

Behavioral Concerns Related to Attention Deficits

In Chapter 3 we dealt with the protean manifestations of attention deficits in children. A youngster's inability to attend selectively to relevant stimuli in the environment is a fundamental ingredient of many learning problems. A number of causes and effects of attention deficits are discussed below. Children with chronically weak attention present a counseling challenge to the pediatrician. Parents are often hungry for advice. A number of books have been written for this purpose, but none should substitute for individualized guidance from a professional.

Poor Selective Attention

The child who seems to tune in and out of focus capriciously throughout the waking day (and sometimes the waking night) is often exasperating to parents and teachers. The child himself frequently shares the frustration.

Clinical Illustrations

1. A youngster may seem unable to listen to or follow directions. When parents or teachers ask him to perform some act, he neglects to do so or omits important steps. Some such children may be labeled "lazy" or "oppositional" if their attention deficits are not diagnosed. In fact they are not lazy or contrary; rather, they have not been able to focus on what is being said to them.

2. The child may seem to daydream. Such a child often is described as "spacy" or "in his own world." At home, he may be sent to perform a chore and never return! In school he may seem to be in a daze while attempting to complete a mathematics or writing assignment.

3. A child's attention may wander aimlessly from one subject to another. Such a youngster may show marked task impersistence. He may listen to something the parents are saying but is easily distracted by a honking car or a chirping bird. Such auditory figure-ground confusion may appear in school, although the pediatrician may not observe some of these behaviors in his office. It is important to stress that sometimes the child attends adequately to high-motivational material (such as television).

General Intervention Strategies. If an inattentive child is to learn effectively and to relate to others in a sustained and meaningful manner, he should be helped through experiences that encourage more focused attention. Initially, this can be done by minimizing the quantity and complexity of information the child has to absorb at any one time. Input can then be gradually increased, staged so that it does not unduly tax the child or "jam his circuits." While one should not expect to "cure" an attention deficit, interventions may have the effect of lessening its impact while they establish a link between problem management and daily routines at home. Parents and children should always be reminded that there may be positive aspects to poorly selective attention, that a "stereoscopic" wide-ranging mind can be creative, inventive, and amusing.

Specific Intervention Strategies

1. Parents should ensure that they have their child's attention when they begin to communicate. Some children require alerting statements such as, "Johnny, come, I have something to say to you right now and I would like you to listen carefully. Okay?" Such comments, delivered in a supportive manner, are helpful in preparing a child to process information and to set appropriate priorities. In addition, as the parents give directions or instructions, at times it may be useful to have the youngster repeat what has been said.

2. Parents can regulate the volume of information that they present to their child in any particular situation. A youngster with attention deficits may not be able to sustain focus for extended periods. Brief, succinct messages are best. More extended communication, or "lecturing," should be abbreviated or split into component parts. Gradually, communications and directions can become longer as a child's attention strength develops.

3. Parents should minimize distractions when communicating with a youngster. Some children are asked to do things while they are watching television, listening to a radio, or playing a game. It is important that, initially, parents talk with the child in a setting that minimizes distraction and maximizes one-to-one interaction. As the child's ability to attend improves, he can be given messages in the presence of competing stimuli.

4. Assigned tasks should consist mainly of activities that can be accomplished in a relatively short period. The child should be able to finish a job soon after he begins it, thereby lessening the possibility of a loss of focus. Having an endpoint that can be reached within the child's duration of attention helps to enhance feelings of effectiveness, which have a beneficial effect on self-esteem. A child who wants to help his parents with household chores might be given the responsibility of emptying the wastepaper basket in his own room. Eventually more complex tasks can be added. If a project is prolonged, requiring several days to complete, it should be divided into stages, each of which can be finished within a specific time span that the child can manage. When a task is segmented into component steps, it is helpful to list "subgoals" and their anticipated time of completion. This kind of experience may be beneficial to a child with task impersistence. It provides a much-sought view of the "light at the end of the tunnel." If, for example, a child has a book-report assignment, his parents may help him develop a schedule, including the number of pages to be read each night and the staging of the writing process.

5. Parents should encourage games that their child likes and that demand selective attention. Most card or board games can help a child focus. In choosing games, a number of variables should be considered, such as how much luck or skill is involved, how well the child can comprehend the rules, and whether the rules must be modified in keeping with the child's abilities. One also needs to consider whether the child can tolerate losing, and whether the games can be played alone or require another person. For example, the board game of checkers and the card game of "war" might increase a child's attention capability. The game of checkers demands more skill than luck. It requires planning, directionality, and spatial orientation. If these skills are beyond the child's capacity, it would be counterproductive to use checkers to induce attention.

Parents should try different games and toys to determine which sustain the child's interest and attention. One should then slowly increase the complexity of the games.

6. Strategic interventions in school are essential, but goals and methods should be consonant with those being employed at home. The pediatrician can help to coordinate such efforts. Some specific suggestions for the management of inattention in school have been described in Chapter 6.

Many of the strategies that are useful in dealing with children who have attention deficits are also applicable to those who have problems with short-term memory and sequential organization. By breaking down materials into small units, giving one-step instructions, and helping children document their work and progress, youngsters who have memory and sequencing disabilities can be assisted.

Impulsivity

As noted in Chapter 3, many children with attention deficits are not reflective; they often respond to tasks, problems, or social situations with little forethought. They act before they think. While an impulsive style often reflects primary attention deficits, sometimes it represents a strategy to abbreviate a difficult or tiresome chore. Thus, both constitutional factors and coping mechanisms may contribute to a child's lack of reflective behavior.

Clinical Illustrations

1. At home, a child may rush through every activity. The frenetic pace is often marked by mistakes and poorly monitored performance. A request to clean up his room may lead a child to dump his toys in a heap in the closet. The child may not plan what he is doing or consider the best approach. Such impulsive children may demonstrate a poor understanding of cause and effect. During a one-to-one pediatric examination, there may be little opportunity to observe an impulsive style unless the child is seen performing developmentally appropriate tasks (see Chapter 5).

2. A child may have problems completing tasks that require reflection. Model building or other projects that of necessity involve planning and delay of gratification may be very frustrating. Difficulty in engaging in reflective activities makes the child susceptible to recurrent failure, eroding self-esteem, and anxiety or frustration.

3. As the demands of school become increasingly complex, a child's nonreflective approach may mediate against success in language arts and mathematics. Difficulty in calculating may arise out of a failure to notice signs for addition, subtraction or multiplication. Impulsive reading may lead to word omissions and poor comprehension or to superficial understanding. Written tasks may be performed in a haphazard, poorly executed manner in an effort to complete the assignment as fast as possible.

General Intervention Strategies. Over the last decade there has been considerable research on techniques to develop reflective cognitive styles in impulsive children (Bash and Camp 1975, Meichenbaum 1977, Palkes et al. 1972,

Santostefano 1978). The major emphasis in these approaches is to have the child decelerate (often both physically and mentally). The youngster is urged to stop and think about what he is doing. It is assumed that such a strategy may help develop a more reflective style. Rapid and poorly considered responses, whatever their bases, are discouraged; the child is asked about the whys and hows of obtaining an answer, so that he must engage in increasingly deliberative thought. The child is taught to verbalize effective learning strategies for almost any task. If successful, such approaches signal internalization of a more reflective cognitive approach.

Specific Intervention Strategies

1. Parents can use games and toys to promote the child's capacity to decelerate and plan. The precise nature of the activities is less important than the manner of engaging in them. As a child assembles a relatively simple snap-together car model in a careless fashion, the parents can point out, in a noncritical way, that the task would go more smoothly if the child would allot additional time. The parents might serve as models by studying the instructions with the child and saying such things as, "The next step is to find piece number 5, which looks like this, and put it on piece number 6, which looks like that. Let's look for the right pieces; no, this isn't number 6, it's number 9. I'm glad I looked carefully so that I didn't make a mistake." The language used should be compatible with the child's age and must not be condescending in tone. Besides serving as a model, the parents can actively, but not intrusively, remind the child to be more reflective and to verbalize what has to be done.

2. As noted earlier, impulsive children may demonstrate poor comprehension of cause-and-effect relationships or of consequences. Parents can help to counteract this by looking for opportunities to ask "why and how" questions, to formulate inquiries that require reflection. For example, if a child mentions briefly a sample of polluted water he saw on a class trip to the science museum, his parents might ask how the water got that way. Could the pollution have been avoided? What is going to happen to all the fish? If the child is playing a game of checkers, the parents can help him understand how some moves lead to countermoves, and how winning requires careful advance planning. A game might be introduced in which an object is placed inside a shoebox and the child tries to guess the contents by shaking the shoebox and asking questions. Such activities provide a model of planning and thinking rather than blurting the first answer that comes to mind.

3. Parents can help in dealing with social impulsivity. If a child recounts a fight between two youngsters in his class, a parent might ask if there was a way either of them could have avoided the confrontation. Could they have stopped to think for a moment? Could one have said or done something differently? Inquiries like these suggest that there are many possible responses from which to select and that the choice of an appropriate option necessitates reflection. Similarly, if a parent sees a child respond to teasing by throwing a rock at a neighbor, the consideration of alternative approaches should be encouraged. Collaborative reflection between parent and child is likely to have a more meaningful impact than a parent's own impulsive condemnation of the act! The time-honored technique of counting to 10 before acting in anger is a useful

strategy. During the course of a day, there may be many interactions between a parent and a child that can be used in a low-key, nonintrusive manner to modify a frenetic, impulsive style. The child can be asked to reflect, to delay, to consider or name alternative solutions, to think of the reasons for situations or events, and to speculate thoughtfully on the consequences of his own and other persons' actions.

4. The pediatrician can help a teacher to manage an impulsive child. School personnel should be encouraged to be process-oriented, showing more interest in how a child obtains a particular answer than in whether the answer is wrong or right. By focusing in this way, the teacher can help the child to become more process-oriented himself and to think through responses. A self-conscious, reflective style learned for one situation can be transferred to other areas and reinforced for many academic activities. When given word problems in mathematics, the student can be assisted to perform while describing what he is doing. Reading comprehension tests are another vehicle for assisting a child to stop and think. Vigilance exercises, in which the child has to find and underline specific rarely occurring letters, words, or names, may be used to adjust the pace of task pursuit. For some school work, the teacher can ask the child to verbalize a strategy before offering an answer.

5. Teachers can present material in ways that minimize a child's impulsivity. For example, rather than assigning an entire page of 20 mathematics problems, which the youngster might rush through in two or three minutes, the teacher can present each problem on a separate index card, giving the child one card every 30 seconds. The teacher can structure a child's day to ensure adequate time for each academic activity. If the youngster knows that he is expected to spend 20 minutes reading a particular chapter, for example, there may be less incentive to finish as soon as possible. The teacher should always feel comfortable discussing why such strategies are being used, in order to gain the collaboration and motivation of the child. A student needs to be reminded occasionally that such interventions reflect neither punishment, criticism, nor disapproval. Instead, they are more like "muscle-building exercises" designed to enhance a child's reflective strength.

6. The teacher can help an impulsive child understand cause-and-effect relationships, especially as they pertain to social interactions. Pictures that have to be arranged in a specific sequence to tell a coherent story can easily serve as a basis for discussion of an ordered event and the effects of individual actions or consequences.

Overactivity

Overactivity may stem from the same sources as poorly selective attention. That is to say, the phenomenon may be primary, secondary, situational, or intentional (see Chapter 3). High levels of activity may be appropriate, exploratory, and generally an asset for certain children at particular times.

Nevertheless, there are a number of youngsters whose "overactivity" impairs productivity and leads to frustration, embarrassment, and sadness. For this group, careful management is imperative. The use of pharmacologic agents to deal with poorly selective activity and attention is discussed in Chapter 7.

Clinical Illustrations

1. Parents may report that at home their child cannot sit still, that he is always on the move and often extremely fidgety. This behavior may be most pronounced when the youngster is attempting to finish homework or sit at the dinner table. The child's ability to sit through a favorite television show does not rule out problems with activity.

2. At school, the child may be out of his seat, constantly running or wandering aimlessly through corridors, frequently unable to settle down. One youngster was described by his teacher as "a fast bowling ball," as he frequently collided with other students during catapults through the building. Some overactive children may remain in their seats but be very fidgety, while others undertake frequent unscheduled excursions throughout the school day.

General Intervention Strategies. A basic goal can be to teach "frenzied" or driven, overactive children to regulate their body actions and to gain greater control over their motor output. Providing activities that allow motor discharge during specified predictable times, but in a relatively controlled and regulated manner, can be helpful. As noted in Chapter 3, some youngsters' overactivity may be secondary to chronic anxiety. In these cases, mastery of feelings that potentiate disorganized and poorly selected activity is an important goal.

Specific Intervention Strategies

1.   If a child appears to require a high level of motor output, his parents can help structure the day, so that activities requiring full use of the body are interspersed with those that demand relative immobility. For instance, one hour of homework each night might be divided into two 30-minute segments. Between these homework periods the child might be allowed to go for a walk, do some running, or perform some indoor exercise. The pediatrician and family can collaborate in selecting activities and allocating times, such that there is a gradual increase in the proportion of each day devoted to activity modulation.

2. Parents and children can play games oriented toward the regulation of body activity (Santostefano 1978). For example, a younger overactive child can be invited to assume the role of different animals who are noted for their fast or slow speeds. As a turtle, the child would be required to walk very slowly; a record book can be kept to show that the turtle can learn to walk increasingly slower each night. As a cheetah, the child moves as quickly as he can, while as a dog he traverses the room at a more regular pace. As he becomes increasingly proficient in representing these three different speeds, the parents can make the task more challenging by asking him to shift abruptly from one animal to another. The more the child can appreciate and regulate different speeds, even in the context of a game, the greater his ability becomes to control overall body activity. At times, when the child becomes extremely active, the parents can suggest, "Why don't you slow down like the turtle?"

Another popular game that can be used with overactive children is "freeze" or "statue." In this game, someone shouts a word like "freeze," and all the participants have to stop and remain perfectly still. As the overactive child

improves in this game, parents can increase its difficulty by having the participants remain in the freeze position for increasingly longer periods. A chart can
be maintained so that the child can gauge his progress.

3. If it appears that the child becomes overactive only at certain times, and
primarily in response to anxiety, the pediatrician should help the parents find
ways to assist the youngster in mastering anxiety-provoking situations. When
necessary, referral to a mental health professional may be indicated. However,
often the parents' interventions will be sufficient to minimize anxiety. For
example, some children become active shortly before bedtime because they are
frightened of having nightmares. A sensitive parent can respond to the child's
anxiety by empathizing about how scary dreams can be but reassuring the
youngster that they are not real, and that the parents are there to help if he
becomes too frightened. Such communication can serve to calm the child and
minimize overactivity. Similar bursts of activity are not uncommon before going
to school in the morning. These may be a response to specific fears about the
school situation (either academic or social). Once again, attending to these
concrete issues may serve to lessen overactivity.

4. The overactive child in school represents a perplexing management issue.
Some of the same techniques used by parents can be applied in the classroom.
For example, if the child shows a propensity toward excessive motoric activity, an
energy "escape valve" period should become a consistently scheduled, regular
part of the program. A youngster can be given specific chores to perform away
from his desk every 15 or 20 minutes, such as taking something to the principal's
office, wiping the blackboard, or putting books and materials back on shelves. As
the child becomes less active, the interval between motor chores can be
lengthened. A second benefit of such responsibilities is that they can give the
child a sense of importance and help increase his self-esteem and social status.

5. An overactive child may benefit from extra time in the gymnasium,
preferably in a small group or even alone. The emphasis should be on
developing body control as well as an ability to regulate his own body tempo.
Physical education teachers can emphasize activities that require motor planning, slow and precise body regulation, and a conscious awareness of accelera-
tion, deceleration, and goal-directed effort. The exercises discussed previously
requiring different speeds may be helpful.

Chronic Insatiability

Insatiability is another characteristic of many children with attention problems
(see Chapter 3). They appear to be in a steady state of hunger and craving for
stimulation or attention. A persistent quest for elusive satisfaction may focus on
food, activity, or material objects. Such children often become whiny and
irritable. They be extremely unpleasant, demanding, and difficult to live with. In
some cases insatiability may be a constitutional trait, first observable in early
infancy. In other cases it can be an acquired behavior, resulting from feelings of
deprivation or "hunger." Insatiability also may be a sign of insecurity, stemming
from humiliating experiences that leave a child feeling so incompetent that he
incessantly desires the input of others.

Clinical Illustrations

1. A child may ask relentlessly for a particular toy or game. Finally he gets it, it loses all its attraction, and a new focus of yearning is quickly developed. This self-perpetuating process can seem endless.
2. A child may reveal an inordinate hunger for adult attention. He may have difficulty tolerating any diversion of adult interest toward a sibling. The youngster may cling in an almost parasitic manner. Although a parent may spend 59 minutes per hour exclusively with a child, the latter resents the one minute that is shared!
3. In some instances feelings of helplessness may lead a child to feel that he is not getting enough support. Such a youngster may demand that the teacher be available constantly and may be perceived by adults as a nag.

General Intervention Strategies. Chronic insatiability is a difficult management problem. Much of the pediatrician's attention may need to be directed toward weary and frustrated parents and teachers. Sometimes his support can relieve feelings of guilt that such a youngster can engender in an adult. Parents may need to recognize that at present no one could satisfy their child, and that incessant cravings do not reflect a failure of their nurturance.

Once the parents can be engaged in this way, several goals can be established. These include (*1*) building the child's capacity to delay receiving gratification; (*2*) helping the child tolerate not having a parent or other adult available at all times; and (*3*) encouraging the sharing of material things with other children. These goals are never easy to achieve, but they should be attempted before referral to a mental health professional.

Specific Intervention Strategies

1. A feeling of deprivation or helplessness may accompany a child's chronic insatiability. Some youngsters experience the momentary loss of a parent's attention as something that will last forever. To deal with this feeling, the parents should set aside specific hours of the day as "special times" for the child. These special times should not be arranged in a rigid or mechanical manner but should be as regular as possible. Parents can tell a child that they realize he likes to be with them, but that this cannot happen all the time, and they would like to have certain periods set aside just for him. If the child reveals a need to control this process, the parents can ask him to select (within reason) those special times.

Once special times are set aside, they may also have to be implemented for siblings. During special times, the parents should try to do what the child wishes—within reason. If the child persists in trying to monopolize the parents' attention at other times, he can be reminded, in a nonrejecting manner, that it is important to delay such intensive interaction until the appropriate special time. The eventual goal is for the child to feel more secure, so that there can be a shift from scheduled times with the parents to natural and spontaneous interactions.

2. Sharing time, possessions, and experiences is not easy for the insatiable child. Parents can attempt to stage situations that progressively promote a capacity to share. These may begin with playing games with the child alone,

gradually progressing to activities in which a sibling or friend is included. The nature of the games should be considered carefully. They should allow for success at the same time that sharing is induced. It may be best to start with more cooperative activities rather than competitive ones. An indoor bowling game with a parent and sibling can be set up so that at first all scores of the participants are combined. As the child learns to wait his turn and to share parent time, the bowling can shift to a more competitive format.

Reading a story alone on some occasions (but at other times with a sibling) can be productive. A friend or a sibling can work with the child to make cookies (an activity that might resonate with the youngster's pervasive hunger). In both cases, emphasis should be on collaboration and the sharing of products.

3. The chronically insatiable child may need to be told repeatedly that desires cannot be satisfied immediately and that some wishes can never be fulfilled. Adults who feel weary and guilty may yield to a child's demands, regardless of their extremity. This may result in momentary relief, but ultimately it reinforces unrealistic expectations. The support of the pediatrician can be crucial in helping parents learn to say no and to find alternative ways of satisfying a child. For example, a child's demand for a very expensive toy may be dealt with by having the parents acknowledge how much the child wants the toy, but that he cannot have it at present because of its price. In some cases, where appropriate, a less expensive object might be substituted. If the child is old enough, he can be told that if a particular item is so desirable, it will have to be earned (perhaps through household chores). Such a strategy nurtures an attitude of responsibility while fostering more realistic goal-setting.

4. Insatiability can be managed in school through the use of "special times," similar to those described for home intervention. In many cases, if the school can foster a child's sense of competence and self-sufficiency, insatiability may diminish. The teacher should search for ways to display the child's work and offer high praise for tasks that are performed independently and with delay of gratification.

Problems with Transitions

Transitional events or changes in routine constitute common impediments for children with learning problems. They may have difficulty switching from one room to another, adapting to different settings, or initiating new activities. Each change carries with it the threat of disorganization or disruption. It seems paradoxical that a child might be impersistent at tasks and yet inflexible when it comes to transitions. There may, in fact, be a fine line between impersistence and perseveration; the two traits often coexist in a youngster. Problems with adaptability may be part of a constitutional picture of inefficient attention and activity. Possibly a child who cannot shift easily is reflecting anxiety linked to issues of loss or fear of failure. Problems with transitions may represent a final common pathway involving cognitive and affective inputs.

Clinical Illustrations

1. A child may find the daily progression of routines difficult to manage. Getting up in the morning, dressing, eating breakfast, and preparing for

school may present problems. The youngster may linger over each activity. The same pattern may appear when the youngster returns from school; there may be problems initiating routines, coming in from play, disengaging from the television set, and preparing for sleep. Parental efforts to induce a shift of activities may result in severe temper tantrums and unbridled anger.

2. A child may persist at an activity, wishing to sustain it beyond a reasonable period. Such a youngster has difficulty suspending a project for continuation tomorrow. Sometimes the behavior reflects a child's wish to pursue some enterprise that is likely to yield success, rather than to move on to a riskier endeavor that might culminate in failure; such tenacity may be an avoidance response. At other times perseveration may be a consequence of cognitive inertia with regard to shifting sets. For example, some children with memory deficits or difficulties in establishing object constancy may experience change as overwhelming.

3. A child may resist any changes in daily routine. His behavior may deteriorate at the prospect of an unexpected visit to a relative. The youngster may be upset by the arrival of cousins for an overnight visit and by having to give up his own bed for the night. Some children crave consistency, or a sameness that helps provide tenuous order in a world that somehow seems chaotic. They do not appreciate surprises and instead insist upon knowing exactly what is going to happen each day.

General Intervention Strategies

A child who has difficulty initiating activities and handling transitions for cognitive reasons should be helped to prepare for a shift by being given adequate advance notice, handling any feelings that are aroused by the change, and providing transitional activities. The latter give the child a sense of control over what happens. Some parents and teachers might argue that it is best not to tell such a child about an altered routine until the last possible moment (so as to minimize anxiety). In most instances, however, it is best for the youngster to know well in advance. This provides experience in managing transitions. The general thrust should be toward helping the child prepare for transitions and assisting him to master changes. At the same time, it is important to meet the child halfway to provide as much consistency as possible, so that frequent surprises will not subvert a developing ability to tolerate change.

Specific Intervention Strategies

1. Parents should provide adequate notice for the child to stop one activity and move on to another. This technique can be implemented by informing the child that, say, in 10 minutes it will be time to stop what he is doing in order to start something else. This same message might be repeated at five and then at two minutes before the shift. Such preparation may minimize the discomfort of the transition. Even with such advance warning, however, some transitions require more active collaboration by the parents. For example, if a youngster is coloring and it is time to get ready for bed, the parents' reminders could be supplemented by helping the child put away the crayons and by preparing the bed.

2. Some shifts in activity, especially those that are apt to be most troublesome (such as dressing in the morning or going to bed at night), are facilitated by transitional activities that promote structure, order, or control. For example, a child who has problems going to sleep at night might be given the responsibility of helping to put out his clothes for the next day, or pulling the shades down and putting a night light on. Actively engaging the child in tasks that signify a transition can help to nurture a sense of mastery, thereby weakening the inherent threat of transition time.

3. Some children are confused by transitions, since they do not have a well-established sense of sequence. Daily routine is a poorly established notion in their lives. What becomes predictable to others remains new and risky for them. The use of a daily schedule chart, with each activity clearly listed, can provide the external structure that some of these children may require. If the child can see that after dinner comes a bath, followed by television, and then bedtime, he may start to assimilate daily sequences and become less overwhelmed by transitions.

4. Some transitions prove difficult for children because it is not clear what is going to transpire. An example might be having to stop playing with friends one afternoon in order to go for a speech and language evaluation. This child, who ordinarily is stressed by transitions, will be even more stressed if subsequent events cannot be anticipated. If the same child is prepared adequately for new situations and given enough time to ask questions, the transition may not be laden with as much anxiety and resistance.

5. There will always be some transitions that are unplanned and do not allow time for preparation. An unanticipated visit to the doctor for a laceration, or the cancellation of a long-awaited baseball game because of rain, may severely tax the child. Whenever there is a disruption in routine, or when anticipation is thwarted, parents should attempt to remain as calm as possible, lessening the child's anxieties by conveying the message that sudden shifts do not necessarily threaten anyone's well-being. If abrupt transitions are managed well, they can actually serve as the foundation for handling similar crises in the future.

6. Problems with transition are also common at school. Some youngsters have difficulty moving from one academic subject to another. Once a routine becomes well established, shifts grow difficult to tolerate. The use of a daily schedule on a child's desk can be helpful. As a particular activity is accomplished, the child can put a checkmark next to it on the sheet.

An added burden for children with learning problems in the school setting is their need to leave the classroom (more often than other youngsters) to spend time in a resource room or other special service facility. These children, in particular, may benefit from a written daily schedule. Such youngsters will need support and assistance with constant changes. They may need to have certain transitional activities built into their schedule.

A case illustration will highlight the management of a child who has difficulty with transitions. A six-year-old boy was said to be overactive and frequently inattentive. During recess, he often became silly and then refused to come back indoors. In part this was an attempt to avoid school work. Consideration was given to keeping him in the classroom during recess, since the latter seemed to be a disorganizing experience. On the other hand, his need for physical activity also was clear. Consequently, he was made "recess monitor," a job that required him to return to the room five minutes before the other children, hold the door open for them, and then ensure that they all came in. The transitional activity worked because it enhanced his self-esteem (the job was a coveted one) and helped him calm down after recess. It tended to nurture his feeling of competence; he took pride in his position. In fact, occasionally he rewarded other children with the privilege of substituting for him!

School Phobia

School phobia may be defined as an inordinate fear of going to school. It should be differentiated from the less intense, less prolonged, and more typical anxiety expressed by children as they begin a new school or dread a threatening event on a particular day.

School phobia affects children from early elementary through high school. Its etiology and pathophysiology are often complicated. A prominent theory advanced in the mental health literature explains school phobia on the basis of a disturbed mother-child interaction (Blackham 1967, Waldfogel et al 1957). It is conceptualized primarily as a child's fear of leaving his mother, rather than as anxiety about school itself. An ambivalent mother-child relationship and serious problems with separation and individuation are seen to be the contributing factors behind the school-phobic child. Given the intensity of the disturbance, referral to a mental health professional is the usual recommendation.

A broader view of school phobia may encompass those children and adolescents who avoid school because of issues other than the classic phenomenon described above. Such an expanded view would include children who seek to avoid school because of anguish over their academic and social performance. In sorting out the issues underlying a school phobia, it is often useful for the pediatrician to obtain an evaluation of the child and family from a mental health professional.

Clinical Illustrations

1. A child may refuse flatly to go to school and may wish to stay in his room all day. Such a youngster may complain of somatic symptoms. Not only does the child refuse to go to school but he curtails almost all outside activities. He may become an exile in a bedroom. This kind of clinical picture generally indicates serious psychopathology; it is the one most likely to reflect separation issues.

2. Alternatively, a child may get to school but on many days becomes ill and is sent home. The child characteristically is well known to the school nurse. Somatic complaints often prevent such a youngster from attending classes. He may wish to remain close to his mother and may desire to avoid certain academic experiences that represent potential humiliation.

3. A child may depart for school without difficulty but never arrive there! Such a pattern is particularly frequent at the junior and senior high school levels, ranging from cutting one or two classes to avoiding most academic subjects. This form of rebellion, or avoidance, may not fall within the more narrow, circumscribed psychoanalytic view of school phobia, but it should be considered within the broader concept of this disorder as it relates to specific

school-related anxieties. Typically, there may be a counterphobic, bravadolike facade, a "macho" often reinforced by peers who are experiencing similar anxieties. Within this group there may be a subgroup who are not particularly anxious about school but feel it is irrelevant. While such a cult would not properly fall under the heading of school phobia, it has a magnetic attraction for youngsters who are trying to contain underlying anxieties.

General Intervention Strategies

Most specialists in mental health and education agree that a fundamental approach to school phobia (regardless of the etiology) is (1) to insure that the school remains in contact with the youngster while he is at home and (2) to help an affected child return to the classroom as quickly as possible. If children do not receive a clear, unambivalent message that they are expected to return to school, their phobias will be prolonged. Continuing contact with the school helps to convey that message. Every morning there should be explicit expectation for the child to attend school

Specific Intervention Strategies

1. If the school phobia seems primarily a function of a disturbed parent-child relationship, the first strategy would be referral to a mental health professional. It is critical that the pediatrician, mental health specialist, school personnel, and family work closely together to help the child or adolescent to return to school.

The initiation of psychotherapy for school phobia is but one step in alleviating the symptom. Helping the parents display less ambivalence in their communication with the child is also important. A parent learns not to allow recurrent abdominal pains to keep a child home. Not infrequently, the child's anxieties are so entrenched that any effort to take him to school becomes overwhelming. The wish to stay within the safe boundaries of home can become obsessional. In such situations, intermediate, well-paced steps may be necessary. These can include:

a. Having the child's teacher and counselor visit the home to convey their wish to have him back in school. Work can be brought home by the teacher.

b. Having the child's parents bring the child to school, even if it is for just a few minutes. If the child only spends these moments in the main office, this still is a step in the right direction. If at first he is unable to go all the way to the school building, that effort may have to be broken down into components. For example, on the first day, the child might walk halfway to school, and the school counselor might meet and talk with him briefly. On the following day the child would be expected to approach even closer to the school. Gradually progress toward the ultimate goal would follow.

c. Having the child spend at least part of the day in the classroom. The school would have to provide a supportive counselor who would remain available to the child if pressures built up too rapidly. The school counselor would attempt to have the child remain in school rather than return home.

d. Having the child spend the entire day at school with whatever backup support is necessary.

2. If a school phobia represents an active fear of school, possible reasons for this response should be elucidated. In many cases, children who have learning problems use avoidance as a way of coping with the painful social or academic situations that remind them of their inadequacy. For such children, helping them to return to school must be coupled with sensitivity in dealing with their feelings of imcompetence. One may need to make modifications in their school programs. For example, if a particular mathematics class is beyond the child's capability, serious consideration should be given to a less demanding program.

3. Some children avoid school because they are being scapegoated by their peers. This predicament demands the combined efforts of a therapist or pediatrician, the family, the child, and the school. The physician can help the youngster learn how his particular social style contributes to scapegoating and rejection. The school can help by engaging the child in supervised small-group activities. This provides an opportunity to experience more appropriate peer interactions and to discuss feelings about social failure. The family must also offer support. The parents can become "coconspirators" in helping overcome social problems. They should not overindulge in reassurance. Instead, they should offer social tutoring—advice on attracting and keeping friends.

4. Although the argument that "school is irrelevant" is overstated by many children (especially adolescents), it should be given serious consideration. Major mismatching may exist between an adolescent's orientation and learning style and what the school's curriculum provides (and demands). A shift to a vocational high school has on occasion brought an antisocial adolescent back to a school setting.

It should be obvious from these examples that much deliberation must enter into determining the optimal approach for managing a student who is reluctant to attend school. Efforts must include consideration of the elements that have led to the school phobia, and the enlistment of the cooperation of all those working with the child.

Homework Avoidance

In many households, parents are constantly prodding their children to finish homework. Often school assignments kindle hostility toward parents, anger toward teachers, frustration about learning, and feelings of helplessness. Homework can become a heated subject within a family. The pediatrician may help tease out the salient factors, including whether the child does no homework at all, or only neglects certain types of assignments or if the homework is too taxing or demanding given the child's learning problems.

Clinical Illustrations

1. A child may refuse to do any homework, either denying its existence or insisting that school is "dumb" and that he would rather watch television.
2. A child may do some homework for some classes but fail to complete all work assigned. The youngster may claim he is given too much to do.

3. A child may be able to do homework assigned on a nightly basis but may be overwhelmed by a paper or project that will require several weeks to complete.

4. Many children attempt to complete homework but are so frustrated by it that they feel defeated. Some resourceful students may enlist the services of a parent to do most of the work for them.

General Intervention Strategies

The first task in developing a general intervention design is to attempt to understand the ingredients of a child's homework avoidance. Is it a reflection of parent-child problems? Is the work actually too great in quantity? Is it so difficult that the child feels overwhelmed? Is the child too disorganized in terms of time and sequence to plan adequately for such work? The homework a child receives should be consistent with his learning and working capacities. If this criterion is satisfied, the goal of intervention is to insure that parental coercion is replaced by self-monitoring of homework, perhaps with the aid of a school counselor. The child may need help to organize his time to permit work to be done within a busy schedule. If necessary, tutoring can be arranged.

Specific Intervention Strategies

1. If it appears that a child's homework problem is only one of many irritants between him and his parents, the pediatrician should attempt to improve communication within the family and should consider referral for more formal counseling. Resolution of certain problems may take months, and it is important not to allow the child's work to deteriorate further. The experience of falling behind on homework assignments may place the child in an untenable position, leading to serious maladaptive behaviors. In the face of extreme conflict between parents and a child, it might be best to recommend that the parents not police homework but rather have it monitored by the child's teacher or counselor, who might then keep them informed. When children are included in the development of such a strategy, it has a good chance of being effective. If necessary, a behavior-modification program that rewards a child for completing homework may serve as a useful replacement for parental threats.

2. The pediatrician can offer to participate in a meeting with the parents, teacher, and child if there is a strong indication that the work is beyond the child's capabilities. A modified homework program may be warranted. The modification may require a simple redistribution of assignments rather than a decrease in total work load during the course of a week.

3. As noted above, some children can manage nightly homework assignments but are defeated by a long-term project. The parents and school personnel can collaborate by demonstrating how even very long assignments can be staged, and how a schedule can be planned to allocate units of work for each evening.

4. If a child has major problems settling down to complete assignments a special "homework time" may be needed each evening and on weekends. Scheduling such a regular hour is especially important for disorganized children who do not have a firm sense of sequence. If the parent-child relationship is a relatively good one, it is appropriate to remind the child about homework time.

The family can determine the optimal hour for it. Some children do best shortly after school, others before dinner. If family relationships are strained, and the parents do not wish to stand vigil over the child, the establishment of a homework time could be incorporated within a behavior-modification program. If the child has no homework on a particular evening, the designated time should be used for other forms of organized learning activity (e.g., reading or using workbooks). This sustains the work habit and thwarts efforts to rush through work at school to free up homework time for television or other less productive pursuits.

5. Many parents ask whether they should tutor their children or assist with their work. While there are no hard and fast rules, several considerations are important: If parents find that they are doing most of their child's homework, there is something wrong (either the work is too difficult or the child has found an excellent means of evading assignments). Such a situation should be rectified.

Tutoring one's own child is often a very difficult task, especially with a dysfunctioning youngster. It is not uncommon for many angry feelings to be aroused, both in the parent and in the child. Acting-out, anger, and frustration may become intensified in the tutoring arena. When this happens, adjustments should be made. Instead of academic tutoring, families might engage in games that promote cognitive development in their children. Such activities generally do not create the tension that often surrounds formal tuition. By the time most youngsters reach adolescence, they are not interested in being tutored by their parents. Nor do they want to play games with them. At this time, it is expecially important that academic help be provided by the school.

Parents should never refrain totally from helping a child who has specific questions while performing homework. The model of a parent as a resource is an important one. The appropriate use of this resource can be a lesson in itself. There can be a wide range of support, short of formalized parental tutoring.

Television "Addiction"

In today's society, many childhood hours pass in front of television sets. Parents frequently ask their pediatrician about the appropriate dosage of televiewing. They express concern about the content of selected shows. The issue is particularly relevant for the parents of a child who has school problems, as they attempt to structure the youngster's day to provide an optimal enviornment for learning.

Clinical Illustrations

1. A child may spend several hours each day watching television, to the detriment of homework or reading. Such a youngster may become accustomed to the passive receipt rather than the active extraction of information. Long hours watching television programs may displace valuable reading experience. Such inactivity might also contribute to a diminished working capacity. The rapid tempo of much television programming may aggravate an underlying impulsivity, impeding efforts to develop reflective behavior.

2. A child may watch aggressive television shows before bedtime. These may excite him, so that he finds it hard to fall asleep.

3. A child may transfer the content of aggressive television shows to sibling or peer relationships. He may overidentify with certain kinds of "superheroes", some of whose most maladaptive traits (such as impulsivity) may lend themselves to imitation.

General Intervention Strategies

Parents need to limit the television consumption of their youngsters, especially before the adolescent years. In determining quotas, parents should insure that television does not preclude school work, that the content of the shows does not serve to disorganize a child, and that the child's ability to distinguish fantasy from reality is such that attempts to be like Superman do not lend to fractured limbs. One should insure that some shows serve to foster cognitive development and that the parent watch some shows with the child in order to exploit these for educational purposes.

Specific Intervention Techniques

1. In establishing daily routines, consideration must be given to television time. This should not assume the highest priority and certainly should not displace homework and household chores. In establishing television hours, parents should consider periods that are likely to be least disruptive. Some children may need a transition that television can provide after a tense school day; a low-keyed program may be appropriate shortly before bedtime.

2. Parents should assess whether television shows with aggressive content provide a vicarious vent for anger, thereby serving a useful psychological function. On the other hand, they need to determine whether certain shows elicit too much excitation and aggression. If feelings of the latter sort are evident, appropriate limits must be set. When a child is permitted to watch such shows, the presence of a parent to preserve calm and to use material to discuss appropriate ways of expressing anger can help promote the development of the child's own controls. Intelligent exposure to television depends greatly on the active involvement of parents.

3. Some children experience great pleasure in viewing programs that are obviously fantasy. Often these shows provide psychologically healthy escapes. However, some children with learning problems may have difficulty discriminating between fantasy and reality. When these children watch wildly imaginative shows, they may need someone with them to help tease out the real-world contents.

Depression and Associated Maladaptive Coping Mechanisms

Some children with learning problems show signs of depression. The symptoms are summarized in Table 1. Such youngsters may have experienced cycles of frustrating situations in their lives. They may have walked away from "battles" feeling defeated, helpless, and dimished.

Some signs of depression are overt, including an unhappy mood, self-deprecatory statements, and loss of energy. In other cases, children succeed in concealing and managing their depression through a number of maladaptive coping styles. They avoid situations that confront them with intense feelings of anxiety. They may retreat from threatening activities or cheat to avoid losing.

Table 1. Direct and Masked Signs of Depression in Children and Adolescence

Direct
Self-deprecatory statements and ideation
Sad affect
Feelings of helplessness and hopelessness
Loss of drive and/or enthusiasm
Intense feelings of boredom
Loneliness and isolation
Suicidal ideation

Masked
Somatic complaints
Sleep disturbance
Eating disturbance
Impulsive behavior
Aggressive behavior (truancy, defiance, rebelliousness)
Drug and alcohol abuse
Excessive quitting, cheating, lying
Poor peer relations
Deterioration in school performance

Occasionally, they attempt to take control and dominate others in order to save face and not feel vulnerable. Some may seriously withdraw, retreating from a world they find humiliating. Still other children may become aggressive and lash out, managing their depression through acting-out behavior that keeps their dysphoric mood well beyond conscious awareness.

In this section we use the term *depression* to describe a condition engendered as a continuing response to loss and failure. This theoretical position diverges from the view held by some investigators (Brumback et al 1977, Cole 1978), who view depression as a primary affective disorder whose diagnosis suggests serious consideration of medication as the treatment of choice. While constitutional predispositions or factors may contribute to a child's depression, environmental variables play a prominent role. Depression may be conceptualized as a complex phenomenon involving cognitive and affective factors growing out of constitutional and environmental antecedents. Before medication is prescribed for childhood depression, counseling approaches should attempt to manage the often overwhelming feelings of inadequacy and incompetence. Ultimately, as more knowledge is gained from basic research, a better understanding of depression as a primary affective disorder will help us distinguish it from reactive symptoms.

The wish to avoid sadness and humiliation is a powerful motivating force and a major determinant of behavior for all school-age children. If a child's unique cognitive style varies significantly from socially based norms, he may need to wage an ongoing defensive war to save face. Such a child may live with an ever-present threat of exposure and peer ridicule. Many adults also are engaged in a constant effort to avoid humiliation and low self-esteem, but for them the task is an easier one. If they can't dance, they don't go to dances! If they are not good at reading, they can go to the movies! Children, however, are required to pursue activities that display weaknesses likely to lead to humiliation.

Very early in the school years (and often earlier) youngsters appropriate strategies to avoid humiliation and consequent depression. Many children with learning problems devise successful mechanisms to maintain self-esteem and fend off embarrassment. These may originate from a sense of humor, an area of particular interest or a form of expertise (e.g., stamp collecting or a musical instrument), the assumption of a leadership role, the vigorous mobilization of discrete strengths (e.g., in sports), or the careful cultivation of social skills. Some children with learning problems hold an excellent track record for selecting the best ways to cope. What it takes to accomplish this is something of a mystery. Parental support, accessible strengths, and good advice (early enough) can facilitate the process.

Some youngsters with learning problems appear to cope in manners that are truly maladaptive. The resultant behavior patterns may lead to alienation from adults and peers. In some cases, the strategies themselves may become a greater problem than the initial developmental dysfunctions. It is common for a child to be referred to a pediatrician or mental health professional, not because of an underlying disability but because of maladaptive coping.

In this section we will consider six commonly encountered maladaptations: quitting, cheating, controlling, aggressing, regressing, and withdrawing. While these six strategies are often recruited to avoid feelings of low self-esteem and fight depression, they may be a consequence of other factors as well. These maladaptations are often intimately tied to the quest to deny sadness and deal with perceived inadequacy, and so they are being considered here along with the issue of depression.

Clinical Illustrations

1. Quitting. A child admitted pathetically to his therapist: "I was born to quit; God made me that way." Such a youngster may denigrate a particular activity, saying it is boring, as a means of averting another setback. He may have difficulty finishing assignments in school and may invoke a quitting strategy to cover this. The pattern of quitting can become a well-ingrained, self-perpetuating, or habit-forming behavior.

2. Cheating. A child may often use the tactic of changing the rules of a game in order to avoid losing. In school, such a youngster who lacks confidence in his own ability may compensate by copying the answers of other children. An older student may submit a report on a designated topic that was written several years ago by another student. Sometimes an extraordinary expenditure of energy goes into the development of cheating techniques. The same output appropriately diverted could obviate the need for cheating.

3. Controlling. A child may feel desperately that he must be "boss," that he must dictate what happens in all situations, and that he needs to be the overseer and the oppressor. It is important to recognize that some children exhibit extreme controlling behavior in an effort to conceal an intense, painful perception of vulnerability and helplessness. A child may dominate other youngsters while playing games in the neighborhood or interacting socially in school. Oppressive tactics are used commonly to achieve social control. These include the scapegoating of other youngsters and the presentation of adult-defying "you-can't-make-me-do-it" facades. Sometimes such youngsters manage to appear "cool" to peers; at other times they may be rejected for their transparent pursuit of power.

4. *Aggressing.* Some children with learning problems deal with failure by becoming aggressive (both verbally and physically). While some of this behavior is a disguise for intense feelings of inadequacy and sadness, other aggressive behavior may represent vindication or striking back at a society that is perceived to be hostile, unrewarding, and rejecting. Some children who have problems with impulsivity may have particular difficulty controlling their anger. They may find themselves driven and dominated by feelings that their cognitive controls cannot dampen. In such cases, the aggressive behavior is manifest by frequent fights, many of which are unprovoked. These may occur when a youngster feels vulnerable and strikes back to get revenge or save face. In other cases, children may use verbal aggressive tactics, criticizing and belittling others. They may indulge in remarks that are cutting, bitter, and antagonistic, that progressively estrange them from peers. Sometimes children direct their anger at objects. They may destroy a school book, overturn a chair, throw a rock through a window, or deface the walls of a building. In some instances these actions may be premeditated, while in other cases there may be a sudden loss of control. Such aggressive tendencies can spiral and intensify, leading ultimately to extreme antisocial behavior and delinquency (Bachara and Zaba 1978, King 1975).

5. *Regressing.* Regression may be used by a child to flee from situations that produce failure, depression, and lowered self-esteem. The youngster may revert to behaviors and actions of a much earlier age. A child confronted with a difficult mathematics assignment may begin giggling or fall on the floor. When he doesn't know a correct answer, the response may be delivered in a baby's voice. A child who has difficulty relating to peers may prefer to engage in the antics of younger children and seek the company of those several years his junior.

A child may also demonstrate cognitive regression. Some skills upon which a youngster has had a tenuous grasp may suddenly weaken. Achievement-test scores actually may fall. This often reflects extreme anxiety, which reduces the capacity to concentrate and organize information. Some children experience this feeling when they take a written examination. They become overwhelmed by its length, complexity, and time constraints. They lose their ability to attend to the questions or to think coherently. Consequently, they may demonstrate a performance one or two years behind their actual skill level.

6. *Withdrawing.* Some children with learning problems seek a strategic retreat; they become isolated and withdrawn. They may talk with family members but have little contact with other children or adults. In group situations, they typically are seen off by themselves, interacting only minimally with others. Such a youngster might occupy the back of a classroom and seldom say a word. Unlike his aggressive counterpart, the child who is withdrawn might not be recognizable by the school as a problem. Consequently, he may be referred late and ultimately receive less service than the acting-out, more blatantly difficult student.

General Intervention Strategies

In analyzing a set of coping mechanisms mobilized by a child to avoid sadness and shame, an empathic approach should be taken, so that the parents, school, and pediatrician communicate to the child that they know things have not been easy. With some children (adolescents especially), initial attempts may seem to fall on deaf ears. The adult world must persevere. The illusory benefits of a particular maladaptive coping style should be pointed out, but such a message must be communicated in a sensitive fashion, lest the child experience it as yet another insult to his integrity.

An attempt should be made to counteract any prevailing sense of hopelessness and defeatism by communicating to the child that, although life has been difficult, positive steps can be taken (with the help of the pediatrician, family, and school). The child should be reassured that he has control and autonomy. This may be unconvincing for such a youngster, but it must be reiterated.

The adults in an affected child's life can suggest alternative approaches to handle problems more adaptively. Parents must help a youngster discover activities in which there is a high probability of success (given the child's specific strengths). Such endeavors can be suggested as an alternative to self-defeating strategies. Methods should be devised that maximize triumphs in learning and social interaction.

If feelings of incompetence are deeply ingrained in a family and child, the input and intervention of a mental health professional is indicated.

Specific Intervention Strategies

1. Quitting. A child needs to be persuaded that tasks or games are not as much fun when they end in the middle. When planning a game at home, parents might want to incorporate a no-quitting rule, which must be adhered to by all participants. Such a rule should be enforced for all children in the family, so as not to single out the youngster with developmental dysfunction. Alternatively, each child might be permitted one quit or two quits a month (but that would be all). This might add some levity (always a useful adjunct to intervention).

Parents should encourage participation in activities that produce immediate, positive results that enhance the child's self-esteem and minimize the compulsion to quit. For example, cooking or baking are endeavors in which any child can succeed and see concrete and relatively immediate results. Specific chores can be assigned well within the reach of a child's own developmental attainment. A youngster might be interested in helping his father paint the exterior of their house. If his fine motor abilities are impaired, however, he might be assigned to paint a part of the house where there are no window panes. Such planned and monitored success experiences can improve self-esteem and diminish the need for quitting.

With adolescents, recurrent quitting sometimes can be avoided by careful selection of jobs that fit his specific abilities. For example, an adolescent with problems in mathematics might not be able to handle a cashier's job at a supermarket. The same adolescent might develop a real feeling of accomplishment by being a stock boy and keeping the shelves in order.

In school, the volume of work may need to be adjusted so that it does not overwhelm the child. Youngsters with diminished working capacity or attention deficits may need to have small doses of work so that closure can be achieved regularly.

Sometimes concrete rewards or positive reinforcements can be used in a very explicit manner to help a child overcome a quitting problem. For younger children, merely earning stars might be reinforcement enough; for older youngsters, the stars might need to have enough purchasing power to obtain hobby supplies, ice cream, or the family car on Saturday evening.

Children with learning problems are likely not to quit a task if it resonates with some of their own emotional needs. For example, a teacher was once confronted with a very needy nine-year-old boy who had extremely low self-esteem and tended to retreat from learning demands. Even when he attempted a task, quitting was the rule. Since hunger was such a significant component of this child's psychological makeup, a decision was made to develop curricula around this need and to provide tasks that would allow him to feed others. He was thus engaged in reading about birds and planning and building a bird feeder. He became a participant in construction—measuring dimensions, buying wood, and offering assistance while not doing the actual work. He was able to wait a day for the paint to dry (not easy for an impulsive child), make a peanut-butter ball of seeds, and place the finished product on a tree for all to admire. This approach offered an active solution to the youngster's more passive longing. Many aspects of this project promoted cognitive and affective development.

2. Cheating. When playing with a child who constantly resorts to cheating, a parent might first ask him if he realizes what he is doing. This provides a good opening for discussion. Parents should point out that when a person changes rules or cheats, the game is not as much fun any more. This should be stated in an empathic and caring manner, but also in a way that challenges the child to evaluate the risks and benefits of cheating. Parents should never let cheating pass without comment. Games need to be selected carefully, so that they do not require skills beyond the child's current level of attainment and thereby encourage rule changing.

School personnel (in a sensitive way) should not tolerate cheating. They should communicate that cheating is unacceptable, but at the same time they should offer to help the child become equipped to handle school work and tests without the need for cheating. Some children have inordinate difficulty tolerating failure or acknowledging mistakes. They need a great deal of reassurance that they will still be accepted and respected despite their errors. If a child is susceptible to cheating, teachers need to be careful to praise at least a portion of each legitimate work effort.

3. Controlling. When a child has an excessive need to be in command, the family and school should seek ways to allow control of certain well-circumscribed aspects of daily life. Rather than always telling the child what to do, they should present choices so the child does not feel that the demands of home and school call for the total surrender of self-determination. With such children, adult attempts to wrest all control meet with renewed resistance and obstinacy. A spirit of compromise must prevail at home and in school.

At home, the child can be put in charge of meaningful, high-motivational chores. If he is interested in cars, it may be possible to have him check the oil or the water in the radiator and the battery. He can keep a notebook in which the checkup is recorded, and he can add more water when necessary. Interest in machines can be linked to use of a power mower or a snow blower. Interest in cooking can be exploited by having the child prepare one meal a week, planning and organizing it several days in advance.

A highly controlling child needs to be offered choices. Whenever possible, jobs or assignments should be presented as options. For example, "You have a choice: you can clean up your room and then take a bath, or first take a bath and then clean your room." Or, "If you don't want to clean your room and someone else has to do it, then it's only fair that you help clean the garage. Which would you rather do?" Such alternatives are likely to lessen the child's resistance.

In school, one can also offer choices in the form of options that can foster feelings of autonomy. One can also use socially acceptable control roles, such as being a monitor at recess or leading the class to the gym. Another kind of control compromise, for older children, involves allowing them to act as tutors or sports instructors for younger students. This not only provides the tutor with an opportunity to feel authoritative but the tutorial situation itself makes the child more aware of the feelings related to learning. Options in school can be presented as they are at home: "This morning we have arithmetic problems to do. We also have a phonics page and paragraphs to read in the blue book. They should all be finished by the end of the morning, but why don't you do them in the order you feel best about. Let me know if you need a hand with any of the work. I'll be around if you do." This approach allows some leeway and enough laxity to lessen any feeling of being constrained and having to fight back for control. An increasingly cooperative attitude hopefully results from this strategy.

Some teachers may fear that offering choices to children or adolescents will weaken their own effectiveness in managing the classroom, but this need not occur if the amount of control and choice are dispensed sensitively. Most important is that the teacher *not* get involved with the child in a competitive battle for control. The learning climate in the classroom will be enhanced if the child and teacher are not defensive about who is the boss. It is the teacher who must take the initiative in offering choices and compromises.

4. Aggressing. A pediatrician can assist parents in determining if a child's aggressive outbursts occur primarily in response to specific situations. If so, some modification of these events can be attempted. For example, if it appears that when a child plays football he becomes frustrated and explosive, another sport might be substituted—one that does not encourage rough physical contact. If parents notice that arithmetic homework is very difficult, leading to outbursts, they might tell the youngster that they can see how upset he gets and that they want to help avoid such unhappiness. Their overt offer of availability when he attempts to do this kind of work might diminish frustration. A general attempt should be made to discern potential precipitants or triggers of aggression and to help remove or modify them.

Parents can help a child become more aware of the early signs of aggressive outbursts. They may note that, before losing control, a youngster begins to clench his fists. If the child is helped to notice this behavior, it might be possible for him to control it by leaving the scene, taking a walk, or just reminding everyone to calm down. In this way, the child experiments with options that replace aggressive behavior.

Parents should help a child focus aggression and verbalize feelings. A mother once reported that her seven-year-old son with a gross motor delay threw sticks at other boys when he became frustrated while playing with them. She was firm in telling him that this was not acceptable, but she added that he could throw sticks at a big tree near the house. This strategy helped the child to learn to delay his anger and to express it more adaptively. Once he gained control, he switched to shouting at the other children, a behavior that still caused him problems but represented a higher level of expression. Also, as he became more verbal, he was able to share his feelings of rejection with his parents, and they helped him deal more effectively with peers.

Parents may use displacement for their children who are acting aggressively toward younger brothers and sisters. The following approach might be employed: "I know you get angry at Johnny, but you can't hit him. If you want to hit, go over and smash that Boppo doll." A punching bag might also be valuable for this purpose.

If a child's aggressive behavior leads to the destruction of property, it is essential that the youngster be held accountable for the damage. Restitution is an important form of intervention. The replacement of a damaged object can be far more relevant than "no television for a week" or "being grounded" for several days. If a child breaks a picture frame during an aggressive outburst, he should accompany the parent to the frame store and pay some amount for a replacement. Discipline in response to aggressive behavior should not represent revenge on the part of the parents, but rather an intervention to help the child learn responsibility and gain control over anger.

It is important for parents to discuss unacceptable aggressive behaviors with a child. However, it may not be possible to do so during an outburst. Instead, an effort should be made to find a relatively calm period within 24 hours of the event in order to review what happened in a dispassionate and supportive manner.

When aggressive behaviors are evolving into serious sociopathic patterns, the pediatrician may have to coordinate meetings with the parents, the child or adolescent, the school, and relevant community agencies. There should be an effort to develop an integrated intervention program. Such efforts must include programming the child for success. After determining the basis of academic lags, school services might be modified to include high-motivational courses, such as those that teach concrete vocational skills. A major effort should be directed toward remediating deficits and developing bypass strategies that provide opportunities for mastery and success. The pediatrician can help parents and teachers negotiate rules and regulations, such as curfews, homework, and the choice of friends.

Aggressive outbursts at school should be observed carefully over time to see if they are situation-specific. For example, one seven-year-old boy became very aggressive only in a small reading group. When this was assessed, it appeared that the combination of reading (a weak area for the child) and sitting on the floor in a small circle contributed to aggression and regression. When given the choice of either sitting in a chair or on the floor, he selected the chair. Also, he was not required to read aloud unless he volunteered to do so. These modifications greatly reduced his aggressive outbursts.

Children who have chronic suppressed anger can be assigned to release areas, such as the gymnasium or woodworking shop. Hammering nails or pummeling a punching bag can serve as exhaust valves for aggression.

When a child loses control in the classroom, the teacher needs to take prompt and appropriate action. This may involve informing the parents or sending the child to the principal's office. This should not be implemented in a punitive way. The child should be told that everyone is trying to figure out the best way to "help you feel better about yourself and get better control of your feelings." It often helps if the child knows that there is a person in the school (such as a counselor) to whom there is access when an outburst seems at hand.

At times (especially with younger children) one may find displacements for aggression targets. One teacher gave a six-year-old boy an "angry pad." The child was told that when he became angry, he was not to throw chairs, but instead to put a big dark X on the pad.

Therapeutic activity groups in schools are becoming common. When handled by a sensitive counselor, they can provide an important intervention for aggressive children or adolescents. Through a combination of collaborative focused activity and discussion, members of the group can learn what their anger represents while working out more adaptive ways of expressing it. Peer pressure can be mobilized for adherence to appropriate social rules, rather than antisocial aggressive behaviors.

Much of the counseling strategy for children with aggressive behavior can also be applied to youngsters who have temper tantrums in the classroom. The teacher must be particularly sensitive to the needs of children who lose control. School personnel must be aware that the loss of control is, in itself, humiliating. When a child regains composure, the teacher needs to help him save face without resorting to even more maladaptive methods.

5. *Regressing.* If parents notice that a child regresses during certain activities, they should not only call this to his attention but also attempt to help him master the difficult activity. For example, if a youngster starts to indulge in baby talk while losing at a game of cards, parents can communicate that they realize it is not fun to lose but that baby talk only makes the situation worse. If the regression represents a disorganization in function, the parents should seek ways to minimize the disruptive situations. If a horror movie frightens and overstimulates a child to the point of regression, the parents can prohibit such viewing and work to help the child distinguish between fantasy and reality. As with all maladaptive coping methods, triggering circumstances should be sought and modified.

A child who regresses in school may need help tolerating specific situations. Some children with attention deficits have a particularly difficult time with recess, and other free periods, because of the lack of structure. Intervention might include clearly defined activities during these periods.

Some regressed children require specifically structured aids, such as the kind of daily schedule suggested earlier. Extreme regressive behaviors should be countered sensitively by the substitution of more appropriate, adultlike activities. Prestigious assignments such as blackboard monitor or messenger may diminish the need for regression.

6. *Withdrawing.* The severely withdrawn child often requires ongoing therapy by a mental health specialist. Working with a withdrawn child is a delicate job, requiring that one not move too quickly into the child's psychological and

physical private space. An adult's frustration and intense desire to draw out the withdrawn child may lead to premature assaults on the child's armor. These, in turn, result in further retreat. Those attempting to engage a withdrawn child must be prepared to accept slow progress. They have to be able to delay their own gratification, while respecting the child's isolating shield until he is ready to lower it. A number of mechanisms can be used to counteract such withdrawal. Nonverbal communication should be tried, including smiles and alterations in tone of voice, while maintaining a comfortable physical distance. One should communicate to the child that adults are there to help and that they really care about and respect him.

At home, parents should seek activities that permit them to be engaged with the child but that also provide enough distance. For example, if a withdrawn child is interested in fish, the parents might buy an aquarium for his room and help him feed the fish and keep the tank clean. Eventually, a withdrawn child may more readily accept the presence of another person if the two are collaborating on a specific project, such as building something, planting vegetables, or playing cards. Not only do these activities serve as a buffer, but they also address issues of self-esteem and confidence. Success experiences render less intense the feelings of anger and sadness.

Sometimes it is easy to begin assuming that a withdrawn child will not assume responsibilities at home. Parents should be helped to avoid such an attitude. They should expect the child to perform certain household chores. When possible, responsibilities should involve collaboration with another member of the family.

When a child appears increasingly ready to relate to others, parents can help to plan activities that involve a sibling or a neighborhood child.

It is important for the pediatrician and parents to understand any underlying fears that promote social withdrawal. A history of rejection by peers because of social imperception might be one such factor. Assisting the child to acquire good social skills may ameliorate this condition. Some children with gross motor problems withdraw because of fear of competition and humiliation. Such youngsters should be helped to avoid specific embarrassing activities without resorting to total withdrawal. They can be aided also to find areas of physical mastery. Some children become socially withdrawn because of language disabilities and problems in controlling conversation. They are likely to be embarrassed by their inability to produce rapid responses and frightened over their own language lapses. Specific counseling and language therapy may be most helpful.

Social withdrawal can be directly related to devastating peer labeling in school. It is important for the pediatrician and parents to know of any specific name-calling. Some children are too ashamed to mention this. Name-calling may be based on physical appearance, actions, or puns involving first or last names. Such indiscriminately used terminology as "fag," "retard," or "red neck" might be driving a child to retreat. The adult world can help find appropriate defenses (and offenses) to deal with these onslaughts. The bland reassurance of an adult (e.g., "Just ignore them") is seldom sufficient. In some cases a teacher may need to conduct a meeting with an entire class to review the dangers of name-calling and to set up a value system in which this activity is condemned by most of the children.

Problems with Interaction

Sibling Relationships

Children with learning disorders commonly have siblings without such disabilities. The disparity may catalyze family conflict and dissension, especially when a younger sibling is surpassing an older disabled child. Pediatricians can serve an important role in sensitizing parents to the feelings of siblings about their dysfunctioning brother or sister, and the reactions of the latter toward the former.

Clinical Illustrations

1. A child with learning problems may attempt all of the challenges a more successful sibling has mastered. These may involve school, athletics, or home-based interests. He becomes increasingly frustrated and resentful when unable to achieve at a comparable level. This, in turn, may engender one or more of the maladaptive coping methods described in earlier sections.

2. The child who is struggling to learn in school demands and often receives more affection and time from parents. Some of this is justified, and some is not. Siblings often feel that the child gets more than his share of attention and perhaps less responsibility and discipline.

3. When siblings feel threatened, they may display their own capabilities more prominently as a way of "putting down" the child with a learning problem. They may stress the As and Bs they received on their report cards, the goals they scored in soccer, or the kudos they won in playing the piano. As they accentuate their accomplishments, they highlight their less fortunate sibling's problems.

4. Some brothers or sisters may express pity or even guilt ("It just as easily could have been me with those problems"). They may become oversolicitous, trying to be too helpful. They may finish the sibling's homework, when they should not, or fight his battles, when he should attempt to handle things by himself.

General Intervention Strategies. A first step for the pediatrician is to promote open and honest discussion of this problem *with the entire family.* At best, such discussion can replace antagonism with support and understanding. Sometimes one or two family meetings will help. If more are required, the pediatrician can make a decision about referral to a mental health professional.

Another general strategy is to help the parents talk honestly with their failing child about his skills and weaknesses. The parents should not compare the child with brothers or sisters. They should seek ways of encouraging him *not* to compete with them but, instead, to find areas of personal excellence. Parents can seek activities that permit siblings to play together on an amiable and equitable level. Games of chance can be used toward this end.

Specific Intervention Strategies

1. Parents should inform a child that he is being unrealistic in struggling to achieve in exactly the same manner as his siblings. For example, if a child with significant gross motor problems wants to play on a neighborhood basketball

team, just as his brother does, the parents can say that they know how badly the child would like to play basketball. They can add that it is fine that he wants to play, and that he *should* keep trying, but that he must realize that some things are much more difficult for one boy than for another. While one should never discourage a child from striving, one should also acknowledge certain realities so that he is not unduly hurt. In this example, it might be possible for the child to practice basketball in the schoolyard, and even play in some "fun games," without entering a competitive league that would be above his abilities and lead to frustration or embarrassment.

2. Parents should encourage the child to engage in activities that are commensurate with his strengths and that are likely to provide a taste of success. A child who would love to play sports might find a niche in swimming rather than basketball or baseball. Another child might do very well with photography rather than in the sibling's area of excellence, gymnastics. The adolescent with school problems might derive satisfaction and recognition from playing the drums rather than through some other activity.

3. It can be a painful experience for an older child to be overtaken by a younger sibling. Parents must become acutely sensitive to this, offering praise for the accomplishments of the younger sibling, but doing so in a way that does not call attention to the slower development of the older child. If the older child is sensitive to and jealous of the sibling's accomplishments, the parents might offer praise to the younger one when his brother or sister is not in the room. It is also important for the pediatrician and the parents to assist the child to accept, but not be defeated by, such shortcomings. The child's realization that even younger children are ahead need not be taken as a signal to suspend effort; rather, it should be perceived as an indication that learning will require more effort and time.

4. Parents should not coerce the siblings of a failing child to look after him or to take him wherever they go. This typically leads to resentment and increased hostility. Nevertheless, they can help siblings understand what the child is experiencing and enlist them in providing support for their brother or sister. They can plan certain family outings that would minimize battles between the siblings.

5. Parents should let their child know why a sibling does not want him around. For example, one boy who had been relatively close to his failing younger brother became more distant as he started congregating with his own friends at the beginning of junior high school. Such behavior is typical, but the younger child sensed rejection. The parents (as well as the older sibling) were helpful in pointing out that when children grow older, especially when they reach junior high school, they like to spend more time with their friends and less time at home.

6. If parents do react differently to one child with regard to expectations and responsibilities, they can discuss this with the other children, offering reasons for the difference. A child who is constitutionally disorganized may be able to handle only half the chores or household responsibilities that his siblings can. The important message for the parents to communicate is that everyone in the home be treated as equally as possible, keeping in mind individual capabilities.

Sibling rivalry exists in every family. No one has invented a way to eliminate it.

At times, it may even serve as a useful arena for expressing anger, resolving differences, and learning the rules of social interaction. Parents have to ensure that the sibling rivalry experienced by a child with a learning problem does not become a destructive force, obliterating supports the child could receive from the family and driving him into self-defeating acts of face saving (i.e., maladaptive coping methods).

7. Teachers who have had several children from the same family should not make comparisions, especially in front of the child with a learning problem. To tell such a child that his brother or sister did not act "hyper," or was able to do the work, intensifies the agony of failure. Teachers must view the child in his own right, so that the programs they develop respect his individuality and unique profile of strengths and weaknesses.

Peer Socialization

As discussed in Chapter 3, some children with learning disorders have significant problems interacting with peers. They may find themselves isolated, teased, scapegoated, manipulated, and ridiculed. They may spend their school years struggling to outlive a "bad reputation." Several pathways lead to this plight.

Clinical Illustrations

1. Because of developmental lags, some children may not perform as quickly as their counterparts in certain prestigious performance areas (such as sports and reading). This may make it difficult for them to achieve social equality and capture the respect of their schoolmates. Nondisabled youngsters may isolate and avoid being seen with a dysfunctioning child, fearing some form of guilt by association.

2. Some children suffer from deficits in social judgment and performance (Bryan 1977, 1978, Kronick 1976). They may misread the social cues emanating from peers, so that they respond inappropriately and thereby alienate other children (see Chapter 3). They may have great difficulty reflecting on social decisions and predicting the social consequences of their actions. Such children often may trigger their own rejection and abuse.

3. Rather than withdrawing from other children in the face of continuing failure, a youngster may assume a counterphobic stance, displaying bravado and attempting to convince everyone of his invulnerability. Unfortunately, bragging may result in further ridicule and isolation. The child then may be left with few, if any, techniques for saving face.

4. When a child experiences difficulty in relating to peers, he may be most comfortable interacting either with younger children, with those of the opposite sex, or primarily with adults (sometimes to the chagrin and annoyance of the elders). This enables the child to compete in a different league, one in which his performance will be admired. The child may imitate the words and actions of his peers but do so before a far less threatening and judgmental audience. For similar reasons, a child may select friends who have disabilities or handicaps that are more severe than his own.

5. A child may struggle to gain recognition through bizarre acts that only add to his reputation as "weird" or "mental." Pejorative labels proliferate ironically,

as the child's desperate bids to win recognition continually backfire. A contributing factor is often the child's impulsivity, inadequate judgment, or limited appreciation of social cause and effect.

6. A child may try to purchase friends by spending his entire allowance on candy, which he then distributes generously to schoolmates. Once the cache is exhausted, so too is the supply of "friends" (possibly replenished when the next shipment arrives). In adolescence, the candy may be replaced by less innocuous delicacies. The child may not understand that he is sought after only for the dole. This may be sensed on some level, but the youngster continues to relish even a fleeting taste of popularity. Behind his back, peers may snicker at his gullibility.

7. Some children with learning problems seek the security of a "tough" clique of peers. They may become victims of exploitation and manipulation by the charismatic prestigious "club." The affected child tolerates this subjugation, since it provides a group identity, a feeling of social acceptance, and some protection against other children.

8. A struggling child may find security and efficacy through a delinquent group that places a high priority on violating taboos. They may indulge in truancy, drug abuse, and disorderly adult-defying behavior. This "cult" often is composed of unsuccessful children, many of whom have suffered from learning difficulty and borne chronic adult ridicule.

General Intervention Strategies. General strategies should be guided by an understanding of the factors underlying a child's social problems. In some instances the involvement of a mental health professional may be warranted, but there are interventions the pediatrician can recommend before making such a referral. Often several objectives need to be addressed simultaneously, such as (*1*) remediating handicaps in social judgment; (*2*) increasing the child's ability to observe his own behavior (especially as his action relates to peer acceptance); and (*3*) highlighting areas of strength to offset debilitating feelings of inadequacy and the need to turn toward antisocial behavior. These goals are not easy to achieve. They often require time and effort, but they are critical.

Specific Intervention Strategies

1. Parents should seek opportunities to point out (in noncritical and nonintrusive ways) those social strategies that are inappropriate and lead to peer rejection. Such messages should be accompanied by specific suggestions that can facilitate the development of positive peer relationships. While such an approach will not prove effective with every child, it will have the best chance of succeeding if it is free from excessive criticism. Children who are unlikely to be helped easily include those for whom the lack of social skill is also a self-defeating drive to confirm their feelings of incompetence.

While alternative ways of behaving are recommended, the child should be told that, even as he changes, it may take the peer group a long time to realize that his efforts are sincere. Some peers may never alter their stance toward a previously "condemned" child, even though the latter makes herculean attempts to demonstrate more acceptable behavior. If the affected child is aware of the difficult task that lies ahead, rather than becoming too downtrodden from continuing ridicule, he may proceed with the strategies that are necessary to gain greater acceptance. In extreme cases, the only "cure" for a bad reputation is a change of school (or neighborhood).

If a child's interactional problems are aggravated by attempts to compete in areas that are beyond his capability, it is important for the parents to introduce activities that will provide greater success and ego satisfaction.

2. The child who desperately tries to gain the attention of others through self-debasing actions (such as playing the role of the class clown) needs assistance in several ways. First, an effort must be made to provide experiences that result in success and recognition and counteract the child's need to engage in inappropriate behavior to obtain credibility. Second, even as parents are searching for the most appropriate activities, they must also point out to the child the self-defeating nature of the present behavior. The task, which should be performed in an empathic and sensitive way, is critical if the child is to learn that he can be effective in determining whether the peer group becomes more accepting. One strategy for facilitating improved peer relations is to ask the child to pretend that he is running for class president. A hypothetical campaign can be planned, touching upon questions of effective and ineffective interactions with others. In seeking votes from peers, the child has the opportunity to begin to learn those social skills that enhance interpersonal relationships.

3. If a child gravitates toward younger children (or those of the opposite sex), parents should use this pattern to help him. Sometimes playing with younger children becomes an exercise in regression or dictatorship, neither of which serves to enhance same-age peer relations. Rather than simply attempting to prevent the child from interacting with younger children, parents may be able to monitor what is occurring and select situations that encourage more mature behavior with such children. If the child has skills in photography, the parents might suggest that he show younger children how to take pictures. To insure that this venture does not fail, the parents can help the child rehearse what he is going to do. They might even stand in the background as the teaching takes place. If the child shows proficiency in kicking a soccer ball, this might be selected as the vehicle through which to develop a sense of competence, first with younger children, and then with contemporaries.

4. Self-destructive sequelae follow when a failing child associates with delin-quent or predelinquent groups. This affiliation often provides the security, safety, and power that have been so elusive. A bonding develops that is difficult to loosen. The group may embody a desire to punish and defy the adult world that has been so critical of them over the years. It may be dedicated to immediate gratification and obliviousness to consequences. In view of the magnetic peer attachment and hypertrophied loyalty that develops, attempts at individual psychotherapy often have less than satisfactory results (assuming the child or adolescent even is willing to visit a therapist).

In these situations, much thought must be given to a comprehensive program involving the school, community agencies, therapist, family, and sometimes the juvenile court. The adolescent may require a high-motivational vocational school program, a total change of environment (e.g., residential school), an adolescent group or family therapy experience, as well as a job in the community. Intensive effort is required to lure a child away from such a self-destructive group identity and to assist him in believing that a more appropriate and equally ego-enhancing status can be achieved.

5. If the school views itself not simply as a purveyor of academic skills but also as a facilitator of the overall development of children, it can serve to enhance the socialization process for the dysfunctioning child. Schools can develop educational programs that (1) help to sensitize children and adolescents to the disabilities of others; (2) help them to become more aware of their own feelings and behavior; and (3) enable them to understand social forces that lead to conformity, isolation, or appropriate integration. If a teacher uses such a program to discuss learning problems or physical disabilities, he can delve into all components related to those problems. Materials can be used to reach both the struggling and the apparently unaffected children in the classroom, focusing on issues of peer ridicule and positive relationships. One can highlight both the self-defeating behaviors to which some failing children resort and the more adaptive ways in which students handle problems. One can also deal with such themes as scapegoating, name-calling, boasting, and excluding.

The teacher can plan activities that will involve the child with increasing numbers of other students. Such a strategy can provide opportunities to learn how to form and sustain relationships. Activities may be academic or oriented toward particular projects. The teacher may be involved directly or as a supervisor. Once the child is able to manage a relationship with one other child, a third and then a fourth might be added to the activity. The teacher should be especially sensitive to the goal of fostering positive relationships and to the need to speak with the child about behaviors that might incur the displeasure of peers. Just as the task of remediating or coping with learning problems may take years, so too may the effort to foster meaningful socialization.

6. Many school counselors conduct groups for children who are having peer problems. These groups often focus on (a) personal feelings related to a disability; (b) reactions of others to the disabled individual; and (c) development of strong socialization skills. Since group members often have endured similar hardships, it is reassuring for them to hear others speak of their experiences. Children and parents often report a sense of relief in discovering that their problems are not unique. If the school offers group counseling, it can be a powerful intervention that the pediatrician can suggest when making recommendations to the family and school. When this is not available, the pediatrician may want to press for the establishment of such programs.

7. Since the child with a learning problem often feels worthless in school, the teacher should attempt to find areas of relative excellence and a means to display these strengths. A child may not be a good reader, but he might be talented at making airplane models or cooking. To have these products displayed, or to show the class how to cook (and then eat) cookies, may help to strengthen the disabled child's self-esteem and also win the respect of peers.

Somatic Functional Issues and Their Impact

Suboptimal controls over autonomic or other body functions sometimes accompany problems with learning. Ineffective somatic regulatory function and learning disorders may stem from the same matrix of constitutional predispositions. In some cases, somatic difficulties may constitute reactive phenomena. Another alternative is that a somatic dysfunction can trigger a learning problem by preoccupying a child and draining selective attention. An example of the latter might be a child who is so concerned about the possibility of soiling in school that it becomes difficult to concentrate on classwork.

In this section we will deal with four clinical pictures of somatic dysfunction: (1) problems with body image and physical mastery; (2) sleep disturbances; (3) issues surrounding eating; and (4) pains and incontinence. These will be considered separately, although they have in common the pathophysiologic model of dysfunction, or the symptom emerging from a final common pathway deriving, in turn, from a complex interplay of constitutional predispositions, environmental factors, and fortuitous events.

Problems with Body Image and Physical Mastery

Some children with learning problems display developmental profiles that include various gross motor inefficiencies, such as problems with directionality and body position sense, difficulties with visually directed physical activities, and generalized lags in motor coordination (see Chapter 3). A child chronically deprived of mastery over the physical world may feel extremely inadequate.

Clinical Illustrations

1. As a result of gross motor problems, a child may be selected last to play in a game: "Why do we have to have George? We had him yesterday. It's not fair." Such resounding refrains of rejection typically aggravate already weak peer relationships. A variety of maladaptive coping methods may supervene.

2. In school, a child may dread physical education and the playground. These two arenas render him most vulnerable. The child may avoid school on a gym day. The fear of humiliation becomes paramount. This phenomenon may take new forms as arenas change; many boys now express great fear of revealing their lack of mastery in newly formed coeducational physical education classes.

3. A child may have significant (and often justifiable) concerns about physical appearance. This may erode his body image. Clinicians must be alert to any physically unusual features, as they may constitute major issues for pediatric counseling. Among the conditions that can potently affect body image are obesity, short stature, delayed puberty, adolescent gynecomastia, acne or eczema, visible birthmarks, prominent ears or noses, and muscular underdevelopment. In some cases, children may overreact to trivial "defects" that no one else even notices. The physican may encounter a relatively thin girl who wishes to lose weight in order to reduce the size of her buttocks. A boy may be very self-conscious because his wrists are too thin or his knees are too knobby. Such preoccupations with body image may precipitate a variety of strategic retreats, including a reluctance to take showers or undress in relatively public places (such as locker rooms), a refusal to wear a bathing suit, or a desire for various kinds of cover-up apparel. The physician working with a school-age child must appreciate the intensity of feelings about such issues. A pediatrician may be the only person who is able to gain access to well-concealed but profoundly felt anxieties about perceived body defectiveness. This opportu-

nity should never be missed, as it can lead to dramatic alleviations of unnecessary, wasteful anxiety.

General Intervention Strategies. A pediatrician should be able to create an atmosphere in which the frank and confidential discussion of body concerns can take place. Too much reassurance, or preaching, should be avoided. The child's concerns should be listened to carefully and respected sincerely. The clinician should offer an honest appraisal of the justifiability of a child's worries. Where possible, every effort should be made to repair obvious defects or cosmetic problems. If this is impossible, the pediatrician can become an important coconspirator in helping the child avoid humiliation. In dealing with problems of gross motor function, the pediatrician can take a careful history, perform gross motor observations, and hopefully write prescriptions for success in areas of physical activity.

Specific Intervention Strategies

1. With very young children, parents may be able to help improve spatial relationships and gross motor coordination through a variety of activities. Treasure hunts using maps and emphasizing directionality might be useful during this period. For children with strong language skills, narrative description can help reinforce the spatial content of such expeditions.

2. Physical activities or various sporting pursuits can strengthen a child's body image and feelings of effectiveness. Typically, a child with gross motor deficits avoids such activities, since they are associated with failure and psychological pain. It is important, however, to find pursuits in which the child can succeed. As a colleague once said, "Any child can hit a home run if the bat is wide enough!" If the child has visual-spatial problems, a sport should be selected that does not require complex visual processing. Swimming, gymnastics, and track are examples. Hiking or mountain climbing are physical endeavors that stress endurance and strong will.

In the acquisition of gross motor skills, an important issue for the dysfunctioning child is privacy. Such a youngster needs protection while acquiring competence. He may be able to master gross motor skills, but relatively slowly by comparison with peers. During this "breaking-in period," training or practice may need to take place in the privacy of a back yard, in a very small group, or on a one-to-one basis in a far corner of a gymnasium. As soon as the child achieves some mastery, there is less risk of humiliation. There can then be a "debut" in which a gross motor performance goes public. One also needs to recognize that certain sports offer more privacy than others. A child with visual-spatial problems playing baseball and assigned as the guardian of right field occupies a position of indisputable accountability with regard to fly balls in that direction. On the other hand, on a soccer field there tends to be more of a crowd where the action is; thus, it is not always quite so clear that a particular child is at fault. For this reason soccer can be a useful sport for children who feel they cannot compete.

One can also recommend certain "equalizer sports." These are activities that no one performs particularly well! For example, in physical education, the teacher can bring out a medicine ball. This is an enormous sphere that children kick about during four-limbed supine locomotion. Since everyone looks ludicrous, the child with motor deficits feels very much the equal of his peers.

3. It certainly is not necessary for all children to be active in sports. Youngsters whose neuromuscular apparatus does not appear to have been designed for such pursuits should be encouraged to develop interests in other areas. Various collections, craft activities, or music and art lessons might be suitable. In certain communities where athletic prowess is the surest path to status, children involved in these alternative avocations will need support and reassurance. They will need to be told that they are building "muscles in their mind" that may, in fact, be more relevant and durable than the limb-strengthening efforts of their athletic peers. One clinician went so far as to suggest that such children be taken to a Little League field and encouraged to laugh at all the foolish youngsters wasting time trying to hit a sphere with a stick! At any rate, it is important to emphasize that most children have the capacity to become great fishermen. In those cases where sustained attention is difficult, an effort should be made to have the child fish where fish are plentiful, using the best possible bait!

4. The pediatrician should be knowledgeable about any special physical education or occupational therapy programs in schools or in the community. A school may offer well-designed adaptive physical activities or gymnastic exercises that enhance a child's body image and strengthen his sense of mastery.

5. In school, physical education activities can either highlight a child's inadequacies or help to develop feelings of competence. Sensitive physical education teachers can foster the latter. Such persons are assuming increasing importance in special education programs throughout the country. They need to be particularly careful to help children avoid excessive peer abuse and humiliation.

6. The child with concerns about body image can be a major challenge for the pediatrician. It is appropriate for the clinician to collaborate with a child in avoiding humiliation. For example, a fifteen-year-old boy who has not yet entered puberty may not wish to take showers after physical education classes. A written excuse from the pediatrician to the school can eliminate a needless stress and help significantly in face-saving and the maintenance of social status. The pediatrician can offer advice about concealing pimples, losing weight, and counteracting the jibes of peers with regard to physical defects. When appropriate, parents and teachers should collaborate in this effort. However, the child should "call the signals" with regard to confidentiality and the sharing of somatic concerns. The physician should never betray a patient by revealing these issues to parents or teachers without the child's consent.

Sleep Disturbances
Typically, sleep patterns become routinized and highly predictable in infancy. However, some children with developmental dysfunction manifest various patterns of sleep disturbance. These might consist of difficulty in falling asleep, a tendency to wake up many times during the night, or excessive fatigue during the day when most children are fully alert.

In assessing a sleep problem, the pediatrician should determine if it is of recent origin, or if the child has never established a consistent pattern. When the onset has been relatively recent, the pediatrician should discern possible triggering events. Among these might be marital tension in the household, fear of nightmares, or the fantasy of never waking up. Sleep problems that have been recurrent or consistent since early infancy may have a constitutional basis. They may be exacerbated by critical events and developmental crises, although their ultimate origins are physiological. Sleep disturbances are common concomitants of attention deficits (see Chapter 3).

Clinical Illustrations

1. A child may have difficulty falling asleep, while seeming to be tense or overwrought. Even if the child can stay in bed, he finds it difficult to fall asleep. Such a child may be discovered night after night roaming the hallways.
2. A child may fall asleep quickly but wake up several times during the night. This may be related to nightmares, night terrors, or anxieties. Such a youngster may plead to sleep in the parents' bed.
3. Some children employ a host of maneuvers to avoid going to sleep. These may range from the commonly invoked extra glass of milk to lamentations over stomach aches or bizarre noises.
4. A child's sleep patterns may be irregular in comparision with those of peers. A youngster may have difficulty falling asleep at night, yet yawn continuously during the day, much to the anguish of parents and teachers.

General Intervention Strategies. Sleep disturbance is one of the most difficult problems for parents and pediatricians to manage, particularly when a child wakes up constantly during the night. If this occurs regularly, the pediatrician often faces parents who are weary, frustrated, and desparate.

If the sleep problem is primarily reactive, the pediatrician should focus on strategies that address the anxiety-provoking issues. Once these are dealt with, the child's insomnia may disappear. Meanwhile, the parents need specific advice on how to address the problem directly. If the condition represents a long-standing inability to develop appropriate rhythms, the pediatrician's recommendations should focus on ways to routinize the sleep pattern.

Specific Intervention Strategies

1. Parents may need to provide a great deal of support and reassurance to frightened children during the night. In one case a four-year-old child who had slept well in the past began to have trouble going to bed and continually awoke screaming. The child expressed dread of an invasion by monsters. The parents were helped to verbalize to the child that sometimes it is frightening to fall asleep because of bad dreams. They informed her that dreams are only dreams, and that adults are always around to help. Sometimes a nightlight in a hallway, or even in the bedroom, can minimize these anxieties. Some children derive comfort from sleeping with a "transitional object" (typically a teddy bear or a particular blanket or piece of clothing). Some children feel relieved by going to bed with a picture of their parents.

Pediatricians often are asked about a child who wakes up screaming and wants to join the parents in their bed. It is more appropriate for a parent to attempt to calm the child in his own room. The parents should be as relaxed as possible and avoid energizing the child's frenzy. If they respond too quickly by taking the child into their own bed, this can further disrupt their own sleep and cause them to feel resentment. Moreover, such a response does not help the child to learn to manage his own anxieties. At most, the parents should spend a short time in the child's room. Sometimes the child can be helped by being moved into a living room or some other bedroom as a temporary escape from threatening nocturnal associations.

2. If the child worries about going to sleep out of fear of not waking up, parents should deal directly with the child's reality distortions and also find concrete ways to help the child feel more in control of waking up. They might, for example, buy the child an alarm clock that can be set each night. Such an action concretely helps to counteract the fear of not waking up, and it gives the child a sense of being in control.

3. In some cases the child's difficulty in falling asleep may reflect a more general problem of handling transitions, as discussed earlier in this chapter.

4. A child may use bedtime as a way of gaining the parents' undivided attention. He may call out constantly. This may be a message that the parents are not providing a reasonable amount of attention during the day. Alternatively, it may be an expression of a child's insatiability. The pediatrician can review the situation with the parents and may recommend "special attention times" before sleep, with the understanding that once the child is in bed, he will not continue to call out for his parents.

5. When the problem is more chronic and appears to have a constitutional basis, the pediatrician might consider medication on a temporary basis (see Chapter 7). Such drugs as chloral hydrate and diphenhydramine (Benadryl) have been used with mixed results. Barbiturates are probably not indicated, especially in view of their aggravating effects on some children with attention deficits.

Alternative strategies should be considered. The parents should create and adhere to a regular schedule regarding when the child gets ready for bed, when there are transitional activities, when there is a period of lying in bed reading or listening to the radio, and when the lights go out. A radio playing in the background or some white noise may help a distractible child filter out stimuli that impair sleep. The use of a schedule may provide the foundation for building a more regular, age-appropriate sleep pattern.

The parents should realize, however, that progress will not be evident immediately. This recognition can minimize some of the frustration that they are likely to experience. A child who has sleep problems on a constitutional basis should not be made to feel guilty. Such children too often are too preoccupied with their sleep failure. Their anxiety actually may worsen the problem. They should be made to understand that their difficulty falling asleep is not their fault and does not endanger their health. It is particularly important that there be no sleep battles between parent and child each evening. Appropriate compromises (such as staying in the room and reading) should be worked out.

Issues Surrounding Eating

Mealtimes constitute a common source of wasteful friction between parents and children. When the child is having functional difficulties in other areas of life, this battleground is particularly inappropriate and needless. The pediatrician should help parents to understand the significance (or lack thereof) of erratic eating patterns in school-age children. It is often important to deemphasize eating as an issue. Feeding battles can be as disruptive to family integrity as warfare over sleep. Parents often need reassurance that self-induced starvation, scurvy, rickets, or beriberi are virtually unheard of in the United States.

Overeating may be more of a problem. It may be a manifestation of insatiability. On the other hand, it may be found in children who are feeling deprived of satisfaction in other areas of life. It is important for the pediatrician to identify the origins of this behavior and to help parents set limits on consumption while substituting other gratifying and more acceptable sources of stimulation. Strategies for providing such substitutions are detailed in other sections of this chapter.

Pains and Incontinence

At the Children's Hospital Medical Center in Boston a clinic called the "Pains and Incontinence Program" (PIP) has been established to deal with four common conditions of dysfunction in the school-age child: enuresis, encopresis, recurrent abdominal pains, and recurrent headaches. A large percentage of the children seen in this program have associated learning problems, including specific information-processing deficits and chronically poor selective attention. Often the symptom formation parallels the mechanisms seen in the production of learning problems.

Clinical Illustrations. The model of somatic dysfunction can be illustrated best by consideration of the most common presenting complaint in the Pains and Incontinence Program—namely, childhood encopresis. This is a condition in which a school-age child regularly soils his underclothing. The child appears to have lost control of defecation. The condition and its treatment have been described elsewhere (Levine 1975, Levine and Bakow 1976).

Children with encopresis may arrive at their symptom via different pathways. Some may be born with a constitutional predisposition toward stool retention. They may have a colonic inertia that makes them vulnerable. They may proceed through life with chronic constipation, resulting in a distended and weak large intestine, whose muscular control and sensory feedback mechanisms are compromised. As a result the child may become incontinent. In other cases, early coercive intervention for simple constipation can lead to a so-called "anal stamp," whose ultimate manifestation is stool retention and overflow incontinence. Diaper rashes, early hospitalizations, and infantile diarrhea all can constitute fortuitous events that lead to bowel dysfunction. Encopresis, like all somatic dysfunctions, is a prime reflector of stress. The condition can continue into adult life in the form of a spastic or irritable colon.

Some children develop bowel incontinence because of an irrational fear of the toilet. They may be frightened of being flushed down, or they may fear a fall from the toilet seat. One youngster proclaimed that he didn't like toilets because of "the fish monsters that bite your rear end whenever you sit down." Between the ages of four and five years, it is developmentally appropriate to acquire certain idiosyncratic avoidance tendencies. Some children will like both peas and mashed potatoes, but they won't eat either of them if they touch each other! Other youngsters avoid lumps in their oatmeal and cracks in sidewalks. Those children who decide that their avoidances will be directed toward toilet bowls may experience dire consequences—specifically, encopresis.

Some school-age children develop encopresis because of the bathrooms in school. The late onset of bowel incontinence in a child who has been fully trained (secondary encopresis) frequently is associated with school-related issues. Many five- to seven-year-old children do not wish anyone to know that they use bathrooms! The absence of a door in front of a toilet in school may precipitate stool retention in such a child. The process of chronic withholding leads ironically to a functional megacolon and resultant incontinence. In schools with doors on toilets, there is still the ever-present threat of peers who climb over or under them, and of children whose lavatory exploits are threatening and potentially humiliating to a vulnerable child.

Children, in general, are highly aware of school bathrooms. It is a subject that is not discussed but that may occupy a reasonably important position in a child's consciousness.

Encopresis can be a direct result of a child's developmental dysfunction. For example, a youngster who is inattentive and impersistent at tasks may have as much difficulty completing defecation as he does finishing a homework assignment! His visits to the bathroom may produce incomplete evacuations, leading ultimately to stool retention and incontinence.

Bowel incontinence can result also from stress events, difficult home situations, or inappropriate parent-child relationships. These causes traditionally have received major emphasis in both the pediatric and psychiatric literature. Although encopresis can certainly be a sign of serious psychopathology, its existence as a manifestation of developmental dysfunction, in a child without serious "emotional illness," needs to be considered.

The child with encopresis experiences a serious plight in school. He is always aware of the threat of exposure and discovery. He worries that other children might find out about the problem and publicize it. When discovered, many such children are abused because of their odors. "Stink pot," "skunk," and other less socially acceptable labels may be applied by peers who seek scapegoats.

Commonly, children with encopresis are aware of *no other youngsters* with the disorder. Parents and teachers often share this lack of awareness. This is surprising, in view of the fact that fecal incontinence in childhood is common.

Many children with encopresis lament that they cannot feel a bowel movement coming. In most cases they are being truthful. A distended bowel wall often impairs the sensory feedback that would otherwise give appropriate "warnings." Often parents chastise such children for not using the bathroom at the right time, which tends to increase their confusion and guilt.

General Intervention Strategies. In discussing intervention, again we will use the example of encopresis. The general philosophy, however, is applicable to other kinds of somatic dysfunction. First, it is important to be honest about the problem. Second, the pediatrician should ask the child not to feel ashamed in front of him, since this is such a common medical problem. Third, there should be an attempt to generalize about the disorder. In dealing with all dysfunctions, it is important to help a child understand that many other youngsters face similar problems. Such destigmatizing can help a child feel less isolated and more optimistic. Fourth, the physician should demystify the problem. Many children sense that their dysfunction has a magical quality that places it beyond their control. Often other professionals and parents inadvertently have fostered this misconception. Informing a child with encopresis that he is messing to win attention or to express hostility is mystifying rather than helpful to him. More appropriately, the clinician can explain the mechanisms of megacolon formation and overflow (with appropriate drawings and analogies), so that the child can begin to understand and feel more in control. Fifth, the pediatrician needs to show the child respect. It is essential to be nonaccusatory and amoral in formulations. There is no need to pin blame on the child, the parents, or the home situation. In most cases, all should be viewed as innocent victims of the dysfunction itself. Accidents should be acknowledged as accidental. In fact, the child might even be helped to see himself as a hero for coping with this socially dangerous condition.

The clinician must be prepared to offer ongoing advice and support to the somatically dysfunctioning child. Children should be invited to call the doctor during telephone hours. The physician can collaborate with the child in face-saving strategies and should be prepared to answer such questions as: "Where should I sit on the school bus if I'm afraid I'm going to have an accident?" He should be prepared to help in crisis situations, such as when the child reports that his brother has told other children in the neighborhood that he messes his pants. Now he is afraid to go to school for fear of humiliation. He would like advice. The physician should not indulge in simple reassurance but instead should help the child develop coping methods that will work in both the short and long run. At the same time, every effort should be made to cure the symptoms of dysfunction. Where a somatic manifestation appears to be reactive or secondary to environmental factors, appropriate interventions should be undertaken.

Specific Intervention Strategies. The treatment of enuresis, encopresis, recurrent abdominal pains, and recurrent headaches is beyond the scope of this book. Each of these conditions subsumes a heterogeneous group of children. One must avoid a priori formulations based only on the chief complaint. After careful description and analysis, appropriate intervention strategies can be developed. One should always look for underlying constitutional predispositions that have been potentiated by environmental factors and critical events. It is never sufficient to declare that a symptom results from "nerves" or emotional prob-lems. The term "psychogenic" may be overused and abused, as it conceals an oversimplification of pathophysiology.

When a child presents with recurrent abdominal pains, the pediatrician needs to consider how he developed abdominal pains (and not headaches). A physiologic predisposition should be sought and, if found, dealt with. At the same time, issues of environment and nurturance should be teased out. A combined medical-counseling intervention may be appropriate. The understanding of a somatic dysfunction can best be achieved by linking multiple fragments of evidence from history, physical examination, interviewing, and appropriate laboratory tests.

One should also avoid rigid application of the paradigm of "organic versus emotional." One can almost always assume that most dysfunctions are neither purely organic nor entirely emotionally based. The physician should bear in mind that if a child has recurrent abdominal pains and his parents are divorced, he may, nevertheless, have lactose deficiency or chronic constipation as mediators of the symptoms! The complex interaction of etiologic factors and the planning of multifaceted interventions constitute a critical pediatric role.

SOME GENERAL CONSIDERATIONS

A recurrent theme in this chapter has been the role of the pediatrician in helping parents develop a positive approach to a child who is failing. It is appropriate to conclude with some general concepts that pertain to all such children, regardless of their behavioral manifestations and the specific nature of their learning problems.

Niche-picking instead of nit-picking. Parents should be encouraged to balance praise and criticism. Children with learning problems may have been showered with criticism. If one were to list their every transgression, there would be a shortage of paper! Parents should be encouraged to counterbalance ridicule with respect. They need to establish priorities, pointing out only major shortcomings or inefficiencies. Adults must find niches for a child that allow for the offerance of praise.

Boasting instead of roasting. Children with learning problems need a sense, not only that their parents love them but that they respect them. They need to overhear boasting about them. A child needs to feel that his parents brag about him. Adults need to make it clear to the child that, although in certain respects they are trying to change him, there is much of him that they now appreciate and respect.

Active collaboration instead of excessive reassurance. Parents may need to be reminded that when a child voices his concerns, they should avoid "reflex reassurance." If a child is being bullied in the hallways at school, the parents should recognize that this is an overwhelmingly humiliating experience. In the adult value system it might be tantamount to losing one's job! If parents respond to such anecdotes by suggesting that a child be brave or ignore the taunts of others, they are not being helpful or sympathetic. Instead, they need to commiserate and offer helpful strategic suggestions. If this does not occur, children will learn early in life that they cannot use their parents as resources.

Open communication instead of hidden agendas. Very early in life it is critical that parents be receptive to children's discussions of problems and incidents. They should show a sincere interest. When a child tends to be noncommunicative, parents should probe in a supportive and interested manner. When communication does not begin early in life, it is likely to be nonexistent during adolescence. A child who has not been taught to express his true feelings at age eight is unlikely to confide in his parents about serious problems later. Often a parent cannot initiate discussions of delicate issues with a child. The pediatrician can suggest specific phraseology and methods of expression to surmount this communication barrier.

Advocacy instead of accusation. A child should perceive his parents as staunch allies. Besides offering their affection and respect, they can help him win rights. They can stand up for his needs in school. in the community, and at home. Federal legislation, such as PL 94-142, supports this concept. The pediatrician can help parents become prime movers or agents for a child. They can be encouraged to visit the school, to take sides with the child whenever possible, to be wise consumers of educational services, and to apply pressure for change when appropriate.

Concerted effort instead of dissension. In cases where parents are not "pulling together," the pediatrician may be able to resolve some differences to facilitate united efforts on behalf of the child. This help may be especially needed where there has been a separation or divorce. The pediatrician should work closely with both parents to assure that they are beaming consistent messages to the child, minimizing any feelings of loss, and not intensifying the conflicts which the child harbors. Sometimes a child's learning problems can become a "rallying point," enabling parents and other family members to cooperate in a manner to which they are unaccustomed.

Appendix A

A Survey
Of Commonly
Employed
Standardized
Examinations

No man can reveal to you aught, but that which already lies
half asleep in the dawning of your knowledge.

The teacher who walks in the shadow of the temple, among his
followers, gives not of his wisdom, but rather of his faith and
his lovingness.

If he is indeed wise he does not bid you into the house of his
wisdom, but rather leads you to the threshold of your own
mind.

Kahlil Gibran, The Prophet

The diagnostic instruments described herein are not an exhaustive compendium; their selection is not an endorsement. Selection has been predicated on the frequency of their use by educators, speech and language therapists, and psychologists. These examinations represent a cross section of procedures typically used to assess intellectual, cognitive, educational, and developmental function. A more comprehensive list of standardized tests may be found in a reference such as *The Mental Measurements Yearbook* (Buros, 1972).

As emphasized throughout this volume, standardized examinations should never be used in isolation from other diagnostic data. The following considerations may be helpful in interpreting tests:

1. One must consider the context of an assessment. Results may reflect a child's anxiety over being removed from a regular classroom in order to be evaluated. Scores may also be affected by the relationship between a child and a tester. The same examination given in a hospital setting or a school may yield discrepant results.

2. Examinations may test a child's test-taking ability. This may not be an accurate reflection of day-to-day performance and attainment.

3. Certain children (particularly those with erratic attention) may perform differently on different occasions. "Test-retest reliability" may be relatively low. Thus, definitive decisions should never be based exclusively on a single-time frame of test performance.

4. Children may respond to examination questions by providing the kind of performance they think one is seeking, rather than the responses that are optimal or preferred by them. In certain examinations this can be particularly misleading. For example, on an oral reading test a child may feel the most important thing is to read fast. His preoccupation with this "mission" may compromise scores on comprehension. Some of these effects can be minimized by explaining carefully to a child what the expectations are.

5. A test-score interpreter needs to be keenly aware of exactly what each test is testing. Achievement tests in the same performance area measure different parameters of development or academic attainment. For example, a multiple-choice test for spelling may tap into a child's recognition memory for discrepancies, while a dictated spelling test requires a very different set of skills (e.g., retrieval or revisualization). Scores may be divergent on these two kinds of spelling tests administered to the same child.

6. Tests administered in a group may yield very different results from those taken individually. Some children exhibit a high level of "social distractibility," which may compromise performance on a group examination.

7. It is important to be aware of cultural and socioeconomic biases in a given examination. If a test originally was standardized on a middle-class, suburban population, normative data may not be applicable in the inner city or may not be relevant to certain socioeconomic or cultural groups. In particular, this can be a problem with examinations that rely heavily on language abilities.

8. One must always be aware that specific tests, subtests, and individual items on an examination usually measure more functions than are purported. For example, although something may be said to measure "auditory-sequential memory," the same set of items also taps sustained attention, emotional composure, and other cognitive and psychological dimensions.

Despite the biases inherent in testing, standardized examinations, used judiciously and interpreted broadly, can help to elucidate specific service needs. As discussed in Chapter 5, the organized collection of data from multiple sources is the best safeguard against unreliable, quick, clinical impressionism on one hand, and rigid psychometric determinism on the other (see also Aliotti, 1977; Brooks, 1979; and Kratochwill, 1977).

TESTS OF INTELLIGENCE*

Wechsler Intelligence Scale for Children-Revised
(The Psycholigical Corporation, 757 Third Avenue, New York, N.Y. 10017).

The WISC-R is an individually administered intelligence test for ages 6–0 to 16–11. Three major IQ scores are obtained: Full Scale, Verbal, and Performance. Five subtests comprise the Verbal IQ and five constitute the Performance IQ. In addition both the Verbal and Performance scales have an optional subtest. In general, the Verbal subtests call on language skills, while the Performance subtests rely on manipulation of materials, stressing motoric and visual-spatial abilities. The subtests include:

Verbal Subtests

Information. This subtest is meant to assess a child's basic fund of information and knowledge of his environment. Questions include "How many days are there in a week?", "Who discovered America?", "What does the stomach do?", "What is a barometer?", and "What are hieroglyphics?" Long-term memory, vocabulary, and experience may also be measured in this subtest.

Similarities. This subtest measures the ability to categorize. The child is requested to tell how two objects go together or are alike. A child's answers may run the spectrum from concrete to abstract thinking. Items include: how are a "wheel-ball," "cat-mouse," "anger-joy," and "salt-water" the same? This subtest may be indicative of higher-order conceptual ability as well as language facility.

Arithmetic. This subtest asks the child to count a specified number of objects or mentally compute answers to such questions as "If I cut an apple in half how many pieces will I have?", "If a boy had twelve newspapers and sold five, how many did he have left?", and "If four boys had 72 pennies and divided them equally among themselves, how many pennies did each boy receive?" This test measures not only arithmetic skills but also a child's capacity to concentrate and attend, since the answers are done mentally without the assistance of paper and pencil.

Vocabulary. This subtest consists of words that the child is asked to define. They begin at a concrete level (such as "bicycle" and "nail") and progress to more abstract or difficult words (such as "affliction" and "imminent"). This subtest measures a child's knowledge of words or receptive vocabulary and also provides an assessment of how concretely or abstractly words are defined. It may assess expressive language ability.

Comprehension. This subtest focuses on a child's ability to reason and to judge, especially in relation to social situations and expectations. Questions include: "What is the thing to do when you cut your finger?", "What is the thing to do if a boy (girl) much smaller than yourself starts to fight with you?", "Why is it usually better to give money to a well-known charity than to a street beggar?" and "Why should a promise be kept?"

---

*The subtests of the Wechsler Intelligence Scale for Children (WISC-R), The Illinois Test of Psycholonguistic Abilities (ITPA) and the Detroit Test of Learning Aptitude are covered in more extensive detail than the subtests of other assessment procedures since these three tests are used very frequently by specialists working with children with developmental dysfunction and learning disorders.

Digit Span (Optional). This subtest measures attention and short-term memory. The child is asked to repeat a series of numbers both forward and backward. Digits repeated forward go from a sequence of three to nine, while digits repeated backward go from a sequence of two through eight. Performance may be impaired by anxiety, relative inexperience with numbers, or problems with sequential organization.

Performance Subtests

Picture Completion. This subtest assesses awareness of visual detail and part-whole relations. The child is shown a series of pictures individually and is asked to tell what important element is missing in each drawing. In the first few pictures the missing parts are more obvious, such as the mouth of a woman, the whiskers of a cat, and the leg of an elephant. Missing details in later pictures are more difficult to discern such as the slot in a screw, the shadow of a tree, and the spokes of an umbrella.

Picture Arangement. This subtest presents the child with a series of pictures that must be placed in the correct order to tell a coherent story. The task assesses visual sequencing, social awareness, planning, anticipation, the ability to relate parts to a synthesized story, and the appreciation of relationships between events. This subtest is scored with respect to the time required to place the pictures in a correct sequence.

Block Design. This subtest asks the child to recreate designs using blocks with sides that are all red, all white, or half red and half white. The test assesses spatial awareness and visual-motor coordination. It requires both an analytic and a synthetic approach. This subtest is timed.

Object Assembly. This subtest requires the child to assemble four jigsawlike puzzles: a child, a horse, a car, and a human face. It measures visual-motor coordination, but, unlike the Block Design subtest, it supplies no pattern or stimulus to guide the child. Thus, the task requires the child to revisualize the object and to construct it from memory. This subtest is timed.

Coding. This subtest requires the child to fill in with a pencil symbols which correspond to a certain number found at the top of the test. There are nine symbols, each paired with one of the numbers one through nine. The numbers are presented in random order in the different rows. This test measures visual-motor coordination and fine motor efficiency. It also involves short-term memory, since it is helpful to memorize the symbol that goes with each number. This subtest is timed.

Mazes (optional). This subtest asks the child to draw a line from the middle of the maze to the exit without going into any blind alleys. It assesses visual-motor skills but also involves planning, directionality, and anticipation. This subtest is timed.

Wechsler Preschool and Primary Scale of Intelligence (WPPSI)

(The Psychological Corporation, 757 Third Avenue, New York, N. Y. 10017)

The WPPSI is an individually administered intelligence test, similar to the WISC-R, with an age range from 3-10 to 6-7. It is dichotomized in terms of Verbal and Performance subtests. The Digit Span subtest is replaced by the

Sentences subtest, in which a child has to repeat sentences rather than numbers. There are no Picture Arrangement and Object Assembly subtests; instead, there are Animal House and Geometric Design subtests. In the Animal House subtest the child is required to match particular colors with a specific animal. This resembles the Coding subtest of the WISC-R. In the Geometric Design subtest the child is asked to copy designs with a pencil. The Mazes subtest of the WPPSI is not an optional test as it is with the WISC-R.

Columbia Mental Maturity Scale
(The Psychological Corporation, 757 Third Avenue, New York, N.Y. 10017)

This is an individually administered, untimed test to measure "global intelligence." Its range extends from three to 12 years. It requires no verbal response and only a minimal motor response. It has special relevance for use with nonverbal or physically handicapped children. The test asks the child to point to a picture that is different in some dimension from other pictures on each card. Differences involve color, shape, size, use, number, missing parts, and symbols.

Leiter International Performance Test
(The Psychological Corporation, 757 Third Avenue, New York, N. Y. 10017).

This individually administered test is a measure of "global intelligence." Its age range is from two to 18 years, and it requires no language for administration or response. It is found to be helpful with deaf, language-impaired, and non-English-speaking children and adolescents. The tasks range from matching of colors and forms to completion of patterns, analogous designs, and classification of objects. Most of the items demand perceptual organization and discrimination.

McCarthy Scales of Children's Abilities
(The Psychological Corporation, 757 Third Avenue, New York, N. Y. 10017)

This is an individually administered intelligence test for children from 2½ to 8½ years. Its subscores include Verbal (the child's capacity to deal with and express verbal concepts), Quantitative (the child's number aptitude), Perceptual Performance (the child's capacity to deal with concrete materials such as blocks and puzzles and to conceptualize information without words), Memory (the child's short-term, immediate recall of words, numbers, and pictures of objects and tonal sequences), and Motor Development (gross and fine motor coordination).

The Slosson Intelligence Test
(Slosson Education Publications, 140 Pine Street, East Aurora, N. Y. 14052)

This is an individually administered intelligence test that can be used with anyone over one month of age. Based in part upon the Stanford-Binet Intelligence Scale and the Gesell Developmental Scales, it is primarily a quick screening device, requiring 10 to 30 minutes to administer. Caution should be taken in using this test in situations that demand precise diagnostic distinctions.

Stanford-Binet Intelligence Scale
(Houghton-Mifflin, 2 Park Street, Boston, Mass. 02107).

This is an individually administered intelligence test with an age range from two years to adult. Unlike the Wechsler, the Stanford-Binet groups dissimilar items into the same age-level tests. Items at younger levels stress visual-perceptual-motor skills, while greater language capacities are required at the older levels. At each age level there are six tasks and one alternate. The test is not dichotomized into different subtests or skill areas.

GENERAL ACHIEVEMENT TESTS

California Achievement Test
(California Test Bureau/McGraw-Hill, Del Monte Research Park, Monterey, Calif. 93940)

This group-administered achievement-test battery requires several hours. Its five levels span grades 1.5 through 12. The Reading subtest is composed of Vocabulary and Comprehension; the Mathematics subtest consists of Concepts, Problems, and Computation; the Language subtest includes Mechanics of Language (involving capitalization and punctuation), Usage and Structure, and Spelling.

Metropolitan Achievement Test
(The Psychological Corporation, 757 Third Avenue, New York, N. Y. 10017)

This group-administered achievement test has six levels from grades one through nine. Subtests include Word Knowledge, Word Discrimination, Reading, Spelling, Language Usage, Punctuation and Capitalization, Study Skills, and Social Studies.

Peabody Individual Achievement Test (PIAT)
(American Guidance Service, Inc., Circle Pines, Minn. 55014)

This individually administered achievement test assesses the following areas: Mathematics, Word Recognition, Reading Comprehension, Spelling, and General Information. It requires no written responses and consists of multiple-choice items to which the child points. The General Information subtest measures overall knowledge, encompassing Science, Social Studies, the Fine Arts, and Sports.

Stanford Achievement Test
(The Psychological Corporation, 757 Third Avenue, New York, N. Y. 10017)

This is a group-administered achievement test spanning grades one through nine. It contains five batteries covering a variety of subjects based on the grade the child is in. Subtests include Word Reading, Paragraph Meaning, Vocabulary, Word Study Skills, Spelling, Language Usage, Arithmetic Computation and Concepts, Science, and Social Studies Concepts.

Wide Range Achievement Test (WRAT)
(The Psychological Corporation, 757 Third Avenue, New York, N. Y. 10017)

This individually administered achievement test surveys skills in Spelling, Word Recognition, and Arithmetic. It has two levels: level one is applicable for children aged five through 12 and level two is intended for those from 12 to adulthood. The Reading subtest involves recognizing letters and pronouncing words, while the Spelling subtest involves copying marks resembling letters, writing your name, and writing single words from dictation. The Arithmetic subtest entails counting, reading number symbols, solving oral problems, and performing written computations. Compared with some of the group achievement tests, the WRAT requires less time to administer (approximately 20 to 30 minutes). Unlike the other achievement tests listed in this section, the WRAT does not have a multiple-choice format. A grade-level score is obtained for each subtest.

READING ACHIEVEMENT TESTS

Botel Reading Inventory
(Follett Publishing Company, 1010 West Washington Boulevard, Chicago, Ill. 60607)

This essentially is an informal test with no normative data. Parts can be administered in a group, while other sections must be presented individually. It spans grades one through 12 and measures reading achievement in the areas of word recognition, word opposites, phonics mastery, and spelling. The test is designed to aid the teacher in estimating a child's independent and "frustration" reading levels and in evaluating phonics and related skills.

Durrell Analysis of Reading Difficulty
(The Psychological Corporation, 757 Third Avenue, New York, N. Y. 10017)

This individually administered reading test spans grades one through six. It is designed to diagnose difficulties in word recognition and comprehension skills. Major subtests include oral and silent reading, listening comprehension (the examiner reads a story to the child and asks questions about that story), word recognition, spelling, and phonics. The norms for oral and silent reading are based on the speed of reading, and only one paragraph is used in each grade level. The Durrell is often seen as a useful screening instrument for the elementary-school child.

Gates-MacGinitie Reading Test
(Teachers College Press, Columbia University, New York, N. Y. 10027)

This is a group-administered reading test, spanning grades one through 12. It is used to assess achievement in silent reading skills, vocabulary, and comprehension; assessment of speed and accuracy starts at the second-grade level.

Gates-McKillop Reading Diagnostic Test
(Teachers College Press, Columbia University, New York, N. Y. 10027)

This is an individually administered reading test spanning grades one through 12. It is used to diagnose difficulties in oral reading, word perception, phrase perception, syllabication, letter names and sounds, blending, and spelling. There are no comprehension measures for the oral reading subtest.

Gilmore Oral Reading Test
(The Psychological Corporation, 757 Third Avenue, New York, N. Y. 10017)

This is an individually administered test spanning grades one through eight. There are four forms, each consisting of ten paragraphs to be read orally, followed by five comprehension questions. Each succeeding paragraph becomes more difficult, representing an increment of about one grade level. This test is used to diagnose difficulties in oral reading accuracy, comprehension, and rate of reading.

The Gray Oral Reading Test
(Bobbs-Merrill Company, Inc., 4300 West 62nd Street, Indianapolis, Ind. 46206)

This is an individually administered reading test, spanning grades one through 12. There are four forms, each containing 13 paragraphs of increasing difficulty and varying content. Each passage is followed by four comprehension questions. The rate of reading is a factor in grade-equivalent scores, but comprehension is not. Like the Gilmore Oral Reading Test, the Gray is used to diagnose difficulties in oral reading, accuracy, and comprehension.

Roswell-Chall Diagnostic Test of Word Analysis Skills
(Essay Press, P.O. Box 5, Planetarium Station, New York, N. Y. 10012)

This individually administered reading test spans grades two through six. It is primarily a brief survey of selected word-attack skills including: single consonants, consonant combinations, short vowels, vowel combinations, and syllabication. It is used to assess a child's phonic knowledge.

Spache Diagnostic Reading Scales
(California Test Bureau, McGraw-Hill Del Monte Research Park, Monterey, Calif. 93940)

This is an individually administered reading test, spanning grades 1.3 to eight. It is used to diagnose difficulties in word recognition, oral reading, and phonics skills.

Woodcock Reading Mastery Test
(American Guidance Service, Inc., Circle Pines, Minn. 55014)

This individually administered reading test spans grades kindergarten through 12. The test is used to measure reading achievement in letter and word identification, word-attack skills using nonsense words, word comprehension using an analogy format, passage comprehension, and a total reading score.

INDIVIDUAL ARITHMETIC TESTS

Key Math Diagnostic Arithmetic Test
(American Guidance Service, Inc., Circle Pines, Minn. 55014)

This is an individually administered mathematics test which relies primarily on oral responses but includes some paper-and-pencil items. It covers from preschool through grade six, although it has no upper limit when used for remedial purposes. The test includes 14 subtests, divided into three main areas: Content

(Numeration; Fractions; Geometry and Symbols), Operations (Addition; Subtraction; Multiplication; Division; Mental Computation; Numerical Reasoning), and Applications (Word Problems; Missing Elements; Money; Measurements; Time).

TESTS TO ASSESS SPECIFIC AREAS OF DEFICITS OR STRENGTHS

Visual-Motor and Spatial-Relation Assessment

Bender-Gestalt Test
(The Psychological Corporation, 757 Third Avenue, New York, N. Y. 10017)

This is an individually administered, untimed test to assess visual-motor function. It spans the ages from five years to adulthood. The child is requested to copy nine geometric designs. When it is used as a visual retention test, the child is asked to reproduce the designs from memory. Koppitz (1964) developed a scoring system for the Bender-Gestalt in order to evaluate perceptual-motor maturity, possible organic impairment, and emotional adjustment. Koppitz highlighted such errors in design construction as distortion of shape; rotation of the design; substitution of circles for dots; perseveration of the design; poor integration of parts; angles instead of curves; and incorrect angles. The Bender-Gestalt is widely used to assess visual-motor function, especially in conjunction with other assessment procedures.

Benton Visual Retention Test
(The Psychological Corporation, 757 Third Avenue, New York, N. Y. 10017)

This is an individually administered test to assess visual memory and visual-motor skills in children beginning at age eight. Geometric designs are shown to a child one at a time. Each is then covered, and the child is requested to reproduce the design with paper and pencil. The amount of time between covering the design and having the child reproduce it can vary. The test is scored in terms of omissions, additions, distortions, perseverations, rotations, misplacement of design figures, and size errors.

Developmental Test of Visual-Motor Integration (Beery)
(Follett Publishing Company, 1010 West Washington Boulevard, Chicago, Ill. 60607).

This test (often called the VMI) can be administered to an individual or to a group and is used to assess visual-motor skills. There are norms covering the ages two through 15 years of age. The child is asked to copy geometric designs selected from other tests including the Bender, Cattell, Gesell, and Stanford-Binet. Each design is copied in the space directly below it in a booklet. This procedure differs from that of the Bender-Gestalt, in which the designs may be copied anywhere on the empty sheet of paper. The Bender-Gestalt may be more sensitive to the organization of space. The VMI designs begin as simple figures, such as a circle or square, and become more complex, integrated figures.

Frostig Development Test of Visual Perception
(Consulting Psychologists Press, 577 College Avenue, Palo Alto, Calif. 94306)

This test, which can be administered individually or to a group, spans the ages three through eight. It is used to assess five visual-perceptual skill areas: (1) eye-motor coordination (the child draws a line between increasingly narrow paths); (2) figure-ground (the child outlines particular embedded figures); (3) constancy of shape (the child selects and outlines circles and squares while ignoring oval and rectangular figures); (4) position in space (the child discerns figures that are either different from or the same as other figures in terms of their position in space); and (5) spatial relationships (the child copies a design by connecting lines between dots). Remedial programs have been developed based on a child's performance on the Frostig, but there is no conclusive evidence to support these programs' effectiveness or their relation to reading abilities.

Body and Motor Assessment

Goodenough-Harris Drawing Test
(The Psychological Corporation, 757 Third Avenue, New York, N. Y. 10017)

This test can be administered both individually and in groups and is applicable to all ages. The child is requested to draw three pictures—one of a man, one of a woman, and one of himself. A full body (not just a face) is required. The scoring system is used to measure intellectual ability and provide a mental age; the test can also be used to assess how well the child represents the human body.

Harris Test of Lateral Dominance
(The Psychological Corporation, 757 Third Avenue, New York, N. Y. 10017)

This test is administered individually and is used to assess lateral dominance in the hand, eye, and foot. It spans the ages seven years to adulthood. To measure hand dominance the child is asked to use scissors, do simultaneous writing, deal cards, tap, write, and show strength of grip. In order to assess eye dominance the child is asked to look through a toy telescope or rifle. Foot dominance is assessed by asking the child to kick an object.

Oseretsky Test of Motor Proficiency
(American Guidance Service, Inc., Circle Pines, Minn. 55014)

This test is administered individually to measure gross and fine motor proficiency. Norms are established from the ages of four through 16. Areas assessed include running speed and agility, balance, bilateral coordination, strength, upper-limb coordination, response speed, visual-motor control, and upper-limb speed and dexterity.

Assessment of Language Skills

Detroit Test of Learning Aptitude
(Bobbs-Merrill Company, Inc., 4300 West 62nd Street, Indianapolis, Ind, 46206)

This individually administered test assesses a variety of learning skills, especially those related to language. It spans from three years to adulthood and yields a general mental age. The test is composed of 19 subtests.

1. *Pictorial Absurdities.* The child looks at a picture and tells what is foolish about it.
2. *Verbal Absurdities.* The child listens to sentences or a story and tells what is foolish about it.
3. *Pictorial Opposites.* After looking at a series of three to five pictures and a model, the child points to a picture that is opposite from the model.
4. *Verbal Opposites.* After the examiner says a word, the child is asked to say a word that is the opposite.
5. *Motor Speed and Precision.* The child is presented with a page with 371 circles of diminishing size and is asked to put an X in as many circles as possible in two minutes.
6. *Auditory Attention Span for Unrelated Words.* The examiner says a series of from two to eight unrelated one-syllable words, and the child is asked to repeat them in the same order.
7. *Oral Commissions.* After hearing a command with one to four parts, the child is asked to perform the actions.
8. *Social Adjustment (A).* The child is requested to tell what he would do after the examiner describes a particular social situation.
9. *Visual Attention Span for Objects.* After viewing a card for as many seconds as there are objects on the card, the child names the objects in linear order once the card is removed. Cards show from two to eight objects.
10. *Orientation.* The child is asked a series of 42 questions requiring a verbal or physical response, drawing on knowledge of orientation in time and space.
11. *Free Association.* The child says as many words as he can as fast as he can. The time limit is one to five minutes, depending on age.
12. *Memory for Designs.* The child is shown geometrical designs and is asked to copy the model, to finish a partial design after having the model removed, and to draw a design from memory after the model is removed.
13. *Auditory Attention Span for Related Syllables.* The examiner says a sentence ranging from five to 22 words, which the child repeats.
14. *Number Ability.* The child is given 12 questions or directions and is asked to respond by pointing, giving the correct numeral, or circling a number.
15. *Social Adjustment (B).* The child is asked to respond to questions requiring social knowledge, such as "What is a jail for?"
16. *Visual Attention Span for Letters.* The child is shown a sheet with from two to seven letters and is asked to recall the letters in the same order once the sheet has been removed.
17. *Disarranged Pictures.* The child is shown a page with parts of a picture disarranged and is asked to place numbers corresponding to the part of the picture in correct position on the paper in order to show the correct placement of the parts to make a whole picture.

18. *Oral Directions.* In 17 sets of letters, figures, words, or digits, the child is given oral directions and asked to mark a certain part or parts of a set in sequence, such as "Put a one in the circle and a cross in the square box."

19. *Likenesses and Differences.* The examiner names two objects, and the child is asked to tell how they are the same and different.

Certain subtests are omitted at specific ages. In addition, it is usually recommended that diagnosticians be selective in terms of which subtests they use to assess a particular learning ability.

Illinois Test of Psycholinguistic Abilities
(University of Illinois Press, Urbana, Ill. 61803)

This is an individually administered test to assess language function in several areas. The age range is from 2-4 to 10-3. The test is composed of 12 subtests designed to delineate deficits in (*1*) three processes of language communication (receptive, organizing, and expressive); (*2*) two levels of language organization (representational and automatic); and (*3*) two channels of language (auditory-vocal and visual-motor).

The 12 subtests include:

1. *Auditory Reception.* This test of simple auditory decoding asks the child such questions as "Do dogs eat?" or "Do dials yawn?"

2. *Visual Reception.* This test of visual decoding requires the child to look at a picture and then find the same object within different pictures on a new page.

3. *Auditory-Vocal Association.* This test focuses on part of the organizing process, and the child is given such verbal analogies as "I cut with a saw, I pound with a _____." Knowledge of vocabulary is required here.

4. *Visual Association.* This test also focuses on part of the organizing process; the child is shown stimulus pictures surrounded by four optional pictures and is asked, "What goes with this?"

5. *Verbal Expression.* The child is given an object such as a block or an envelope and is asked "Tell me all about this." This test is helpful in determining the child's ability to express concepts.

6. *Manual Expression.* The child is given 15 pictures of common objects presented one at a time and asked, "Show me what we do with the telephone." No verbal response is required.

7. *Grammatic Closure.* This test evaluates the child's level of syntactic development. An example would be: "This dog likes to bark. Here he is _____." The examiner shows the child a picture of what the dog is doing.

8. *Auditory Closure.* The child is asked to fill in missing parts and sounds of a word, such as "tele--one."

9. *Sound Blending.* Words are divided into from two to seven sounds and presented with picture clues. The words range in difficulty from sh-e to nonsense words such as r-u-s-o-p.

10. *Visual Closure.* The child is requested to mark embedded figures within a 30-second time limit. This test assesses not only visual figure-ground

capacities but also the ability to generalize an object from seeing just parts of it.

11. *Auditory Sequential Memory.* The child is asked to repeat from two to eight digits from memory.

12. *Visual Sequential Memory.* The child is shown a sequence of from two to 17 plastic chips with geometric forms for five seconds and then must reproduce this sequence.

The Boston Naming Test
(This test has been developed by Sylvia Kaplan of the Boston University Graduate School of Education)

This is an individually administered test, spanning approximately the ages four through 11. The child is shown pictures and is asked to name the objects as quickly as he can.

Goldman-Fristoe-Woodcock Test of Auditory Discrimination
(American Guidance Service, Inc., Circle Pines, Minn. 55014)

This is an individually administered test to assess speech-sound discrimination ability with and without background distractions. The age range is from four years to adulthood. The test has three parts: (*1*) a Training Procedure to familiarize the child with the word-picture associations to be used; (*2*) a Quiet Subtest, which provides a measure of auditory discrimination in the absence of background noise; the child is asked to point to an object that is said over a tape ; (*3*) a Noise Subtest, in which the object is named over the tape against a background of distracting noises. The child must listen closely to what word is being said and point to the correct object on the page.

Careful attention is paid to the differential performance of children under the quiet and distracting-noise conditions.

Myklebust Picture Story Language Test
(Western Psychological Services, Box 775, Beverly Hills, Calif. 90213)

This is an individually administered test to measure the level of a child's writing ability. It is appropriate from ages seven through 17. The child is shown a picture and asked to write a story about it. The child's story is assessed by: (*1*) productivity as measured by the number of words, sentences, and words in a sentence; (*2*) syntax, or how grammatically correct the written production is; and (*3*) abstract-concrete level of language, or the nature, meaning, and richness of the ideas expressed.

Northwestern Syntax Screening Test
(Northwestern University Press, Evanston, Ill.)

This individually administered test is for screening purposes only. It is designed to assess syntactic sophistication in receptive and expressive language. Its norms cover ages three through eight. The test is divided into two sections. In the section measuring receptive language skills, a child is given a set of two related pictures and two decoy pictures on one page and a pair of contrasting syntactical sentences spoken by the examiner. The child is asked to point to the picture that corresponds to the meaning of the spoken sentence. In the section assessing expressive language skills, the child is given a set of two related pictures on one page and a pair of contrasting syntactical sentences spoken by the examiner. The child is requested to repeat the sentences exactly as the examiner says them.

Peabody Picture Vocabulary Test
(American Guidance Service, Inc. Circle Pines, Minn. 55014)

This is an individually administered test to assess receptive language skills as well as an estimate of overall intelligence. The age range is from 2-3 to 18-6. No verbal response is required. The examiner says a stimulus word and the child must respond by pointing to the one of four pictures on a page that best illustrates the word. The test is particularly useful for measuring receptive language in nonverbal children.

Slingerland Screening Test for Identifying Children with Specific Language Disability
(Educators Publishing Service, Inc., 75 Moulton Street, Cambridge, Mass. 02138).

This test, which can be administered individually or in groups, is used to assess strengths and weaknesses in perceptual-motor functions, visual, auditory, kinesthetic functions, and receptive and expressive language. The range is from grades one through four. There is a similar test called the Malcomesius for grades six, seven, and eight. These tests stress auditory, visual, and kinesthetic perceptual processes rather than more abstract language function.

Wepman Auditory Discrimination Test
(Western Psychological Services, Box 775, Beverly Hills, Calif. 90213)

This is an individually administered procedure, which is used to assess the child's ability to detect differences in spoken word pairs. The child is asked to indicate whether word pairs are the same or different (e.g., web-wed, chew-chew, shot-shop, pit-kit). This test is useful only as a screening device and in children under eight.

Tests of Cognitive Function

Cognitive Control Battery
(A series of tests developed by Dr. Sebastiano Santostefano of the Hall-Mercer Children's Center of McLean Hospital, 115 Mill Street, Belmont, Mass. 02178)

This battery is used to assess cognitive controls or information-processing strategies. The tests are individually administered and can be used with preschool children up to adulthood. They measure such cognitive functions as body ego, body tempo regulation, scanning, selective attention, memory, and conceptual thinking. Results from this battery are used to plan cognitive control therapy programs, which focus on both cognitive remediation and emotional function (see Chapter 8). The test in the Cognitive Control Battery used to assess conceptual thinking is the Goldstein-Scheerer Object Sort test, which is published by The Psychological Corporation.

Raven Progressive Matrices
(The Psychological Corporation, 757 Third Avenue, New York, N. Y. 10017)

This is an individually administered test, spanning ages five to adulthood. It measures conceptual thinking within a perceptual field. No verbal response is required. The child is asked to choose from multiple-choice options the design or design part that best fits a pattern. The fit may be based strictly on a perceptual quality or on qualities involving concepts. While the test may be useful with some groups who have language disorders, a procedure such as the Leiter discussed above would probably yield more information about the process of thinking.

Assessment of Readiness Skills

Boehm Test of Basic Concepts
(The Psychological Corporation, 757 Third Avenue, New York, N. Y. 10017)

This test, which may be administered either individually or in groups, spans kindergarten through grade two. It can also be adapted for prekindergarten children. Designed as a screening instrument to assess a child's overall level of concept mastery, it consists of 50 items concerning a child's understanding of space (location, direction, orientation, dimensions), time, quantity (number), and a few miscellaneous concepts. It is thought to be useful for teachers in the detection and remediation of the verbal understanding of basic concepts.

Carrow Test of Auditory Comprehension of Language
(Learning Concepts, Inc., 2501 North Lamar, Austin, Tex. 78705)

This is an individually administered test for ages three through six. It is used to assess the auditory comprehension of language structures. It consists of three line drawings, which represent certain linguistic references. The child is asked to point to the picture that represents a word, phrase, or sentence presented verbally by the examiner. The score comprises vocabulary, morphology, and syntax, offering the teacher a quick assessment of general problem areas requiring intervention.

Basic Concept Inventory
(Follett Publishing Company, 1010 West Washington Boulevard, Chicago, Ill. 60607)

This is an individual or group-administered test for preschool and kindergarten children. It may, however, be given to children as old as 10 years. It is used to evaluate knowledge of basic concepts found in the kindergarten and first-grade classroom. Several of the tests do not require verbal responses.

Gates-MacGinitie Reading Readiness Test
(Teachers College Press, Columbia University, New York, N. Y. 10027)

This test is typically administered in groups and is applicable in kindergarten and early first grade. It is used to measure the child's ability to follow picture directions, match words, rhyme, read, and name letters and numbers. There are eight subtests: (1) Listening Comprehension; (2) Auditory Discrimination; (3) Visual Discrimination; (4) Following Directions; (5) Letter Recognition; (6) Visual-Motor Coordination; (7) Auditory Blending; and (8) Word Recognition.

Meeting Street School Screening Test
(Meeting Street School, 333 Grotto Avenue, Providence, R.I. 02906)

This is an individually administered test for kindergarten and first-grade children; its purpose is to screen for learning problems in the areas of motor patterning, visual-perceptual-motor ability, and language development. Specific tests involve following the examiner's body movements; following directions, especially involving spatial relations; visual memory and visual matching; auditory memory; copying forms; repeating words and sentences; and telling a story.

Metropolitan Readiness Test
(The Psychological Corportation, 757 Third Avenue, New York, N. Y. 10017)

This is a group-administered test for kindergarten and first-grade children. There are six subtests: (1) Word Meaning; (2) Listening Comprehension; (3) Matching (visual perception); (4) Alphabet (knowledge of names of lower-case letters); (5) Numbers; and (6) Copying.

Stanford Early School Achievement Test
(The Psychological Corporation, 757 Third Avenue, New York, N. Y. 10017)

This is a group-administered test for kindergarten and first grade. There are two levels. Subtests for both levels include: (1) The Environment (involving the social and natural sciences); (2) Mathematics; (3) Letters and Sounds; and (4) Oral Comprehension (the child is asked to read a paragraph and then answer questions about it). Level two, which is for first grade, also contains subtests in Word Meaning and Sentence Meaning.

Appendix B

Glossary

The bird would cease and be as other birds
But that he knows in singing not to sing.
The question that he frames in all but words
Is what to make of a diminished thing.

Robert Frost, The Oven Bird

This glossary contains words and phrases that frequently are encountered by physicians working with children who have learning problems. Interdisciplinary teams are teeming with multidisciplinary jargon—perhaps a necessary "growing pain" during this historical period. The inclusion herein of specific terms does not necessarily constitute an endorsement of them by the authors!

Achievement test.   A standardized examination designed to document a child's basic level of attainment in academic areas, such as arithmetic, reading, spelling, and vocabulary. Scores may be reported as grade equivalents or as local or national percentile ranks. These tests vary widely in their scope and design; therefore their interpretation requires caution.

Affect.   The observable signs of a child's mood or handling of feelings. Inappropriateness, "flatness," and extreme lability of affect may be signs of turmoil or maladaptation.

Agnosia.   An inability to process information through a particular input channel or sense. This difficulty exists despite the fact that the sensory organs themselves are likely to be operating appropriately, which suggests a problem with central processing. Difficulty localizing one's fingers (finger agnosia) is an example.

Anomia (or Dysnomia).   Difficulty with the retrieval of names or objects. It can constitute a significant handicap for writing and speaking.

Apraxia (or Dyspraxia).   Difficulty in planning and carrying out a particular act. Apraxias can affect both verbal and nonverbal functions. An apraxia is an impairment of output, in contrast to an agnosia, which represents impaired input.

Associated movements.   Extraneous motor activities that accompany a particular motor performance. These movements appear irrelevant to the act in question. For example, a child, while performing an exercise involving

290

finger tapping, may show a great deal of movement of his tongue and mouth. A synkinesia, or mirror movement, is one kind of associated movement. Associated movements sometimes are called "overflow phenomena."

Attention deficits.   Handicapping conditions that cause difficulty in selecting purposeful stimuli on which to focus or concentrate and in remaining focused on these stimuli for appropriate periods to accomplish a particular aim. Children with attentional disorders may vary between showing short attention spans or perseverating. They may be impulsive, and they may be unusually susceptible to distractions, either visual, auditory, or internal. Such children may or may not show overactivity.

Auditory discrimination.   The ability of the brain to tell the difference between very similar sounds. Children with problems in auditory discrimination may have difficulty distinguishing words that sound alike. Such words as "fluid" and "fluent," "dim" and "din," may sound identical to children with auditory discrimination problems, which can interfere with comprehension in the classroom and with the development of good reading skills and can also cause a child to appear inattentive or hyperactive.

Auditory memory.   The ability to store and retrieve information presented verbally, or as sounds, or in the form of sound-symbols, which may entail remembering details in a particular order (auditory-sequential memory). A child's auditory memory may relate to the acquisition and use of vocabulary. His receptive vocabulary (i.e., understanding of words) may constitute a form of auditory recognition and association. His expressive vocabulary (i.e. words he can use appropriately) may depend on an ability to recall or retrieve exact words at the appropriate times.

Auditory perception.   The ability of the brain to interpret information coming in through the ears. Auditory perception is not directly related to auditory acuity. The ability of the brain to discriminate sounds from each other and to identify meaningful units of sound are involved in auditory perception.

Auditory-sequential memory.   The capacity to retain in the right order a span of information presented verbally. A child with deficits in auditory-sequential memory may have difficulty following a series of instructions in the classroom or at home. He may need to be presented simpler verbal commands. Auditory-sequential memory can be tested in a number of ways, including a digit span, tests of sentence memory, and memory of nonsense syllables.

Choreiform movements.   Involuntary rotational and arrhythmic tremors. These movements are seen most commonly in the outstretched fingers or the protruded tongue. A number of studies have shown associations of these with learning and behavior problems.

Closure.   The ability to recognize an entire word or sentence when one or more parts of it are missing, which can depend to some extent on the child's overall awareness of the structure of language and the use of context.

Cognitive function (Cognition).   The various kinds of "thinking skills" that are involved in the processes of acquiring and utilizing knowledge.

Cognitive style.   Individual methods by which a child appears to learn best. A particular child may be said to be a visual learner or an auditory learner, meaning that he may learn best through visual or through auditory modalities. Many other forms of cognitive style can be discerned by careful description of a child's relative strengths and weaknesses.

Continuous performance.   The ability to sustain a motor act over a period of time without significant deterioration in the quality of the activity. The antonym is impersistence. Some children with attentional disorders or "hyperactivity" may have difficulty with this kind of sustained performance.

Decoding.   A process whereby symbols are converted by the brain. The act of reading is one such form of deciphering ideas from visual symbols. The interpretation of spoken words, facial expressions, and social cues might also be considered forms of decoding.

Depression.   A mental state of chronic sadness from which it is difficult to rebound. Common signs of childhood depression include self-deprecatory remarks, loss of appetite, sad affect, chronic fatigue, sleep problems, somatic symptoms, and generalized slowness of tempo. Depression commonly may represent a reaction to loss or to chronic failure. It may be a manifestation of reduced self-esteem. It is also thought that in certain cases depression may be a primary pathologic disorder (i.e., not secondary to any particular circumstance).

Diodochokinesis.   Rapid alternating movements, most commonly sequential pronation and supination of the hands. Some children have difficulty suppressing activity in proximal muscle groups while performing in this way, thereby leading to excessive flailing of the arms or marked deviation of the elbows from the trunk. This is a normal finding in preschool children but is said to be associated with dysfunction in older age groups (dysdiadochokinesis).

Dominance.   A tendency to use preferentially one side of the body. In many cases it reflects a preferred development of one side of the brain for particular functions. Hand dominance is usually well established by age six. Eye dominance can also be evaluated. Children who are delayed in establishing clear dominance are sometimes said to have neuromaturational delays.

Dyscalculia.   An inability to perform various mathematical functions. It may be associated with other kinds of learning problems and neurodevelopmental findings. Children said to have dyscalculia represent a heterogeneous group with regard to specific disabilities.

Dysgraphia.   An inability to perform the fine motor movements necessary for handwriting. Children with dysgraphia may show extreme illegibility, a slow rate of writing, and basic problems with letter formation. The mechanical aspects of writing are sometimes included in the term *graphomotor function.*

Dyslexia.   The symptom of inability to read. The basis is usually thought to be organic or neurologic. The literal meaning is "difficulty with words"; however, the term has been used and abused widely and has come to have little real meaning with regard to etiology, prognosis, or treatment.

Dystonic posturing. An awkward, often writhing, associated movement (commonly of the upper limbs) that may be seen especially during gross motor acts and may indicate immaturity or gross motor and/or neurologic dysfunction.

Encoding. A process whereby ideas are transformed into symbols for purposes of communication. Spoken or written words, body gestures, sign language, and pantomime are examples that entail encoding.

Encopresis. A condition in which children over four years old soil their underwear and appear to have little control over defecation. It is a common concomitant of school maladaptation or learning disorders. It may result from multiple factors (psychological, developmental, and fortuitous).

Enuresis. Urinary incontinence. A child may have daytime, nocturnal, or day and night wetting. There can be many sources for this dysfunction.

Expressive language function. The ability to code ideas into words, phrases, and sentences. Children with expressive language disorders may appear to be very sparse, hesitant, or awkward in their speech. They may have difficulty narrating an incident or story, and they may be reluctant to participate in class discussions. Such children require thorough evaluations by a speech and language pathologist.

Figure-ground discrimination. The differentiation between foreground and background in the context of any given set of stimuli. Thus, children with auditory figure-ground problems may have difficulty distinguishing between a teacher's voice and certain background noises in the classroom. Children with visual figure-ground problems may even confuse printed words with the background of paper on which they are seen. Both auditory and visual figure-ground problems can form part of a perceptual disorder or attentional handicap.

Fine motor function. The ability to use small muscles smoothly, quickly, and efficiently. It is especially relevant to functions involving the fingers. Children with fine motor problems may have difficulties in eye-hand coordination and may be handicapped in handwriting. Some children with fine motor disorders have difficulty writing rapidly enough and tend to fatigue easily during written tasks.

Finger agnosia. Difficulty in perceiving and naming the position of one's fingers in the absence of visual cues. In assessing this, a child may be asked to fingers are between two of the examiner's fingers. The child keeps his eyes closed during this test. Difficulty with finger awareness has been commonly recognized as having some predictive validity in tests of educational readiness. Finger agnosia may be a sign of proprioceptive or kinesthetic imperception.

Gestalt processing. The ability to perceive nearly simultaneous stimuli that together form a configuration or pattern. The instantaneous appreciation of a particular geometric shape, a familiar face, or an object may represent examples of such processing. This is in contrast to sequential or segmental processing, in which the information is received essentially in a series of successive stimuli or in a sequence.

Grapheme.   The orthographic (written) representation of a speech sound (phoneme).

Graphesthesia.   The ability to recognize shapes, numbers, or letters that are drawn on the skin while a child keeps his eyes closed—an ability thought to have some relation to intersensory integration. Poor graphesthesia has, in some studies, been linked to specific learning disorders.

Graphomotor function.   The ability to express oneself in written language. Children with graphomotor problems may have difficulties with handwriting because of fine motor problems, disorders of word finding, problems in coding ideas into words, or other combinations of deficits. Graphomotor problems (dysgraphias) become increasingly handicapping as children get older and the school requires increasing written output.

Gross motor function.   The ability to use large muscle masses in a coordinated and efficient manner. Included in gross motor function are such elements as body position sense, balance, coordination, the ability to pattern movements appropriately, and the capacity to utilize appropriate muscle groups for specific activities. Gross motor problems may reflect more basic central nervous system disorganization. Children with gross motor deficits may have difficulty in sports and may appear to be clumsy, awkward and sometimes physically unattractive. Some children with gross motor problems have, accompanying them, significant visual-perceptual and visual-perceptual-motor problems, but these deficits do not necessarily go together.

Haptic function.   The sense of touch and the interpretation of sensory data coming from touch receptors in the skin. The sensory component is commonly called *tactile sensation*.

Hyperactivity.   A symptom described in children who do not function properly and demonstrate increased levels of motor output. A great deal of confusion has accompanied this term, since many people automatically associate it with some form of organic brain damage. In addition, looking merely at activity levels can be quite misleading, since some overactive children can be quite productive, and some underactive children can have a great deal of inefficiency, impulsivity, and distractibility. The quality of activity may be more worthy of evaluation than the quantity.

Impulsivity.   A tendency to do things without adequate reflection. Children who are impulsive may show destructive behavioral manifestations, as well as learning problems, because of their inability to plan what they are doing.

Independent evaluation.   A process whereby a second opinion is offered outside of the public school. It may be requested by the parents, the school, or students over the age of majority. It may be performed by a single professional consultant or an interdisciplinary team.

Individualized education plan.   A "blueprint" designed to offer intervention for a child who requires special education and related services. It is the product of an interdisciplinary diagnostic team, usually based in a public school system, which defines the educational goals and objectives for a student.

Intelligence test.   An examination that measures various specific strengths and weaknesses in order to derive a composite rating of overall cognitive ability. There is considerable controversy about the value and potential dangers of such examinations. Some observers are concerned about labeling and an oversimplistic or rigid view of human competence. At best, however, such examinations can help define specific strengths and/or cognitive deficits.

Intersensory integration.   The capacity to process information through more than one sensory pathway simultaneously or in close sequence in order to derive information. For example, a child may require good feedback from proprioceptive and kinesthetic pathways as well as visual channels while attempting to button a shirt.

Kinesthetic function.   The ability to interpret stimuli from sensory end organs in and around muscles, which provide information about body movements through space.

Laterality.   The ability to discriminate between the two sides of the midline. Before school, children become aware of the fact that there are "two sides to things." By age seven, most children can identify left and right. Between seven and eight, they know how to touch their left knee with their right hand. Shortly after that, they can identify the left and right of a person sitting opposite them. Children with problems of laterality sometimes have difficulty learning. Some of them have other forms of visual-spatial disorientation.

Mainstreaming.   A process in which children with handicaps are encouraged to spend as much time as possible in a regular educational program with their chronological peers.

Metalinguistic awareness.   Overall appreciation of the function and structure of language. It suggests an inner sense of the way meaning and language interrelate. Presumably a child with a high level of metalinguistic awareness can be particularly adept at performing tasks of closure and of efficient processing of language.

Minimal cerebral dysfunction.   A controversial "syndrome," consisting of a variety of possible learning problems, attention problems, behavioral disorders, and minor neurologic findings that result in poor performance in life, thought to be based largely on central nervous system deficits. There are dozens of synonyms for minimal brain dysfunction, such as specific learning disabilities, hyperactivity syndrome, and hyperkinetic impulse disorder.

Mixed dominance.   A discrepancy between the preferred lateralization of different functions. A child who is left-handed and right-eyed is said to have mixed dominance. In some studies, mixed dominance has been associated with increased incidences of learning problems. However, this is quite controversial, and findings have been contradictory.

Monitoring ability.   A child's capacity to exercise quality control over his performance. A child who has difficulty monitoring may make careless mistakes and not be aware of his own errors. Many children who have attentional problems demonstrate poor self-monitoring skills.

Morpheme.   The smallest meaning-bearing unit in a language. In most cases it is a word.

Motor impersistence.   An inability to maintain a posture, or sustained activity, over a given period of time. For example, if a child is asked to stand with his hands outstretched, his mouth open, and his tongue protruding for 30 seconds, one might find that the motor-impersistent youngster shows deviation of his arms and that his tongue darts in and out of his mouth during this period. This tendency to be impersistent can be seen in children with attentional disorders, learning problems, and presumed brain injury.

Neurodevelopmental examination.   An integrated evaluation of the maturation of a child's nervous system and of his developmental status in a number of areas. Developmental components of such an assessment might include screening of gross motor function, fine motor function, temporal-sequential organization, visual perceptual-motor function, and auditory-language ability. These are all looked at from the point of view of the child's developmental level or age. A neurodevelopmental examination can help to determine the extent to which issues of maturation, development, and constitutional characteristics contribute to a child's behavioral and learning problems. A traditional neurologic examination looks for specific diseases or lesions in the nervous system, while a neurodevelopmental examination focuses on assessing aspects of function in the nervous system.

Neuromaturation.   A process whereby the central nervous system progressively acquires increasing efficiency. The concept is based on empirical observations of the gradual disappearance of certain neurologic indicators (e.g., associated movements, stimulus extinction), especially between ages seven and nine. The delayed disappearance of such signs is thought to be associated with learning and behavior problems and suggests a constitutional basis (at least in part) for these problems.

Noncategorical.   A system of clustering handicapped children for services without regard to any particular label or category of disability.

Perception.   The interpretation of sensory input. (See *sensation*.)

Perseveration.   A tendency to focus too long on a particular stimulus, so that it interferes with adaptation to a new task or focus. This tendency is commonly seen in some children with attentional disorders. A child who perseverates may, when offered a new task, continue to follow the directions from a previous activity.

Phonemes.   The smallest sound units in any language. In learning to read, a child may be expected to break a word down into its phonemes and then reblend them to re-create the word.

Phonetics.   The study of all of the particular sounds connected with any given language. It includes evaluation of how these sounds are produced.

Phonics.   The application of phonetics to the teaching of reading, particularly in English. It involves efforts to form rich associations between sounds (phonemes) and written symbols (graphemes).

Phonology.   The system of sounds of speech within a particular language. A collection of unique sounds that make up a particular language represents its phonology.

Praxis.   The process through which particular motor acts are planned and carried out. A praxis can be a motor plan, such as that which one might develop for tying shoelaces. Children who have difficulty deriving and applying such plans are said to have *apraxia* or *dyspraxia.*

Projective Test.   A standardized examination designed to elicit information about a child's personality, subconscious feelings, and sources of conflict. A child may be asked to tell a story based on a provocative picture or to say what an ink blot resembles.

Proprioception.   A perceptual process whereby data from sensory nerve endings in joints enable one to acquire information about body position or the location of individual parts of one's body in space.

Propriokinesthetic function.   The ability to interpret information coming from the sensory end organs in muscles and joints. Propriokinesthetic stimuli can be interpreted by the brain to yield information about body position, movement, form recognition, and balance.

Receptive language function.   A child's ability to process and understand verbal information coming in through the ears. The accuracy and rate of decoding words and syntactical constructs into ideas contribute to a child's receptive language capacity. Children with disorders of receptive language may have difficulty understanding instructions and lessons in a classroom and may appear inattentive. There are multiple possible combinations and types of receptive language disorders. When such a problem is suspected, a child should have a thorough language evaluation.

Resource teacher.   A specialist who works closely with children who have learning disorders. This person can also act as a consultant to other teachers, providing various materials and techniques to help children who are struggling in the regular classroom. Ordinarily such a teacher works from a centralized "resource room" or "learning center" in which special curriculum materials are kept.

School phobia.   A condition in which a child develops an extreme fear of going to school. In many cases this may reflect separation anxiety. In other instances it may result from specific fears (e.g., gym class, a particular teacher, or the abuse of peers).

Segmental analytic processing.   The form of processing in which bits of data enter the brain in succession or in a predictable sequence. The serial order of the information is germane to its interpretation. The precise syntax of a sentence or the order of digits in a telephone number are examples of information whose content needs to be appreciated as a series of segments in a particular order. This is in contrast to Gestalt processing, in which an appreciation of simultaneity is critical.

Self-esteem.   An individual's feelings of worthiness and adequacy. Diminished self-esteem may stem from chronic failure and may result in clinical depression.

Semantics.   The system of word meanings in a language. A child with language difficulties may have problems in matching appropriate words with meanings.

Sensation.   The "lowest level" of receptive behavior, which refers only to the activation of sensory-neural structures. Deficits at this level would include deafness, blindness, and other involvements of the peripheral nervous system. It contrasts with perception, which involves the interpretation of sensory information. Children with perceptual disorders have an ongoing neurologic deficit that may involve the inadequate interpretation or processing of sensory input.

Soft neurologic signs.   A series of findings on an examination that indicate inefficient or immature function of the central nervous system. Such signs represent a kind of "window" on the development of the nervous system. Some are normal at very early ages and become increasingly unusual and more likely to be associated with learning problems as children mature. They contrast with hard neurologic signs, which indicate a specific brain lesion or disease of the nervous system. There is considerable misunderstanding about these signs, with some professionals believing that the term "soft" means equivocal. This is not the case, since such findings are reliable and well documented. We prefer to use the term "minor neurological indicators" for these signs.

Somesthetic function.   The sum total of perceptual and sensory feedback from end organs in muscles, joints, and skin, all contributing to a total sense of body awareness in space.

Sound blending.   The ability to synthesize the specific sound components (phonemes) of a word so that it can be recognized and pronounced in its entirety. The process of segmenting words into their individual sounds and reassembling them is an important aspect of developing word-analysis skills in childhood.

Specific learning disability.   HEW definition: "Children with specific learning disabilities exhibit a disorder in one or more of the basic psychological processes involved in understanding or in using spoken or written language. These may be manifested in disorders of listening, thinking, talking, reading, writing, spelling, or arithmetic. These include conditions which have been referred to as perceptual handicaps, brain injuries, minimal brain dysfunction, dyslexia, developmental aphasia, etc. They do not include learning problems which are due primarily to visual, hearing, or motor handicaps; mental retardation, emotional disturbance; or to environmental disadvantages."

Stereognosis.   The ability to recognize and match or identify shapes grasped in the hand without visual assistance. Difficulty with form recognition can be associated with kinesthetic or proprioceptive deficits in a child and may be correlated with learning difficulties.

Stimulus extinction.   A tendency for a child to be unable to perceive a distal sensory stimulus when he is simultaneously presented with a more proximal one. Thus, a youngster may not be able to appreciate the fact that you are touching his hand when you are simultaneously touching his cheek. In older children, this can be looked on as a sign of neurologic inefficiency or immaturity. This sign is sometimes said to reflect "rostral dominance."

Synkinesia.   A particular motor phenomenon in which one side of the body mimics closely an activity being carried out by the contralateral side. This may also be called a mirror movement. This type of motor activity is sometimes a manifestation of neuromaturational delay, as it is a normal finding in younger children but, depending upon the complexity of the motor act, becomes increasingly rare as children grow older. Synkinetic movements in older children are associated with learning and behavioral disorders in many studies.

Syntax.   The system of grammar in a particular language. It includes very specific rules about word order and the functions of particular words within a sentence.

Tachistoscope.   A machine that exposes words or sentences for very short periods. It is intended to improve the rate of word identification by children and is sometimes said to help with visual tracking and visual memory.

Task analysis.   The technique of analyzing a particular task to discover the elements that are within it and the process that is required to perform it. One can select any developmental or academic task and dissect out those underlying functions that are necessary for its achievement. This is an important part of interpreting functioning of children.

Temporal-sequential organization (Sequencing ability).   The ability to orient oneself and the outside world in dimensions of time. Children with sequencing problems may have difficulty perceiving auditory or visual stimuli in a particular order. In addition, they may have major problems with short-term auditory or visual-sequential memory and with motor activities involving a rhythm or definite stepwise progression. Sequencing deficits are becoming recognized increasingly as a cause of serious learning disorders in childhood.

Visual memory.   The capacity to retain information originally presented through visual sensory and perceptual pathways. The ability to retain the visual configuration of a word (e.g., for spelling) or the image of a face may relate to visual memory. It is often useful to separate visual recognition from the ability to revisualize or retrieve specific images from memory when needed.

Visual perception.   The ability to interpret visual information. Visual perception is not related directly to visual acuity or eye movements. It represents the brains's discrimination of information coming into it. Such determinations as position in space, relative size, foreground and background, and relative locations of objects may all be components of visual perception. Children with visual-perceptual problems may have great difficulties recognizing letters and remembering the Gestalt, or overall appearance, of words.

Visual-perceptual-motor function.   The ability to interpret and integrate visual information in such a way that a motor act can be performed based on that information. This ability is most commonly assessed by having a child copy forms. Such tests as the Beery VMI and the Bender-Gestalt help to assess visual-perceptual-motor function. Children with fine motor problems or visual-perceptual problems can show difficulty with visual-perceptual-motor performance.

Visual-spatial orientation.   A capacity closely related to visual perception and involving a child's orientation in space and understanding of such factors as body position, left-right discrimination, and farness versus nearness.

Visual tracking.   The ability to follow visual stimuli through space with the eyes. Children with problems in visual tracking may have difficulty following a line of print with their eyes; consequently, they may lose their place frequently. Visual tracking depends both on the coordination of extraocular muscles and on central nervous system integration. Some children with tracking problems have particular difficulty crossing the midline.

Word finding.   The capacity to associate an image or idea with an appropriate word and to retrieve that word from a "memory bank" at an appropriate rapid rate. Children with word-finding problems may have difficulty participating in class discussions and expressing their ideas. They may tend to substitute pronouns and general nouns (for example, "that thing," "whatchamacallit") for specific nouns.

Appendix C

Parent and School Data Collection Systems

The child is not only the offspring of the race as a species, but of the individual bearing the traces and consequences of his parentage throughout the whole of his compound nature—his body, his soul, and spirit—and as a serious corollary to this, that the career of that child for good and evil, for personal advantages or the contrary, for intellect, or imbecility, and even for moral tendencies, if not written before his birth, with pen of adamant, on tablet of brass, is at least marked out for him by boundary lines, which to overpass, if unfavorable, will require more than ordinary courage, resolution, and a concurrence of favorable circumstances not often to be looked for.

A. K. Gardner, M.D., Our Children: Their Physical and Mental Development
(1872)

THE CHILDREN'S HOSPITAL MEDICAL CENTER

Parent Questionnaire
For Functional and Developmental Assessments

CHILD'S NAME _____ DATE OF BIRTH _____

PERSON COMPLETING FORM _____ DATE _____

NAME OF SCHOOL _____ GRADE _____

TOWN _____ TEACHER(S) _____

A. Please list child's major problems with which you want help:

    1. _____

    2. _____

    3. _____

    4. _____

    5. _____

B. To whom would you like reports sent?

    _____

    _____

    _____

C. What have you said to the child about this evaluation?

    _____

    _____

    _____

    _____

D. Whose idea was it that you come in for an evaluation?

    _____

    _____

    _____

    _____

Levine 12/74, 7/77

302

E. Has this child had previous evaluations outside of school?

Yes ☐   No ☐

If so, where and when? _____

_____

_____

_____

F. Has this child received any special treatments (diet, medications, psychological
counselling, psychiatric help, etc.) outside of school?

Yes ☐   No ☐

If so, please describe below:

APPROXIMATE DATE(S)	TYPE(S) OF TREATMENT (include name of any medicine if you remember)

G. Please attach a recent photograph of the child, if available, in the space below.
This will help us remember him or her if there is an inquiry from you after the
evaluation. It is not essential, but it can be very useful. Any size is
acceptable.

Levine 12/74, 7/77

303

The following checklists help us to decide whether there are any early medical factors that might relate to this child. The checklist entitled "Pregnancy Problems" is all about the mother while she was pregnant <u>with</u> <u>this</u> <u>child</u>, except for items 1.12 and 1.13, which refer to her previous pregnancies. "The Newborn Infant (Problems)" checklist is about the baby <u>during</u> <u>the</u> <u>first</u> <u>month</u> <u>of</u> <u>life</u>. Please review each complete list, and then put an X in the appropriate column following each item.

1.0	PREGNANCY PROBLEMS	TRUE	NOT TRUE	CANNOT SAY
1.1	Had bleeding during first three months			
1.2	Had bleeding during second three months			
1.3	Had bleeding during last three months			
1.4	Gained 25 or more pounds			
1.5	Had toxemia			
1.6	Had to take medications			
1.7	Vomited often			
1.8	Got hurt			
1.9	Gained less than 15 pounds			
1.10	Took narcotic drugs			
1.11	Drank much alcohol			
1.12	Had previous miscarriages			
1.13	Had previous immature babies			
1.14	Had an infection			
1.15	Had other illness(es)			
1.16	Labor lasted longer than 12 hours			
1.17	Had a Cesaerean section			
1.18	Had a difficult delivery			
1.19	Was put to sleep for delivery			
1.20	Labor lasted less than two hours			
1.21	Length of Pregnancy _____			

Levine 12/74, 7/77

304

2.0	THE NEWBORN INFANT (PROBLEMS)	TRUE	NOT TRUE	CANNOT SAY
2.1	Born with cord around neck			
2.2	Injured during birth			
2.3	Had trouble breathing			
2.4	Got yellow (jaundice)			
2.5	Turned blue (cyanosis)			
2.6	Was a twin			
2.7	Had an infection			
2.8	Was given medications			
2.9	Had seizures (fits, convulsions)			
2.10	Had diarrhea			
2.11	Needed oxygen			
2.12	In hospital more than seven days			
2.13	Gagged often			
2.14	Vomited often			
2.15	Born with heart defect			
2.16	Born with other defect(s)			
2.17	Had trouble sucking			
2.18	Had skin problems			
2.19	Was very jittery			
2.20	Had other problem(s)			
2.21	Baby's birth weight _____			

Levine 12/74, 7/77

305

Following are two checklists about problems parents sometimes have with very young children. The checklist entitled "Early Health Problems" is about any medical problems the child may have had during the first five years of life. The "Early Functional Problems" checklist includes functional problems the child may have had, other than health problems. For each list, if the child has had any of these problems, please put an X in the column under the age at which the problem(s) occurred. If a problem occurred over a long period or over and over again, please check the columns for each age during which the problem existed. If the child has never had any of these, put an X in the "Never" column.

3.0	EARLY HEALTH PROBLEMS	Never	0-3 Months	4-6 Months	7-12 Months	13-18 Months	19-24 Months	2-3 Years	3-4 Years	4-5 Years	Cannot Say
3.1	Ear Infection(s)										
3.2	Rashes										
3.3	Meningitis										
3.4	Seizures (convulsions) or spells										
3.5	High fevers (over 103°)										
3.6	Pneumonia										
3.7	Asthma										
3.8	Slow weight gain										
3.9	Trouble with hearing										
3.10	Trouble with eyes										
3.11	Diarrhea										
3.12	Hospitalization(s)										
3.13	Surgery (operations)										
3.14	Serious injury										
3.15	Food allergies										
3.16	Other allergies										
3.17	Anemia (low blood count)										
3.18	Lead poisoning										
3.19	Other poisoning or overdose										
3.20	Heart problem										
3.21	Kidney Problem										

Levine 12/74, 7/77

306

3.0	EARLY HEALTH PROBLEMS (continued)	Never	0-3 Months	4-6 Months	7-12 Months	13-18 Months	19-24 Months	2-3 Years	3-4 Years	4-5 Years	Cannot Say
3.22	Got sick after a shot (immunization)										
3.23	Other important illnesses (specify):										
	a.										
	b.										
3.24	Medications used over long period (specify):										
	a.										
	b.										

4.0	EARLY FUNCTIONAL PROBLEMS	Never	0-3 Months	4-6 Months	7-12 Months	13-18 Months	19-24 Months	2-3 Years	3-4 Years	4-5 Years	Cannot Say
4.1	Feeding difficulty										
4.2	Poor appetite										
4.3	Unwillingness to try new foods										
4.4	Very unpredictable appetite										
4.5	Extreme hunger										
4.6	Colic										
4.7	Constipation										
4.8	Bellyaches										
4.9	Trouble falling asleep										
4.10	Trouble staying asleep										
4.11	Very unpredictable length of sleep										
4.12	Very heavy sleeping										
4.13	Overactivity										
4.14	Head banging										
4.15	Rocking in bed										

Levine   12/74, 7/77

307

4.0	EARLY FUNCTIONAL PROBLEMS (continued)	Never	0-3 Months	4-6 Months	7-12 Months	13-18 Months	19-24 Months	2-3 Years	3-4 Years	4-5 Years	Cannot Say
4.16	Temper tantrums										
4.17	Self-destructive behavior										
4.18	Difficulty in being comforted or consoled										
4.19	Stiffness or rigidity										
4.20	Looseness or floppiness										
4.21	Crying often and easily										
4.22	Shyness with strangers										
4.23	Bashfulness with new children										
4.24	Irritability										
4.25	Extreme reaction to noise or sudden movement										
4.26	Difficulty in keeping to a schedule										
4.27	Trouble getting satisfied										
4.28	Desire to be held too often										
4.29	Failure to be affectionate toward parents										
4.30	Unwillingness to go along with change in daily routine										

Levine 12/74, 7/77

308

Following is a checklist of early accomplishments of children. Please put an X
next to each item under the column giving the age at which this "milestone" first
occurred. If there are items the child still cannot do, please leave all the
columns blank.

		0-3 Months	4-6 Months	7-12 Months	13-18 Months	19-24 Months	2-3 Years	3-4 Years	4-5 Years	Cannot Say
5.0	EARLY DEVELOPMENT									
5.1	Sat up without help									
5.2	Crawled									
5.3	Walked alone (10-15 steps)									
5.4	Walked up stairs									
5.5	Rode a tricycle									
5.6	Caught a big ball									
5.7	Spoke first words (Mama, Dada, etc)									
5.8	Put words together (Daddy bye-bye, Mama home, etc.)									
5.9	Spoke 2-3 word sentences									
5.10	Spoke clearly so strangers understood									
5.11	Used fingers to feed self									
5.12	Used a spoon									
5.13	Fully bowel trained									
5.14	Fully bladder trained									
5.15	Able to dress self									
5.16	Able to tie shoelaces									
5.17	Able to separate easily from mother (for school, play, etc.)									

Levine 12/74, 7/77

Following is a checklist of seven school problems. We are interested in whether anyone in the family other than this child has or has had any of these. Please put an X in the column of the family member(s) who have or have had each problem. If more than one brother or sister has or has had one of these difficulties, put an X <u>for each one</u> in the appropriate column (for example, if there were two brothers who had trouble learning how to read, you would put two X's next to item 6.2 under the column "Child's Brothers"). The "Others" column (for family members such as cousins, aunts, uncles, grandparents) should be used in the same way.

6.0	FAMILY HISTORY	Child's Mother	Child's Father	Child's Brother(s)	Child's Sister(s)	Others (Specify)
6.1	Hyperactive as a child					
6.2	Trouble learning to read					
6.3	Trouble with arithmetic					
6.4	Speech problems					
6.5	Behavior problems in childhood					
6.6	In trouble as a teenager					
6.7	Kept back in school					

6.8   Father's Present Age _____ School Level Completed _____

Present Occupation _____

6.9   Mother's Present Age _____ School Level Completed _____

Present Occupation _____

6.10   Brother(s):   Age(s) _____

_____

6.11   Sister(s):   Age(s) _____

_____

Levine   12/74, 7/77

310

Following is a checklist of skills and interests. Please put an X in the box in the column which best describes how well this child performs each skill. In considering each of these, it is useful to compare the child to other children of his or her own age.

	SKILLS AND INTERESTS				
8.1	BALANCING	Falls easily	Seldom loses balance	Has excellent balance	Cannot Say
8.2	THROWING A BALL	Has difficulty	Can do this	Very good for age	Cannot Say
8.3	CARRYING THINGS	Often spills things	Sometimes spills things	Rarely spills things	Cannot Say
8.4	RUNNING	Slow or awkward	Average for age	Fast and excellent	Cannot Say
8.5	PLAYING SPORTS	Poor	Average for age	Excellent	Cannot Say
8.6	USING A PENCIL	Poor	Average for age	Excellent	Cannot Say
8.7	TYING SHOELACES	Poor or unable	Adequate	Does easily	Cannot Say
8.8	DRESSING SELF	Poor or unable	Adequate	Fast and easy	Cannot Say
8.9	PUTTING THINGS TOGETHER	Poor	Average	Excellent	Cannot Say
8.10	UNDERSTANDING SPOKEN INSTRUCTIONS	Often confused	Sometimes confused	Understands well	Cannot Say
8.11	TELLING A STORY	Often confused	Sometimes confused	Does it easily	Cannot Say
8.12	FINDING THE RIGHT WORDS FOR THINGS	Trouble finding words	No problems	Exceptionally good	Cannot Say
8.13	PRONOUNCING WORDS	Often mispronounces	Rarely mispronounces	Never mispronounces	Cannot Say
8.14	REMEMBERING SPOKEN INSTRUCTIONS	Often forgets	Sometimes forgets	Rarely forgets	Cannot Say
8.15	REMEMBERING PHONE NUMBERS	Often forgets	Sometimes forgets	Rarely forgets	Cannot Say
8.16	REMEMBERING FAMILIAR PLACES	Often forgets	Usually remembers	Remembers very well	Cannot Say
8.17	READING	Has difficulty	Does adequately	Does very well	Cannot Say
8.18	SPELLING	Has difficulty	Does adequately	Does very well	Cannot Say
8.19	TELLING TIME	Has difficulty	Does adequately	Does very well	Cannot Say
8.20	COUNTING MONEY	Has difficulty	Does adequately	Does very well	Cannot Say
8.21	TELLING LEFT FROM RIGHT	Has difficulty	Does adequately	Does very well	Cannot Say
8.22	REMEMBERING THINGS IN THE RIGHT ORDER	Has difficulty	Does adequately	Does very well	Cannot Say

Levine 12/74, 7/77

311

In this section, there is a list of sentences that parents use to describe their children. Please read each of these statements and check off the appropriate square in the right-hand columns.

KEY

Definitely Applies = Is _much_ _more_ frequent and/or extreme than in others of the same age

Applies Somewhat = Is sometimes more extreme than in others of the same age

Does Not Apply = Is usually appropriate or better than average for his or her age

---

9.0	ACTIVITY-ATTENTION PROBLEMS	Definitely Applies	Applies Somewhat	Does Not Apply	Cannot Say
9.1	His/her body is in constant motion.				
9.2	His/her body is underactive.				
9.3	His/her mind seems overactive.				
9.4	He/she has trouble sitting through a meal.				
9.5	He/she does things without thinking.				
9.6	He/she starts things, but doesn't finish them.				
9.7	At times, he/she doesn't seem to hear what you say.				
9.8	He/she does things in the wrong order.				
9.9	He/she doesn't realize when he/she has made a mistake.				
9.10	He/she has trouble _falling_ asleep at night.				
9.11	He/she has trouble _staying_ asleep at night.				
9.12	He/she yawns often during the day.				
9.13	He/she breaks things around the home.				
9.14	He/she seems to do things the hard way.				
9.15	He/she stares at things for long periods.				
9.16	He/she listens to outside noises for long periods.				
9.17	He/she gets distracted easily.				
9.18	He/she likes to keep changing games.				
9.19	He/she is hard to control on a long car trip.				
9.20	He/she can't keep his/her hands to himself/herself.				
9.21	He/she seems to want things all the time (is seldom satisfied).				

Levine   12/74, 7/77

Following is a list of behaviors and characteristics. All children show some of these at some time during their lives. To the right of each item, please put an X in the column which best describes this child <u>during the past six months</u>. If a particular item does not describe the child, put an X in the column "Not Applicable or Cannot Say".

<u>KEY</u>

<u>Definitely Applies</u> = Is <u>much more</u> frequent and/or extreme than in others of the same age

<u>Applies Somewhat</u>　　= Is sometimes more extreme than in others of the same age

<u>Does Not Apply</u>　　　= Is usually appropriate or better than average for his or her age

10.0	ASSOCIATED PROBLEM AREAS	Definitely Applies	Applies Somewhat	Does Not Apply	Not Applicable or Cannot Say
10.1	Is moody				
10.2	Has a bad temper				
10.3	Cries easily				
10.4	Is a worrier				
10.5	Has bad dreams				
10.6	Is often sad				
10.7	Is often very quiet				
10.8	Is fearful of new situations, people, places				
10.9	Is fearful of being alone				
10.10	Is often tired				
10.11	Speaks unclearly, stutters, or stammers				
10.12	Has stomach aches often				
10.13	Wets bed or pants often				
10.14	Soils underwear or has accidents with bowel movements				
10.15	Often has headaches				
10.16	Overeats often				
10.17	Bites nails				
10.18	Often complains of pains in arms or legs				
10.19	Has nervous twitches				

Levine 12/74, 7/77

313

KEY

Definitely Applies = Is _much_ _more_ frequent and/or extreme than in others of the same age

Applies Somewhat   = Is sometimes more extreme than in others of the same age

Does Not Apply   = Is usually appropriate or better tnan average for his or her age

10.0	ASSOCIATED PROBLEM AREAS (continued)	Definitely Applies	Applies Somewhat	Does Not Apply	Not Applicable or Cannot Say
10.20	Complains of feeling ill often				
10.21	Has constipation				
10.22	Is often too neat or orderly				
10.23	Is often too concerned about cleanliness				
10.24	Tells lies				
10.25	Steals things at home				
10.26	Often plays with matches				
10.27	Bullies other children				
10.28	Is fresh, sassy to grownups				
10.29	Destroys objects at home				
10.30	Destroys objects away from home				
10.31	Is fearless				
10.32	Is mean				
10.33	Deliberately tries to make parents angry				
10.34	Gets in trouble with neighbors				
10.35	Is cruel to animals				
10.36	Is a "loner"				
10.37	Has no real friends				
10.38	Loses friends easily				
10.39	Has mostly younger friends				
10.40	Has mostly older friends				

Levine 12/74, 7/77

314

		Definitely Applies	Applies Somewhat	Does Not Apply	Not Applicable or Cannot Say
10.0	ASSOCIATED PROBLEM AREAS (continued)				
10.41	Gets bossed by other children				
10.42	Prefers to play alone				
10.43	Is slow to trust adults				
10.44	Gets picked on				
10.45	Demands to be the center of attention				
10.46	Is not liked by other children				
10.47	Is slow to make friends				
10.48	Will not play alone				
10.49	Will not follow a leader in games				
10.50	Fights with brothers and/or sisters				

Levine   12/74, 7/77

315

Below is a list of positive or good behaviors. Please indicate which of these pertain to your child by putting an X in the appropriate column to the right of each item.

		Often True	Occasionally True	Seldom True	Cannot Say
11.0	ASSOCIATED STRENGTHS				
11.1	Has an even disposition, is easy to live with				
11.2	Usually seems happy				
11.3	Enjoys new experiences				
11.4	Easily becomes involved in many activities				
11.5	Takes pleasure in many activities				
11.6	Is friendly and outgoing				
11.7	Tolerates minor bumps or scratches without much complaint				
11.8	Usually feels well				
11.9	Plays well with other children				
11.10	Shares or cooperates with others				
11.11	Accepts rules easily				
11.12	Is affectionate				
11.13	Is kind or sympathetic if someone else is sad or hurt				
11.14	Compromises easily				
11.15	Plays gently with smaller children or animals				
11.16	Makes friends easily				
11.17	Enjoys playing with other children				
11.18	Has many friends				
11.19	Stands up for himself/herself when necessary				
11.20	Takes turns well				

Levine 12/74, 7/77

If you have any additional comments, please write them in the space below. Thank you very much for your assistance.

Levine 12/74, 7/77

THE CHILDREN'S HOSPITAL MEDICAL CENTER

School Data Collection Form

CHILD'S NAME _____ GRADE _____

SCHOOL _____

FORM COMPLETED BY _____ POSITION _____

WITH HELP FROM _____

A. Please describe this child's school difficulties and strengths as you see them:

_____

_____

_____

_____

_____

_____

B. Please list any specific questions and/or areas in which you would like help with this child:

_____

_____

_____

_____

C. Which of the following services does your school provide? (Check appropriate box)

☐	Learning Disabilities Tutor	Full-Time ☐	Part-Time ☐
☐	Remedial Reading	Full-Time ☐	Part-Time ☐
☐	Remedial Arithmetic	Full-Time ☐	Part-Time ☐
☐	Speech and Language Therapy	Full-Time ☐	Part-Time ☐
☐	School Psychologist	Full-Time ☐	Part-Time ☐
☐	Guidance Counsellor	Full-Time ☐	Part-Time ☐
☐	Adjustment Counsellor	Full-Time ☐	Part-Time ☐
☐	Social Worker	Full-Time ☐	Part-Time ☐
☐	Other (please specify)	Full-Time ☐	Part-Time ☐

_____

_____

Does your school have any self-contained classes for children with special needs?

☐ Yes   ☐ No

If so, please describe: _____

_____

_____

Does your school have any resource rooms for children with special needs?

☐ Yes   ☐ No

If so, please describe: _____

_____

_____

D. Please describe briefly this child's present educational program (include size and nature of classroom, description of time outside of regular classroom, special help):

_____

_____

_____

_____

_____

_____

_____

E. Please record below or attach scores of any individual or group testing that has been performed:

_____

_____

_____

_____

_____

_____

_____

In this section, there are a number of items that deal with this child's performance in various educational areas. In assessing the child's performance in each of these areas, we would like you to consider two basic measurements. First, we would like you to rate the child's typical performance in each area as compared to other children of the same age. To do this, one should put an X in one of the first four columns under "Typical Performance". We would also like you to rate the child in terms of variability of performance in each area. Those children whose abilities seem to change from day to day or hour to hour should be scored at "Highly Unpredictable"; those who show minor degrees of variation in the quality of their performance should be considered "Somewhat Variable"; and those who have the amount of consistency that we would expect from children of that age should be marked under "Consistent Performance". Thus, for each performance area, we would like both a typical performance rating and a variability rating.

		TYPICAL PERFORMANCE				VARIABILITY OF PERFORMANCE			
1.0	PERFORMANCE AREA	Strong for age	Appropriate for age	Delayed less than one year	Delayed more than one year	Consistent Performance	Somewhat Variable	Highly Unpredictable	Cannot Say
1.1	Reading Comprehension								
1.2	Reading Rate								
1.3	Oral Reading								
1.4	Silent Reading								
1.5	Word Analysis Skills								
1.6	Sight Vocabulary								
1.7	Spelling								
1.8	Arithmetic								
1.9	General Knowledge								
1.10	Written Language								
1.11	Music								
1.12	Art								
1.13	Playing Sports								
1.14	Handwriting or Crayon Use								
1.15	Balance								
1.16	Coordination								
1.17	Mechanical Skills								

320

1.0	PERFORMANCE AREA (continued)	TYPICAL PERFORMANCE				VARIABILITY OF PERFORMANCE			
		Strong for age	Appropriate for age	Delayed less than one year	Delayed more than one year	Consistent Performance	Somewhat Variable	Highly Unpredictable	Cannot Say
1.18	Word Pronounciation								
1.19	Sound Differentiation								
1.20	Oral Sentence Structure								
1.21	Vocabulary								
1.22	Writing from Dictation								
1.23	Copying Written Material								
1.24	Orienting Letters (b-d, etc.)								
1.25	Keeping Place in Reading								
1.26	Knowing Left from Right								
1.27	Discriminating Similar Words/Letters								
1.28	Following Series of Directions								
1.29	Retaining Yesterday's Lessons								
1.30	Retaining Skills								
1.31	Visual Memory								
1.32	Relating an Experience								
1.33	Remembering Routines								
1.34	Using Numbers								
1.35	Performing Tasks in Correct Order								
1.36	Getting Letters in Correct Order								
1.37	Getting Words in Correct Order								
1.38	Understanding Time								
1.39	Motivation								
1.40	Imagination								
1.41	Creativity								
1.42	Sense of Humor								
1.43	Enthusiasm								

The twenty items on this page should be scored with respect to the way in which this child compares to other children of the same age and sex. Clearly, all of the items on this page are true of all children, at least occasionally. Therefore, we are particularly interested in whether this child shows these behaviors either more or less frequently than other children. Please indicate this by placing an X in the appropriate column to the right of each item. We would also like you to indicate any item(s) on this page which you would consider to be major problems for this child in the classroom by placing an X in the box to the left of the specific item(s).

2.0		BEHAVIORAL OBSERVATIONS (Activity-Attention)	Less often than other children	As often as other children	More often than other children	Cannot Say
2.1		Keeps getting out of seat				
2.2		Seems to do things without thinking				
2.3		Learns best on a one-to-one basis				
2.4		Is unaware of own mistakes				
2.5		Seems to have too much energy				
2.6		Has trouble finishing a task				
2.7		Seems to "tune out" intermittently				
2.8		Is not sensitive to punishment				
2.9		Is very impatient for rewards or approval				
2.10		Is easily distracted from work				
2.11		Does tasks at the wrong times				
2.12		Hands and/or feet in motion				
2.13		Tires easily during a task				
2.14		Does not plan work				
2.15		Has marked variation in moods				
2.16		Stares for long periods				
2.17		Seems underactive or lethargic				
2.18		Is slow to take up a new task				
2.19		Makes careless mistakes				
2.20		Has trouble during unstructured time				

Following is a list of behaviors as they are observed in school. Please put an X in the appropriate column to the right of each item.

		Does not apply	Applies somewhat	Certainly Applies	Cannot Say
3.0	BEHAVIORAL OBSERVATIONS (Associated)				
3.1	Often sucks thumb or bites nails				
3.2	Often complains of pains or aches				
3.3	Stutters or stammers				
3.4	Misses school for trivial reasons				
3.5	Has wet or soiled self at school				
3.6	Is not much liked by other children				
3.7	Is solitary -- Does things alone				
3.8	Friends mostly of opposite sex				
3.9	Prefers younger children				
3.10	Loses friends easily				
3.11	Bullies other children				
3.12	Often tells lies				
3.13	Frequently fights with other children				
3.14	Has stolen things				
3.15	Destroys own or others' belongings				
3.16	Often worried, worries about many things				
3.17	Cries easily, is often tearful				
3.18	Often appears unhappy or distressed				
3.19	Is fussy or over-particular				
3.20	Is afraid of new situations				
3.21	Is a class clown				
3.22	Doesn't care after making mistakes				
3.23	Tries to copy work of others				
3.24	Is quick to "fly off the handle"				
3.25	Is defiant toward teacher(s)				

323

References

Aliotti NC: Covert assessment in psychoeducational testing. *Psychol in the Schools* **14**:438, 1977.

American Academy of Cerebral Palsy: Statement of The Executive Committee. Feb 15, 1965.

American Academy of Pediatrics Committee on Nutrition: Proposed changes in Food and Drug Administration regulations concerning formula products and vitamin-mineral dietary supplements for infants. *Pediatrics* **40**:916, 1967.

American Academy of Pediatrics Committee on Nutrition: Megavitamin therapy for childhood psychoses and learning disabilities. *Pediatrics* **58**:910, 1976.

American Academy of Pediatrics, Joint Organizational Statement: The eye and learning disabilities. *Pediatrics* **49**:454, 1972.

American Academy of Pediatrics: Statement of The Executive Board. *AAP Newsletter* **16**:1, 1965.

American Psychiatric Association Task Force on Vitamin Therapy In Psychiatry: *Megavitamin and Orthomolecular Therapy in Psychiatry.* Washington, DC, American Psychiatric Association, 1973.

Arnold E, Kirilcuk V, Corson S, and Corson E: Levoamphetamine and dextroamphetamine: Differential effect on aggression and hyperkinesis in children and dogs. *Am J Psychiat* **130**:165, 1973.

Arnold L, Barnebey N, McManus J, Smeltzer D, Conrad A, Winer G, and Desgranges L: Prevention by specific perceptual remediation for vulnerable first graders. *Arch Gen Psychiat* **34**:1279, 1977.

Arter J and Jenkins J: Examining the benefits and prevalence of modality considerations in special education. *J Sp Educ* **11**:281, 1977.

Ayres AJ: Patterns of perceptual motor dysfunction in children: A factor analytic study. *Percept Motor Skills* **20**:335, 1965.

Ayres AJ: Deficits in sensory integration in educationally handicapped children. *J Learn Disabil* **2**:160, 1969.

Ayres AJ: Improving academic scores through integration. *J Learn Dis* **5**:330, 1972(a).

Ayres AJ: *Sensory Integration and Learning Disorders.* Los Angeles Western Psych Services, 1972(b).

Bachara GH and Zaba JN: Learning disabilities and juvenile delinquency. *J Learning Disabil* **11**:242, 1978.

Baddeley A: *The Psychology of Memory.* New York: Basic Books, 1976.

Bain AM: Written expression—the last acquired skill. *Bull Orton Soc* **26**:79, 1976.

324

Baldessarini R: Pharmacology of the amphetamines. *Pediatrics* **49**:694, 1972.

Bandura A and Adams NE: Analysis of self-efficacy theory of behavioral change. *Cog Ther Research* **1**:287, 1977.

Baratz, JC: Relationship of Black English to reading: A review of research. In Laffey J and Shuy R (eds): *Language Differences: Do They Interfere?* Newark: International Reading Association, 1973.

Barcai A: Predicting the response of children with learning disabilities and behavior problems to dextroamphetamine sulfate. *Pediatrics* **47**:73, 1971.

Barkley R: Predicting the response of hyperkinetic children to stimulant drugs: A review. *J Abnormal Child Psychol* **4**(4):327, 1976.

Barkley R: A review of stimulant drug research with hyperactive children. *J Child Psychol Psychiat* **18**:137, 1977.

Barkley R and Jackson T: *The Effects of Methylphenidate on the Autonomic Arousal, Activity level, and Attention Span of Hyperkinetic Children.* Unpublished manuscript, Bowling Green State University, Ohio, 1976.

Barsch R: *A Movigenic Curriculum.* Madison, Wisconsin, Bureau for Handicapped Children, 1965.

Barsch R: *Achieving Perceptual-Motor Efficiency: A Space-Oriented Approach to Learning.* Seattle, Special Child Publications, 1967.

Bartel N, Grill J, and Bryen D: Language characteristics of black children: Implications for assessment. *J School Psych* **11**:351, 1973.

Bash M and Camp B: *Think Aloud Program: Group Manual.* Unpublished manuscript, University of Colorado Medical School, 1975.

Bax M and MacKeith R (eds): *Minimal Cerebral Dysfunction,* Little Club Clinics in Developmental Medicine 10. London, William Heineman, 1963.

Beall J: Food additives and hyperactivity in children. *Cong. Record* 519736, Oct 30, 1973.

Beck AT: *Cognitive Therapy and the Emotional Disorders.* New York, International Universities Press, 1976.

Becker L: Training pediatricians to serve learning disabled children and their families. *Clin Pediatr* **17**:355, 1978.

Belmont L and Birch H: Lateral dominance, lateral awareness, and reading disability. *Child Development* **34**:257, 1963.

Belmont L and Birch H: The effect of supplemental intervention on children with low reading readiness scores. *J Sp Ed* **8**:81, 1974.

Benton A: Right-left discrimination and finger localization in defective children. *Arch Neurol & Psychiat* **74**:583, 1955a.

Benton A: Development of finger localization capacity in school children. *Child Dev* **26**:225, 1955b.

Benton A: Finger localization and finger praxis. *Quart J Exper Psychol* **11**:39, 1959a.

Benton A: *Right-left discrimination and finger localization development and pathology.* New York, Hoeber Medical Division, Harper & Row, 1959b.

Benton A: *The Revised Visual Retention Test: Clinical and Experimental Applications* (3d Ed). New York, Psychological Corporation, 1963.

Benton C: Comment: The eye and learning disabilities. *J Learn Disabil* **6**:334, 1973.

Berges J and Lezine T: The imitation of gestures, *Clinics in Developmental Medicine, No. 18.* London, Heinemann, 1965.

Berlin R: *Eine Besondere Art Der Wortblindheit* (Dyslexia). Wiesbaden, 1887.

Betts E: Physiological approach to the analysis of reading disabilities. *Educ Res Bull* **13**:135, 1934.

Binet A and Simon T: *Mentally Defective Children,* Trans Drummond WB. London, Edward Arnold, 1914.

Birch H: The problem of "brain damage" in children, in Birch H (ed): *Brain Damage in Children,* Baltimore, Williams and Wilkins, 1964.

Blackham GJ: *The Deviant Child in the Classroom.* Belmont, Calif., Wadsworth Publishing Company, Inc, 1967.

Boder E: Developmental dyslexia: A diagnostic approach based on three atypical reading-spelling patterns. *Dev. Med Child Neurol* **15**:661, 1973.

Boder E: School failure—evaluation and treatment, *Pediatrics* **58**:394, 1976.

Bradley C: The behavior of children receiving benezedrine. *Am J Psychiat* **94**:577, 1937.

Brazelton TB: Anticipatory guidance, *Pediat Clin N Am* **533**:22, 1975.

Bronfenbrenner U: *Is early intervention effective: A report on longitudinal evaluations of preschool programs,* vol II, DHEW Publication No. (OHD) 76–30025, 1974.

Brooks R: Psychoeducational assessment: A broader perspective. *Prof Psychol* **10**:708, 1979.

Brown D, Winsberg B, Bailer I, and Press M: Imipramine therapy and seizures: Three children treated for hyperactive behavior disorders. *Am J Psychiat* **130**:210, 1973.

Brumback RA, Dietz—Schmidt SG, and Weinberg WA: Depression in children referred to an educational diagnostic center: Diagnosis and treatment and analysis of criteria and literature review. *Dis Nerv Sys* **38**:529, 1977.

Bryan TH: Learning disabled children's comprehension of nonverbal communication. *J Learning Disabil* **10**:501, 1977.

Bryan TH: Social relationships and verbal interactions of learning disabled children. *J Learning Disabil* **11**:107, 1978.

Bryden M: Auditory–visual sequential–spatial matching in relation to reading ability. *Child Development* **43**:824, 1972.

Buchsbaum M and Wender P: Average evoked responses in normal and minimally brain dysfunctioned children treated with amphetamine. *Arch Gen Psychiat* **29**:764, 1973.

Budoff M: Engendering change in special education practices. *Harvard Educational Review* **45**:507, 1975.

Burdé B and Choate M: Early asymptomatic lead exposure and development at school age. *J Pediat* **87**:638, 1975.

Buros OK (ed): *The Seventh Mental Measurements Yearbook.* Highland Park, N.J. The Gryphon Press, 1972.

Buscaglia L: *The Disabled and Their Parents: A Counselling Challenge.* Thorofare, N.J, Charles Slack, 1975.

Caputo D and Mandell W: Consequences of low birth weight. *Develop Psychol* **3**:363, 1970.

Carey W, Fox M, and McDevitt S: Temperament as a factor in early school adjustment. *Pediatrics* **60**:621, 1977.

Carroll J: The nature of the reading process. In Singer H and Ruddell R (eds): *Theoretical Models and Processes of Reading.* Newark, International Reading Association, 1976.

Cazden C: Play with language and metalinguistic awareness. In Bruner J, Jolly A, and Sylva K (eds): *Play–Its Role in Development and Evolution.* New York, Basic Books, 1976.

Chalfant J and Scheffelin M: *Central Processing Dysfunctions in Children: A Review of Research.* Ninds Monograph No. 9, Bethesda, US Dept HEW, 1969.

Chall J: *Learning to Read: The Great Debate.* New York, McGraw-Hill, 1976.

Chess S: Neurological dysfunction and behavioral pathology. *J Autism and Childhood Schizophrenia* **2**(3):299, 1972.

Chomsky C: *The Acquisition of Syntax in Children from 5 to 10*. Cambridge, Mass: MIT Press, 1969.

Christensen D and Sprague R: Reduction of hyperactive behavior by conditioning procedures alone and combined with methylphenidate. *Behav Res Ther* **11**:331, 1973.

Clements S: *Minimal Brain Dysfunction in Children: Terminology and Identification*. Ninds Monograph No. 3. Public Health Service Publ No. 1415. Washington, DC US Government Printing Office, 1966.

Clements S and Peters J: Minimal brain dysfunction in the school age child. *Arch Gen Psychiat* **6**:185, 1962.

Cohen H, Taft L, Mahadeviah, M, and Birch H: Developmental changes in overflow in normal and aberrantly functioning children. *J Pediatr* **71**:39, 1967.

Cohen S, Semmes M, Guralnick M: Public Law 94-142 and the education of preschool handicapped children. *Exceptional Children* **45**:279, 1979.

Cohn R: Dyscalculia. *Arch Neurol* **4**:301, 1961.

Cole JO: Drug therapy of adult minimal brain dysfunction. *McLean Hosp J* **3**:37, 1978.

Conners C: A teacher rating scale for use with drug studies with children. *Am J Psychiat* **126**:884, 1969.

Conners C: The effect of stimulant drugs on human figure drawings in children with minimal brain dysfunction. *Psychopharmacologia* **19**:329, 1971.

Conners C: Psychological effects of stimulant drugs in children with minimal brain dysfunction. *Pediatrics* **49**:702, 1972a.

Conners C: Pharmacotherapy of psychopathology in children. In Quay H and Werry J (eds): *Psychopathological Disorders of Childhood*. New York, John Wiley & Sons, 1972b.

Conners C: Rating scales for use in drug studies with children. *Psychopharmacol Bull,* Special Issue: **24**, 1972.

Conners C: Psychological assessment of children with minimal brain dysfunction. *Ann NY Acad Sci* **205**:283, 1973.

Conners C, Goyette C, Southwick D, Lees J, and Andrulonis P: Food additives and hyperkinesis: A controlled double-blind experiment. *Pediatrics* **58**:154, 1976.

Conners C, Rothschild, G, Eisenberg L, Stone L, and Robinson E: Dextroamphetamine sulfate in children with learning disorders. *Arch Gen Psychiat* **21**:182, 1969.

Connolly K and Stratton P: Developmental changes in associated movements. *Dev Med Child Neurol* **10**:49, 1968.

Connolly AJ, Nachtman W, and Pritchett EM: *Key Math Diagnostic Arithmetic Test*. Circle Pines, Minn, American Guidance Service, Inc, 1976.

Conrad W and Insel J: Anticipating the response to amphetamine therapy in the treatment of hyperkinetic children. *Pediatrics* **40**:96, 1967.

Cook P and Woodhill J: The Feingold dietary treatment of the hyperkinetic syndrome. *Med J Australia* **2**:85, 1976.

Council on Child Health, American Academy of Pediatrics: *Statement on Early Identification of Children with Learning Disabilities: The Preschool Child*. 1973.

Council on Child Health, American Academy of Pediatrics. Medication for hyperkinetic children. *Pediatrics* **55**:560, 1975.

Corballis MC and Beale IL: *The psychology of left and right*. New York: John Wiley & Sons, 1976, p 169.

Cott A: Orthomolecular approach to the treatment of learning disabilities. *Schizophrenia* **3**:95, 1971.

Critchley M: *The Dyslexic Child,* 2d Edition of Developmental Dyslexia. London, William Heinemann Medical Books Ltd, 1970.

Croxen ME and Lytton H: Reading disabilities and difficulties in finger localization and right-left discrimination. *Developmental Psychology* **5**:256, 1971.

Cruickshank W: The psychoeducational match. In Cruickshank W and Hallahan D (eds): *Perceptual and Learning Disabilities in Children.* Syracuse, NY, Syracuse University Press, 1975, pp 71–114.

Cruickshank W, Bentzen F, Ratzeburg F, and Tannhausser M: *A Teaching Method for Brain-Injured and Hyperactive Children.* Syracuse, NY, Syracuse Univ Press, 1961.

Cruickshank W and Dolphin J: The educational implications of psychological studies of cerebral palsied children. *Except Child* **18**:3, 1951.

Davie R, Butler N, and Goldstein H: *From Birth to Seven.* London: Longmans, 1972.

Davis, FB: Research in comprehension in reading. *Reading Research Quarterly* **68**:499, 1967.

deHirsch K: Specific dyslexia or strephosymbolia. *Folia Phoniatrica* **4**:231, 1952.

deHirsch K, Jansky J, and Langford W: *Predicting Reading Failure.* New York: Harper & Row, 1966.

deHirsch, K: Clinical spectrum of reading disabilities: Diagnosis and treatment. *Bull NY Acad Med* **44**:470, 1968.

deHirsch K: Interactions between educational therapist and child. *Bull Orten Soc* **27**:88, 1978.

Delacato C: *The Treatment and Prevention of Reading Problems: The Neurological Approach.* Springfield, Ill, Charles C Thomas, 1959.

Delozier JE: *National Ambulatory Medical Care Survey: 1973 Summary United States, May 1973–April 1974* (Vital and Health Statistics Series 13, Data from the National Health Survey; No. 71), DPEW Publication No. (HRA) 76-17772, October 1972.

Denhoff E, Hainsworth P, and Hainsworth M: Learning disabilities and early childhood education: An information-processing approach. In Myklebust H (ed): *Progress in Learning Disabilities,* Vol II. New York, Grune & Stratton, 1971.

Denckla M: Color-naming defects in dyslexic boys. *Cortex* **8**:164, 1972.

Denckla M: Naming of object-drawings by dyslexic and other learning disabled children. *Brain and Language* **3**:1, 1976.

Denckla M and Rudel R: Anomalies of motor development in hyperactive boys. *Ann Neurol* **3**:231, 1978a.

Denckla M: Minimal brain dysfunction. *In Education and the Brain.* Chicago, The National Society for the Study of Education, 1978b.

Dolphin J and Cruickshank W: The figure-background relationship in children with cerebral palsy. *J Clin Psychol* **7**:228, 1951a.

Dolphin J and Cruickshank W: Pathology of concept formation in children with cerebral palsy. *Am J Ment Def* **56**:386, 1951b.

Dolphin J and Cruickshank W: Visuo-motor perception of children with cerebral palsy. *Quart J Child Behavior* **3**:198, 1951c.

Dolphin J and Cruickshank W: Tactual-motor perception of children with cerebral palsy. *J Personality* **20**:466, 1952.

Doman R, Spitz E, Zuckman E, Delacato C, and Doman G: Children with severe brain injuries: Neurological organization in terms of mobility. *J Amer Med Assn* **174**:257, 1960.

Douglas V: Stop, look and listen: The problem of sustained attention and impulse control in hyperactive and normal children. *Can J Behav Sci* **4**:259, 1972.

Durkin D: *Children Who Read Early.* New York, Teachers College Press, 1966.

Dworkin P and Levine M: The preschool child: Prescribing the practical management. In Scheiner A and Abroms I (eds): *The Practical Management of the Developmentally Disabled Child.* St. Louis, CV Mosby, 1980.

Dworkin P, Shonkoff J, Leviton A, and Levine M: Training in developmental pediatrics: How practitioners perceive the gaps. *Am J Dis Child* **133**:709, 1979.

Dykman R, Ackerman P, Clements S, and Peters J: Specific learning disabilities: An attentional deficit syndrome. In Myklebust H (ed): *Progress in Learning Disabilities,* Vol II. New York, Grune & Stratton, 1971.

Eckhardt LO and Rabin RA: A proposed new model for training pediatric residents in the psychosocial aspects of pediatrics. *J Clin Child Psychol* **7**:73, 1978.

Eisenberg L: Office evaluation of specific reading disability in children. *Pediatrics* **23**:997, 1959.

Eisenberg L: Reading retardation. I. Psychiatric and sociologic aspects. *Pediatrics* **37**:352, 1966.

Eisenberg L: Principles of drug therapy in child psychiatry with special reference to stimulant drugs. *Amer J Orthopsychiat* **41**(3):371, 1971.

Eisenberg L: The clinical use of stimulant drugs in children. *Pediatrics* **49**:709, 1972.

Epstein L, Lasagna L, Conners C, and Rodriquez A: Correlation of dextroamphetamine excretion and drug response in hyperkinetic children. *J Nerv Ment Dis* **146**:136, 1968.

Fantz R: Visual experience in infants: Decreased attention to familiar patterns relative to novel ones. *Science* **146**:668, 1964.

Farris L: Visual defects as factors influencing achievement in reading. *Cal J Sec Educ* **10**:50, 1934.

Feingold B: *Why Your Child Is Hyperactive.* New York, Random House, 1975.

Feingold B, German D, Braham R, and Simmers E. Adverse reaction to food additives. Read Before the Annual Convention of the American Medical Association, New York, 1973.

Fendrick P: Visual characteristics of poor readers. *Teach Coll Contr Educ* **656**:54, 1935.

Fish B: The "one child, one drug" myth of stimulants in hyperkinesis. *Arch Gen Psychiat* **25**:193, 1971.

Fisher JA: Congenital word-blindness (Inability to learn to read). *Trans OPH Soc UK* **30**:216, 1910.

Flax N: The eye and learning disabilities. *J. Learn Disabil* **6**:328, 1973.

Frame P: The use of art in remedial tutoring with an 8 year old boy. *Am J Art Ther* **13**(3):205, 1974.

Frank JD: Psychotherapy and the sense of mastery. In Spitzer RL and Klein DF (eds): *Evaluation of Psychological Therapies.* Baltimore, The Johns Hopkins University Press, 1976, p 47.

Frankl, Hellman I: Symposium on child analysis. II. The ego's participation in the therapeutic alliance. *Int J Psychoanal* **43**:333, 1962.

Freeman R: Controversey over "patterning" as a treatment of brain damage in children. *J Amer Med Assoc* **202**:383, 1967.

Freud A: *The Ego and the Mechanisms of Defense.* London, the Hogarth Press, 1936.

Friedus E: The needs of teachers for special information on number concepts. In Cruickshank (ed): *The Teacher of Brain-injured Children.* Syracuse, NY: Syracuse University Press, 1966.

Frostig M, Lefever D, and Whittlesey J: A developmental test of visual perception for evaluating normal and neurologically handicapped children. *Percept Motor Skills* **12**:383, 1961.

Frostig M, Maslow P, Lefever D, and Whittlesey J: *The Marianne Frostig Developmental Test of Visual Perception,* 1963 Standarization. Palo Alto, Consulting Psychology Press, 1964.

Frostig M and Horne D: *The Frostig Program for the Development of Visual Perception: Teacher's Guide.* Chicago, Follett, 1964.

Frostig M and Maslow P: *Learning Problems in the Classroom: Prevention and Remediation.* New York, Grune & Stratton, 1973.

Garfield J: Motor impersistence in normal and brain damaged children. *Neurology* **14**:623, 1964.

Garfinkel B, Webster C, and Sloman L: Methylphenidate and caffeine in the treatment of children with minimal brain dysfunction. *Am J Psych* **132:**723, 1975.

Gascon G and Goodglass H: Reading retardation and the information content of stimuli in paired-associated learning. *Cortex* **6**:417, 1970.

Gearhegart B: *Learning Disabilities–Educational Strategies.* St. Louis, CV Mosby, 1973.

Gesell A and Amatruda K: *Developmental Diagnosis.* New York, PB Hoeber, 1941.

Getman G, Kane F, Halgren M, and McKee G: *The Physiology of Readiness, an action program for the development of perception for children.* Minneapolis, Programs to Accelerate School Success, 1964.

Getman G: The visuomotor complex in the acquisition of learning skills. In Hellmuth J (ed): *Learning Disorders,* Vol 1. Seattle, Special Child Publications, 1965.

Gibson E and Levin H: *The Psychology of Reading.* Cambridge, Mass: MIT Press, 1975, p 400 ff.

Gillingham A, and Stillman B: *Remedial Training for Children with Specific Disability in Reading, Spelling, and Penmanship,* 5th ed. New York, Sackett and Wilhelms Litho Corp, 1956.

Gittleman-Klein R, Klein D, Katz S, Saraf K, and Pollack E. Comparative effects of methylphenidate and thioridazine in hyperkinetic children. *Arch Gen Psychiat* **33**:1217, 1976.

Glaser K and Clemmons R: School Failure. *Pediatrics* **35**:128, 1965.

Goddard H: What can the public school do for subnormal children? *The Training School* **7**(5):242, 1910.

Goldstein K: The modifications of behavior consequent to cerebral lesions. *Psychiatric Quarterly* **10**:586, 1936.

Goldstein K: *The Organism.* New York, American Book, 1939.

Gonick-Barris S: Art for children with minimal brain dysfunction. *Am J Art Ther* **15**(3):67, 1976.

Goodman L and Gilman A: *The Pharmacological Basis of Therapeutics.* New York, Macmillan, 1975.

Grant Q: Psychopharmacology in childhood emotional and mental disorders. *J Pediat* **61**:626, 1962.

Grant W, Boelsche A, and Zin D: Developmental patterns of two motor functions. *Develop Med Ch Neurol* **15**:171, 1973.

Greene HH and Perry WT: Developing spelling skills. In Rubin L. (ed): *Curriculum Handbook*. Boston, Allyn & Bacon, 1977.

Greenhill L, Rieder R, Wender P, Buchsbaum M, and Zahn T: Lithium carbonate in the treatment of hyperactive children. *Arch Gen Psychiat* **28**:636, 1973.

Gross M: Imipramine in the treatment of minimal brain dysfunction in children. *Psychosomatics* **14**:283, 1973.

Gross M: Caffeine in the treatment of children with minimal brain dysfunction or hyperkinetic syndrome. *Psychosomatics* **16**(1):26, 1975.

Gross M: Growth of hyperkinetic children taking methylphenidate, dextroamphetamine, or imipramine/desipramine. *Pediatrics* **58**:423, 1976.

Gross M: Case report—improvement with L-dopa in a hyperkinetic child. *Dis Nervous System* **38**:556, 1977.

Guthrie J: Models of reading and reading disability. *J Educ Psych* **65**:9, 1973.

Hagen JW and Hale GH: The development of attention in children. In Pick AD (ed): *Minnesota Symposium on Child Psychology*, Vol. 7. Minneapolis, Univ of Minnesota Press, 1973, pp 117–140.

Hallahan D and Cruickshank W: *Psychoeducational Foundations of Learning Disabilities*. Englewood Cliffs, NJ, Prentice-Hall, Inc, 1973.

Harley JP, Ray R, Tomasi L, Eichman P, Matthews C, Chun R, Cleeland C, and Traisman E: Hyperkinesis and food additives: Testing the Feingold hypothesis. *Pediatrics* **61**:818, 1978.

Helper M, Wilcott R, and Garfield S: Effects of chlorpromazine on learning and related processes in emotionally distrubed children. *J Consult Psychol* **27**:1, 1963.

Hinshelwood J: Word-blindness and visual memory. *Lancet* **2**:1564, 1895.

Hinshelwood J: A case of dyslexia: A peculiar form of word-blindness. *Lancet* **2**:1451, 1896.

Hoffer A and Osmond H: *The Chemical Bases of Clinical Psychiatry*. Springfield, Charles C Thomas, 1960.

Hoffman S, Englehardt D, Margolis R, Polizos P, Waizer J, and Rosenfeld R: Response to methylphenidate in low socioeconomic hyperactive children. *Arch Gen Psychiat* **30**:354, 1974.

Hagenson D: Reading failure and juvenile delinquency. *Bull Orten Soc* **24**:164, 1974.

Holt LE: *The Diseases of Infancy and Childhood*, 1st ed. New York, Appleton & Co, 1897.

Hook P and Johnson D: Metalinguistic awareness and reading strategies. *Bull Orton Soc* **28**:62, 1978.

Hornsby JL: Teaching behavioral science in a family practice residency training program. *J Clin Child Psychol* **7**:80, 1978.

Huessy HR and Wright AL: The use of imipramine in children's behavior disorders. *Acta Paedopsychiatrica* **37**:194, 1970.

Hurwitz I, Bibace R, Wolff P, and Rowbotham B: Neuropsychological function of normal boys, delinquent boys, and boys with learning problems. *Perceptual and Motor Skills* **35**:387, 1972.

Ingram T: Intermittent hearing loss in young children. *Dev Med and Ch Neurol* **18**:239, 1976.

Interagency Collaborative group on Hyperkinesis: *First Report of the Preliminary Findings and Recommendations to the Assistant Secretary for Health*. US Dept of HEW, 1976.

Jameson MC and Hicks WV: *Elementary School Curriculum from Theory to Practice.* New York, American Book Company, 1960.

Johnson D and Myklebust H: *Learning Disabilities: Educational Principles and Practices.* New York, Grune & Stratton, 1967.

Johnstone ER: The defective child. *The Training School* **6**(1):1, 1909.

Johnson D: The language continuum. *Bull Orton Soc* **18**:1, 1968.

Kagan J: Impulsive and reflective children: Significance of conceptual tempo. In Krumholtz (ed): *Learning and the Educational Process.* Chicago, Rand McNally, 1965.

Karlin R: *Teaching Elementary Reading.* New York, Harcourt Brace Jovanovich, 1975.

Keith CR: The therapeutic alliance in child psychotherapy. *J Am Acad Child Psychia* **7**:31, 1968.

Kenny T, Clemmons R, Hudson B, Lentz G, Cicci R, and Nair P. Characteristics of children referred because of hyperactivity. *J Pediatr* **79**:618, 1971.

Kenny T, Clemmens R, Cicci R, Levitz G, Nair P, and Hudson B: The medical evaluation of children with reading problems (dyslexia). *Pediatrics* **49**:438, 1972.

Keogh B: Optometric vision training programs for children with learning disabilities; review of issues and research. *J Learn Disabil* **7**:36, 1974.

Kephart NC: *The slow learner in the classroom.* Columbus, Ohio, Charles E Merrill, 1971.

King CH: The ego and the integration of violence in homicidal youth. *Am J Orthopsychia* **45**:134, 1975.

Kinsbourne M: School problems. *Pediatrics* **52**:697, 1973.

Kinsbourne M and Warrington E: The development of finger differentiation. *Quart J Exp Psychol* **15**:132, 1963.

Kirk S: Behavioral diagnosis and remediation of learning disabilities. In *Proceedings of the Conference on Exploration into the Problems of the Perceptually Handicapped Child,* First Annual Meeting, Vol 1. Chicago, April 6, 1963.

Kirk S, McCarthy J, and Kirk W: *Illinois Test of Psycholinguistic Abilities,* rev ed. Urbana, Univ of Illinois Press, 1968.

Kittler F and Baldwin D: The role of allergic factors in the child with minimal brain dysfunction. *Ann Allergy* **28**:203, 1970.

Klein S and Deffenbacher J: Relaxation and exercise for hyperactive impulsive children. *Percept Motor Skills* **45**:1159, 1977.

Knights R and Hinton G: The effects of methylphenidate (Ritalin) on the motor skills and behavior of children with learning problems. *J Nerv Ment Dis* **148**:643, 1969.

Knopp W, Arnold L, Andras R, and Smeltzer D: Predicting amphetamine response in hyperkinetic children by electronic pupilography. *Pharmakopsychiatrie* **6**:158, 1973.

Koppitz EM: *The Bender Gestalt Test for Young Children.* New York, Grune & Stratton, 1964.

Korsch BM, Gozzi EK, and Francis V: Gaps in doctor-patient communication. I. Doctor-patient interaction and patient satisfaction. *Ped* **42**:855, 1968.

Korsch BM and Negrete VF: Doctor-patient communication. *Sci Am* **227**:66, 1972.

Kosc L: Developmental dyscalculia. *J Learn Disabil* **7**:164, 1974.

Kraft M: The face-hand test. *Devel Med Ch Neurol* **10**:214, 1968.

Krager J and Safer D: Type and prevalence of medication used in the treatment of hyperactive children. *New Eng J Med* **291**:1118, 1974.

Kramer K: The search for improved programs. In Rubin L. (ed): *Curriculum Handbook.* Boston, Allyn & Bacon, 1977.

Kratochwill TR: The movement of psychological extras into ability assessment. *J Spec Educ* **11**:299, 1977.

Kronick D: *Three Families.* San Rafael, Calif, Academic Therapy Publications, 1976.

Kussmaul A: Diseases of the nervous system and disturbances of speech. In Von Ziemssen H (ed): *Cyclopaedia of the Practice of Medicine,* Vol 14. New York, W Wood, 1877.

LaBerge D and Samuels SJ: Toward a theory of automatic information processing in reading. *Cognitive Psych* **6**:293, 1974.

Laufer M and Denhoff E: Hyperkinetic behavior syndrome in children. *J Pediat* **50**:463, 1957.

Leahy S and Sands I: Mental disorders in children following epidemic encephalitis. *J Amer Med Ass* **76**:373, 1921.

Lerer R, Lerer M, and Artner J: The effects of methylphenidate on the handwriting of children with minimal brain dysfunction. *J Pediatr.* **91**:127, 1977.

Lerner J: *Children with learning disabilities,* 2d ed. Boston, Houghton Mifflin, 1976.

Levine M: Children with encopresis: A descriptive analysis. *Pediatrics* **56**:412, 1975.

Levine M and Bakow H: Children with encopresis: A study of treatment outcome. *Pediatrics* **58**:845, 1976.

Levine M and Liden C: Food for inefficient thought. *Pediatrics* **58**:145, 1976.

Levine M, Palfrey J, Lamb G, Weisberg H, and Bryk A: Infants in a public school system: The indicators of early health and educational need. *Pediatrics* 60(suppl):579, 1977.

Lilienfeld A and Parkhurst E: A study of the association of factors of pregnancy and parturition with the development of cerebral palsy: A preliminary report. *Am J Hygiene* **53**:262, 1951.

Loney J, Comly H, and Simon B: Parental management, self-concept, and drug response in minimal brain dysfunction. *J Learn Dis* **8**:187, 1975.

Lubar J and Shouse N: EEG and behavioral change in a hyperkinetic child concurrent with training of the sensorimotor rhythm (SMR). *Biofeedback and Self Regulation* **1**(3):293, 1976.

Luria AR: *Higher Cortical Functions in Man.* New York, Basic Books, 1966.

Mann L: Perceptual training revisited—the training of nothing at all. *Rehab Lit* **32**(11):322, 1971.

Martin JZ: The reading counselor: A method of counseling the reading disabled child. *J Learning Disabil* **10**:271, 1977.

Mattis S, French J, and Rapin I: Dyslexia in children and young adults: Three independent neuropsychological syndromes. *Develop Med Child Neurol* **17**:150, 1975.

Mauser A: Learning disabilities and delinquent youths, *Academic Therapy* **9**:389, 1974.

Maynard R: Omaha pupils given "behavior" drugs. *Washington Post,* June 29, 1970.

Medical Letter **20**(12):55, 1978.

Meeks JE: *The Fragile Alliance.* Baltimore, Williams & Wilkins Company, 1971.

Mechenbaum D: *Cognitive-Behavior Modification.* New York, Plenum Press, 1977.

Menkes J: On failing in school. *Pediatrics* **58**:392, 1976.

Menyuk P: Bases of language acquisition—some questions. *J Autism and Childhood Schizophrenia* **4**:325, 1975.

Millichap J, Egan R, Hart Z, and Sturgis L: Auditory perceptual deficit correlated with EEG dysrythmias: Response to diphenylaydantoin sodium. *Neurology* **18**:870, 1969.

Millichap JG: Drugs in management of minimal brain dysfunction, *Ann NY Acad Sci* **205**:321, 1973.

Millichap JG (ed): *Learning Disabilities and Related Disorders: Facts and Current Issues.* Chicago, Year Book Medical Publishers, 1977.

Millman M, Campbell M, Wright K, and Johnson A: Allergy and learning disabilities in children. *Ann Allergy* **36**:149, 1976.

Minde K, Weiss G, and Mendelson N: A 5-year follow-up of 91 hyperactive school children. *J Am Acad Child Psychiat* **11**:595, 1972.

Minskoff JG: Differential approaches to prevalence estimates of learning disabilities. *Ann NY Acad Sci* **205**:139, 1973.

Money J: *The disabled reader.* Baltimore, The Johns Hopkins Press, 1966.

Morgan WP: A case of congenital word-blindness. *Brit Med J* **2**:1378, 1896.

Myklebust H: Learning disabilities: definition and overview. In Myklebust H (ed): *Progress in Learning Disabilities,* Vol 1. New York, Grune & Stratton, 1968.

Mykelbust H: *Development and Disorders of Written Language,* Vol 2. New York, Grune & Stratton, 1973.

McLeod T and Crump W: The relationship of visuospatial skills and verbal ability to learning disabilities in mathematics. *J Learning Disabil* **11**:237, 1978.

McSpadden J and Strain P: Memory thresholds and overload effects between learning disabled and achieving pupils. *Exceptional Children* **44**:35, 1977.

Nall A: Alpha training and the hyperkinetic child—is it Effective? *Acad Ther* **9**:5, 1973.

Nathan L and Andelman M: The use of a tranquilizer in the management of behavior programs in a private pediatric practice. *Illinois Med J* **112**:171, 1957.

National Advisory Committee on Hyperkinesis and Food Additives: *Report to the Nutrition Foundation.* New York, The Nutrition Foundation, 1975.

Navelet Y, Anders T, and Guilleminault C: Narcolepsy. In Guilleminault C, Dement W, and Passouant P: *Advances in Sleep Research,* Vol. 3. New York, Spectrum Publications, 1976.

Needleman HL, Gunnoe C, Leviton A, Reed R, Peresie H, Maher C, and Barrett P: Deficits in psychological and classroom performance in children with elevated dentine lead levels. *New Eng J Med,* **300**:689, 1979.

Nelson WE, et al: *Textbook of Pediatrics,* 6th ed 1954, 7th ed 1959. Philadelphia, WB Saunders.

Nolan E and Kagan J: Psychological factors in the face-hand test. *Arch Neurol* **35**:41, 1978.

Ogbu J: *Minority education and casts.* New York, Academic Press, 1978, pp 217–237.

Orton S: Specific reading disability—strephosymbolia. *J Amer Med Assn* **90**:1095, 1928.

Orton S: *Reading, Writing and Speech Problems in Children.* New York, WW Norton & Co, 1937.

O'Sullivan M and Pryles C: Reading disability in children. *J Pediat* **60**:369, 1962.

O'Tauma L, Swisher C, Reichler R, and Routh D: Lack of effect of TRH in minimal brain dysfunction. *Pediatrics* **59**:955, 1977.

Palfrey J, Mervis R, and Butler J: New directions in the evaluation and education of handicapped children. *New Eng J Med* **298**:819, 1978a.

Palfrey J, Hanson M, Norton S, et al: Selective hearing screening for very young children. Presentation at the Region I meeting of the Ambulatory Pediatric Association, September 1978b.

Palkes H, Stewart M, Freedman J: Improvement in maze performance of hyperactive boys as a function of verbal training procedures. *J Spec Educ* **5**:337, 1972.

Pasamanick B and Knobloch H: Epidemiologic studies on the complications of pregnancy and the birth process. In Caplan G (ed): *Prevention of Mental Disorders in Children.* New York, Basic Books, 1961.

Pauling L: Orthomolecular psychiatry. *Science* **160**:265, 1968.

Peters JE, Romine JS, and Dykman RA: A special neurological examination of children with learning disabilities. *Dev Med Child Neurol* **17**:63, 1975.

Piaget J and Inhelder B: *The Psychology of the Child.* New York, Basic Books, 1969.

Pick A, Frankel D, and Hess V: Children's attention: The development of selectivity. In Hetherington E (ed): *Review of Child Development Research,* Vol 5. Chicago, Univ of Chicago Press, 1975, pp 325–383.

Pless IB and Pinkerton P: *Chronic childhood disorder—promoting patterns of adjustment.* Chicago, Year Book Medical Publishers, 1975.

Popp H: Selecting initial reading instruction for high risk children: A theoretical approach. *Bull Orton Soc* **28**:15, 1978.

Porges S, Walter G, Korb R, and Sprague R: The influences of methylphenidate on heart rate and behavioral measures of attention in hyperactive children. *Child Develop* **46**:727, 1975.

Prechtl H and Stemmer C: The choreiform syndrome in children. *Dev Med Ch Neurol* **4**:119, 1962.

Quinn P and Rappaport L: Minor physical anomalies and neurologic status in hyperactive boys. *Pediatrics* **53**:742, 1974.

Randolph T: Allergy as a causative factor of fatigue, irritability and behavior problems of children. *J Pediatr* **31**:560, 1947.

Rapoport J, Abramson A, Alexander D, and Lott I: Playroom observations of hyperactive children on medication. *J Amer Acad Child Psychiat* **10**:524, 1971.

Rapoport J, Buchsbaum M, Zahn T, Weingartner H, Ludlow C, and Mikkelsen E: Dextramphetamine: Cognitive and behavioral effect in normal prepubertal boys. *Science* **199**:560, 1978.

Rapoport J, Quinn P, Bradbard G, Riddle K, and Brooks E: Imipramine and methylphenidate: Treatments of hyperactive boys. *Arch Gen Psychiat* **30**:789, 1974.

Reichard C and Elder S: The effects of caffeine on reaction time in hyperkinetic and normal children. *Am J Psychiat* **134**(2):144, 1977.

Rie HE: Therapeutic tutoring for underachieving children. *Prof Psychol* **5**:70, 1974.

Rie H, Rie F, Stewart S, and Ambuel J: Effects of methylphenidate on underachieving children. *J Consult Clin Psychol* **44**:250, 1976.

Ring B: Memory problems and children with learning problems. *Academic Therapy* **11**:111, 1975.

Robeck M and Wilson J: *Psychology of Reading: Foundations of Instructions.* New York: John Wiley & Sons, 1974.

Robbins M and Glass C: The Doman-Delacato rationale: A critical analysis. In Hellmuth J (ed): *Educational Therapy,* Vol II. Seattle, Special Child Publications, 1969.

Ross AO: *Psychological Aspects of Learning Disabilities and Reading Disorders.* New York, McGraw-Hill, 1976.

Ross D and Ross S: *Hyperactivity: Research, Theory, and Action.* New York, John Wiley & Sons, 1976.

Routh D, Schroeder C, and O'Tauma L: Development of activity level in children. *Develop Psychol* **10**:163, 1974.

Rudel R and Denckla M: Relationship of IQ and reading score to visual, spatial, and temporal matching tasks. *J Learning Disabil* **9**:169, 1976a.

Rudel R, Denckla M, and Spalten E: Paired associate learning of Morse code and Braille letter names by dyslexic and normal children. *Cortex* **12**:61, 1976b.

Rutter M, Tizard J, and Whitmore K: *Education, Health, and Behavior.* New York, John Wiley & Sons, 1970.

Safer D and Allen R: Factors influencing the suppressant effects of two stimulant drugs on the growth of hyperactive children. *Pediatrics* **51**:660, 1973.

Safer D, Allen R, and Barre E: Growth rebound after termination of stimulant drugs. *J Pediatr* **86**:113, 1975.

Salzman L: Allergy testing, psychological assessment and dietary treatment of the hyperactive child syndrome. *Med J Aust* **2**:248, 1976.

Sameroff A and Chandler M: Reproductive risk and the continuum of caretaking casualty. In Horowitz F (ed): *Review of Child Development Research,* Vol 4. Chicago, Univ of Chicago Press, 1975.

Samuels SJ: Hierarchical subskills in the reading acquisition process. In Guthrie J (ed): *Aspects of Reading Acquisition.* Baltimore, Johns Hopkins University Press, 1976.

Santostefano S: The assessment of motives in children. *Psychol Rep* **26**:639, 1970.

Santostefano S: MBD: Time to take a new look. *Med Times* **103**:82, 1975.

Santostefano S: *A Biodevelopmental Approach to Clinical Child Psychology: Cognitive Controls and Cognitive Control Therapy.* New York, John Wiley & Sons, 1978.

Satterfield J, Cantwell D, Lesser L, and Podosin R: Physiological studies of the hyperactive child: I. *Am J Psychiat* **128**:1418, 1972.

Satterfield J, Cantwell D, Saul R, Lesser L, and Podosin R: Response to stimulant drug treament in hyperactive children: Prediction from EEG and neurological findings. *J Autism Childhood Schizo* **3**:36, 1973.

Satterfield J: EEG issues in children with minimal brain dysfunction. In Walzer S and Wolff P (eds): *Minimal Cerebral Dysfunction in Children.* New York: Grune & Stratton, 1973, pp 35–46.

Satz P, Friel J, and Goebel R: Some predictive antecedents of specific reading disability: A three year follow-up. *Bull Orton Soc* **25**:91, 1975.

Schain R and Reynard C: Observations of effects of a central stimulant drug (methylphenidate) in children with hyperactive behavior. *Pediatrics* **55**:709, 1975.

Schleifer M, Weiss G, Cohen N, Elman M, Cyejic H, and Kruger E: Hyperactivity in preschoolers and the effect of methylphenidate. *Am J Orthopsychiat* **45**:38, 1975.

Schnackenberg, R: Caffeine as a substitute for schedule II stimulants in hyperkinetic children. *Am J Psychiat* **130**(7):796, 1973.

Schrag P and Divoky D: *The Myth of the Hyperactive Child.* New York, Pantheon, 1975.

Shannon W: Neuropathic manifestations in infants and children as a result of anaphylactic reactions to foods contained in their dietary. *Amer J Dis Child* **24**:89, 1922.

Shaywitz S, Cohen D, and Shaywitz B: The biochemical basis of minimal brain dysfunction. *J Peds* **92**(2):179, 1978.

Shonkoff J, Dworkin P, Leviton A, and Levine M: Primary care approaches to developmental disabilities. *Pediatrics:* **64**:506, 1979.

Silberberg N and Silberberg M: Myths in remedial education. *J Learn Disab* **2**:209, 1969.

Silver L: Acceptable and controversial approaches to treating the child with learning disabilities. *Pediatrics* **55**:406, 1975.

Smith NB: Cultural dialects: Current problems and solutions. *The Reading Teacher* **29**:137, 1975.

Snyder R and Mortimer J: Diagnosis and treatment: Dyslexia. *Pediatrics* **44**:601, 1969.

Spache GD and Spache EB: *Reading in the Elementary School.* Boston, Allyn & Bacon, 1973.

Speer F: The allergic tension-fatigue syndrome. *Ped Clin N Amer* **1**:1029, 1954.

Speer F: The allergic tension-fatigue syndrome in children. *Int Arch Allerg* **12**:207, 1958.

Spitzer HG: *Teaching Elementary School Mathematics*. Boston: Houghton Mifflin, 1967.

Sprague R and Werry J: Methodology of psychopharmacological studies with the retarded. In Ellis NR (ed): *International Review of Research in Mental Retardation*, Vol 5. New York, Academic Press, 1971.

Sprague R and Sleator E: Methylphenidate in hyperkinetic children: Differences in dose effects on learning and social behavior. *Science* **198**:1274, 1977.

Spring C, Yellin A, and Greenberg L: Effects of imipramine and methylphenidate on perceptual motor performance of hyperactive children. *Percept Motor Skills* **43**:459, 1976.

Sroufe L: Drug treatment of children with behavior problems. In Horowitz F (ed): *Review of Child Development Research*, Vol 4. Chicago, Univ of Chicago Press, 1975, pp 371–374.

Steele A: Music in a special way. *Child Today* **2**(4):8, 1973.

Still GF: The Coulstonian Lectures on some abnormal physical conditions in Children. *Lancet* **1**:10008 (1077, 1163), 1902.

Stine J: Symptom alleviation in the hyperactive child by dietary modification: A report of two cases. *Am J Orthopsychiat* **46**:637, 1976.

Stott DH: *The Hard-to-Teach Child: A Diagnostic-Remedial Approach*. Baltimore, University Park Press, 1978.

Strauss A and Lehtinen L: *Psychopathology and Education of the Brain-Injured Child*. New York, Grune & Stratton, 1947.

Strauss AA and Kephart NC: *Psychopathology and Education of the Brain-Injured Child, Vol 2: Progress in Theory and Clinic*. New York: Grune & Stratton, 1955.

Strother CR: Minimal cerebral dysfunction: A historical overview. *Ann NY Acad Sci* **205**:6, 1973.

Solnit A and Stark M: Pediatric management of school learning problems of under-achievement. *New Eng J Med* **261**:988, 1959.

Sykes D, Douglas V, and Morgenstern G: The effect of methylphenidate (Ritalin) on sustained attention in hyperactive children. *Psychopharmacologia* **25**:262, 1972.

Tarver S and Hallahan D: Attention deficits in children with learning disabilities: A review. *J Learn Dis* **7**(9):560, 1974.

The Task Force on Pediatric Education: *The Future of Pediatric Education*, monograph, 1978.

Thomas A: Significance of temperamental individuality for school functioning. In Hellmuth J (ed): *Learning Disorders*, Vol 3. Seattle, Special Child Publications, 1965.

Thomas A, Chess S, Birch H, Hertzig M, and Korn S: *Behavioral Individuality in Early Childhood*. New York, New York Univ Press, 1963.

Thomas A, Chess S, and Birch H: *Temperament and Behavior Disorders in Children*. New York, New York Univ Press, 1968.

Tiwary C, Rosenbloom A, Robertson M, and Parker J: Effects of thyroidtropin-releasing hormone in minimal brain dysfunction. *Pediatrics* **56**:119, 1975.

Torgesen J: Learning disabilities: A theoretical assessment. *J Learning Dis* **10**:1, 1977.

Touwen B and Prechtl H: *The Neurological Examination of the Child with Minor Nervous Dysfunction*. Little Club Clinics in Devel Med No. 38. London, Spastics Society (Heineman), 1970.

Town CH: Congenital aphasia. *Psychological Clinic* **5**(6):167, 1911.

The Training School: Health and development supervision in California. Unsigned editorial. *The Training School* **7**(2):248, 1910.

Twarog W, Levine M, and Berkeley T: *Pediatric Participation in Public Law 94-142*. Report for the Bureau of Education for the Handicapped. Boston, 1979.

Venezky R: Prerequisites for learning to read. In Levin J and Allen V (eds): *Cognitive Learning in Children: Theories and Strategies*. New York, Academic Press, 1976.

Vernon MD: *Backwardness in Reading* (2d ed). Cambridge: Cambridge Univ Press, 1960.

Waldfogel S, Collidge J, Hahn P: The development, meaning, and management of school phobia. *Am J Orthopsychiat* **27**:754, 1957.

Waizer J, Hoffman S, Polizos P, and Engelhardt D: Outpatient treatment of hyperactive school children with imipramine. *Am J Psych* **131**:587, 1974.

Waldrop MF and Halverson CF: Minor physical anomalies and hyperactive behavior in young children. In Helmuth J (ed): *Exceptional Infant,* Vol II. New York, Bruner/Mazel, 1971.

Warner F: *The Nervous System of the Child—Its Growth and Health in Children.* New York, Macmillan, 1900.

Watson JB: *Psychological Care of Infant and Child.* New York, Norton & Co, 1928.

Weaver P: Comprehension, recall, and dyslexia: A proposal for the application of schema theory. *Bull Orton Soc* **28**:92, 1978.

Weaver P and Shonkoff F: *Research Within Reach: A Research-Guided Response to Concerns of Reading Educators.* St. Louis, Cemrel, Inc, Washington, DC, National Institute of Education, 1978.

Weikart D et al: *Longitudinal Results of the Ypsilanti Perry Preschool Project.* Ypsilanti, Mich, High Scope Educational Research Foundation, 1970.

Weinberg W, Penick E, Hammerman M, et al: An evaluation of a summer remedial reading program. *Am J Dis Child* **122**:494, 1971.

Weiss G, Minde K, Douglas V, Werry J, and Sykes D: Comparison of the effects of chlorpromazine, dextroamphetamine, and methylphenidate on the behavior and intellectual functioning of hyperactive children. *Can Med Assoc J* **104**:20, 1971.

Wender PH: *Minimal Brain Dysfunction in Children.* New York: Wiley Interscience, 1971.

Werner H and Strauss A: Problems and methods of functional analysis in mentally deficient children. *J Abnormal and Social Psychol* **34**:37, 1939.

Werner E, Bierman J, and French F: *The Children of Kauai.* Honolulu, Univ of Hawaii Press, 1971.

Werry, J: Some clinical and laboratory studies of psychotrophic drugs in children: An overview. In Smith WL (ed): *Drugs and Cerebral Function.* Springfield, Ill, Charles C Thomas, 1970.

Werry J, Weiss G, Douglas V, and Martin J: Studies on the hyperactive child: III. The effect of chlorpromazine upon behavior and learning ability. *J Am Acad Child Psych* **5**:292, 1966.

Werry J and Aman M: Methylphenidate and haloperidol in children. *Arch Gen Psych* **32**:790, 1975.

Werry J, Aman M, and Lampen E: Haloperidol and methylphenidate in hyperactive children. *Acta Paedopsychiatrica* **42**:26, 1976.

Werry J: Developmental hyperactivity. *Ped Clin NA* **15**:581, 1968.

Werry J and Sprague R: Methylphenidate in children—effect of dosage. *Aust and New Zealand J Psychiat* **8**:9, 1974.

Werry J and Quay H: The prevalence of behavior symptoms in younger elementary school children. *Am J Orthopsychiat* **41**:136, 1971.

Westcott AM and Smith JA: Basic principles of mathematics programs. In Rubin L (ed): *Curriculum Handbook.* Boston, Allyn & Bacon, 1977.

White R: Motivation reconsidered: The concept of competence. *Psychol Rev* **66**:297, 1959.

Wiederholt J: Historical perspectives on the education of the learning disabled. In Mann L and Sabatino D (eds): *The Second Review of Special Education*. Philadelphia, Journal of Special Education Press, 1974.

Wiig E and Semel E: *Language Disabilities in Children and Adolescents,* Columbus, Ohio: Charles E Merrill, 1976.

Williams JI, Cram D, Tausig F, and Webster E: Relative effects of drugs and diet on hyperactive behaviors: An experimental study. *Pediatrics* **61**:811, 1978.

Wilson S, Harris C, and Harris M: Effects of an auditory perceptual program on reading performance. *J Learning Disabil* **9**:670, 1976.

Winsberg B, Goldstein S, Yepes L, and Perel J: Imipramine electrocardiographic abnormalities in hyperactive children. *Am J Psychiatry* **132**:542, 1975.

Winter S and Boyer J: Hepatic toxicity from large doses of vitamin B_3 (nicotinamide). *N Eng J Med* **289**:1180, 1973.

Witty P and Kopel D: Studies of eye muscle imbalance and poor fusion in reading disability, and evaluation. *J Educ Psychol* **27**:663, 1936.

Wolff P and Hurwitz I: The choreiform syndrome. *Dev Med Ch Neurol* **8**:160, 1966.

Wolraich M: Stimulant drug therapy in hyperactive children: Research and clinical impressions. *Pediatrics* **60**:512, 1977.

Yoss R and Moyers N: The pupillogram of the hyperkinetic child and the underachiever. Abstracts for 7th Colloquium on the Pupil, The Mayo Clinic, Rochester, Minn, 1971.

Zahn T, Abate F, Little B, and Wender P: Minimal brain dysfunction, stimulant drugs, and autonomic nervous system activity. *Arch Gen Psychiat* **32**:381, 1975.

Zintz MV: *The Reading Process*. Dubuque, Iowa, William C Brown, 1975.

Zuckerman B, Carper J, Alpert J: Mental health training for pediatricians. *J Clin Child Psychol* **7**:43, 1978.

INDEX